GEORGE MELNYK

One Hundred Years of Canadian Cinema

UNIVERSITY OF TORONTO PRESS
Toronto Buffalo London

University of Toronto Press Incorporated
Toronto Buffalo London
Printed in Canada

ISBN 0-8020-3568-X (cloth)
ISBN 0-8020-8444-3 (paper)

Printed on acid-free paper

National Library of Canada Cataloguing in Publication

Melnyk, George
One hundred years of Canadian cinema / George Melnyk.

Includes bibliographical references and index.
ISBN 0-8020-3568-X (bound)   ISBN 0-8020-8444-3 (pbk.)

1. Motion pictures – Canada – History.   I. Title.

PN1993.5.C3M44 2004   791.43'0971   C2004-900621-5

University of Toronto Press acknowledges the financial assistance to
its publishing program of the Canada Council for the Arts and the
Ontario Arts Council.

University of Toronto Press acknowledges the financial support for
its publishing activities of the Government of Canada through the
Book Publishing Industry Development Program (BPIDP).

To Peter Harcourt,
a pioneer of Canadian film studies

Contents

Acknowledgments

In 2000 I was teaching a course in Canadian film culture and using a collection of readings I had pulled together because there was no history of Canadian film available. So I decided to write that history. Little did I realize what a major multi-year project it would become. The most important assistance I received during the four years of preparing this book for publication came from my wife, Julia, who carried out many tasks, including the translation of French-language texts, proofreading, creating the bibliography, organizing the photographs, and reviewing the copy-edited manuscript. Most importantly, she provided moral support during an unusually busy period of book writing for me, which included at one point four other books besides this one. Without her commitment to getting this book completed on time, I would have faltered.

During the revisions of the manuscript, I had the good fortune to have a six-month sabbatical leave from my teaching in the Faculty of Communication and Culture, University of Calgary. The time allowed me to make major revisions and add significant new material. I am grateful to Wendy Stephens, copyright officer at the University of Calgary, for her assistance in tracing photographs and their copyright holders, and in obtaining permission to publish them in this book. Her help came at a crucial time, when I felt overwhelmed and unable to go on. Scott Forsyth of *Cineaction* magazine published two chapters from the manuscript-in-progress, both about Quebec, in special Canadian film issues of the magazine (nos. 57 and 61), which he edited.

Siobhan McMenemy, acquisitions editor, cultural studies, film, literature, and book history at University of Toronto Press, moved the manuscript along in a timely manner through the various stages of peer review with professional efficiency and commitment to the Press's high scholarly standards. Frances Mundy, managing editor, University of Toronto Press, was understanding in preparing the manuscript for production. Ken Lewis proved to be a conscientious copy editor. Elizabeth Bell and Andrea Palmer made an exceptional effort to produce an exemplary index in a short period of time. Proofreader Mairi Babey was diligent in tracking down errors. I appreciate everything that they have done for the book.

I am also greatful to Dave Barber and Matthew Etches of the Winnipeg Film Group for photographs and to Claude Lord of the National Film Board for his kind assistance in locating suitable photographs from the NFB collection. Sean Lancaster of the National Archives of Canada was most helpful in locating crucial photographs. Their inclusion in the book helps the reader visualize historical reality.

A special thank-you goes to my students in Canadian Studies 331 (Canadian Film Culture) at the University of Calgary. Their enthusiasm for Canadian film has been an inspiration and my guiding spirit. Finally, I want to acknowledge all those who granted me interviews, provided photographs, and assisted me in my research. A book such as this contains so many dates, names, and references that the occasional error is bound to creep in, despite one's best efforts and those of others. I regret any errors that the book may contain, and I accept sole responsibility for them.

ONE HUNDRED YEARS OF CANADIAN CINEMA

Introduction

From the perspective of the twenty-first century, understanding the past of Canadian film has grown complicated because of the intellectual currents of recent times and the changing political and social nature of the country. A nation's cultural identity is often summed up in simplistic concepts associated with 'who we are.' But a nation state's traditional concepts about identity have been challenged by those who emphasize other national identities within the state and by those who claim issues surrounding gender, race, ethnicity, and region are their primary allegiances.[1] Intellectually, the prominence of various theoretical approaches such as feminism, postcolonial theory, and postmodernist cultural studies has made issues of diverse perspectives and themes of subjugation central to cultural analysis.

The feminist critique views film production as formed by a patriarchal society, its messages and restrictions. A Marxist critique views film in terms of capitalist modes of production and their generation of class subjugation. Postcolonialists are concerned about the cinematic portrayal of racial stereotypes, formerly colonized peoples, and their repressed languages and cultures. Queer theorists expose the heterosexual bias of mainstream cinema and provide an alternative gay reading of films. The new field of cultural studies has synthesized and superceded these previous schools of thought in a wide-ranging critique that seeks to valorize counter-hegemonic theories and practices that unmask the ideological myths dominating popular thought.[2] The age of grand narratives, which viewed the world in a simple, one-dimensional way may be behind us, but the proliferation of debate over the dark side of those narratives, and what is to replace them as the ideology of choice, continues.

When writing a history of one nation state's cinema today, the historian must acknowledge the demands made by formerly subjugated nationalities and critical ideologies. Material changes in Canadian society and politics have swept aside the old verities about what constitutes Canada, being Canadian, and, therefore, Canadian film. What constitutes being Canadian is now hotly debated. There are primarily five historical factors that have brought this about, and each reflects the efforts of a minority to change the status quo. The first and most powerful is the political success of the pro-independence movement in Quebec. The Parti Québécois and the Bloc Québécois have replaced Quebec's former 'French-Canadian' identity with that of the secular, dynamic, nation-building 'Québécois.' With this change has come a proactive, self-reflective, and redefining Quebec cinema. The second major factor is the rise of a new ethnic and racial mix in Canada based on extensive non-European immigration from various regions of the globe. In the largest urban centres, the established Euro-Canadian reality has been challenged by a major new demographic that is creating a multiracial society of great diversity. At the same time as this diversity has swept Canada, the country's Aboriginal peoples have demanded redress for a legacy of oppression and exclusion. First Nations cultural self-consciousness and goal of political self-government are redefining Canada's political and cultural landscape in a way that has brought a new, affirmative Aboriginal identity to the screen. The fourth factor comes from the feminist challenge to the privileges and mores of patriarchal society. The feminist reinterpretation of social roles, sexual identity, and the institutions that govern gender relations is in the ascendancy. Finally, the increasing social prominence of equality issues for gay, lesbian, bisexual, and transgendered Canadians has made sexuality an emerging theme in the social imaginary of Canadian cinema, as it reflects newly acknowledged realities.

As well as the influence of new social and political ideologies, cinema has been moulded by technological innovation. The recent reconfiguration of cultural communication through computer-based digital technologies is just the latest step in a century of change that began with the movie theatres of 1910 and continues with the large-screen home entertainment systems of today. Technological change influences who makes and controls films, who watches them and where they are watched, what subject matter is preferred, the ideologies they express, and the desired impact that cinematic art is expected to have on its audiences. Technology also affects an audience's perceptual experiences and encourages change in the cultural medium itself. An example of this is the contrast between the narrative experience presented by rapidly intercut music videos and the more reserved and linear editing of conventional cinematic storytelling. The influence of new media forms has caused some theorists to marginalize cinema because they consider it an 'old' technology whose language is increasingly irrelevant to new modes of communication. Cinema, at one time the dominant visual mode of representation in the world, was first challenged by television a half-century ago and most recently by video games and the Internet. Looking back on the golden age of film dominance from the vantage point of today's visually saturated and media diverse universe, one can only wonder about the future of film as a distinct cultural form.

Added to these material changes is the evolution of the theory of film, which offers ever expanding insights into the subliminal workings of the medium and its messages. While the film historian is not necessarily a film theorist, there is little doubt that historical narrative is a discourse informed by prevailing theoretical approaches. Because cinema was such a widespread cultural reality even during the era of silent film, theories of film arose quickly. The Soviet montage theories of the 1920s made film a distinct artistic genre; the 1940s Frankfurt School idea of culture as 'mass deception' raised the issue of film's role in propaganda and public delusion; and the 1950s fascination with the film-maker as 'auteur' on a par with the grandeur of literary novelists pushed cinema toward the top of the cultural food chain. Understandably there was a reaction. Various psychoanalytic and linguistic theories applied to the language and imagery of film sought to dethrone film from its exalted place in the cultural pantheon. In the 1960s and 1970s the philosophy and methodologies of European poststructuralism emerged to deconstruct the conventional practices of cinema, exposing its 'subliminal ideological underpinnings.'[3] The academic disciplines of film studies and cultural studies have flourished since the 1980s, creating an ever-expanding body of literature analysing cinema from the perspective of theory-oriented intellectuals. As a result, today's historian of film has an extensive menu from which to choose: ranging from conventional chronological accounts, through ideological prisms of various kinds and techno-sociological explanations, to theories of aesthetics and narrative structure based in linguistics.

In Canada these intellectual, social, political, and technological changes have been simultaneously profound and superficial: superficial because the historical reality of American dominance of Canadian film screens has continued unabated; and profound because the content of Canadian cinema has grown, become diversified, and matured so that today the feature film industry in Canada and its documentary predecessor, the National Film Board of Canada, can point proudly to a legacy of achievement and acclaim. It is the task of this book to explain this contradiction between Canadian film's artistic accomplishment and its acknowledged public invisibility by outlining the history of cinema in Canada, its main players and developers, and the trends that have evolved into underlying themes.[4]

The author of this narrative is not a product of the dominant theoretical schools of thought outlined above. Instead, he writes from the diffuse, interdisciplinary universe of Canadian studies, a discipline framed in the 1970s by scholars concerned with the national question. It is the very relevance of the national question and its evolving nature that is challenged by these newer schools of thought and disciplinarity. They associate interest in the national question with patriarchal concerns, colonialism, and imperialism, and they view the construction of nationality as something that is suspect. A recent example of this framing is Christopher E. Gittings's *Canadian National Cinema* (2002), which seeks to unveil 'the masquerades of Canadian nation' as it was constructed by an imperialist, racist, and sexist cinematic practice.[5] Canadian studies as a discipline does not embrace the ideology of nationalism. It acknowledges the historical nationalist representation of peoples and issues as flawed and, in some cases, seriously deficient. Nevertheless, Canadian studies finds the nation state to be a useful framework for understanding the project of national cultural autonomy in which an imagined community fosters its own creative interpretation in order to create a sense of a bordered self. The nation as cultural phenomenon, whether it be First Nations, Canadian, or Québécois, cannot be divorced from social, economic, and political issues at the heart of each community's struggle in an age of global integration, First World dominance, and renewed American imperialism.[6] Even while there is much discussion of the concept of our living in a post-national age, nationally based cultural production, including film, was and still remains a site of resistance to multinational capitalism and globalization in spite of those who reject and deplore the protective mantle of nationalism as something reactionary. In an essay titled 'The Dilemmas of Canadian Identity,' the editors of a 2001 textbook on Canadian studies state: 'Aspects of the new globalization are so threatening because Canada does not have the mechanisms for national integration normally associated with strong nation building. Many of our leading national institutions ... either no longer command the loyalty they once did or seem to be in need of drastic reform.'[7]

Framing film in terms of nationality and dividing Canadian film primarily into a narrative of two competing cultural entities will not appeal to those for whom this division is outdated, irrelevant to contemporary concerns, and profoundly conservative because the older narrative ignored and negatively stereotyped minorities.[8] A prominent Canadian film critic disagrees with this charge of irrelevance. In 2003, Brian D. Johnson wrote: 'We talk about Canadian cinema, as if it exists. But even if the "two nations" concept has run its course politically, there are two distinct cinemas in this country – English and French – and their personalities are poles apart.'[9] In his 2002 Martin Walsh Memorial Lecture for the Film Studies Association of Canada, Canadian film scholar Jim Leach qualified this interpretation when he stated: 'The old questions of national duality and the influence of U.S. popular culture continue to preoccupy English-Canadian and Québécois filmmakers in their different cultural contexts. However, these themes now often become entangled with the interest in cultural diversity ...'[10]

Highlighting 'English-Canadian and Quebec cinema,' as this text does, must not be construed as a belief that contemporary Canadian cinema exists solely in the contested paradigm of the famous 'two solitudes' of modernist construction. Rather it means that the history of Canadian cinema up to the 1980s, when this paradigm began to crumble historically, represents two distinct cultural streams that had their roots in two non-Canadian realities – the European and the American. These two cultural streams drew on the power and influence of non-Canadian realities in their battle to create national distinctiveness for themselves. They fought with each other and with their metropolitan cultures for recognition. But it was not until Canadian elements that felt excluded by the dominant paradigm challenged this dualistic tradition that the possibility of other senses of 'nationality' could emerge toward the end of the twentieth century.

Contemporary challenges to the traditions represented by English and French Canada have been raised by formerly marginalized voices who want to instil new possibilities into the core of Canadian cinema. This is a perfectly valid objective, but it is equally valid to use the concept of two national cinemas when writing a book of Canadian film history simply because this was the route of historical development.

Using the idea of nationality and exploring differing national idioms in film does not undermine contemporary theories of historiography or cinema if one takes into account the insights offered by them into the limitations of nationality. In the current debate between what the past established (and its meaning) and what the present is trying to achieve is the foundation of the future of cinema in a country where film has yet to achieve a prominent place in the pantheon of cultural expression.

The articulation of cultural history is not just a matter of a retrospective gaze coloured by the narrator's current situation; it is also a matter of a factual, chronological evolution that constructs periods, points out seminal personalities, generates schools of thought and expression, and, in the broadest sense, addresses numerous texts and works of art that have spoken to audiences with the sensibilities of their differing communities and their creators. This history of cinema in Canada respects both elements – those asserting contemporary perspectives that define our present moment and critique the past, and the historical reality that has been constructed and interpreted over time by others. This text balances the perspectives of the past with contemporary interpretations of that past. The historian who seeks to find the links among a multiplicity of events tries to do so without invention. A quick look at the beginnings of cinema in Canada shows how the two 'national' traditions were born. That, a century later, their trajectory would come to be viewed as hegemonic by those it excluded and oppressed is not surprising. A history of twentieth-century cinema in Canada outlines both the persistence of long-held attitudes and their moments of change.

In June 1896, scarcely six months after its premiere in Paris, the Lumière brothers' Cinématographe was entertaining astonished audiences in Montreal with its moving pictures of scenes from Europe. A month later in Ottawa, Edison's Vitascope brought its version of this new entertainment marvel, using American scenes. This division in content symbolized the conflicting universes, European and American, that were Canada's attachments at the time. The two events also serve as a metaphor for the evolution of cinema in the Canadian state. For cinema produced in English Canada, the result has been a continual struggle to imitate, however poorly, the enormous success of the American film industry and to differentiate itself from its domineering cultural norms. For Quebec cinema, the result has been a different struggle, in which national aspirations and cultural differences based in religion and language have been used to build a distinct film identity on the basis of a relationship with France and Europe. That Quebec was first off the mark in viewing moving pictures gave it a certain symbolic head start as far as feature films are concerned. This book argues that this head start, even a century later, remains intact. English Canada has fought valiantly but with much less success than Quebec to carve out a distinct niche for itself in the overpowering shadow of Hollywood. The differing cultural requirements of these competing national projects are the cause of this dissimilarity.

Spanning the period from the triumph of mechanized industrial society in the late nineteenth century to the digital post-industrial reality of today's First World countries, the cinema industry has been primarily an urban phenomenon. As the history of Canadian cinema evolved in the twentieth century, Ontario and Quebec and their primary cities, Toronto and Montreal, came to embody the two great protagonists of Canada's former bicultural identity. Supporting roles for Toronto were played by a few other cities, but the fulcrum of this balancing act was Ottawa, the nation's capital and the country's legislative and bureaucratic heart. Ottawa kept the protagonists and the supporting cast performing on the same single-state stage, while letting each side use distinct scripts. If Montreal and Toronto were the entrepreneurial hearts of their respective cultures, Ottawa was the Machiavellian brain. Whatever was to happen to Canadian cinema in the twentieth century would be touched, evaluated, and muddied by the politicians and mandarins of the federal government and their desire to appease public expectations, while keeping the state central to the enterprise. If we think of Ottawa as the director and Montreal and Toronto as the principal actors in this drama, then the rest of Canada served in supporting roles, as walk-ons, and as a cast of extras.

Using the analogy of a Greek play, we might consider Canadian film history as a circle of mortals surrounded by the mythic powers of various gods who wreaked havoc on the aspirations and actions of the players. At the top of the pantheon was the god of Hollywood, almighty Zeus, who sent his thunderbolts of money and political power to unnerve terrified Canadians. Then there was the god of France, the beautiful and powerful Athena, who had her own agenda and brought European cinematic values to Canada. Of late, another god has appeared to unseat those he considers usurpers of his former omnipotence. Trickster Coyote, who comes from the Aboriginal pantheon, has emerged from his long, voiceless exile during the period of Euro-Canadian conquest to reject both Zeus and Athena and remind the world of the resurgence of First Nations nationalisms within Canadian identity. He is the god of Canada's postcolonial reality come to haunt and displace the dominance of those who became masters. His goal is to unseat the national cinemas of the earlier gods from their place of prominence because of their colonialism toward First Nations identities and their subservience to non-indigenous cinematic models.

A century ago the diverse cultures of Canada were reduced in the public mind to promoting racial unity within British imperialism or clinging to a tradition of French-Canadian perseverance. A hundred years later, Canada's relationship to its colonial heritage is much different. While Anglo-Canadian identity has been engaged in a self-conscious nationalism energized by an ongoing struggle with American hegemony, French-Canadian identity has transformed itself into a Quebec nationalism that seeks a greater or lesser degree of separation from the rest of Canada. Both Anglo-Canadian and Quebec nationalism look inward for inspiration, but what is 'inside' is no longer the old norm. National identity for both entities has engendered a greater sense of a distinct self that seeks to differentiate itself from, rather than integrate with, the other. This confrontational self-identification purposefully ignored those groups that it sought to assimilate under its own monolithic banner. Behind the English-French conflict were forgotten elements that are now resurfacing to challenge the validity of singular national identities. Resurgent First Nations identities, ongoing regional aspirations, and the increasing challenges offered by cyberspace culture and electronically linked communities are the cutting edge of cultural discourse. For Canadian capitalism, the inviting continentalism of the North American Free Trade Agreement is a fait accompli that reconfigures Anglo-Canadian and Quebec cultural discourse into an increasingly North/South rather than an East/West polarity.

The nature of cinema, its economic role, its cultural impact, its locus as a battleground among aesthetics, politics, and commerce are part of global cultural history. Anglo-Canadian cinema and its Quebec partner have created distinct places for themselves within the overall history of global cinema that are little known by Canadians, Quebeckers, and non-Canadians. As well, knowledge of each other's national cinemas by both traditions is almost non-existent outside small circles of film aficionados. In general, Quebec audiences see as few Anglo-Canadian films as Anglo-Canadian audiences see Quebec films. There is more influence from abroad on these cinemas than from each other. Canadian cinema prefers to respond and adapt to forces that are global rather than national in nature. This adaptation contains its share of farce, its moments of individual heroics, its elements of pettiness and greatness, and, finally, an amazing rapprochement with American domination. Canada was viewed throughout much of the twentieth century as being marginal to major cultural trends, an enthusiastic follower but seldom a leader. When it did contribute to a global agenda in film, beginning in the 1940s, it did so in two secondary modes – the documentary and animation – a reflection of its established secondary political status.

Some will read the narrative of Anglo-Canadian and Quebec cinema as an allegorical tale of two Davids against a single American Goliath. Others will read it as a pathetic expression of dependent capitalism concerned more with making a quick buck than fostering cultural integrity. And yet others will read it as the story of an ambivalent and restricted nation state (Canada) and a would-be nation state (Quebec) trying to find some validation in cinema for each of their political aspirations for sovereignty. There will be those who view Canadian film history in terms of technological change that creates both great opportunities and serious problems for cultures that feel they lack sufficient room for self-expression. Finally, there will be those who view Anglo-Canadian and Quebec cinema as cinemas of obliteration, cinemas that purposefully 'forgot' vast areas of national identity because remembering certain peoples or events would have created a threat to established power and ideology.[11]

No matter which viewpoint or interpretation one adopts, we are looking at Canadian film history from the experience of the early twenty-first century and the current impact of Canadian cinema on Canadians and non-Canadians. Since the mid-1980s both Anglo-Canadian and Quebec feature films have received international recognition. It is from the perspective of an increasingly important feature film industry that this text is written rather than from an earlier perspective when the NFB documentary and animation were valorized as Canada's greatest achievements. In today's digitalized universe, both in television and the Internet, there is an insatiable demand for content that has given Canada its most productive and profitable period in a hundred years.

This narrative begins when moving pictures, along with the automobile, were a major technological innovation of the late nineteenth century. What the automobile was to the train and the telephone was to the telegraph, the moving pictures were to nineteenth-century photography. All three pushed the public universe toward a culture of mass appeal. From the beginning, film was a social art that developed its own mores, myths, and customs. The later privatization of the consumption of film through home video and then DVD formats, and the televizing of films on a daily basis in a multi-channel universe, all add to the ongoing impact of films on public consciousness. While the movie theatre as a locale may no longer be the dominant venue for film viewing or film profit, it retains its iconic presence in popular life and its requirements continue to frame the art.

This history of cinema in Canada does not aspire to be comprehensive, much less definitive. It omits far more than it includes. But what it does aspire to is an interpretive overview that interweaves the cinematic stories of English and French Canada into a single narrative, showing their similarities and differences, while exploring their serious omissions. These omissions have left open a vast space where varieties of multicultural, gender-based, and experimental consciousness may express themselves. What was done in film in Canada by resident filmmakers rather than the work of those who went elsewhere is the focus of this text. The result, for better or for worse, is the cinema that Canada created. And that creation must be understood in the context of what was happening in cinema worldwide – technologically, economically, politically, and aesthetically. If we are to understand both the achievements and the failures of Canadian cinema in the twentieth century, we need to know and understand the evolution of the art itself and the industry it was based in. That is why this text integrates an understanding of certain key developments outside of Canada with the situation inside Canada. As a result, readers do not need to possess a general knowledge of film history to appreciate developments in Canada. The historical framework is alluded to here.

Providing a reading of Canadian cinema using the rubric of nationality, as mentioned above, is problematic. Understanding the differences and respecting the diversity between and within the two 'national' cinemas raises the thorny question of 'national' cinema and its formulation as a theoretical or ideological construct. The task of the cultural historian in using the concept of national cinemas is that of a framer putting up the framework for a house. The reader cannot live under its empty spaces. Something other than nationalism must complete the structure. That 'something other' consists of various perspectives initiated by the practitioners and followers of the ideologies and theories mentioned previously.

Readers of film history need to understand that the construction of a critically examined history of film has more to do with the craft of historiography than the art of film-making or the experience of viewing films. The historian is not a film critic who reveals the hidden meanings and artistic secrets of a film or group of films. The historian is dependent on the theoretical insights of those for whom the study of film is a passion. He uses both criticism and theory to flesh out a narrative canvas filled with numerous figures, their creations, and interrelationships, but he paints primarily from the conventional historical imperative of providing information about who, when, where, why, and how, as provided by previous historians. In doing this, he is aware of how the language he uses creates distance between itself and the phenomenon it is meant to describe. In reading a history of film, one does not enter film as such, nor the minds of its creators and analysts, whose truncated statements about a film or films appear in the text. Unfortunately, the reader of a text about film can be lulled into accepting the validity and even primacy of the secondary printed text over that of the primary visual text. The narrator achieves this by weaving a rational construct that seems to make sense. But the historian's dependence on the writing of others (scholars, theoreticians, and critics) means a history of film is based more in other texts than in the films themselves.[12] So a film history is actually twice removed from the object that it purports to describe, be it a film or an event. Readers who experience Canadian film through a text of cultural history are receiving a *tertiary* reality compared to the primary experience of viewing the films themselves. While theoreticians and critics can dissect a film or a film-maker with their analytical tools, the historian only observes and records what they have done. It is not surprising that reading a history of Anglo-Canadian and Quebec film is normally accompanied by the viewing of major films in those traditions. Films themselves are a necessary balance to any film text.

It is the secret dream of all non-film-making writers of film history to have their narrative creation somehow equal the art of the original, which, of course, is an impossibility. In the end, what matters most is not the historical text but the films themselves and their impact on the viewer. What the individual reader brings to the text and to the films is as vital as what the historian brings. The reader comes from innumerable points on the intellectual, cultural, and emotional compass of human experience. It is the reader's universe that sits in judgment on what is read. It may be disturbing to some readers, especially those who are cinephiles, to realize that the main sources of a text of film history are other texts and not films, and that the practice of history involves the provision of an 'interpretation of interpretations.'[13] The scepticism that this may encourage is a good starting point for critical thinking rooted in the reader's own experience and intellectual heritage. The reader need only ask herself or himself how a paragraph in this text on any one film or a page on any film-maker can be anything more than a paltry glance at a two-hour visual and aural reality or a lifetime of creative work. Nevertheless, one can argue that a few lines of information or analysis can help lift the veil on a subject that may be completely unknown. Experiencing film directly and the indirect experience of reading about film are not necessarily incompatible, especially when one considers how different is the experience of a contemporary audience watching a fifty-year-old black and white film and the experience of the audience of its day. The historical contexts are radically different and so the meaning derived from the film necessarily changes. The historical text serves as a useful intermediary between today's reader/viewer and the subject, helping to acclimatize viewers using a language they comprehend.

One should think of this text as a kind of translation of the writings of others on Canadian film into a synthesized narrative. The historian acknowledges that historical writing is a representation of history whose cognitive mapping is framed by the historian's ideological mindset. Deciphering that mindset is not always easy because even one person's attitudes and approaches are often varied, interconnected, contradictory, and overlapping. Because the failings of a particular ideological approach tend to be exposed by competing ideologies, all exposition is ladened with the struggle for primacy. The historian's recycling of others' concepts and evaluations while offering the odd, previously unwritten insight is the best that can be hoped for. The text she or he creates is only a bare bones signpost, like the kind we see on the highway that says x number of kilometres to a destination. The sign is neither the destination nor the experience of getting there. It simply points the way to a much richer experience that may be discovered within the body of films that have come to define this nation state's cinematic eye. In the end, the historian's imagined reader and the reader's imagined historian meet through the text that is the reading of each other. Just as a film is the point of intersection between film-maker and viewer, a historical text is a point of intersection between writer and reader. They meet, exchange words, and go on.

CHAPTER ONE

Foundations of the Silver Screen

Canada's first indigenous cinematographer was James Freer (1855–1933), a farmer from the Brandon area of Manitoba, who began filming agricultural subjects in 1897. Freer's films became part of the Canadian Pacific Railway's and the Canadian government's push to attract settlers to the West when Canada had a population of only five million. As a result of the intense drive for settlers, the population increased by another three million in the period up to the First World War. From the Canadian government's point of view, too many of these immigrants were coming from the United States, thereby undermining Canada's imperial connection and its British identity. Freer's portrayals of the agricultural bounty that awaited the loyal Englishman in Western Canada were an attempt to overcome the advantage of easy cross-border access available to American settlers. First in 1899 under the sponsorship of the CPR and then again in 1902 under the sponsorship of the Department of the Interior, Freer toured Great Britain with his moving pictures that displayed the riches of the West.

This foray into promotional propaganda became a cornerstone of Canada's early experience with cinema production. Later, documentary film propaganda evolved into a hallmark of the Canadian industry when it made a name for itself in the early days of the National Film Board. Freer's subject matter served as a basic metaphor for early Canadian cinema – the figure in the landscape, with an emphasis on landscape. In 1902 the CPR hired Joe Rosenthal, who was considered 'the most famous cameraman of his day,' to make a promotional series about the natural resources and beauty of Canada titled *Living Canada*.[1] Rosenthal was later to be the cameraman for *Hiawatha, the Messiah of the Ojibway* (1903), the first film drama to be made in Canada. The CPR's involvement in Canadian promotional documentaries culminated in 1910 when it contracted with the Edison Company to do a dramatized series of thirteen films set in Western Canada. The CPR and the Canadian state had become inextricably linked ever since the building of Canada's transcontinental railway in the 1880s. Their joint sponsorship of immigration films resulted in a Canadian tradition of large corporate and state interests coalescing.

Rivalling these early films sponsored by corporate and government interests were numerous ad hoc shorts made about Canada's natural wonders. Subjects ranged from such perennial tourist attractions as Niagara Falls all the way to the joys of moose hunting in New Brunswick. The Canadian film historian Peter Morris has noted that this subject matter generated a cinematic image of Canada worldwide as 'a piece of exotic scenery.'[2] The term for these films was appropriately 'scenics.' The short scenic was a product of limited technology (the single-reel film), which severely restricted the length of films, and the format of the weekly or monthly 'illustrated news' magazines read by middle-class audiences, which set the cultural standard for the visualization of distant places and events. Audiences of the day were accustomed to accepting the reality of 'scenes' beyond their immediate surroundings as they were presented by journalistic descriptions and visual reproductions in pictorial magazines, postcards based on photographs, or the novelty of three-dimensional reproductions of photographic stills in hand-held devices called stereoscopes. The acceptance of early films depended on their being 'read' as an extension of the established cultural framework of these non-cinematic forms. Since the films were 'silent,' they were associated with the world of photography and pictures, and so films were termed 'moving pictures.' Eventually the prominence of the medium resulted in the shortening of the name to 'movies.'

Another cultural medium that was understood by late nineteenth- and early twentieth-century audiences was vaudeville, a live theatrical entertainment consisting of various individual acts such as magic tricks, dancing, and gymnastics. The first films were often added to vaudeville shows as another form of performance placed between live acts. One might think of it as an early form of virtual reality. Since early films were very short, they emulated the time frame used by vaudeville acts, in which variety was enhanced by numerous brief performances. When film first appeared, its novelty was translated into a version of what turn-of-the-century audiences already knew – a combination of pictorials (the photographic image) and theatricals (costumed acting or performance).[3] This made moving pictures into a valid expression of what was already known and accepted. As magazines and photographs provided information and variety shows provided entertainment, so these two elements became the parameters of the new medium.

As a result of the ownership of proprietary inventions, the film industry came to be dominated by two major national players – France and the United States. 'It was above all the French, followed by the Americans, who were the most ardent exporters of the new invention,' writes the editor of *The Oxford History of World Cinema*. 'In terms of artistic development it was again the French and the Americans who took the lead.'[4] Because cinema was 'from the outset an international business,' cinema in Canada became a reflection of the battle between Europe and the Americans.[5] Right from the start, the market for silent films was multinational, and producers sent their films from one country to another for viewing. The initial winners of the contest were the French, even though the Americans had been first off the mark with their kinetoscope, a peep-show device that allowed a single viewer at a time to view a 35 mm strip of moving images. Although vast numbers of kinetoscope devices were sold, the market that was emerging for film was a public and social one in which people would come together to view movies in a theatrical setting. The kinetoscope consequently died out.[6]

The French played to and developed the mass market audience more quickly than the Americans. The Lumière Cinématographe was a camera projector that weighed a mere seven kilograms and could make films and project them. In comparison, the American Kinetograph projector weighed over a hundred kilograms.[7] Both machines created the marvel of realistic motion that appealed to audiences everywhere. Montreal's *La Presse* concluded its commentary on the first screening in Canada with this prediction: 'All that was needed to complete the illusion was colour and a phonograph to reproduce sounds. That is soon to come, we are to believe.'[8]

The most popular of the very early images was Lumière's single-shot film of a train entering a station.[9] But quickly the audience sought something more complex. Pathé, the soon-to-be-famous French newsreel company, was formed in 1896 and quickly became the world leader in film production. By 1906 the firm was releasing six new film titles per week, printing 30,000 metres of positive film per day (15 metres per minute of a film), and making a minimum of seventy-five copies of each of its titles for the U.S. market alone.[10] Most films made prior to

1910 were one-reelers (one reel of film was 1,000 feet or 300 metres) and at 50 feet per minute ran for twenty minutes or less. One reel might contain six different subjects.[11] The average film was shot in one day at a cost of $200 to $500.[12] Of the 1,200 films released in the United States in 1907, only 400 were American-made.[13] The rest were primarily French.[14] No wonder that the film inventor Edison called for an American response to this commercial and cultural onslaught.[15]

The overall selection of films available for viewing in Canada was not much different from that in the United States, except for an even greater proportion of French production because of Quebec's French-speaking audience. Early on, French firms began to specialize in pious religious and historical tableaux for conservative audiences. The touring mother-and-son team of the Countess and Vicomte Grandsaignes d'Hauterives from France brought film treatments of biblical material to various parts of Quebec as early as the late 1890s.[16] The established French tradition of the 'tableau vivant' (costumed representations of particular biblical or historical scenes) was the basis for this form of early film approved by the Catholic Church, which saw it as contributing to piety. There was no such argument required in English Canada. Two worlds were developing in Canadian cinema – a Quebec-based French Catholic one, with an emphasis on approved mythologies (entertainment) for personal edification, and an English Protestant one with an emphasis on promotional documentary realism (information) for achieving financial objectives. While Quebec was ideologically reflective, hierarchical, and inward-looking, English Canada was expansionist, financially motivated, and interested in film as an adjunct to nation-building. The former tradition sought the preservation of piety, while the latter sought immigration. When the CPR was touting its advertising scenics of Canada for its own materialist goals, Ernest Ouimet (1877–1972), Quebec's pioneer film theatre owner, was showing *La Vie et la passion de Jésus Christ* (1906) to impress the clergy. While the vastness of the land and its possibilities became a signature of Anglo-Canadian film-making during the first decade of the twentieth century, French-Canadian sensibilities turned to mythological and historical subjects as determined by European taste and religious norms. This difference between a film of the spirit and a film of the body was to have major repercussions decades later when Quebec outpaced English Canada in the production of feature films.

A comparison between the careers of Ernest Ouimet in Quebec and the Allen brothers of Brantford, Ontario, encapsulates the divergence that was occurring. Ouimet was a Montreal theatre electrician who got into film as a projectionist and then opened his own cinema in Montreal in 1906. Within a few years, he was producing his own short films and newsreels of local events. In 1907 he opened North America's first movie palace – the thousand-seat Ouimetoscope – years ahead of the Americans.[17] Ouimet was able to show his films on Sundays, something that was not allowed in other Canadian or American cities for some time to come. Using religious subjects in his screenings no doubt helped make him Quebec's premiere film exhibitor.

The Allen brothers were two Americans who opened a theatre in Brantford, Ontario, in 1906 and went on to create a nationwide chain of fifty theatres that dominated film exhibition across Canada until the early 1920s, when, under duress, they sold out to Hollywood studio interests. In contrast, Ouimet was successful within the Quebec milieu until he sold his distribution company and tried his hand at producing films in Hollywood, with tragic results. When the Allen brothers opened their first film theatre, the only concept for a permanent venue for films was the nickelodeon, a converted storefront, where admission was initially five cents. Because of public demand, thousands of storefront businesses in North America converted from retail use to nickelodeons showing single-reel fifteen-minute movies.[18] Prior to the nickelodeon phenomenon, films were viewed outdoors in amusement parks or in regular theatres that specialized in vaudeville-type entertainment. Nickelodeons created a mass market for film that attracted the working class.[19] They were small ad hoc venues, requiring little capital, that were meant to cash in on a craze. Ouimet's revolutionary leap to the movie palace format, offering two hours of film entertainment for one dollar, could only work when there was sufficient content to sustain a full program. The movie palace concept required a longer narrative structure than was present in the short films made for nickelodeons. The interaction between film space and film time would soon undergo a quantum leap equal to the nickelodeon's victory of group viewing over the individuality of the kinetoscope salon.

Early cinema spoke to spectators very differently from the way spectators were addressed by later classical cinema with its coherent fictional world, its characters and stars.[20] Early silent films were what historians call 'a cinema of attractions.'[21] Single shots of a juggler performing or the single-shot historical tableau scene emulated the entertainments of the day, especially for the lower classes. Film was not grand opera because it took its cues from journalism, photography, and vaudeville. Likewise, at this very early stage of popular cinema, any conception of 'Canadian' content beyond figures moving in a Canadian landscape was completely unthinkable. It was not until the narrative feature film came into existence, with its links to middle-class ticket prices (one dollar versus five cents) and elegant theatre surroundings, that content would be an issue. In the first decade of cinema, films circulated internationally and 'the concept of a national cinema was largely unarticulated.'[22] Films played to a common popular taste in Europe and North America. The demand for a disaster film about the San Francisco earthquake or Edison's 1906 *The Life of a Fireman* was universal. But already the cultural differences between English and French Canada were at play. Even during the internationalist silent era, 'national' cultural norms were not far below the surface.

A good example of early internationalism was the amazing work of French producer and director Georges Méliès, who in 1902 made a thirteen-minute film titled *Voyage to the Moon*, which was inspired by the work of his fellow countryman, the world famous novelist and science fiction writer Jules Verne. The film used thirty sets. He followed this triumph with a 1904 sequel titled *Voyage beyond the Possible*, about a space trip to the sun, and *Twenty Thousand Leagues under the Sea* in 1906. Méliès became the father of cinematic special effects and the master of primitively constructed illusions. Not only was the literary material on which the films were based popularly known among literate audiences in the Western world, but the subject matter appealed to audiences of all nationalities. Méliès's films were a success wherever they were shown, including Canada. He was honoured for his achievements by being elected president of the International Congress of Film Producers in 1909.

Early attempts at narrative structure remained within the single-reel format and the time frame linked to singing, dancing, and magic acts. An important reflection of this format and the popular taste that it formed was the fact that in 1907 fully 70 per cent of films were comedies.[23] Slapstick humour, contorted facial expressions, ridiculous costumes, and silly activities fitted the vaudevillian universe that audiences inhabited comfortably. Film as escapist entertainment was the norm, and comedy was the transitional vehicle that moved audiences toward fictional films.

The first developments in narrative feature film came from a combination of European and American experiments and were fed by film versions of stage plays such as Shakespeare's *Taming of the Shrew* (1908) and adaptations of novels such as Victor Hugo's *Les Misérables* (1911). Cinema historian Douglas Gomery describes how film companies in this period (1905–10) 'raided pulp magazines, public domain novels and successful plays for plots.'[24] At the same time, the typical tableau camera angle of full-frame figures with space below and above was being augmented by close-ups and other differently framed shots, so that character, mood, and actions could be more effectively displayed. The turn to fiction and away from documenting reality made film a more complex phenomenon both in production terms and in its impact on audiences. What had once been simple awe at the marvel of moving pictures became a thirst for laughter and eventually a desire for tears. Film became an emotional experience comparable to that generated by live drama.

Cinema was beginning to develop its own visual language distinct from its roots in pictorials and theatricals. The narrative feature film used editing to create its own illusion of reality in its representation of both space and time. The single piano player of the nickelodeon was soon to be surpassed by movie palace orchestral arrangements and performances that gave silent cinema a richer, more complex sound. Dialogue frames were added between scenes, so that audiences could read what the actors were imagined to be saying to each other.

Hiawatha, the Messiah of the Ojibway (1903) was a single-reeler filmed on location in Ontario using Native performers. It was based on the renowned American poet Henry Wadsworth Longfellow's *The Song of Hiawatha*. The film displayed the characteristics that would soon dominate Canada's relationship to cinema. First, it was filmed on a First Nations reserve, using a Canadian location to add realism, thereby furthering Canada's connection to locale, landscape, and wilderness. Second, it was based on an American topic and author's work. That Canadian readers and viewers would be well aware of this famous poem only added to the cultural interplay between the two countries. American interpretation of the real Canadian setting as their own imagined one simply confirmed the increasing division between the original content of a story and how it was visually and culturally constructed.

The choice of an Aboriginal theme was not surprising given the mythologized view of Canada as a place of wilderness and the supposedly retained authenticity of its Native peoples compared to those of the United States. This interpretation fitted the colonizing culture's late nineteenth- and early twentieth-century fascination with Native Americans and their supposed doomed way of life. At the time, this theme was central to the valorization of technologically superior Euro-American civilization and its self-generated antithesis – the desire to find salvation from industrialism in Nature. This desire manifested itself in everything from the popularity of the Boy Scout movement to the romantic fascination with Buffalo Bill Cody's globe-trotting Wild West Show. While *Hiawatha* fulfilled the tragic expectations of its contemporary non-Aboriginal North American audiences, its subject matter launched a thematic trajectory of Canada as an on-going site of wilderness and retained pre-contact Aboriginal authenticity, which has remained until the end of the twentieth century and the beginning of the twenty-first (see chapters 11 and 17). While Canada would continue to serve almost exclusively as a simple locale for films on the theme of White–Native relationships, especially in the heyday of the American western (1910–60), its own perspective and that of its Native peoples were awaiting liberation from a Euro-Canadian understanding.

There were three different ways in which Canada came to be presented in early narrative films. The first was in Hollywood productions; the second was in American productions of Canadian subjects shot in Canada; and the third was in the productions of Canadian firms shooting Canadian materials in Canada. Up to 1910, global film production was dominated by the French, but in the decade of the 1910s the Americans took over. As demand for more complex, lengthier, and narrative-oriented films increased, the technique of creating cinematic illusion with indoor studio sets and the need for a sunny year-round climate for outdoor shooting coalesced in the creation of a film studio system based in Hollywood, California. There were numerous independent firms making films, but these were soon to merge into a half-dozen key players. An example of the size of American operations just prior to the First World War is the Vitagraph Company, which in 1912 had a gross income of $6 million and was making three hundred one- and two-reel films per year.[25] Canada had nothing comparable, but it did have a surfeit of wilderness landscape (not the CPR's wheat fields of Saskatchewan but forests, rivers, and mountains) and its own adventure identity in popular pulp fiction. American firms, in their hunger for material, actually developed an early film genre about Canada termed 'the northwoods melodrama' that was a take-off on the American western.

At the same time that Canadians were using film to populate their own West with agrarian immigrants, the Americans were conscious of the end of their western frontier. In the film genre of the 'western,' they created a glorified interpretation of American national character based on the subjugation of Native Americans and the supposed heroism and sacrifice of the subjugators, while vilifying their opponents. Building on this image from their own culture, American film companies created Canadian spin-offs in which the stock figure of the law-enforcing sheriff became a Mountie, the happy-go-lucky cowboy became a lumberjack or a prospector, and the ne'er-do-well Mexican villain became a shifty-eyed, dark French Canadian.[26] The 'Mountie novel,' which began to appear in the 1890s, was considered to be part of the American 'Wild West' pulp fiction genre, which provided the impetus for film equivalents. Written by ex-Mounties and others, these texts, popular in Europe and North America, became the basis for Hollywood's film imagination.[27] The resulting portrayal of Canada in American feature films used Hollywood sets and California locations to create stereotypical imagery in which an American-styled fictional world overwhelmed the image of Canada created by Canadian 'scenics.' Because of the sheer volume of these movies and their popularity, an American-created cinematic stereotype of Canada was born.[28]

American romanticized and racist melodramas triumphed over indigenous realism and filled the world's imagination with their characterization of a country and its peoples. What is equally disturbing is that the racism toward Aboriginal peoples in these 'northwoods' melodramas was echoed in the Anglo-American treatment of French Canadians, who, like their Catholic counterparts in Mexico, were portrayed as sinister, slovenly, and racially inferior.[29] But the indigenous realism of the CPR's 'documentary' mode could not claim innocence either. It was also an idealized fiction using actors and stories that eliminated the Aboriginal presence in the agrarian West and replaced it with a purely Euro-Canadian one of boundless prosperity. Some American companies actually went to Canada to film melodramas. The first of these was *The Cattle Thieves* (1909). The same firm went on to make nine more films, including *Wolfe or the Conquest of Quebec* (1914), shot on location in Quebec City. This latter film suggested that popular subject matter could be taken from Canadian history and attract non-Canadian audiences, holding out the promise of a countervailing influence over the dominant fictional stereotype.

There were four film companies who attempted to create a different, Canadian-based fictional narrative in the brief period from 1912 to 1914. All of these companies had heavy American involvement. The British American Film Company produced *The Battle of the Long Sault*, which was a two-reeler about a 1660 Iroquois attack on Montreal. It was the only film the company made. A Montreal producer drew on the same period to make *Madeleine de Verchères*, an account of the Quebec heroine's defence of a fort against the Iroquois. It was his only production. Obviously, these films fitted in the 'good' Whites over 'nasty' Natives theme that was, unfortunately, the contemporary norm. It was the norm because it glorified those with whom the audience felt affinity. There was a departure when the All-Red Feather Company moved into a pro-Canadian, pro-British mode with a three-reeler about the War of 1812 titled *The War Pigeon*. Based on a story by the Canadian writer Arthur Stringer, it was released at the outbreak of the First World War, and failed. The final film company that operated in the pre-war period was the Canadian Bioscope Company, which was British-owned. Canadian Bioscope made *Evangeline* in 1913, based on Henry Wadsworth Longfellow's poem about the expulsion of the Acadians in the mideighteenth century. The seventy-five-minutes-long film was tinted for colour. It did very well, and the company went on to make a half-dozen other films, none of which was successful. The company closed with the coming of the war.[30]

Evangeline represented a high point in Canadian fictional film prior to the First World War. It starred known American actors – Laura Lyman as Evangeline and John F. Carlton as Gabriel, her beloved – and was shot on location in the Annapolis Valley of Nova Scotia. The reviewer for the New York trade journal *Moving Picture World* explained that the five-reel film was about 'a real Canadian subject' that was known worldwide because Longfellow's poem had been translated into a multitude of languages.[31] If Evangeline was the high point, what kind of high point was it, one may ask, when the leading Canadian feature film of its day was made by a British-owned Canadian company, used American actors, and was based on a work by an American writer? Only the subject matter and the locations were Canadian. Playing to the American market as a formula for Canadian cinematic success was to be repeated in the future. The economics of feature film-making created a formidable obstacle to the development of an indigenous narrative identity in Canadian film. It seems that the Canadian ability to mythologize itself had not come anywhere near what the Americans were capable of doing about themselves, their history, and the history of their neighbours. Many years later, this failure to mythologize was to prove a blessing of sorts, when it helped Canadian cinema follow its own path, distinct from that of Hollywood.

Other British colonies were making headway in cinema. In 1904 Charles Tait, an Australian director, developed a seventy-minute epic about the notorious Australian outlaw Ned Kelly, using a Canadian actor in the lead role.[32] Even an occupied colony like India was making fictional films based on Hindu legends by 1912.[33] In the rest of the film world, other nationalities were furthering the language of film. The Italians were pioneering *film d'arte*, a lavish form of historical film drama using thousands of extras and elaborate sets and costumes (the major example was the nine-reel *Quo Vadis* of 1913). But none of these other countries had to deal, as Canada had to, with the proximity of the major production centres of New York and Hollywood, which continued to be the cinematic leaders.

In 1911 a proposal to sign a reciprocity treaty with the United States was defeated by a wave of Canadian nationalism, which was soon augmented by Canada's entrance as Britain's ally into the First World War, while the United States stayed neutral. Since newly introduced provincial censor boards were upset with the amount of American flag-waving in films shown in Canada at the very moment that the country was trying to fan patriotic fervour, the time seemed right for a new Canadian film initiative. The Conner Till Film Company of Toronto was a Canadian-American joint operation with its own studio. It released its first drama in early 1915, followed by the release of a new short film weekly. Within several months, the studio burned and the company closed down to become just another short-lived experiment in Canadian film. With Hollywood filling public demand for films because Europe was embroiled in a terrible war, Canada fell increasingly under American influence.

In the battle between American fictional narrative film and Canadian promotional 'documentaries,' realistic portrayal of Canada lost out. The two great economic powers in Canadian society at the time – large corporate entities like the CPR and the government – wanted to use film for non-cinematic economic benefit rather than for the expansion of cinema. With a colonial mentality like Canada's that was always looking elsewhere for greatness there was little hope for the creation of a vibrant cinema, though sporadic attempts were made. The Canadian popular cinematic imagination prior to the First World War was already being moulded by images from outside the country, and indigenous attempts to create a counterbalancing vision failed to achieve any critical mass. The pliability of silent cinema, in which different language frames for titles and dialogue could be easily inserted, made film an international medium that crossed linguistic and cultural borders. The growing stature of the United States as the premiere film producer in the world after the outbreak of the First World War, when the European film industry temporarily collapsed, meant that Canadian audiences were receiving more and more American content. The rise of the Hollywood studio system and its oligopolistic practices led to a diminution of Canadian film exhibiting power. It was Hollywood that was making easily accessible films about Canada with formulaic attributes, rather than Canadians making feature films about Canadian subjects. As a result, Canadian moving picture imagery became linked primarily to landscape, wilderness, and nature.

The 1905 figure in the landscape of CPR scenics was replaced by 1915 with the stereotypical characters in a Hollywood setting purporting to be Canadian. Without a studio system of its own or even a single centre that could focus the country's film production as had occurred in European countries, Canada remained the home of a cinema colonized by another sensibility. As for Quebec, the temporary collapse of the French film industry and exports during the First World War meant a break in cultural continuity between itself and Europe. Because, in the words of one film theorist, 'the beginnings of cinema coincided precisely with the very height of imperialism,' Canada's colonial heritage did not augur well for an indigenous cinema.[34] With Canada officially a proud member of the world's then most extensive and powerful empire, the country's colonial mentality was a major player in formulating and limiting its cultural identity. The worldview of the day, from the perspective of Euro-Canadians, was generally racist, self-congratulatory, and attuned to an ideology of superiority. This view played into the national stereotypes of Hollywood's 'northwoods' genre with its easily identifiable French-Canadian and Aboriginal villains and its handsome nordic Mountie heroes representing the vanguard of Euro-Canadian values.

The importance of the rise of silent narrative feature film should not be underestimated. What the Americans were developing as a standard in the industry between 1910 and 1920 set the norm for cinema until the end of the silent era and beyond. Artistically the parameters of film changed during the teens. The feature film was aimed at middle-class audiences attending large, new movie palaces like the eight-hundred-seat Allen Theatre in Calgary. The class tastes of this audience moved the medium beyond its vaudevillian roots and toward epic themes. The finest and most controversial example of the narrative film that the

Americans produced was D.W. Griffith's silent classic *The Birth of a Nation*, released in 1915, which was denounced as racist by African Americans. The film was twelve reels, took four months to make, cost $100,000 to shoot, advertise, and distribute, and lasted three hours. Filmgoers had to pay a special admission.[35] The spectacle that it offered its viewing audience was so superior to anything else that its creation propelled the American industry to a new level. Considering what passed for Canadian film-making at the same time, it is not surprising that Canada did not develop a competitive product for its own audiences. Nor could Canadian firms compete with the vertically integrating practices of the American industry in Hollywood, with its film factory studios geared to non-stop production, a large domestic market (2,000 movie palaces and 18,000 small theatres by 1920), control of the distribution networks, and a movie star system.[36]

The star system was particularly problematic for the development of an indigenous Canadian feature film industry because it resulted in Canadian talent heading to Hollywood. The most famous of the Canadian-born stars was Mary Pickford (1893–1979), who, in the exalting words of one critic, 'parlayed a precociously fearless innocence into the most popular screen persona of the silent era.'[37] As a cinema star, she was known as 'America's Sweetheart' and began her rise to stardom under the direction of D.W. Griffith. With the likes of Douglas Fairbanks and Charlie Chaplin, she rose to the front ranks of the new cult of cinematic celebrities. While Fairbanks exemplified clean-shaven virile masculinity, Pickford expressed the ideal of female vulnerability and youthful feminine beauty. To balance this idealization, Chaplin's character captured the comic travails of the naïve everyman. The star system became an essential ingredient in winning public attention because it came to represent cultural and social ideals, both the conscious and the repressed. The film star personified the power of the new medium to create a unified culture for a mass audience.

'It is clear,' film historians have concluded, 'that stardom, along with narrative and the classic Hollywood style, became institutionalized during the second decade of the century.'[38] This institutionalization did not include Canada in any creative manner other than America's magnetic power to attract exceptional talent such as that of Mary Pickford or Mack Sennett (1880–1960), the famous creator of the 'Keystone Cops' slapstick comedies that entertained tens of millions of cinemagoers around the world. As film audiences became more and more attuned to looking for Hollywood stars on marquees and playbills, the more difficult it became for firms without recognized stars to create a profitable film.

The final barrier to Canadian feature film production was the lack of a Canadian business class that was willing to invest in such a risky enterprise. It was much more profitable to distribute and exhibit films made outside Canada than to take a chance on making a feature. By the 1910s, the size of film budgets had grown exponentially, the cost of stars had increased dramatically, and exhibition in the American market, where such costs could be recuperated, was problematic and difficult for non-American firms. Isolated and idiosyncratic attempts at 'making it in the movies' were more commonly failures than successes. A good example is Ernest Ouimet, who tried his luck producing Canadian material in Hollywood and lost everything.

That the foundations of the silent screen ended up being anti-Canadian was not surprising considering that Canada at this time was part of the British Empire. Its colonial mentality was filled with political, cultural, and economic links to the mother country that precluded a concerted nationalistic desire to create a competitive, world-class film industry. The evolution of the industry from the standard documentary or dramatic fifteen-minute short to the multi-hour feature film with recognized movie actors left Canadian narrative lying in the dust, except when that narrative was created by Hollywood. The further evolution of Canadian cinema was to be stymied by the new realities of cinema production and its major centres. Canadians willingly succumbed to outside material. One must remember that this was the era prior to a nationalist concept of Canadian literature, or even the recognition of the Group of Seven as producing the first self-conscious Canadian iconography.

What the narrative feature film heralded was the importance of fantasy and illusion for the popular imagination. Its fictive nature expressed a culturally agreed upon stereotyping and mythology. The government- and corporate-sponsored advertisements for Canada were no match for heroic and melodramatic fantasy, especially after 1910. When Federico Fellini, the post–Second World War Italian director, stated that 'two things always look good in a film – a train and snow,' one might be led to conclude that Canada ought to have been a cinematic success because it had an abundance of both.[39] But Fellini's observations do not take into account the human desire for escapism and dreams nor the realities of economic power. Hollywood understood the human psyche and how to pander to its needs. It sought to create a narrative with universal appeal, and its high investment in production values and promotion ensured a wide acceptance.

Culture operates on the unity of a *mythos* (story) and a *logos* (rationalizing structure), ergo, the concept of the *mytho-logical*. Myth is a story of characters that is structured in a meaningful way because it affirms a common, underlying understanding shared by the creators of cultural products (art) and its observers and consumers (audience). The cultural embodiments in narrative film have to fit a common discourse that is shared by all the participants in order to make sense and win approval. When a culture does not have a sufficient mass of its own interpreters of its own stories, it ends up receiving and absorbing interpretations offered by others. These interpretations are then internalized into a collective consciousness. The result is a conflict in which the internal identity that is self-generated is opposed to the external image that is generated by others. That conflict occurred not only for Quebec and Anglo-Canadian society but for those excluded from the mythological paradigms or demonized by them. Hollywood's Canada may have contained the positive English-Canadian Mountie, which appealed to a certain part of Canadian society, but it also represented French-Canadian and Aboriginal figures as villains, thereby leaving these groups alienated and disheartened. As well, it omitted a large number of immigrant groups who were asked to assimilate to the stereotypical norm.

The historical reality of colonialism, racism, and imperialism in Canada during the first two decades of the twentieth century made Canada open to American cinematic consciousness. This enhanced the dependency and subordination of national identities in Canada, but it also set in motion antithetical currents. While national cinemas in Canada awaited their moment in history, cultural self-awareness proceeded. The lack of strong national cinemas in Canada early on did not block the eventual rise of cultural nationalism in other fields. The limited power of cinema to set a whole culture's agenda signalled that cinema was a place of contest and struggle. The content of universally appealing paradigms of human myth, when presented through an outsider's cultural interpretations and configurations, could be challenged and deconstructed when communities gained the power for self-expression.

CHAPTER TWO

Back to God's Country: The Shipman Saga

The struggle against Germany and its allies was the main concern of Canadians from 1914 to 1918. War creates an outpouring of nationalism that seeks a public stage for its display of patriotic fervour, and cinema was one of its venues. In this period, when radio was still in its infancy, print was the dominant public format for expressing nationalist sentiments, but cinema played an increasingly important role in propaganda with the newsreels that preceded feature films in movie theatres. Audiences were able to visualize and 'experience' historic events through newsreels, whose makers framed these events from the point of view of the viewing audience. Beginning with the Boer War at the turn of the century, then with the Russo-Japanese War of 1905 and the Balkan conflicts of 1910–11, audiences around the world were able to be 'witness' to actual events from the perspective of the cinematographer and his employers. An example of the importance of newsreels during the First World War was the famous footage of the British officer known as Lawrence of Arabia as he led camel-mounted Arab tribesmen in their guerrilla war against Germany's allies, the Turks, who controlled Palestine and the Arabian peninsula.

Initially, governments in Canada naturally favoured British newsreels and censored American ones because the United States was officially neutral until 1917, but they were not above using Hollywood for their own ends. For example, when the Americans produced a Mary Pickford film titled *100 Percent American*, which was used to sell war bonds, the Canadian government had it retitled *100 Percent Canadian* and used the same film to sell their own war bonds.[1] In 1916 a Toronto promoter, George Brownridge, built a studio in Trenton, Ontario, and made two feature films that led to his bankruptcy. He then resurrected himself as Adanac Producing Company, which distributed the earlier films and went on to make *The Great Shadow* (1919), which was part of a short-lived genre called 'Red scare' films. The motivation for these films originated with American anti-communism, a response to the Russian Revolution of 1917. Panic about the spread of communism and proletarian rule was also strong in Canada's ruling classes, who were particularly fearful of agitation among unemployed veterans.

In Canada the most notable political event of the time was the Winnipeg General Strike of 1919, which paralyzed the city. In this atmosphere of class conflict, the Canadian Pacific Railway and the Employers of Labour funded Brownridge to make *The Great Shadow*. It was filmed in factories in Montreal and featured an 'honest,' some might say compliant, labour leader almost succumbing to subversive elements. The film industry magazine *Moving Picture World* of New York characterized the film as excellent 'propaganda against industrial unrest.' [2] But the film did not do that well because it was released at the tail-end of the Red scare phenomenon. A few years later, Brownridge sold his Trenton studio to the Ontario government to house its motion picture bureau. The Brownridge saga continued the linkage between independent film producers, large corporate interests, and the state which had begun at the turn of the century.

One man who tried to work outside this structure, and for a time seemed to be successful, was Ernest Shipman, born in Hull, Quebec, in 1871. He worked in the amusement industry as a promoter. In 1910 he met and married eighteen-year-old Helen Foster Barham of Victoria, who later became the movie star Nell Shipman. They lived in southern California, where Ernest made films and Nell became a scenario writer and actress.[3] Her breakthrough film was *God's Country and the Woman* (1916), based on the work of James Oliver Curwood, the American writer who popularized the 'northwoods' genre in fiction and film. *God's Country and the Woman* made Nell Shipman a star. The Shipmans used this first-hand American film experience to launch their own made-in-Canada features aimed at the American market. The first was *Back to God's Country*, which went into production in 1919 using a Calgary-incorporated company with Ernest as the producer, Nell as the film's leading lady, and Curwood as the storyteller. Basically, *Back to God's Country* was a sequel to the hugely popular *God's Country and the Woman*.

In 1919 Calgary may have seemed like a strange location for funding and producing a Canadian film, but it must be remembered that Calgary was the corporate headquarters of the Allen movie theatre chain, the single largest one in Canada. Besides, Ernest Shipman decided to shoot the winter scenes on location in northern Alberta to capture a degree of authenticity often lacking in Hollywood studio productions. Shooting in mid-March on Lesser Slave Lake was problematic, not only technically because of the impact of the extreme cold on the equipment, but because the lead actor died of pneumonia working in such a harsh environment. The rest of the film was shot in California and released to the North American market by First National. Nell, as the script/ scenario writer, changed the Curwood story by expanding the heroine's role, while reducing that of the canine hero in the original story.[4] This led to a break between the Shipmans and Curwood, and as a result, Ernest Shipman turned to Canadian-authored material for his later films. The Canadian film historian Peter Morris writes that the film was 'an enormous financial success, grossing over half-a-million dollars in its first year of release, and netting the Calgary backers a three hundred percent return on their investment.'[5] It seemed that 'God's Country' was heaven for investors.

With this kind of result, the Shipmans felt they were on a roll. Ernest had been adept at promoting the film by emphasizing a swimming scene with Nell in the nude. 'Is the Nude Rude?' asked the ads teasingly. The scene itself was discretely filmed. But it was evident that Ernest's showmanship (sex sells) was able to take Nell's innovative approach to women heroines (protagonists not victims) and make it work for a mass audience. Nell herself not only was a talented and original scenario writer, but she also developed a rapport with the animals used in the film. She was presented as an innocent and beautiful Eve in a wilderness Garden of Eden in touch with and befriending wild animals. A year after their mutual triumph, Nell and Ernest divorced. With the Curwood connection also broken, their twice-successful formula came to an end. Nell Shipman set up her own production company, but things did not go well for her. Her major effort was *The Girl from God's Country* (1921), a sequel that bankrupted her firm and caused her to set up operations in Idaho, where she made several other films on wildlife themes using her own scripts.[6] Curwood kept writing the 'northwoods' genre, of which he was a master, while Ernest Shipman, ever the showman, used the example of *Back to God's Country* as proof-positive that Canadian-made films had a great future.

In 1919 Ernest Shipman signed a contract with Canada's best-selling author Charles William Gordon (1860–1937), who used the pen-name of

Nell Shipman in *Back to God's Country* (1919).

Ralph Connor, to film Connor's novels using capital raised from investors in Connor's home city of Winnipeg. The money was then funnelled through Shipman's New York company. The first film was *God's Crucible*, based on Connor's 1909 novel *The Foreigner*, a moralistic story of a Slavic immigrant who transforms himself from a youthful rowdy to a responsible Canadian man. It was shot, using the Shipman formula, on location in Winnipeg and in the Alberta foothills, where Connor had spent a few years as a Presbyterian clergyman in the 1890s and where he received his inspiration for much of his popular fiction. More films followed, of which the most successful was *Cameron of the Royal Mounted*, based on Connor's 1912 novel *Corporal Cameron of the North West Mounted Police: A Tale of the Macleod Trail*. Always keen on authentic location as a key ingredient for both his fund-raising and his film-making, Shipman even got a squad of real Mounties based in Fort Macleod, Alberta, to participate.

Connor also wrote about nineteenth-century frontier life in Ontario in two famous works, *The Man from Glengarry* (1901) and its sequel, *Glengarry School Days* (1902). Shipman went to Ottawa, where the novels were set, to raise money from local investors, among them Canadian writers Robert Stead and Duncan Campbell Scott.[7] The films were directed by a Canadian, Henry McRae, who had directed Shipman's previous two films. The first Ottawa film used the title of the novel, but the second was retitled *The Critical Age*. Neither of these 1922 films was a box office success. The Shipman saga was coming to an abrupt and dismal end. The Canadian-owned Allen movie theatre chain was sold at fire sale prices to American interests in 1923, the same year that Brownridge sold his Trenton studio to the Ontario government. The four-year post-war run of Canadian feature film-making was over. Its short lifespan replicated the equally brief upsurge in Canadian dramatic film just prior to the First World War.

While serving as a symbol of Canadian cinema entrepreneurship, Shipman made a speech to the London, Ontario, chapter of the Canadian Club in which he waxed eloquent on the national spirit embodied in Canadian literature and how that spirit needed to be translated into motion pictures. Playing on the appeal of nature as a symbol of purity, he called this spirit 'real and free and wholesome as Canadian life at its best.'[8] The cultural nationalism of morale-boosting speeches, such as Shipman's, is one thing; the efficacy of cultural nationalism as a force in a specific historical reality is something else. At this point, cultural nationalism was insufficient to sustain a Canadian feature film indus-

Ernest Shipman, Canadian film producer from the silent era.

try. The American film industry was taking control of Canadian movie theatres; the few Canadian feature films that were being produced did not do well enough at the box office to sustain ongoing production; and the entrepreneurial model of film-making was an increasingly poor option under the pervasive influence of the Hollywood studios, whose budgets kept increasing and whose stars were major drawing cards for an acculturated public.

What had Ernest Shipman accomplished? His siren call of patriotic nationalism may have appealed to the national elite and, during war-time, to the masses, but it could not compete with American budgets and the fantasies purveyed by Hollywood. Shipman was successful at the Canadian box office with his Canadian-made films when he used Hollywood formulas of the Mountie or the 'northwoods' melodrama. He was successful when he did his own variant on what Canadians were already accustomed to watching and what the American public readily accepted. But the time of independent producers was over. Their approach of using private investors for each film couldn't work in a world increasingly filled with well-financed corporations. That Shipman ended his career trying to make films in Florida is a reminder of the lack of depth to his nationalist sermonizing.

As long as the short-lived Americanized troika of Curwood, Ernest, and Nell worked together, they could use the Canadian wilderness as a spectacular locale to give distinctness and enhanced value to their product. But when they split apart, each one taking a piece of the formula, their individual replacements were inadequate. Even if they had stayed together, their films would have represented Canada through an American author's view. The expatriate Canadian director Allan Dawn wrote in a 1920 article in *Maclean's* that what Canada had to offer silent film was nothing but location: 'Why, I could do the best movie I ever put on if I could work around Lake Louise, or Banff. Montreal and Quebec offer the best backgrounds on this side of the ocean. They have been used, but not as often as they deserve. Many a time I have looked up at the buildings at the top of the bluff at Quebec, and thought what a wonderful location it would be for the story of a mythical kingdom.'[9] These real locations were backdrops where mythical (but not real) kingdoms could be created for the screen. Films in which the locale is memorable result in a glorification of the physical environment, while lessening the importance of the mythical.

Joseph Campbell, the American mythologist, who wrote about the importance of elemental myth to the human psyche, explained that casting off 'the [mere] shell of the local, historical inflection, one comes to the elementary idea which is the path to one's own innermost heart.'[10] Hollywood had learned how to exploit elemental images and myths that appealed to the heart. While Canadian literature had a Canadian audience in book and magazine form, the film tastes of the general public were not attuned to stories with a national setting. It was Hollywood's power to create a mythological universe, however inaccurate, that worked. The dean of popular Canadian historians, Pierre Berton, wrote *Hollywood's Canada* in the 1970s, in which he described how Hollywood had created an unreal image of Canada geographically and culturally in numerous films.[11] By the mid-1920s, he relates, the RCMP was refusing to cooperate with Hollywood because of its bizarre image of the force.[12] This glamourized, pulp-fiction, and American image of Canada, while so different from what the CPR and the Department of the Interior were doing in their non-fictional documentaries a few years earlier, found a national and international audience, where its images lingered for a long time.

Since the universal language of cinema is mythological, the appeal of films about the real depends on their degree of mythologization, that is, their recasting of real people in heroic roles. Berton's belief that Canadians could have created a more 'realistic' image of Canadian life than the Americans is probably true, but it needs to be balanced with the so-called 'realistic' portrayals that non-American national cinemas have created of their own identities. The mythologizing of the self by oneself remains mythologizing. It needs to be asked if Canada in the 1920s had a sufficiently distinctive national identity that it could have created its own visual style and cinematic image and so advanced cinematic art. The answer is, not likely. A Canadian cinema that grew out of Canada's dominant British heritage would be different from the Hollywood product if it had developed, but the history of Ernest and Nell Shipman's links to the U.S. market is indicative of the reality of film-making in the 1920s. Canada's cinema of self-absence was not just a product of American power in cinema. Even if Canada had had a successful feature film industry, it would have omitted important elements in Canadian society because of the dominant ideologies of the time. What Canadian identity was to Canadians in the 1920s was something today's Canadians would hardly recognize as inclusive and fully representative of the reality of the time. It was a narrow colonized consciousness intent on assimilating its peoples to British imperial values.

This is not to deny that Ernest Shipman's films had a distinctive approach because of their use of authentic location and Canadian literary material, but their final form had to satisfy the acquired tastes of Canada's Hollywood audiences. If the Shipman approach was the 'best' that Canadian nationalism could put forward at the time, how different was it from the Hollywood product? Not as radically different as one might have hoped. Using the American 'northwoods' genre, Shipman tried to express a distinctly Canadian national identity, an identity fully framed by the metaphor of wilderness and the North American penchant for natural subjects. Equally, the Hollywood representation of Canadian subjects as a sub-genre of the American western captured certain aspects of Canadian identity, however inaccurately. First, the genre recognized the bilingual nature of Canada. Second, it played up the distinctive redcoat identity of the country and its national police. Third, it acknowledged and glorified the vast wilderness that Canada possessed. Fourth, it described Canada as a northern country defined by snow and cold. These features were real aspects of Canada, even if they were presented in an unreal and distorted way. If nothing else, Hollywood films gave Canada a distinct identity, which Shipman simply built on by filming on location.

The structural issues that American cinema created to block an indigenous Canadian industry were real enough, but they also existed for many other countries struggling to recreate national cinemas after the First World War. Britain, for example, was the second largest film market in the world after the United States. In 1927 the British made 44 feature films in comparison to the 723 American films that were screened in Britain.[13] In response to this small quantity of home-made product, the British government passed the British Film Act (1928), which established a quota for domestic film screening of 7.5 per cent (up from the 4.85 per cent in 1927). Nothing similar happened in Canada. In Asia, Japan produced 875 silent features for its domestic industry in 1924![14] These historical realities laid the groundwork for a national feature film industry in both countries. Other countries were doing something to promote indigenous film production. If Canada's natural advantage in film-making was its magnificent wilderness locale, why did this not become the basis of an industry when there was definitely a global market for such material?

An excellent example of how non-Canadians were able to make a mark for themselves using Canadian material was the 1922 classic *Nanook of the North*, by Robert J. Flaherty. Here was a fictionalized ethnographic documentary on a Canadian subject – the life of an Inuit family – viewed by millions around the world, but made by a foreigner. Where was the indigenous creative energy and the long-term political and commercial will to create a Canadian cinematic image? If the Shipman films were the most innovative and original product that Canada produced, how did they compare with what was happening in other countries, such as Russia, Germany, and France? They were certainly lacking in any aesthetic innovation that was significant enough to influence other film cultures. The political conservatism and colonial mentality of pro-British and Hollywood-centric Canada were a sterile environment for substantive originality.

In stark contrast was Russia, which had recently gone through the Bolshevik Revolution (1917), overthrown the autocratic czarist system, and replaced it with the world's first communist government. The country was aflame with a vibrant, messianic ideology, revolutionary artistic movements, and the birth of a new class structure forged in the conflict and tragedy of a brutal civil war. The Soviet Union, as it came to be called, was alive with a new belief system, at least before the Stalinist dictatorship was totally institutionalized. Both the artistic intelligentsia and the state apparatus wanted to express this new beginning through cinema, both as art and as propaganda. The most famous of Soviet film directors was Sergei Eisenstein, who founded the Soviet school of montage film by making impressive and cinematically important works such as *Battleship Potemkin* (1925) and *October* (1928), both about the Russian Revolution. Obviously, Canada was not a country experiencing social upheaval the way Russia was, but it should be noted that Canada might very well have required events of such revolutionary magnitude in order to build a fully realized, non-Hollywood sensibility in Canada.

Germany is another example of a country that contributed in a significant way to furthering cinematic art. *The Cabinet of Dr Caligari* (1920), directed by Robert Wiene, became a milestone of the horror genre with its German Expressionism–influenced abstract sets and unusual lighting. The popularity of the genre resulted in the chilling film *Nosferatu, the Vampire* (1922), based on the 1897 novel *Dracula*. But the culmination of German Expressionism in cinema came with Fritz Lang's monumental *Metropolis*, released in 1927. This three-and-a-half-hour work of science fiction about a futuristic universe of enslaved factory workers, robots, and revolt was a major international hit. German films offered a dark interpretation of the human condition that played well to a broad audience in the industrialized world. The result for Germany was a large export business and minority status for Hollywood films on German screens. Nothing like this existed in Canada.

Unlike German Expressionism, the Canadian art considered avant-garde at the time was the landscape art of the Group of Seven, which preferred glorifying Canada's virile natural beauty over the human figure or social issues. The Group's southern Ontario–based artists offered wild, windswept wilderness as a metaphor for the hardiness of a 'northern' people, whose identity was expressed by the harshness of northern Ontario's Precambrian Shield. If one attempts to equate Shipman's 'northwoods' films with the iconic status attained by this Canadian art movement, one is left to wonder why the latter became prominent and the former disappeared. It would seem that the medium of film operated in a different way culturally than the traditional arts. Film was considered a matter of mass appeal, while, for instance, original painting appealed to the elite, who, once they were convinced of its validity, had the power to institutionalize it. In comparison to the work of the Group of Seven, German Expressionist art, which was rooted in a despairing view of the human condition caused by economic and social turmoil in the aftermath of war, was first translated into innovative stage design and from there into cinema, where its aesthetics caused a revolution. Canada in the 1920s lacked a revolutionary political culture like Russia's to stimulate its own cinematic expression, and it lacked an immediately influential art movement like Germany's which fostered a new cinematic style. The importance of art movements influencing film was also evident in France, where the surrealist art movement created a film avant-garde of outrage and scandal.[15] For instance, Luis Buñuel's 1928 *Un chien andalou* (An Andalusian Dog) displayed a razor slicing an eyeball and a collage of imagery composed of priests, donkeys, and grand pianos.[16]

For their part, the Americans had the financial resources to produce grand spectacles such as Cecil B. De Mille's *The Ten Commandments* (1923), with a budget of $1.5 million, which was quickly surpassed by the $4-million budget for MGM's *Ben Hur* (1925). Not only did Canada lack a cultural or political avant-garde like those in Russia, Germany, and France, it also lacked the depth of historical identity of a country like France, which could draw on epic history when it produced films such as *Napoleon* (1927), and it certainly did not have the economic power of the Hollywood studio system. These historical factors mitigated against a Canadian feature film industry and limited the expression of a distinctive idiom in cinema. Canada's nascent cultural nationalism was insufficiently developed at this stage of Canada's national identity to propel it toward either a national cinema or even a variety of cinemas with distinctive characteristics. The result was a dependence on the state for Canadian film production, and the Canadian state was not interested in creating a feature film industry; its natural inclination was propaganda.

Peter Morris considers Canadian government involvement in film production as something 'unique' and 'among the most significant defining characteristics of film in Canada.'[17] This uniqueness was rooted in the Canadian government's early adoption of film as a tool of promotional propaganda to attract immigrants who might otherwise be destined for the United States. It was also linked to the lack of feature film production in the country. Canadian government 'scenics' and 'shorts' became a nationalistic substitute for Canadian feature films. Media historian and critic Michael Dorland described the sources of these creations of the late teens as 'film production agencies ... devoted to military and industrial propaganda films, informational films for government departments ... and occasionally documentaries dealing with topics of broad civil interest such as the coronation of British kings and queens.'[18]

The first of these agencies was the Ontario Motion Picture Bureau established in 1917. The next year the federal Department of Trade and Commerce set up an Exhibits and Publicity Bureau, later renamed the Motion Picture Bureau, and known popularly as the Canadian Government Motion Picture Bureau. Headed by Ben Norrish, the Bureau quickly began releasing shorts, such as its *Seeing Canada* series, to both theatres and non-theatrical audiences. Thirty years before television, film audiences visualized current events and other non-fictional topics through these cinematic shorts. The market for the one- and two-reel silent films that preceded the showing of the main feature or features was extensive and global because the short was an established part of the theatrical film experience in most countries of the world. The short was the equivalent of the warm-up act in musical shows. It was there to quickly draw the audience out of its mundane universe and accustom it to the mood and magic of the silver screen. In its first full year of operation (1919), the Bureau had start-up costs of $90,000 and revenue of $1,600.[19] Twenty years later, when the Bureau was being amalgamated into the National Film Board, its expenses were $85,000 and its income, $29,000.[20] In 1927 it had over one thousand prints circulating in the United States alone.[21] These statistics indicate a lively entity with a sizeable demand for its products, and suggest also that its films were well made, entertaining, and competitive with other shorts and newsreels produced by private firms.

In 1924 the deputy minister of the Department of Trade and Commerce explained that the purpose of the Bureau was 'advertising abroad Canadian scenic attractions, agricultural resources and industrial development.'[22] For 'scenic attractions,' one can read tourism; for agricultural resources, immigration; and for industrial development, trade. Tourism, immigration, and trade were the kinds of interests a government agency could conceive as its mandate. And that mandate was completely satisfying to both the political and bureaucratic mind, especially when it was encouraged by corporate interests, who could reap its benefits at no cost.

The Ontario Motion Picture Bureau began by contracting films to the private sector. Their purpose was educational, especially in the field of agriculture with such films as *Marketing of Livestock* being aimed at farmers. In 1923 the Ontario government purchased the Trenton studio of Adanac Films to begin making its own educational films, and by 1925 the Bureau was distributing 1,500 reels of film monthly.[23] But the situation began to deteriorate later in the 1920s when the 28 mm film used by the Bureau for non-theatrical release gave way to the 16 mm format and sound became essential for audience acceptance. In 1934 a newly elected Ontario government dissolved the Bureau.

Government forays into film-making with their educational and propagandist goals created the illusion of an active Canadian film industry and furthered the cinematic image of Canada as a place of wilderness and scenic wonders. These government film bureaus also established a tradition of state involvement in film-making, a tradition that came to both define and limit Canadian cinema in years to come. The resulting interplay of the state and private film entrepreneurship was most evident in 'Canadian cinema's most expensive flop.'[24] *Carry on Sergeant!* was a 1928 silent feature film, written and produced by British principals in Canada, that told the story of a Canadian war hero. By the time the film was released, sound was quickly becoming the standard. The film was condemned by prudish Canadian critics for its suggested immorality, and its distribution was undermined by the American-controlled Famous Players Canadian Corporation.[25] *Carry on Sergeant!* was conceived by a British distribution company that had received the right to distribute the Ontario Motion Picture Bureau's films. The company's owners, Colonel W.F. Clarke and R.T. Cranfield, realized

Movie poster for *Carry on Sergeant!* (1928).

that Canadians were tired of seeing war films glorifying Americans. British playwright Bruce Bairnsfather, whose work was known in Canada in film version, was hired to create a script on the theme of Canadian war heroism.[26] After the money was raised in Canada from private investors, the film was made at the Ontario government's Trenton studio. Its disastrous release was the final straw for feature filmmaking in Canada in the 1920s. What had begun so hopefully with Ernest Shipman's profitable sequel *Back to God's Country* ended so ignominiously with Bairnsfather's film, itself a kind of sequel that was sold on the basis of an earlier success (*Carry On!* was Bairnsfather's original 1918 film hit distributed by the Allen brothers).

In the case of both Shipman's and Bairnsfather's films, a Canadian story was dependent on foreign elements. This dualism was an indicator of the underlying problems facing the creation of a national cinema in the 1920s. In neither case was there a possibility of cinematic success without external elements being featured prominently, whether stories, writers, or stars. When this dependency is added to the prevalence of government involvement in documentary films, one can quickly see the uncertainty surrounding the creation of a successful stand-alone feature film industry.

The situation in Quebec was as difficult as the situation in Ontario. In January 1927 a tragic fire at the Laurier Palace theatre in Montreal resulted in seventy-eight deaths, mostly children. A shocked public demanded that something be done, and so the province passed a law that no one under the age of sixteen could attend the cinema. The law remained in effect until 1967! After the fire, those in the francophone community who in the 1920s had tried to pioneer a Quebec feature film industry turned to other pursuits, leaving the same vacuum in feature film production as existed in English Canada. These pioneers had made ten features in Quebec between 1920 and 1926, surpassing the body of work produced by Ernest Shipman in English Canada. Quebec silent cinema historian Germain Lacasse described this as 'une formidable expansion.'[27]

Montreal at this time was a francophone city under the economic and social control of an anglophone elite. It was Canada's leading city economically and culturally because of its connection to transatlantic shipping on the St Lawrence. (Toronto did not gain pre-eminence over Montreal until the 1960s when the St Lawrence Seaway was built and allowed ocean freighters to enter the Great Lakes.) Montreal's premiere corporate entity was the Canadian Pacific Railway, the country's pre-eminent capitalist enterprise. The 1919 'Red scare' film *The Great Shadow* was shot in part at its local manufacturing facilities. The CPR also assisted in getting financial backing for the film. In 1920 the CPR founded Associated Screen News in Montreal to do newsreels, several of which were about Quebec. The first feature film of the 1920s was *Hicks and Vamps*. It was a comedy starring 'Fatty Canuck,' an imitator of the popular American screen comedian Fatty Arbuckle. Then came *The Lonely Trail*, described by an American critic as 'the worst film ever made.'[28] It was followed in 1923 by Ernest Ouimet's *Why Get Married*. Ouimet, the successful Montreal theatre owner, had made a popular dramatic documentary in 1918 about the city's firemen and then decided to get into feature films. He sold his film importing business and moved to California to make the film using Hollywood actors and resources. The film was a failure and Ouimet stopped making films.

In 1922 a company called Le Bon Cinéma National Limitée was founded by French-Canadian cinematographer Joseph-Arthur Homier. Its first feature was a comedy titled *Oh! Oh!* It starred Maurice Castel, a well-known Montreal comedian. Six months later, Homier produced *Madeleine de Verchères*, the story of a heroine from the days of New France. It was shot on location at the Khanawake Reserve near Montreal with a script by eighteen-year-old journalist Emma Gendron, based on a popular book about the heroine. Homier's last film was *La Drogue fatale*, which received no distribution outside of Quebec. In a curious turn of events, the French-language Montreal daily *La Presse* launched a competition in 1923 offering a prize for a film script based on life at a newspaper. The resulting film, *La Primeur volée*, received national distribution, and *La Presse* ran a second contest, out of which came a family comedy titled *Diligamus Vos* (later renamed *Aimez-vous*). But the fire of 1927 brought all this to an end. Homier and Ouimet were already out of the business. The talented Emma Gendron returned to journalism, and Jean Arsin, the creator of *Aimez-vous*, returned to making documentaries.

Quebec also suffered from a robust, anti-cinema mentality fostered by elements in the Catholic Church. It was one of the first provinces to have a censor board because of concerns about morality on the screen. In 1925 Quebec film censors banned 20 per cent of films destined for theatres and edited a further 40 per cent.[29] The cleric and historian Lionel Groulx, an ideologue of traditionalism, said in a speech in 1918 that 'le cinema est devenu le premier et l'unique livre, le catéchisme de la déformation populaire' [Cinema has become the primary text for popular corruption].[30] This campaign against Hollywood films helped create a space for Canadian productions that could meet the restrictive standards of the Church.

Innocuous comedies and historical melodramas were a safe haven until 1927. That year was a milestone for world cinema: it was the year when the 'talkies' were born with Al Jolson singing in *The Jazz Singer*. The next year, Walt Disney's cartoon *Steamboat Willie* featured a talking Mickey Mouse. And in 1929 the Academy Awards were launched. If anything, the end of the decade brought a sense of American dominance in cinema that, for Canada at least, seemed unassailable. What had begun with such promise after the First World War ended with a sense of complete failure in 1927. Only Canadian documentaries produced under the auspices of government seemed to have any future at all. That pessimism was framed by a number of factors. First there was Hollywood's increasing monopoly of distribution in the 1920s. Second there was the failure of Canadian cultural nationalism to convince the government of the importance of feature films for national identity. This failure was a by-product of the state's overall satisfaction with its restrictive role as a producer of documentaries and a censor of movies. Third, the introduction of sound, with its increased costs and the need for studio sound stages, played into the hands of Hollywood, whose studios were sufficiently capitalized to meet market demands. In the silent era, Canada produced less than two dozen feature films in the decade between 1919 and 1929. At the same time, Hollywood was making and distributing hundreds of films annually in Canada, and other countries were making names for themselves as innovators in the art. Canada's colonial heritage, with its deep sense of Canadian cultural subservience and the state's interest in the practical economic and social results of documentaries, allowed Hollywood's domination of feature film.

Ted Madger, in *Canada's Hollywood: The Canadian State and Feature Film*, concludes that Canada's dependency on the Hollywood feature film industry dates from the silent era because there was no substantial demand for an indigenous feature film industry at this time.[31] When Pierre Berton bemoaned Canada's lack of a home-grown cinematically created mythology a quarter of a century ago, he touched on the failure of Canadian feature film-making to become established during a period when film was becoming the prime entertainment in the industrialized world, but he also alluded to the possibility that this very failure would foster renewed efforts to address the issue from the Canadian perspective.[32] While the Canadian public seemed content with Hollywood's monopoly and the state felt unmotivated to act, there were a few in Canada who found this disturbing and therefore a challenge that needed to be met. That Shipman and his Quebec counterparts made a serious effort to create a feature film industry during the 1920s, using Canadian material, was a sign that both English-Canadian and Quebec identities were seeking a cinematic expression.

CHAPTER THREE

The Dirty Thirties: The British Quota Era

In Canada the Great Depression that swept the industrialized world after the stock market collapse of 1929 was also known as the 'Dirty Thirties,' a reference to the dust-bowl conditions that existed in the West. The Depression was a global phenomenon that shook the foundations of industrial capitalism, gave rise to powerful movements for social and economic reform, and ushered in fascist dictatorships in Spain, Italy, and Germany. In these terrible conditions, cinema was one of the few affordable amenities.

The Depression was an economic and social backdrop to two important cinema-related developments that set a special agenda for film in Canada. The first was a reaction in various countries to the dominant position of Hollywood on world screens. The second was the immediate success of the 'talkies,' when sound became the norm in feature films. In 1929 France established its first quota for national films, while a few years earlier political leaders at the Imperial Conference of 1926 in London agreed that a quota system be established for 'imperial' films, that is, films made in the British Empire. The British and the Australians went on to establish quotas, but Canada did not. The country preferred to benefit from the new restrictions on Hollywood films screened in the British Empire by making itself available as a film location that made 'Canadian' production part of the British quota. And since the British film market was the second largest in the world after the United States, this was no small consideration in film-making and distribution.

There had been one failed attempt to challenge Hollywood's monopoly of distribution in Canada. In 1930 the Ontario government established an inquiry into film distribution using the Combines Investigation Act. The report exposed the way film booking practices marginalized independent producers and claimed that this practice was against the public interest. However, the resulting actions came to naught. First Ontario (1931), then Quebec (1932), and finally Alberta (1933) brought forward provincial legislation establishing quotas for imperial films in each province, but none of these provinces turned these acts into law. The primacy of other pressing economic concerns, public demand for Hollywood product, and the lack of an established industry crying for protection meant that quotas were not a popular priority. Instead Canada became home to 'quota quickies' destined specifically for the British market. These feature films were Hollywood-inspired, -funded, and -distributed for the sole purpose of furthering Hollywood's dominance in Britain.

Film historian Peter Morris has concluded that the Canadian government colluded with 'Hollywood producers to establish subsidiaries in Canada and thereby circumvent the clear intent of the British quota.'[1] Ray Peck, the head of the Canadian Government Motion Picture Bureau, was the main emissary for this approach. He believed, and was supported in his belief by the government, that feature films were the preserve of Hollywood and that Canada could not and should not compete. The state felt it had no interests to protect by bringing in quotas since there was no indigenous feature film industry in Canada, and using quotas to create an opportunity for indigenous production was too far-sighted even to be considered. Besides, government documentary products were doing well enough, and feature film-making was not culturally significant. Hollywood could feel at home in Canada to do what it pleased.

Hollywood's strategy of subverting the quotas was simple and effective. It would produce cheap films in Canada (and later in Britain itself) that would qualify under the quota system and then screen them in British theatres at obscure times so that the letter of the law would be observed, while British audiences attending prime-time screenings would remain wedded to the Hollywood product. In 1930 the quota for domestic titles in Great Britain was only 15 per cent, leaving the remaining 85 per cent to Hollywood and the occasional Continental film. It must be remembered that sound was now the norm, so that French and German films were being made in their own languages, thereby limiting their markets.

Between 1928 and 1938, the year when the British changed the law to rid themselves of pirate productions, Hollywood produced twenty-two quota films in Canada. 'None of the quota films produced during that decade,' writes Peter Morris, 'can be considered Canadian in any cultural sense.'[2] And yet, in a curious way, they were Canadian because the quota quickies were precursors of 'Canadian' films made in the 1970s when the Canadian government sponsored a system of tax shelters that resulted in a flood of low-budget Hollywood imitation films starring superannuated American actors. Quota films represented the economics of the quick buck and the illusory glamour of Hollywood's coat-tails, which is precisely the same culture that reared its head five decades later in Vancouver.

The first quota film was initiated in Calgary, the home of Ernest Shipman's 1919 success, *Back to God's Country*. British Canadian Pictures Ltd was locally controlled but tied to a New York distributor. Their one film, *His Destiny* (1928), renamed *North of 49* in its sound version, was a ranching story based on a local script and shot on location in Alberta, featuring the Calgary Stampede and an aging Hollywood western star, Neal Hart. The film was a financial failure for its investors and the company folded. Other films were made in other venues, but the prime locale for quota films turned out to be Victoria, the capital of British Columbia.

Repatriated Canadian Kenneth Bishop made fourteen films here from 1932 to 1937, first as Commonwealth Productions and then as Central Films. His first film, *Crimson Paradise*, was based on a British Columbia novel set in a logging camp, but it failed to meet British quota standards. The same thing happened to his second film, *The Secrets of Chinatown* (1934), which had to be completed by another company. The film played to the racist attitudes of the time, when Chinese immigration to Canada was banned. According to Christopher Gittings, the film 'demonized' the Chinese community and represented Chinatown as a site of evil, drugs, violence, and sexual threat.[3] After these two failures, Bishop got a contract from Columbia Pictures to make quota films. He used Hollywood actors of British birth for leading roles and filled in the rest with local talent. All the film processing and editing was done in Hollywood. When Britain's 1938 Cinematographic Films Act excluded Canadian production from the quota, Bishop's operation came to an abrupt end.

What did this episode in Canadian film-making mean? Morris concludes that the quota quickies 'contributed absolutely nothing to the creation of a domestic film identity and the effort to make them sapped the drive of those Canadians who might have been able to take advantage of the positive possibilities the British quota law offered to Canadian production.'[4] This harsh judgment has a certain relevance to the grand descendant of quota quickies, today's American-driven film industry based in Vancouver. One production after another of mostly American television movies of the week is cranked out by eager union-ized cinema workers, who depend on this production for their liveli-hood.[5] Rather than beating quotas, this time the motivation for using a Canadian location for production of American films is the low value of the Canadian dollar. In both situations, the Americans were the driving force and the main beneficiaries. Canada was a convenient economic location and nothing more.

While the quota quickies prefigured both the tax shelter mentality of the 1970s and the American-led success of Vancouver production in the 1990s, they played their own historical role in marking Canada's transi-tion from its British colonial past to its new imperial master, the United States. The British Empire was already in substantial decline after the First World War, and Canada's connections to Britain, while superfi-cially strong on a cultural, social, and political level, were economically weakened by the Depression. After the Second World War, when the British Empire came to an end and was turned into a loosely related 'Commonwealth,' Canada found itself a willing adjunct of the United States. The way in which Canada played with the quota system to the advantage of Hollywood rather than to its own cultural advantage, much less that of Britain, was a signal of a major geopolitical shift. Cinema may not have been viewed as a core cultural necessity requir-ing national control as it was in other countries, but it was a political bell-wether of Canada's continentalist reorientation. While some may conclude that allowing quota quickies to be made in Canada was not against the national interest since it encouraged production, Morris's judgment stands. If the quota quickies had led to an industry that was self-sustaining, their role would have been positive. The situation re-peats itself in British Columbia today, when the film industry takes a nosedive whenever the Americans pull back, because they fund two-thirds of production.

Canada's poor record of indigenous films during the 1930s included more than just the quota films. The major films made about Canada in Canada were the works of foreign film-makers. The first was Douglas Burden's *The Silent Enemy*, a story of a pre-contact Ojibway triumph over famine, which began shooting in 1927 in Ontario's Temagami Provincial Forest and was released in 1930 without synchronized dialogue. The American-born Chief Buffalo Child Long Lance of Calgary, exposed decades later as a Native imposter, played the lead. The use of ethnographic Aboriginal material continued the underlying association of the 'noble savage' theme with the Canadian wilderness that began with *Hiawatha* (1903), reached popular acclaim in *Nanook of the North* (1922), and was now embodied in *The Silent Enemy*. The continued interest in Aboriginal subjects using an ethnographic approach that was outside the cowboy western was to remain an enduring feature of Canadian cinema for the simple reason that the history of Euro-Canadian interaction with the Native peoples differed from that of the Americans.

The second film, *The Viking*, was released in 1931. The film was a dramatization of the bitterly dangerous life of the seal hunters of Newfoundland and was directed by the American explorer and adventurer Varick Frissell, who lost his life while gathering post-production material on the icefloes off Labrador. It was a triumph of intense realism. Both of these films emphasized authentic location shots and 'real' participants as actors. Both were docudramas, like *Nanook of the North*, but they also captured the spirit and practice of Shipman's *Back to God's Country*, in which the human struggle for survival in a harsh climate was an important theme. Regrettably, the energy for these Canadian subjects came from non-Canadians, who seemed more enthralled with the stories of the country's inhabitants than were Canadians themselves. This was not an uncommon situation: Canada had been 'defined' in a similar way by numerous foreign travel writers of the nineteenth and early twentieth centuries who wanted to explore the exotic and the wild.[6] These non-quota films continued an established literary tradition.

While Canada was languishing in cinematic obscurity during the Depression, the rest of the world was continuing to develop film both as an industry and an art. The first decade of sound brought new stars to the fore, whose voices matched their good looks. Greta Garbo, Mae West, and Marlene Dietrich were the new female stars, while Clark Gable was one of the male leads who appealed to North American audiences. Child stars like Shirley Temple and the Canadian-born Deanna Durbin were enormously popular. Even a new film genre, the musical, was born. Hollywood survived the Depression intact with productions of glittering song-and-dance spectacles that entertained Depression-weary audiences with escapist glamour. Hollywood also developed the gangster film, based on the Prohibition-era urban reality of warring gangs, and then balanced these action films with sentimental melodramas and romantic comedies. Technicolor made its debut with the film *Becky Sharp* (1935). By the end of the decade, colour was being used to memorable effect in some of Hollywood's most celebrated films, including the feature-length Disney cartoon *Snow White and the Seven Dwarfs* (1937), the Civil War epic *Gone with the Wind* (1939), and the delightful fantasy *The Wizard of Oz* (1939). Against this flood of technical innovation and Hollywood glitter, Canada could only stand in silence and awe.

Hollywood also attracted famous figures from Europe (Fritz Lang, for example) who were fleeing Nazism and fascism. Many found a refuge, if not a home, in the world's foremost film production centre. But if Hollywood dominated, other countries continued to produce impressive numbers of films. For example, France produced an average of 130 per year during the 1930s, while Japan had an annual output of almost 500 films.[7] Even impoverished Mexico made 38 features in 1937.[8] But the most important challenger was Great Britain, whose quota system laid the groundwork for indigenous sound studio productions. In 1937, ten years after the introduction of quotas, the British made 200 feature films mitigating, to some degree, Hollywood's dominance.[9] The British had directors of world stature, such as Alfred Hitchcock, who later went to Hollywood, and the Hungarian-born Alexander Korda, who specialized in historical themes. It would seem that the introduction of synchronized sound actually helped the British industry because it allowed it to highlight the speech of its theatrically trained actors such as Laurence Olivier.

During the 1930s, Hollywood's foreign sales brought in between a third and a half of the industry's income, while in 1939 65 per cent of films exhibited worldwide were American.[10] That meant that up to the Second World War about one-third of the films made globally were non-American, a respectable enough figure to ensure multidimensionality in the art form. In Britain the Cinematographic Films Act (the quota act) had allowed the country 'to emulate the American pattern of vertical integration with the same monopolistic organization producing, distributing and exhibiting its own films.'[11] Two companies, for example, controlled four hundred cinemas, while the well-equipped Ealing Studios allowed the production of numerous sound films. In Canada's sister colony of Australia, film production had been more frequent in the 1920s, with an average of nine features per year, while in the period of sound and quotas it was only two per year.[12] Like Canada,

Australia did not benefit culturally from the quota system. In the end, it worked best for Britain.

Quebec was not interested or involved in the quota racket. It went its own way and, in so doing, laid the foundation for its own identity in cinema. In 1928 Herbert Berliner created a company called Apex Film Parlant, which did a series of documentary sound films of popular Quebec folksingers. Most of what was happening in Quebec documentary was being done by the English firm of Associated Screen News of Canada Limited (ASN), which had been started by the CPR in 1920 with a staff of two and a capital investment of $250,000. By 1930 it had a staff of one hundred.[13] The company owned a film lab in Montreal, which did the release prints for American films in Canada, and in 1936 it built Canada's first sound stage. ASN was a profitable enterprise that did not reflect French-Canadian culture or society, but it did provide English Canadians and foreign audiences with the only contemporary cinematic images of Canada being produced in the country. The most famous of ASN films was the *Canadian Cameos* series conceived and directed by Gordon Sparling (1900–94). In total, eighty-five of these ten-minute shorts were made between 1932 and 1953, and were widely distributed in theatres around the world. This emphasis on the niche marketing of documentary realism was a commercial success for Canadian firms.

The French majority in Quebec was not without several key players in the documentary mode. Two clerics created a Quebec 'voice' in documentary that was distinct from the subject matter of ASN films. Albert Tessier (1885–1976) and Maurice Proulx (1902–88) were both Catholic priests who took an 'amateur' interest in film-making because they were not paid as film-makers, and yet their films were of professional quality. L'Abbé Tessier did the majority of his documentaries from 1927 to 1937. His films were silent documentaries infused with a lyrical spirit that glorified the natural landscapes of Quebec and the simple life of its country people. He provided an in-person narration at each screening as an educational aid.

L'Abbé Proulx, while saluting the valour of rural life, was more ambitious. His 1937 *En pays neuf* was a feature-length documentary about the settling of the Abitibi region of Quebec by pioneering farmers. A later version had a soundtrack. The film promoted the benefits and virtue of leaving established communities for the excitement and rewards of the frontier. Both film-makers pursued their didactic purposes in a Catholic context. The Church and its numerous clergy were a

L'Abbé Albert Tessier, early Quebec film-maker.

dominant social force in Quebec, tightly controlling not only religious institutions but also the province's francophone education and social services.[14] Their use of film as propaganda for Church interests could be expected.

The ideology of these documentaries reflected the clergy's emphasis on how the French language, the Catholic faith, the Quebec landscape, and popular – especially rural – folk culture were crucial to maintaining a distinct identity in an economic universe controlled by corporate English Canada. While the documentaries exhibited aspects of social realism, their spirit represented a profound traditionalism that mystified elements in the culture. Nevertheless, their work stood outside the English-speaking cinematic culture in Quebec and so has come to be classified as 'the first expression of a Québécois national cinema.'[15] Their work possessed a unity of expression that established Quebec's interest in itself from the point of view of francophone identity.

While the Tessier/Proulx documentaries were as propagandistic as earlier CPR / Canadian government immigration films, one might ask how fundamental the documentary mode of film is in establishing a cultural identity. Is a role as a 'precious archive' of a historical period, as one Quebec commentator calls these films,[16] sufficient to influence a cinematic tradition? On the one hand, anything done from within the perspective of a people is important to its identity, especially when the film genre had so few practitioners. On the other hand, only the influence of these documentaries on future Quebec film-makers reflects their true value in an evolving film tradition. Tessier and Proulx have been turned into icons of Quebec's national tradition by later generations because of their Quebec orientation. Yet Quebec was to move beyond the documentary much sooner than English Canada. The need for 'realism' to express national identity was a sign of the ideological control favoured by the state or the Church, while the feature film represented a wider mythological appeal because it spoke to audiences in an unauthorized way.

Considering the overall failure of an indigenous feature film industry to establish itself in the Dominion of Canada between 1910 and 1940, one must acknowledge the profound lateness of Canada's arrival on the main stage of feature film history (post-1970). For all the reasons discussed earlier, Canada's permanent entry into feature film-making was developmentally delayed. The glorification of the documentary mode, which the next chapter reveals to be English Canada's cinematic *raison d'être* for almost three decades, was one of the main reasons for this backwardness. Pushing the documentary mode to the side, as Quebec did in the 1940s, allowed an exciting discovery – a non-propagandist identity in fictional films. While enthusiasm for the documentary in English Canada in the 1940s, spearheaded by John Grierson of the National Film Board, fostered an anti-feature film tradition, Quebec's rejection of the documentary in the same decade would lead to the birth of a half-century of dynamic feature film production. The Second World War was about to create this basic divide.[17]

The tension between a successful documentary and a failed feature film tradition had been a key characteristic of English-Canadian and Quebec cinema throughout the twentieth century to this point. While the quota films and their modus operandi contributed to the devaluing of indigenous feature film-making within English Canada, Quebec's lack of participation in quota film production allowed it to embrace a new, self-conscious fictional identity. Quota films compromised Canadian feature cinema of the 1930s. Instead of joining Great Britain's cinematic rival, Canada preferred to let the Americans use its political status as a Dominion to bypass the system. While Quebec was about to build on its documentaries of the 1930s toward a greater and more complex self-expression fundamental to feature films, English Canada in 1939 was simply standing pat, awaiting another foreign saviour.

CHAPTER FOUR

The Rise of the NFB: Grierson and McLaren

The quick evaporation of Canada's Hollywood-dependent feature film industry, the lack of any feature film production in Quebec, and the dullness of government documentaries created an imploding universe that set the stage for an unexpected and remarkable rebirth of Canadian cinema during the Second World War. Canada had been turned into a cinematic 'desert' that awaited a heavy rain for its desert plants to blossom.[1] That rain came swiftly in the form of two Scotsmen – John Grierson and Norman McLaren – who individually and together established a new cinematic identity for Canada. These two provided the structure for and the character of the achievement that would give Canada a specific pre-eminence in the film world that it had never before possessed. Grierson was the warrior; McLaren was the pacifist. Together they created the legacy of the National Film Board, with its success in the documentary tradition and in animation.

John Grierson (1898–1972) was a native of Stirling, Scotland, who came to be recognized internationally as the father of the documentary. 'I suppose I coined the word [documentary], saying it was an ugly word that nobody would steal, and it always was one of our defences against commercialism,' he related in an interview a few years before his death.[2] This son of a Scottish schoolmaster was a navy veteran of the First World War and a philosophy graduate, who went to Chicago on a scholarship in 1924 to study the media and their impact on public discourse. It was in the United States that he was converted to his lifelong commitment to cinema and its influence on public opinion. Initially interested in the power of journalism, he quickly moved into studying film audiences after being introduced to influential people in the American studio system. He spent three years in the United States researching and writing on the impact of film before returning to Britain to make documentaries. These American years liberated him from the restrictions of his upbringing and the encrusted class-consciousness of Great Britain. This spirit of liberation repeated itself more than a decade later in his greatest achievement – the National Film Board of Canada.

Grierson had formulated his approach to cinema by combining a standard of innovative artistry with a populist interest in everyday life. He wanted to tell the story of the masses through an artful cinema. He was inspired by the docudramas made by the American Robert Flaherty, especially his world-renowned study of the Inuit titled *Nanook of the North* (1922) and *Moana* (1926), a film about South Pacific islanders. At the same time, Grierson was enthralled with the revolutionary style of the new Soviet cinema developed in the 1920s, in particular Sergei Eisenstein's *Battleship Potemkin*, with its radical use of counterpoint montage, expressionist camera angles, and evocative lighting. He applied both influences to his first documentary, *Drifters* (1929), a film about ordinary fishermen. Making everyday work artistically alive was his way of critiquing British culture and what he called its divorce 'from the actual.'[3] Later in life, he boasted that he was 'the first guy to put the working class on the screen.'[4]

Drifters was produced by the Empire Marketing Board (EMB), where Grierson was employed. Its mandate was the projection of England in a positive way to the colonies and dominions, and thereby to promote imperial trade and commerce.[5] In short, its mandate was propaganda, something Grierson felt was important in human affairs. 'I look on cinema as a pulpit,' he readily acknowledged, 'and use it as a propagandist.'[6] When the EMB film unit was disbanded a few years later, Grierson moved over to the General Post Office film unit, where he continued his energizing of documentaries of interest to the state. He refused to accept that filming reality meant dullness. During the 1930s, the struggle for hearts and minds was serious business, as Leni Riefenstahl's 1935 masterpiece *Triumph of the Will*, glorifying Hitler and his Nazi party, readily attests. Grierson's attachment to, and promotion of, the importance of the documentary mode was based on his belief that it was the real that mattered in human affairs. What he wanted was to apply elements of feature film technique to the documentary in order to raise it from its clichéd newsreel format.[7] In 1935 he wrote:

Commercial cinema, being the monstrous undisciplined force it is, has done a great deal of harm. It has also done a great deal of simple good. Even in the world of sentimentality and sensationalism its narrative is racy, its wit is keen, and its types have more honest human gusto than their brothers and sisters of the stage and popular novel.[8]

Grierson despised the content of feature films, but he admired their form. A 1930s study of the characters in Hollywood films showed that almost half of the heroes and the villains were 'wealthy or ultra-wealthy.'[9] A fictional portrayal of a society to its members in which 80 per cent of films dealt with sex and crime irritated him immensely because of its utter escapism. What he wanted for the real world documentary was a dramatic style comparable to Hollywood's.

The model had been gestating within Grierson from as early as 1929 when his documentary *Drifters* was used as the short for the London premiere of the feature film *Battleship Potemkin*. Here was the perfect format for Grierson – a powerful and moving documentary about the culture of the cinema's audience placed just prior to an entertaining and captivating foreign feature film. It was by marrying the documentary and the feature film at the same showing that Grierson achieved his desire to have cinema 'command its audience.'[10] He had developed a reputation in Britain for this new genre, the documentary, with *Drifters* and such classics as *Night Mail* made for the General Post Office, which was a film about overnight mail trains speeding to all parts of the United Kingdom, set to the text of a riveting poem by W.H. Auden. The voice of the narrator with its dynamic musical rhythm, and the dramatic close-ups of spinning train engine wheels – edited to match the rhythm of words suggesting the pumping of the wheel rods – fuelled a sense of excitement about something as mundane as mail delivery. It was pure Grierson. But it wasn't just the quality of the films he worked on or had produced that brought him to the attention of Canadian authorities; it was also his salesmanship of, and advocacy for, the documentary, and his prodigious administrative talents. He knew how to be an innovative servant of the state who created products that enhanced the reputations of his political masters. He articulated ideas about the use of film that politicians and civil servants could understand, and he knew how to make the documentary indispensable to their purposes.

In 1938 Grierson was invited by the Canadian government to make a report on the state of film-making in the country. The forty-year-old

John Grierson (left), chairman of the Wartime Information Board, meeting with Ralph Foster, head of graphics, National Film Board of Canada, to examine a series of posters produced by the National Film Board of Canada (1944).

Grierson toured from east to west and met with the prime minister and other notables. His report called for a new film agency under the control of the federal government that would coordinate and direct all government film-making, as well as work to unite the country and project the life of Canada to the world. The federal government liked his viewpoint because it presented documentary film as a useful tool for the state in the dissemination of general knowledge and information on government department activities, as well as in the promotion of trade and, finally, national prestige.[11] Mackenzie King, the Liberal prime minister, agreed to implement the report through an act of Parliament, drafted by Grierson, titled the National Film Act, which was passed in the spring of 1939. The National Film Board of Canada was born a few months later, and Grierson became its first commissioner.

The Second World War created an instant imperative for the NFB because of the need for government propaganda to mobilize the population on behalf of the war effort. In John Grierson, Canada had the most able film propagandist on the Allied side. In the first year, a dozen staff were hired; the next year, he took over the Motion Picture Bureau's staff of thirty-five; and then a year later, staffing had increased fivefold to almost three hundred. When the war ended in 1945 there were almost eight hundred people working at the National Film Board production facilities in Ottawa.[12] In 1940 the NFB made 40 films; in 1943, 200 films; and in 1945 over 300.[13] One could rightly say that in 1945, having released over 500 short films in five years, the NFB had become 'one of the world's largest film studios.'[14] This exponential growth, which stopped in 1945 with the end of the war and Grierson's departure, was more than just a story of great quantity generated by the heat of national mobilization. It also contained superior quality that only Grierson's energetic vision for the documentary could foster. It was this standard of quality production that the NFB maintained for decades.[15]

Grierson himself had no time to make documentaries. He found others to make them. He imported an accomplished documentary film-maker, Stuart Legg, from England to direct major productions, and later brought in the quiet artist Norman McLaren to create a new animation element. The vast majority of the new staff were young, inexperienced, and completely dedicated to the novelty of film work, and probably to Grierson, who could mould them into the fighting force that he wanted. Historian Peter Morris rather grandly described Grierson's modus operandi as 'a Messianic father figure gathering his children round him and teaching the laws of the land.'[16] A more apt metaphor would be of a colonel creating a special battalion by restricting the power of the old guard and filling key positions with officers totally loyal to him.

One example of the many women and men whom Grierson inaugurated into the mysteries of the documentary was the neophyte Grant McLean (1921–2002), a native of Yorkton, Saskatchewan, who began as an assistant cameraman in 1941 (his father was controller of the NFB at the time) and rose to the position of acting commissioner decades later. His early career at the NFB took him on a bombing raid over Berlin, later to the stronghold of the Chinese communists in Hunan province, and finally to several run-ins with Ottawa mandarins who banned documentaries he made or produced. In his conflicts, he was a worthy protégé of the wily and idealistic Grierson.[17]

Louis de Rochemont's *March of Time* was a popular American newsreel series doing the rounds of movie theatres during the Second World War, which became the model for two series that Grierson initiated at the NFB. *Canada Carries On* and *The World in Action* were monthly releases that played in theatres across North America and abroad, where they were dubbed into Spanish and Portuguese for the neutral South American market. Euphemistically termed 'public information,' these documentaries were pure propaganda, a rousing tribute to everyone from influential politicians to ordinary folk engaged in a holy crusade. They were sold on a 'commercial' basis, with foreign distribution by the American studio United Artists. The international series had such titles as *Freighters under Fire* and *Inside Fighting China*, while the Canadian series included the 1942 Academy Award–winning *Churchill's Island* (1941), and later mobilization films such as *Universities at War* (1944). At the same time, Grierson and his staff set up nontheatrical distribution in Canada through libraries and churches. In the pre-television era, Grierson made certain that even the most far-flung territory was covered by his hardy band of seventy travelling projectionists and their 16 mm equipment.[18] The voice-overs for the films were also done in French for Quebec audiences. It was the didactic voice-over format that served as the essential Grierson teacher/preacher technique because it interpreted events, encouraged right thinking, condemned wrong, and generally led the audience to believe what the makers of the documentary wanted it to believe. The sonorous voice of the Canadian actor Lorne Greene was the perfect tool for the job, and his narrative style set the standard in numerous NFB documentaries.

This was the 'classic' documentary style, based on the voice-over news-reels that played prior to feature films.

Grierson wanted the NFB documentary to have the power of his alter ego – Hollywood. In a 1940 broadcast he said: '... beside me in Holly-wood was one of the greatest potential munition factories on earth. There, in the vast machinery of film production, of theatres spread across the earth with an audience of a hundred million in a week, was one of the great new instruments of war propaganda.'[19] In the end, Grierson created just such an instrument for the Canadian government, and he did so in collaboration with Hollywood's distribution system, while riding on the coat-tails of its cinematic appeal, the very appeal that he had denounced earlier as the opiate of the masses. Grierson was not interested in a dull, rational approach to the public. He wanted his documentaries to emulate Hollywood's emotional appeal. Effective documentaries were ones that pressed the right buttons in the collective psyche with expertly edited images and with unambiguous mono-logue.[20] Documentaries were meant to rouse people to action. In his 1942 Oscar acceptance speech for *Churchill's Island*, he spoke of how 'the enormous power of the film medium ... must not be used solely for entertainment.'[21]

Since he described himself as a 'missionary,'[22] it is worthwhile asking what faith he was advocating? Was his task the revitalization of a moribund Canadian government film propaganda section? Was he here simply as a fortuitous accident of history? One journalist stated that in 1946 Grierson revealed to him that his 'real mission' in Canada was 'to help bring the United States into the war.'[23] If true, this is quite a revelation because it implies that Grierson's work in war films was directed by the military and political interests of Britain and its Cana-dian ally, or it could be that this was simply Grierson's overblown view of his own importance in the war effort. Since propaganda is political, it may very well have been some sort of political mission in which he was to try to have the United States, then neutral, become sympathetic to its beleaguered European forebears. His earlier association with Holly-wood in the 1920s and his connections in the American film world during the Second World War had him thinking in continental and international terms. At one point, he confirmed that it had been put to him on going to Canada from Britain that his job was to improve 'inter-communication, particularly between the Dominions and England on a film level.'[24] In the end, his film work fostered the wartime 'North American Triangle,' as it came to be called, between the United States

and Britain, with Canada serving as the convenient geopolitical intermediary. So the official goal of projecting Canada to Canadians and to
the world also had an unofficial goal of first building international
economic liaisons, and then political and military connections. Many
years later, Grierson's international orientation in film propaganda was
described critically by one Canadian scholar as a championing of 'emer-
gent multinational capitalism.'[25] This may be a harsh judgment, but
considering the full extent of Grierson's career from the Empire Marketing Board to the films of the Second World War, it may not be so far
off the mark. This was most likely not the result that he, as a left-winger,
envisaged, but it was a result nonetheless. The defeat of fascism in 1945
divided the world into capitalist and communist camps, and Grierson
spent the balance of his time in the capitalist world.

But there was more than politics to Grierson's role. He had a distinct
and innovative film philosophy that made the documentary much
more than an obvious tool of state interests. He wanted to replace the
actor with ordinary people and the studio with the real world. He
wanted the power of non-fiction to triumph over the power of fiction.
Ian Aitken, who made a detailed and exhaustive study of Grierson's
intellectual contribution to film theory, claims that 'Grierson's ideas constitute the most important British contribution to film theory.'[26] Since
those ideas had their fullest expression in Canada and also their greatest
and longest impact, how they played out in Canada is important.

Grierson taught that the documentary must not deal with the socially
superficial. It must reach to the heart of the matter. For him the heart of
the matter was associated with uplifting values such as 'strength, sim-
plicity, energy, directness, hardness, decency, courage, duty, upstand-
ing power' and so on.[27] These words convey an almost tyrannical
puritanism that is suited to the thrift and sacrifice that a state at war
demands.[28] Grierson was comfortable in this atmosphere. It suited him
and his personal values. One telling observation on this stringent devotion points out that Grierson's approach in films was to show ordinary
people doing nothing but working, as if people did nothing else in their
lives worth recording.[29] The focus on productive labour may appeal to
state interests and their view of the happy citizen, but, other than the
excitement of war exploits, the general public can be excused for wanting something escapist in place of earnest documentaries.

Grierson's populism was not an up-from-the-masses viewpoint. It
was a manipulative one that promoted the energy and self-sacrificing
dynamism of people from an ideology of leadership. People must be

educated and mobilized for their own good.[30] What Grierson couldn't stand was a smug, self-congratulatory social and political status quo. People had to be pushed, cajoled, and propagandized into being noble. Teaching people 'civic appreciation, civic faith, and civic duty' was the mission he gave Canadian cinema.[31] Canadian authorities embraced this message, but any government would, if it had as skilful a propagandist as Grierson in its service. He had worked a decade earlier in Britain for the Empire Marketing Board constructing 'a broad discourse of imperialist ideology which would cement the Empire together.'[32] Now he was in Canada, a safe haven, organizing an English-language documentary film *blitzkrieg* that would swamp the screens of North America, Britain, her dominions, and colonies with Allied propaganda. Grierson believed that the education of the public meant making films about the real world and not about fantasy or dreams. But that 'real' world had to be 'actualized' through the film-maker's understanding of what was really going on. 'By romanticizing and dramatizing the issues of life,' he wrote, '[the documentary] creates or crystallizes the loyalties on which people make their decisions.'[33]

That NFB films were generally very successful in the war context indicates that Grierson got it right in terms of persuasion. If Grierson's message was, in the words of one film analyst, 'man's nobility when facing a hostile environment,' then Canada was a perfect place for Grierson.[34] Canada was a country where the glorification of the explorer and the pioneer was the stuff of school textbooks and official ideology. From the treacherous cold weather to the endless wilderness of the desolate North to the historical 'taming' of the country, the triumphant nobility of human survival, so eloquently created by Robert Flaherty in *Nanook of the North*, was a myth that Canadians had already been taught. It was the positive myth balancing the negative myth of a people on the margins of history. Grierson built on that paradoxical inferiority/superiority syndrome by transferring the concept of a hostile environment to the great threat of the Axis powers, who could only be defeated by human nobility. He gave Canada an international mission that enhanced popular self-esteem for as long as the war lasted. That esteem was not reserved for great celebrities or individual heroes, but for everyone who felt that he or she could contribute to the collective 'greatness.' In Grierson's Canadian world, everyone could and should be a star. The image of everyman and -woman as self-sacrificing hero was perfect for the times.

Grierson left the NFB as the war ended. He was temporarily embroiled in the Gouzenko spy scandal that fed the Cold War in Canada and contributed to the anti-communist fervour of the 1950s. Since the Axis was defeated, a new enemy was required, and this enemy was Soviet and Chinese communism. Although Grierson was not aligned with the communists, he was unable to pursue a career in either Canada or the United States: the times had changed quickly, and he was ideologically suspect. For a year, he worked for UNESCO and then did some feature film work in Britain, finally ending up hosting a weekly Scottish television program that featured documentaries about the world. In the late 1960s, he returned to Canada to lecture at McGill University, where he was very popular among students. He died in Scotland in 1972.

The impact and meaning of Grierson's legacy have been debated since the 1960s and will continue to be debated. When he left, Grierson described the NFB as going 'great guns.'[35] But it quickly sank into what one astute observer termed 'a slightly stuffy and sober official institution filled with earnest and anonymous workers dutifully cranking out the documents of social concern that we would see at school assemblies.'[36] For several decades, the NFB became the dominant expression of Canadian cinema to the exclusion of all else. Grierson's vision and creation, perhaps diminished by his Canadian disciples because they were only disciples, nevertheless continued with such national prominence because they fitted so well into Canada's cultural landscape – a landscape of worldly modesty. During the Second World War, Canada's modest military role and the role of its NFB documentaries reflected the country's political status in international relations. The NFB flourished in Canada because it was the film equivalent of the nation's identity as a handmaiden of greater powers who was allowed a temporary rise in status in a specific field that did not threaten the real hegemony.

That Grierson's documentary ideology did not take root in Britain, where it was sidetracked, is indicative of this secondary nature.[37] 'It was in Canada,' writes Ian Aitken, 'that he was at last able to establish the sort of documentary film movement which he had been unable to establish in Britain.'[38] Stuart Legg, his longtime associate, said that Grierson would never have been allowed to establish anything as powerful as the National Film Board if he had remained in Britain.[39] The role of Canada for Grierson is captured best by Forsyth Hardy: '... the restrictions that had hampered his ambitions for the social use of film fell away [in Canada]. Here was a new country, a clean slate. Here above all ... was the commitment of government, coming from the top.'[40] Grierson had become a big fish in a small pond. Canada became his site of liberation from the class-ridden, hierarchical establishment of Britain that mistrusted his democratic impulses. He was given a freedom by the Canadian government to operate and to create which was not possible for him in either Britain or the United States. He was the missionary who had found his mission in Canada. But what did that mission mean for the development of film in Canada? How did such a sweet cinematic triumph get absorbed into the body politic and the cultural consciousness of a nation for whom Hollywood was still the true grail? Did the NFB represent a bureaucratically convenient construction of film in Canada that generated inevitable lethargy and self-satisfaction? Was the NFB such an overwhelming privileging of the documentary and state support that it became the greatest obstacle to feature film production ever created in Canada? The answers to these questions are at the heart of the debate over English-Canadian cinema.

Canada's leading film historian, Peter Morris, has concluded that 'John Grierson was a key architect of Canada's marginalization in the film world ...'[41] This conclusion is the very opposite of Grierson's own assessment of how the NFB put Canada on the world stage of film history. The issue revolves around the status of the documentary mode in film history. Grierson saw the documentary as a superior mode, while film history indicates that it is a minor art form. Morris refers to Grierson's writings on Canada's relationship to film in which Grierson claimed that it is impossible for Canada to compete with Hollywood in feature film production.[42] He considers this attitude a continuation of the policy capitulation that the Canadian government had already adopted since the 1920s.[43] Morris also exposes the inflated figures for wartime distribution in the United States that the NFB produced and the rather low non-theatrical distribution figures for Canada.[44] He argues that American feature films on the subject of war were better received by Canadians than were Grierson's documentaries. It would seem that the schoolmaster's moralizing received superficial public acknowledgment and lots of government approval, but the public's heart was elsewhere.

In comparison with NFB war documentaries, what did Hollywood produce during the Second World War that had immediate impact and lasting value? Classics of social criticism such as Orson Welles's *Citizen Kane* (1941) and the espionage melodrama *Casablanca*, released in 1943, were just two films of note. Who among today's Canadian public has ever heard of *Churchill's Island*? How often is it replayed? If wartime

Canadian audiences were looking for 'moral superiority' and 'combat heroism' and the absolutes of good and evil, they could find them in the four hundred or so war-related American feature films released between 1941 and 1944.[45] The documentary in its interpreted manipulation of reality certainly played a role in making history, but it also became a victim of that same history in the same way that Grierson himself was to become. It was used in the moment and then forgotten.

There is support for Morris's viewpoint in the British experience. The British documentary during the Second World War paled in comparision to that of the NFB, but after the war the British got right back into making feature films. The Rank Organisation became a significant feature film producer in Britain. In Canada, however, the NFB came to monopolize and symbolize Canadian film identity. Joyce Nelson points out that Grierson, while advising Canada not to have a feature film industry, was simultaneously telling the British government to do the opposite – to get into feature film production, which it did and to which he himself contributed.[46] It would seem that in Grierson's world the antipathy between documentary and feature film was such that a culture that seeks to excel in one cannot excel in the other. The ideological animosity that Grierson posited between their two worlds stuck in Canada for a long time. But the post-Grierson peacetime documentary film-makers who inhabited the NFB were not enamoured of the 'clear distinction between documentary and fiction,' and this resulted in an inevitable questioning of the documentary's 'claims to moral superiority and even its truth claims.'[47] The craft of non-fiction always had to face the beckoning power of fictional art.

While some would argue that the practice of documentary cemented Canada's reputation on the international scene, it is legitimate to ask what kind of reputation this was. Achievement in a minor area of film may be laudatory, but at what price did this achievement come? It can be argued that it is the feature film that has made the greatest impact on a nationality's popular psyche and not the documentary. The experience of France after the Second World War is a case in point. The Americans forced the French to sign an agreement restricting French feature film production in favour of American films, in exchange for forgiveness of French war debts and postwar loans. The end result was over 1,500 American feature films being screened in France between 1946 and 1948 compared to 233 French films.[48] Obviously, this formation of popular consciousness far exceeded any influence that documentaries had on art or politics. Whereas allegory and myth inform the feature film and give its best examples artistic longevity, the informing of documentary by history results in a radical subordination to time and shifts in public interest.

The role that the NFB had in developing another minor film form provides a point of comparison with the documentary that is distinct from its comparison with feature films. In 1941 a youthful Norman McLaren (1914–87) joined the NFB after Grierson had persuaded him to leave a job in New York. Grierson had been impressed with McLaren's abilities as early as 1936 when he saw McLaren's animated short *Colour Cocktail.* McLaren was then still a student at the Glasgow School of Art, and Grierson offered him a position in the General Post Office film unit upon graduation.[49] A colleague of theirs describes the link between the two as 'one of the most fascinating stories.'[50] What was it about the shy, introverted, and skinny animator that made the brusque, no-nonsense Grierson invite him to the NFB? First, they were both frugal, hard-working, and old-fashioned men from the same area of Scotland, and Grierson liked working with those he knew and respected. Second, Grierson recognized artistic talent. As Grierson himself said later in life, 'I hold an absolute reservation in favour of the special freedoms due to seers and artists.'[51] Third, Grierson felt McLaren could be used in the propaganda war. 'I am one who believes in personal creative talent,' Grierson explained with his characteristic frankness, 'and in the obligation of society to employ it and develop it, but under conditions ... [such as] the duty of the person to serve men's needs.'[52]

This may have been Grierson's viewpoint about McLaren, but McLaren's was not the same. In his recollection of coming to the NFB, he related: 'The war was coming and I visualized myself doing hard-sell war propaganda film. I hated the thought of it so much that I wanted to escape and I thought of America.'[53] But the warrior Grierson discovered where in the United States the pacifist McLaren was hiding, and, using threats of getting him fired, dragged him into his project much against McLaren's will. McLaren's first four animations were for the War Savings Campaign. *Dollar Dance, Five for Four, V for Victory*, and *Hen Hop* were all drawn by hand directly on 35 mm clear leader. There was no script other than the music, to which McLaren created corresponding movement using a frame counter to match the length of each note.[54] If a drawing did not work, he just wiped it off the leader using a wet cloth or his own saliva! Working improvisationally on leader allowed him to achieve his philosophy for 'the

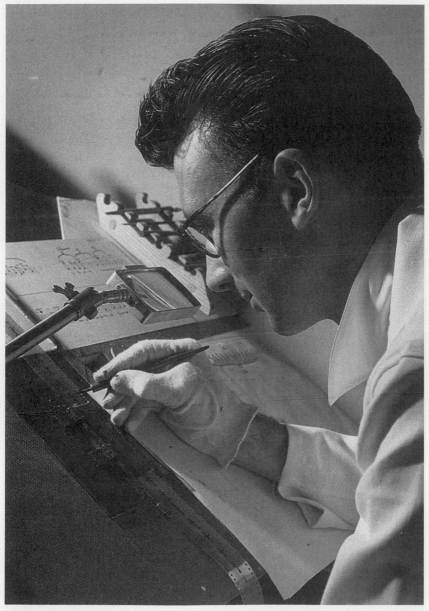

Norman McLaren, of the animation department, National Film Board of Canada, drawing directly on film (1944).

simple hand-made movie' and realize an artistic desire to maintain 'my intimacy with celluloid.'[55]

McLaren's artistic vision was a stark contrast to Grierson's documentary vision. Here was the solitary artist in a dark room working alone to create something entertaining, while the NFB's documentary production was the epitome of collective creation and the glorification of real life and events outside the studio. But McLaren's animations were very important to the success of the NFB. James Beveridge makes the point that McLaren was not some sort of extravagance that was tolerated, that his animations actually helped sell the documentaries to theatres because the screening of both newsreels and cartoons prior to a feature film was the norm at the time.[56] While there is no doubt that McLaren and animation were given a secondary role during wartime, McLaren's later role and the role of animated films evolved into a more equal partnership with the documentary. In terms of continuing audience appeal, animation was closer to the feature film than the in-the-moment documentary.

Not that the staff of the animation unit was large; rather, it was the impressive artistic imagination that gave it such importance. In 1952 McLaren received an Academy Award for *Neighbours*, a film that used his innovative single-frame 'pixillation' technique. The silent film used two actors (actually staff) and had them portray an ever escalating argument over property as a metaphor for war and peace. The novel use of a camera technique to animate real human beings represented McLaren's commitment to innovation, while the topic reflected his strong views on violence and war. In *Beyond Dull Care* (1949), McLaren began 'by smearing paints and dyes in long streaks on a length of film' to harmonize with and interpret visually a jazz piece by the Oscar Peterson Trio.[57] The use of real human figures in *Neighbours* was an equally dramatic innovation in animation, which culminated in such marvellous, sublimely expressive films as the Academy Award nominee *Pas de deux* (1968) and *Ballet Adagio* (1971). In *Pas de deux* McLaren used a slow-motion, multi-imaging technique to follow the figures of two dancing ballet performers set to Romanian panpipe music. The result was a flowing and layering black and white image that seemed like a silky X-ray study of a mesmerizing motion. *Ballet Adagio* was described as 'a work of exquisite beauty, a hymn of flesh, muscle and grace, which is both deeply erotic and sublimely moving.'[58] McLaren would duplicate a certain bodily movement up to eleven times with time lapses to create this special effect.[59]

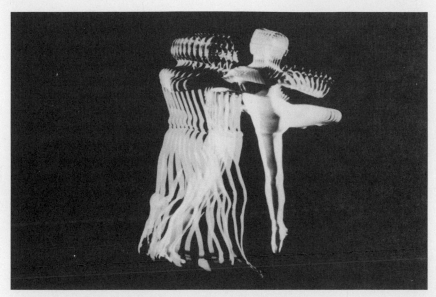

Pas de deux (1968), directed and produced by Norman McLaren.

While Grierson was the king of reality, McLaren was the king of abstraction. The institution of the NFB housed both in balance and harmony because both forms were outside the domain of feature film. The reputation of the NFB came from its balancing of the teacher role (Grierson) with the role of the artist (McLaren). That its space could be home to the conflicting visions of both an introspective poet whom one critic has termed 'a shy, absorbed trafficker in the fantastic' and a sophisticated ideologue is a tribute to its institutional magnanimity.[60]

After the Second World War, the NFB settled into a comfortable state-supported rhythm (except for a brief panic about communist sympathizers in its ranks), producing documentaries and animated shorts (a total of almost eight thousand by the late 1980s), occasionally winning major awards (and innumerable minor ones) and international recognition and eventually moving to Montreal in 1956, where it remained, along with the CBC and French Radio-Canada, as a pillar of Canadian government involvement in media and the arts.[61] Early views of the NFB's grandeur as a national institution of world renown have given way to more critical appraisals.[62] Scholars no longer accept Grierson's personal view that without the NFB, Canada would not have had a film industry or culture of its own.[63] In fact, knowledgeable historians like

Peter Morris see the NFB as having been a decisive barrier to the evolution of the Canadian film industry by its institutionalization of a state-funded documentary status quo.[64] The meaning of the NFB for the Canadian film industry and the importance of Grierson and McLaren in defining the trajectory of Canadian film in mid-century are dependent on the perspective one has on film and its social and artistic role. If the NFB's near-monopoly on film production in Canada until the early 1970s and its devotion to the documentary and animation prevented feature film-making, then those who value the feature film as an expression of creative identity have cause for criticism.

Toward the end of his life, Grierson stated with typical rhetorical flourish that the NFB 'was there to invoke the strengths of Canadians, the imagination of Canadians in respect of creating their present and their future.'[65] Of course, Grierson, using his politically and socially utilitarian view of film, was speaking of the role of documentary in creating a national identity. But Grierson's limiting of the Canadian imagination to the documentary and the occasional work of animation was a severe restriction. His eagerness to leave feature film-making to Hollywood and other traditional film centres betrayed a certain colonialist attitude that may have made sense in his historical context. Yet the long-term ramifications of the institutionalization of his philosophy by Canadian bureaucrats could be described today as short-sighted and narrow and of ultimate benefit to Hollywood, which did not have to face any Canadian competition in the home market. The NFB did provide a world-class institutional framework for a very limited form of cinema production. In time it became the highest pinnacle of the established Canadian tradition of state film involvement. For a brief period in the 1960s, the NFB allowed the production of a few feature films, but this was soon quashed. The feature film industry that emerged in Canada after 1970 was privately based. The NFB has continued to exist into the twenty-first century with an ever diminishing budget and profile.[66] It holds to its original mandate of provocative documentary and innovative animation, while receiving less and less attention from Canadian film-makers and the public.

Morris makes the point that Grierson's ideology worked in Canada because the kind of corporatism that it espoused (the state knows best) melded well with the historical view of the Canadian state as the fundamental bulwark preserving the national identity.[67] This attitude held that only state intervention and protectionism could sustain Canadian culture. It was a perfect example of Canada's age-old 'garrison mentality' so eloquently defined by Northrop Frye.[68] Ironically, Grierson used Canada's preservationist state nationalism for his own internationalist purposes of binding the United States to Britain in a military and political alliance.

The house that John Grierson built and that Norman McLaren decorated was not replicated in other places to the extent achieved in Canada. Although some thought that the film board idea was adaptable and '[could] take root and grow in a variety of national climates,'[69] the truth is that the NFB became a model that others poorly emulated. Was there some kind of symbiosis between the documentary mode, the nature of the Canadian polity, and the Grierson vision that allowed it to work best in Canada? It may be argued that the whole tradition of realism that evolved in Canadian feature films of the 1960s and early 1970s, when the country was undergoing a spate of nationalist fervour, was an outcome of the powerful legacy of award-winning documentary production. Or the opposite could be argued – the NFB-induced absence of feature film production was a vacuum crying out to be filled. In the United States, the historical domination of feature film production put serious restrictions on the achievement and appeal of the American documentary until the end of the twentieth century, when it made a comeback on public television. That Grierson made his two cinematic opposites complement each other in wartime theatres was a strategic success, but his marriage of convenience did not constitute a healthy long-term relationship of mutual learning and growth. That the Canadian feature film eventually emerged either 'out of' or 'in reaction' to the NFB monopoly was a reflection of wider historical changes that demanded a new paradigm beyond the one that Grierson and the Canadian state had created.

There are numerous conflicting metaphors that can express the Grierson enigma. One might conclude that he was a pragmatic and realistic leader who waged a valiant guerilla war on behalf of the documentary against the overwhelming cultural might of feature films and that Canada, not having a feature film industry of its own, was the perfect place to base such a war. Or one could say that he was a secret agent of a conscious cinematic colonialism that sidetracked Canada from its own cultural expression to serve grander interests and so keep Canada in a subservient position. Likewise, he could be seen as a film revolutionary, who put the common man on the screen and glorified the meaning of the everyday without succumbing to the siren call of profit. Finally, he could be portrayed as the eager beaver civil servant

building an impenetrable, yet cozy, bureaucratic lodge to survive what
he considered to be the long cold winter of Hollywood dominance.
Each metaphor tries to capture Grierson's Canadian work in a simple
way and must be used cautiously. What is fascinating to contemplate,
however, is the staying power of his vision when compared to the
brevity of his own time in the Canada. Grierson's general direction held
fast for film-makers, the general public, and the state for decades after
he left. Such longevity can only come about when a society's basic
identity is reflected in an institution.

Ultimately, one is thrown back on the 'educational' model of cinema
that Grierson put up against what he considered the decadence of the
feature film. The didactic mode combines the hierarchical idea of im-
parting superior knowledge from above, the democratic goal of individual and collective improvement, and the public concept of fostering
socially useful identity. It was in the thousands of classrooms of the
nation, before innumerable students, that the NFB found its greatest
captive audience. In the world of education, NFB documentaries were
the film equivalent of a well thought out school lunch, balancing earnest wholesomeness with colourful appeal.

Of course, the NFB worked best within a unitary model of Canadian
nationalism. When that model began to fragment, the NFB had to
change. The first serious cultural critique came from a burgeoning
Quebec nationalism in the late 1950s. It was from within the bosom of
the NFB, now headquartered in Montreal, that the Griersonian model
was called to task by young Quebec film-makers who claimed it was
restrictive of and alien to the Quebec identity. The film-maker Jean
Pierre Lefebvre described the NFB as the English-speaking voice of the
Canadian state in cinema, whose goal was the creation of a political,
social, and cultural mode of communication that *acted on* Canadians
and Quebeckers.[70] A rebellion against the Griersonian formula of putting a French-language gloss on an Anglo model ensued. In the 1960s,
the Quebec state became proactive and began a seemingly inexorable
move toward independence. The demands of this movement were
based on the concept of being 'masters in our own house,' a concept
that required Quebeckers to set the cinematic agenda rather than the
bureaucrats of Ottawa. As soon as Quebec demanded national equality,
the Grierson model wavered significantly. Just as the NFB was never
translated successfully into any national entity outside of Canada, so
the new Quebec nationalism rejected the model as inappropriate for its
aspirations. In a conflicted state, the political function of the documen-

tary became its greatest weakness. In the end, neither the Scots warrior nor the Scots pacifist was able to speak for a nation within a nation. The NFB monopoly on both the documentary and animation, which matched Hollywood's monopoly on feature films, inspired an anti-hegemonic practice that transformed the very nature of film in Canada. Neither Ottawa nor Hollywood was prepared for the rise of Quebec nationalism in film.

CHAPTER FIVE

Quebec Goes to the Movies

When synchronized sound films quickly became the standard in the market place, the era of silent films was over. With 'the talkies' came an emphasis on speech as a key to cinematic communication. With Hollywood producing only English-language films, non–English-speaking audiences around the world had to interpret these films with only visual clues, the way they would a silent film, or through tone of voice. Because dubbing and subtitles were not yet available, the only alternative was watching talkies produced in the language of the audience. Language in film was an issue in francophone Quebec, where only a small percentage of the population was bilingual. At the time, the francophone community was dominated by a traditional nationalism that clung to the importance of the family, Catholicism, rural life, and, of course, the French language as the only valid allegiances for the people of Quebec. This ideology was a product of centuries of Church dominance, which was embraced by the reigning political party, the ultra-conservative Union Nationale, which took office in 1936. At the same time, Quebec society was filled with the products and tastes of contemporary North America, especially in cinema. Movie theatres were the most accessible and popular form of entertainment outside of radio for Quebeckers. Yet this culturally and linguistically distinct society produced no feature films of its own at the very moment when cinema was a crucial factor in defining social values and interests. In such a situation, what nation-building role, if any, could film play in a culture whose powerful clerical elite viewed cinema with suspicion and even animosity because it reflected the alien culture of America? War, as always, heralded a new stage.

The Second World War resulted in two major changes to the film scene in Canada. First, the war established the overpowering domination of the National Film Board, and second, it created a linguistic vacuum on Quebec screens that was more serious than the one that had occurred during the First World War, when the mannered, melodramatic acting style of silent cinema generated a universally accessible imagery for audiences. Because of the war, French-language films no longer arrived from France, part of which was occupied by Germany and part of which was under the control of the collaborating Vichy regime. Not the uplifting documentaries of Quebec's intrepid clerical cinematographers (Tessier and Proulx), nor the sonorous French voice-overs of NFB war propaganda, nor the happy-go-lucky animated shorts in Norman McLaren's *Chants populaires* series could match the power of Hollywood or fill the space vacated by French cinema.[1]

'Le cinéma en français,' writes Louise Carrière, 'se présente comme un rempart contre l'assimilation culturelle anglo-états-unienne.'[2] Because of this cultural defensiveness, French-language cinema was viewed as a guardian of Quebec's identity.[3] France-Film, under the direction of Joseph-Alexandre DeSève, monopolized the importation and distribution of French-language films after 1932. Initially these films played on about 10 per cent of screens in the province.[4] Even so, Quebec's French-language magazine about films that France-Film published had a weekly circulation of 28,000 copies.[5] Soon the entrepreneurial DeSève was to play a pivotal role in creating an indigenous Quebec feature film industry.

In 1939 DeSève invested in a French feature production titled *Notre-Dame de la Mouise*, about one of France's first Catholic worker-priests. Made by Fiat Films in Paris and directed by René Delacroix, who later came to Quebec, the film and the studio that made it were a response to the 1936 papal encyclical *Vigilanti Cura*, which called for a morally uplifting Catholic feature film industry to counteract Hollywood. DeSève had begun to build a direct relationship with French producers as early as 1934 when he sold 70,000 tickets to *Maria Chapdelaine*, a French-made film based on a French-written novel relating to New France, which was shot partially in Quebec.[6] It was this success that gave birth to the distributor France-Film. In its 1934 annual report, France-Film claimed to have distributed 250 French-language films in the previous four years (a figure that included the work of earlier distributors that it had bought up).[7] The demand for French films made the Quebec market distinct from the rest of the Canadian market, and it was this distinctness that set the stage for Quebec's very own feature film industry.

Another development that was to prove vital to a Quebec feature film industry was the creation of Radio-Canada in 1933. This French-language arm of the Canadian Broadcasting Corporation (CBC) developed a large popular audience for radio drama with a Quebec focus. Quebeckers now had their own comic and soap opera characters and familiar situations to enjoy on a weekly basis. Paul L'Anglais was a radio drama producer who became a key player in film when he took to adapting popular material from radio to film in the 1940s. He and DeSève became at first competing, and then cooperating, godfathers of an indigenous feature film industry for francophone Quebec. They created two separate production companies that made feature films between 1944 and 1953.

The first film was *Le Père Chopin*, produced in Montreal by Charles Philippe, a French national, and directed by the Russian-trained émigré director Fédor Ozep, who had come to Canada from Hollywood. Released in the spring of 1945, the film was instantly popular and led to DeSève's buying up the company and creating Renaissance Film Distribution with the aim of making films of 'Christian inspiration.'[8] *Le Père Chopin* had a respectable budget of $240,000 in the same year the NFB made 310 short films with a budget of $2.5 million.[9] For Quebec's national identity, *Le Père Chopin* was much more important than anything the NFB produced. It was a typical family melodrama of the sort popularized on radio. Curiously, in its review, the English-language *Montreal Gazette* decried the abundance of 'Parisian French' that was spoken in the film and pined for more Quebec joual.[10] The plot revolved around two brothers in a small town, one of whom was its villainous and greedy mayor, while the other was poor and happy. The film valorized the role of the clergy (Father Chopin) and the triumph of unassuming good over ambitious evil.

Right after the war, Paul L'Anglais established Quebec Productions Corporation to make a film shot in both French and English versions. *La Forteresse* was released in an English version (different lead actors) as *Whispering City*. The total cost was $750,000, of which two-thirds went into the English version.[11] L'Anglais used Fédor Ozep to direct. The film was a typical Hollywood-style crime thriller in the *film noir* genre, with a plot involving murder and blackmail in an urban setting and a female journalist of U.S. birth as the hero.[12] *La Forteresse* was described by one critic as a Canadian film that spoke in French but thought in American.[13] The feminist critic Louise Carrière perceptively claims that a strong, non-traditional female hero could only be justified in this period through foreign birth.[14] L'Anglais saw Quebec as a linchpin for making films in two languages that would sell in both the North American and European markets. He claimed in a speech that 'nous sommes bien favorisés parce que nous vivons dans un pays bilingue ...'[15] While *La Forteresse* showed in Paris for three weeks, *Whispering City* was effectively locked out of the U.S. market. In Quebec the film had 100,000 viewers in six weeks.[16] L'Anglais realized that the anglophone film market was too difficult to penetrate, and so he turned specifically to the Quebec market for his next set of films. Later on, his 'bilingual' approach was continued in other Quebec-made films.

Un homme et son péché (A Man and His Sin), released in 1949, continued in the tradition of *Le Père Chopin*. The village curé, a historical figure named Labelle, takes on an oppressive, miserly mayor during the colonization of 'northern' Quebec. The film was based on Quebec's most popular radio serial, scripted by Claude-Henri Grignon, who had done the radio serial, and directed by Paul Gury Le Gouriadec (1888-1974). Gury was a comedian, originally from France, who wrote Quebec radio dramas. *Un homme et son péché* was the first of a trilogy of films based on a similar theme. The second film, *Le Curé de village*, was also released in 1949 and was based on another radio drama. The third, *Séraphim*, returned to the characters of *Un homme et son péché* and was also under the direction of Paul Gury. The distinguished Quebec film historian Pierre Véronneau described these films as an entertaining glorification of 'cowboys in cassocks.'[17] The radio serial *Un homme et son péché* was itself based on a 1933 novel by Claude-Henri Grignon, affirming the film's solid roots in the indigenous literary imagination. The three main secular characters in the film (and the radio drama) are Alexis, a big-hearted man with a fondness for the bottle, Séraphin, the local bad guy, and Donalda, his self-sacrificing, victimized wife. Made for only $137,000, the film won a special award at the first annual Canadian Film Awards held in Ottawa in 1949 for 'making a definite advance in Canadian film history.'[18] It was the only feature film entered along with twenty-eight shorts. With its low budget, it made money for L'Anglais in the Quebec market alone.

Meanwhile, DeSève set up his own studio with the help of l'abbé Aloysius Vachet of Fiat Films in Paris. Renaissance Film Distribution, now renamed Les Productions Renaissance, made its first film, *Le Gros Bill* in 1949. It was directed by René Delacroix, who had come from Fiat Films in Paris. In various ways, the two studios, Renaissance Productions and Quebec Productions, went in opposite directions, with

Quebec Productions using radio drama material already popular with the Quebec audience and Renaissance seeking new stories with a decidedly Catholic orientation. *Le Gros Bill* was the story of a Texan (Big Bill) who comes to Quebec to inherit some land and faces numerous misadventures in the pursuit of love. This was followed by *Docteur Louise*, an anti-abortion film, which was advertised as being approved by ecclesiastical authority and had l'abbé Vachet listed in the credits as a scriptwriter. The leading French daily in Montreal, *Le Devoir*, had warned in a 1947 article about the dangers of religious propaganda in film.[19] The warning went unheeded, and the next film in 1950 proved to be the last for Renaissance.

Les Lumières de ma ville (City Lights) was an urban love story presented as a musical comedy that marked the end. What was interesting about the film was its director – Jean-Yves Bigras, a thirty-year-old francophone Canadian with NFB training. He signalled the inauguration of Quebec directorial talent. Funds for Renaissance Productions had been raised in Quebec by ardent pleas from the pulpit and in the press by l'abbé Vachet, but the end result was bankruptcy.[20] Nevertheless, it is obvious that there was sufficient local capital and interest to fund an indigenous industry with two competing studios, that Quebec actors had local appeal, that there were sufficient literary properties, and that locally controlled distribution of French-language films did not upset the Hollywood majors. In fact, DeSève continued with France-Film, and his experience as a producer did not dissuade him from trying again. Production of Quebec-based films increased popular demand, which resulted in 20 per cent of Quebec screens showing French-language–only films in 1950, compared to 10 per cent in 1940.[21]

In 1952, DeSève released a disturbing film titled *La Petite Aurore, l'enfant martyre*, directed by the talented Bigras under the aegis of a new company, Alliance Films. Made for a miserly $59,000 and shot in a few weeks, the film became a *cause célèbre*.[22] It was a sadomasochistic story of a ten-year-old girl who knows that her stepmother poisoned her mother in order to marry her father. Because of this forbidden knowledge, she is brutally tortured and beaten. Her father is a weak and passive figure, while the stepmother is evil incarnate and eventually hanged for her crimes.

In a major study of distinctly Quebec aspects in film, Heinz Weinmann believes that *La Petite Aurore* truly reflects the collective imagination of Quebec.[23] He focuses on the 'orphan' image in the film, claiming that it is an expression of the orphan theme in Quebec identity, with the province playing the role of an innocent orphan abandoned by France to an alien power and crying out for sympathy and pity.[24] Since almost all of Quebec viewed the film, one has to conclude it elicited a powerful response from the collective psyche.[25] The humiliation, physical pain, and death of an innocent child certainly has a superficial sensationalist appeal, but, if Weinmann is right, it may also touch a deeper nerve. He asks rhetorically how there could be such an obsession with the film, considering its themes, unless there was already a strong element of sadomasochism in Quebec society.[26] Véronneau also believes Quebec's preoccupation with the film expresses the 'collective morbidity' of the Duplessis era.[27] He places it squarely inside the political spirit of the day. Duplessis's Union Nationale government had been elected for one term prior to the Second World War, and then re-elected at the end of the war, remaining in power throughout the 1950s. Its rhetoric was obsessed with communism and threats to traditional identity. In fact, the regime banned the showing of NFB films in the school system because they were judged pro-communist. The closest international example of the repressive atmosphere in Duplessis's Quebec would be the staunchly Catholic, obsessively anti-communist Franco dictatorship in fascist Spain.

Obviously, martyrdom is a theme close to Quebec's heart, and the painful tortures associated with martyrdom are a staple of traditional Catholic piety. But, in the end, it may have simply been the shocking subject of the film that was appealing – a universal attribute rather than a specifically Quebec one. Even so, images that feed sadomasochism and collective morbidity point out the troubled reality that underlies politically constructed ideals. Yves Lever provides a graphic description of the underlying and subversive message of *Aurore*:

... it is one of the explicit films of the period: the countryside is the site of the martyrdom of children, a place where there is no united family, in which marriage brings only unhappiness, and in which religion is completely ineffective. And this whole approach enters into an absolute contradiction with official ideology.[28]

In affirming its own Quebec identity, Quebec cinema undermined official ideology and expressed, perhaps unwittingly, a deep undercurrent of discontent with the status quo. And *Aurore* was not the only film to do so.

If *Aurore* expressed the underbelly of Quebec's psyche, the film *Tit-*

Coq (1953) expressed a spirit of positive rebellion, a harbinger of political and social change. Later hailed as 'one of the most important classics of Québécois cinema,'[29] *Tit-Coq* provided an unusually strong male character as its lead. The heroic feistiness of Tit-Coq, a returning veteran who has lost his true love to someone else because of a forced marriage, captivated Quebec audiences. But the underlying themes are similar to *Aurore*. The hero is an orphan born out of wedlock, who challenges conventional morality by affirming the value of a 'nation of bastards.' He speaks freely and passionately about his desires and his own anti-establishment morality in the face of injustice. Lever considers Tit-Coq a model for the self-affirming attitudes that were percolating throughout the dark days of Duplessis and burst forth in Quebec's Quiet Revolution in the early 1960s with the Liberal party slogan 'masters in our own house.'[30] Weinmann admits that in the swirling Freudian subtext that infected Quebec society, Tit-Coq was 'le premier héros québécois authentiquement, affectivement, autonome et indépendant.'[31] In fact, he coins the term 'Tit-Coquébec' to capture this new manifestation of autonomy and independence.[32]

Tit-Coq was based on a popular play of the same name written and performed by Gratien Gélinas, a multi-talented artist who became a central figure for the Quebec stage after his play premiered in 1948. Gélinas had been approached by Paul L'Anglais to do a film version, and L'Anglais, having left Quebec Productions, then convinced DeSève to finance the film. Gélinas set up his own film company to produce the film. He worked with René Delacroix on adapting a screenplay, and then the two men co-directed, with Gélinas playing the lead role. The film won 'Film of the Year' at the Canadian Film Awards of 1953. The awards ceremony was held for the first time in Montreal, and Gélinas received the award from a popular Hollywood actor of the day, Dorothy Lamour. The flashiness of the approach was a sign of a newly found sense of glamour associated with feature films, which replaced the government-dominated ceremony previously held in Ottawa.

There were a number of key events at the time that showed the growing gap between official attitudes and rising disenchantment. In 1948 the Quebec abstract artist Emile Borduas (one of the founders of the radical Automatiste art movement) published his manifesto *Refus global*, which condemned Church-oriented artistic realism; he then went into exile. In 1949, Quebec experienced a bitter strike by asbestos miners, which pitted ordinary francophone workers against the English mine owners and the Duplessis police. A new post-war generation of intellectuals founded *Cité Libre*, a dissident journal of liberal views that symbolized anti-Duplessis attitudes. It was in this ideological battlefield that Quebec's first realized feature film industry came to play a supporting role.

There were other feature films, not as prominent, that added to the overall effect of a society with a distinct cinematic expression. Shortly before Quebec Productions folded, the company did a Quebec-France co-production titled *Son copain* (1950), which was also made in English under the title *The Unknown from Montreal*. Both of these films and *Les Rossignols et les cloches* (1952) were directed by René Delacroix. *Etienne Brûlé, gibier de potence* was also done in English as *The Immortal Scoundrel* (1952). Quebec films were now being done as 'one-off' productions because the two studios had closed. Among the last of the films to be made was *Coeur de maman* (1953), the story of a woman abandoned by her children. It too was directed by Delacroix. France-Film provided complimentary tissues for weeping patrons.[33] The same year, Jean-Yves Bigras directed *L'Esprit du mal*, another film about an evil mother figure, released in 1954. None of these films was profitable, and the industry came to an end. It was to be another decade before a new wave of Quebec film-making made it to the screen in a totally new political environment. Even so, the decade between 1944 and 1954 inaugurated an independent feature film industry in Quebec, whose closest English-Canadian counterpart up to that point had been the films of the Shipman era in the 1920s. This inaugural wave of sound films even encouraged the making of two strictly English-language features in Quebec – a spy-thriller, *Forbidden Journey*, and *The Butler's Night Off*. Neither film left a mark.

While Quebec was going to the movies, English Canada was making a deal with Hollywood that would preclude the creation of an English-Canadian feature film industry for another two decades. The infamous Canadian Co-operation Project, developed by the Motion Picture Association of America, was agreed to by the Canadian government in 1948 and lasted for ten years. After the war, Canada faced a serious balance of payments crisis with the United States and there was talk about limiting the funds that could be repatriated to Hollywood in American dollars. The MPAA convinced the Canadian government that the best way to assist with the balance of payments problem was to have Hollywood encourage American tourism to Canada by mentioning the country favourably in its feature films and producing documentaries on Canada, which would be shown as shorts in theatres across the United

States. There was even a promise to encourage Hollywood to shoot more films in Canada. The Canadian government agreed, with the end result that the Canadian Co-operation Project, in the words of the head of the Association professionnelle des cinéastes du Québec, 'sold the potential Canadian post-war film industry down the river.'[34] Hollywood continued its domination, and no one was really able to determine whether the CCP ever contributed to the solution of the balance of payments problem.

Ted Madger, in his study *Canada's Hollywood*, concludes that the CCP was just another reflection of the 'dependency that deeply penetrated Canadian society.'[35] It was the latest episode in the history of the Canadian government's ongoing complicity with the American film industry. He points out that Britain, facing a similar situation after the war, was able to impose restrictions on U.S. remittances. Manjunath Pendakur, in *Canadian Dreams and American Control*, considers the Canadian government's support of the CCP as 'a way of covering up their lack of policy initiatives to encourage the production of indigenous film.'[36] These harsh judgments need to be balanced with the continued support of the NFB, the rise of independent film producers in Quebec that were obviously not affected by the CCP, and the creation of the Canada Council in the early 1950s as a key player in fostering Canadian culture. The history of Canadian political and bureaucratic cooperation with Hollywood reflected Grierson's earlier dismissal of feature films as just mindless entertainment created purely for commercial profit. The Canadian government did not see any psychological depth or profound meaning in feature films or their impact on the social imagination in the way later critics and historians have viewed Quebec feature films of the period. Instead, it heard a few self-interested film-makers crying out for subsidy and protection, looked over a history of false starts, and concluded that there was no place for the state in the studios of the nation outside the documentary and its educational mandate. In short, Canadian nationalism, which was still rather British-oriented at the time, had yet to convince the Canadian government that a feature film industry of its own was a cultural necessity for an entity like Canada.

While leaving its support to film production solidly in the hands of the NFB, the Canadian government decided to invest in Canadianizing the fundamental new medium of television. In 1952 television came to Canada under the control of the state-owned Canadian Broadcasting Corporation. It was this publicly supported television network that was the Liberal government's priority. It already had a successful model in radio (the CBC), and it was following the British model of the BBC, which incorporated both radio and television production and dissemination. The public was moving rapidly toward television in terms of visual entertainment and information.

In 1952, Quebec had a population of nearly 4 million, and film theatre ticket sales for that year were 60 million or an average of 14 admissions per capita.[37] Canada as a whole had 263 million ticket sales that year for a population of 14.5 million, or 18 per person.[38] The lower figure for Quebec was a result of the provincial law that did not allow children under sixteen to attend movie theatres. As television made rapid inroads, movie attendance dropped off drastically. By 1969 movie theatre ticket sales were only 19 million in Quebec, or 3 per person.[39] The Canadian government got involved in the medium (television) that really mattered in terms of popular culture, rather than in a medium (film) whose influence was beginning a precipitous decline.

The viability of a national cinema, which Canada did not believe in, but Quebec did, depends for its success on a film industry's capacity '... to sustain production in sufficient volume to support the requisite infrastructure and audience familiarity; on the power of local cultural traditions; and on how strongly these are articulated by film relative to other artistic practices.'[40] In the case of Quebec, not all these factors were achieved. Certainly, Quebec films articulated local culture but there was insufficient volume to maintain 'the requisite infrastructure.' When the last Quebec feature was screened in 1954, the new medium of television was surpassing the earlier speed of radio's penetration of every home. The radio dramas that were listened to by vast audiences in French in the 1940s were transferred to television, where their comedy and melodramatic flair delighted television viewers. Quebeckers, including children, could now see themselves on the television screen just as they had earlier listened to themselves on radio. The neophyte Quebec film industry could not compete for talent and audience against the power of the new medium.

So what did the decade-long upsurge of feature film production represent and how much further ahead of English Canada did the Quebec film industry get because of what happened between 1944 and 1954? Quebec film historian Yves Lever concludes that this era produced 'une pensée mythologique' about Quebec.[41] In Weinmann's view, this mythologizing was contradictory because of its pathology – a valorization of traditional beliefs and attitudes riddled with failings and contradictions. For every affirmation of the ideology of clerical nationalism in such films as *Le Père Chopin*, there were films like *La Petite Aurore* which pointed out the impotence of the Church.[42] It would seem that what these films reflected was a popular imagination that embraced repression and liberating fantasies at the same time.[43] Lever believes that the contradictory messages of the films indicated how Quebec society was looking for a new model, which came into being with the Quiet Revolution.[44] If this is the case, then we must view these films as prescient expressions of the future. The two film studios represented the conflicting viewpoints of conservatism and radicalism present in the same society and within the collective personality. On the one hand, the traditional Catholic personality clung to the past and reactionary piety through the spirit of martyrdom and victimhood; on the other hand, that same personality sought to rebel by viewing the forbidden.

Since Quebec audiences had been raised on a steady diet of Hollywood genres, from musicals to crime thrillers, they already had another world within themselves, a world that was not Catholic, not pious, not French. Through cinema and Anglo commercial domination, Quebec was already Americanized to a degree. Traditional French-Canadian identity was both inadequate for the modern world and surprisingly resilient. The desire for melodrama and comedy in these films served as a safety valve at a time when repression covered over an underlying social insecurity and instability.[45] Eventually this contradiction would allow the emergence of a whole new cinematic voice and a new identity that subsumed the old French-Canadian idea into that of the autonomous Québécois. Michel Houle has argued, not altogether convincingly, that 'the most obvious and consistent theme [in these films] ... is unquestionably the omnipresence and the near omniscience of the clergy.'[46] This theme, according to him, was not overcome until the anti-clerical Quiet Revolution of 1960, which inaugurated a process of deep secularization that turned Quebec into the least religious province in Confederation by the end of the century. If this secularization was not already germinating within Quebec society, its later revelation and triumph would not have occurred.

While this decade of film-making has been interpreted as having no notable films other than *Tit-Coq*, it must also be seen as an amazing beginning for Quebec cinema. In 1981, Christiane Tremblay-Daviault published a 350-page book analysing the films of this period, which is surely a sign of their importance to Quebec culture. *Un cinéma orphelin* (An Orphan Cinema) argued that the cult of victimhood and alienation found in these films was based on a Jansenistic pessimism about the human condition and prognosis for change.[47] At the same time, the sociological process of urbanization and industrialization launched by the Second World War, and which continued into the 1950s and beyond, undermined the official ideology of clerical conservatism. The result was a kind of social and cultural schizophrenia.[48]

In the almost twenty films (French with English versions) that were made in this period there was a genuine expression of Quebec's conflicted cultural values and the turmoil that would lead to the Quiet Revolution and the next wave of Quebec film-making. Although foreign directors played a dominant role, it was local capital and distribution networks that brought these films to large numbers of Quebec cinema patrons. The material itself was rooted, for the most part, in identifiable Quebec subject matter and based, in part, in Quebec literature. Nothing like this was happening in English Canada. There were no independent Anglo-Canadian feature film producers at that time. Everyone in English Canada looked to government and the National Film Board for 'national' cinematic expression. Since, in the words of film theorist and historian Geoffrey Nowell-Smith, national cinemas are able to 'speak for social groups and interests under-represented in Hollywood or the mainstream of European cinema itself,'[49] one could say that Quebec was doing just that in this period. In short, it had a national cinema when Canada did not.

The genre-oriented, as opposed to art-house, cinema of this period only highlighted the mainstream imagination represented by these films. Canadian film commentator Johanna Schneller confirmed this point about genre films, in general, when she wrote that film audiences 'go to a thriller because they want to be challenged, to a romance because they want to dream, to a horror flick because their lives feel too ordinary, and they want to be shaken awake.'[50] This is what Quebec audiences got from their brief foray into feature films. In the same way that world audiences enjoyed a British thriller like *The Third Man* (1949) or John Huston's American classic *The African Queen* (1951), so Quebec audiences lost themselves in the not so imaginary and perhaps uncomfortably identifiable universe of *Un homme et son péché* and *La Petite Aurore*. Although Italian national cinema of the day was breaking new ground with the neo-realism of Roberto Rossellini and Federico Fellini, and France was preparing for its 'New Wave' cinema of the 1960s, Quebec's modest body of genre films laid the cornerstone of a unified and distinct cinematic identity – putting it far ahead of anything else in Canada, albeit far behind the rest of the world. By having to turn to private entrepreneurship for feature film production, Quebec was able to bypass the lethargy and restrictions of English Canada's state-sponsored model. In terms of feature film-making, Quebec was a quarter-century ahead of the rest of the country.

CHAPTER SIX

Budge Crawley and the Other Documentary Tradition

Shortly before the founding of the National Film Board in 1939, a young newly married couple created an independent documentary film company that became a vital counterpoint to the domination of the NFB. Twenty-seven-year-old Frank Radford Crawley, known as 'Budge,' and Judith Crawley (née Sparks) spent their 1938 honeymoon on Quebec's Île d'Orléans making a silent documentary, which won the Hiram Percy Maxim Award for best amateur film in the United States. Their creative and business partnership was to last through thirty years of marriage, and for another decade after their divorce.

Prior to the formation of the National Film Board, Canada had a tradition of public and private sector collaboration in the making of promotional films, starting with those of the Canadian Pacific Railway. These films served both a public policy purpose and commercial interests in attracting immigrants and tourists. It was this tradition that the Ottawa-born Crawley came to exemplify. He was considered a native Canadian in his sensibility, in contrast to the work of Grierson and his foreign directors, who brought a more aggressive approach to the documentary as compared to Crawley's lyricism. Whereas Crawley was soft and relaxed in his approach, Grierson was hard and demanding. Crawley, as a native Canadian, was considered a film-maker who dealt with the beauty of landscape and idyllic nature. This, of course, was the major theme of tourism promotion films made earlier by government bureaus. Grierson, by contrast, was the father of the stern and morally uplifting human action films that depicted the triumph of brains and brawn – the hammer and the anvil.

Budge had received his first film camera in 1927 as a gift from his accountant father for the purpose of improving his teenage son's swimming stroke. Eight years later, Budge made a silent short titled *Glimpses of a Canoe Trip*, based on a summer adventure in northern Quebec. The film was judged one of the top ten amateur films in the Amateur Cinema League's 1937 film festival in the United States. It was this award that spurred the aspiring film-maker to do *L'Île d'Orléans*. The idea for the honeymoon location had come from the Canadian ethnographer Marius Barbeau, who had given a presentation on the simple life of the island's rural inhabitants and their preservation of ancient customs at a talk that the Crawleys had attended. The success of the resulting film convinced Budge's father, Arthur A. Crawley, to loan Budge $3,000 and establish a partnership between himself (Arthur) and Budge's wife, Judy, that would produce films. Budge's father was to play a crucial role in managing and expanding the business.

It was Grierson who gave the Crawleys their first assignments. *Study of Spring Flowers* and *Birds of Canada*, both made in 1939, were done as commissions from the NFB because Crawley had refused to be a state employee. It was this initial refusal and the goal of building his own company that set Budge Crawley apart and allowed him to make his own distinct mark on the Canadian documentary. In 1946, when Crawley Films was about to become a limited company, the operation had six staff. Three years later, it employed thirty-three people (a tenth the size of the NFB), and by the mid-1950s, almost a hundred.[1] It had moved out of the Crawley residence in 1943 and had its own substantial facilities in Ottawa.

An important early film by the Crawleys was *Canadian Landscape*, a 1941 film on the already famous Canadian artist A.Y. Jackson, a member of the Group of Seven. Crawley's biographer, Barbara Wade Rose, describes Budge's lens as dwelling 'on the rocks, trees, and rivers of the Canadian wilderness, unhurried and at home,' much in the way a painting by the Group of Seven might dwell on the Canadian Shield.[2] Since this was the landscape of Budge's own outdoor adventures and, by the 1940s, an integral part of the official Canadian aesthetic created by the Group of Seven, the film's subject matter and technique reflected a bond between nationalist cultural ideology and popular sentiment. In a way, Crawley was the English-Canadian counterpart of Quebec's cleric film-makers, Tessier and Proulx, who glorified their own land and people in the 1930s.

Canadian Landscape led to the Crawleys' first professional triumph. While filming A.Y. Jackson, Judy Crawley had spotted a West Coast mask in his studio. She had a keen interest in Native folklore because of the influence of Marius Barbeau, who had published highly popular collections of translated Native legends. The Crawleys' *The Loon's Necklace* used masks collected by Barbeau and cast their own staff as the film's actors. The film told the story of a blind shaman whose sight is restored by a loon, which is rewarded by a necklace of shells that turn into the white spots on its throat. Barbeau sang a Native song to accompany the film; sets were constructed at the Crawley studio; and the whole thing was filmed in a semi-animated, dream-like style befitting a mythological imagination. The film cost between $7,000 and $10,000 to make and was considered a tax loss by Arthur A. Crawley because the NFB refused to buy it.[3] Budge and Judy's revenge on the NFB's short-sightedness came in 1949, when the film won first prize at the Venice Film Festival and a citation at the Festival of Documentary Films in Edinburgh. The film's awards culminated that same year with the winning of the 'Film of the Year' prize at the first Canadian Film Awards. Tens of millions have viewed the film since then, and it earned the company $1.5 million over thirty years.[4]

This laudatory reception is questioned by a postcolonial critique that challenges the cultural appropriation of Native cultures by non-Aboriginals and the White mystification of these cultures in the interests of continuing racial stereotyping promoted by Euro-Canadian ethnographers like Barbeau. Makers of *The Loon's Necklace* may have felt that they had achieved Native authenticity within the ideological limits of the times and so considered their work ground-breaking, but their dependence on the interpretations offered by Barbeau makes their work open to critical reappraisal. The story and its fable-like presentation ossified Aboriginal culture in a mythological universe that deprived the viewer of any historical context that might show the cultural onslaught that the dominant society had been waging against the very culture that the film claimed to glorify.

The role of the film in confirming Euro-Canadian values and domination became evident with the sale of the film to Imperial Oil of Canada (Esso), Canada's largest oil company and a pillar of Canada's WASP corporate establishment. The company bought the film for $5,000 from Crawley and gave it to the Canadian Educational Association because it was viewed as suitable for children. This reflected the popular view of the time that Native peoples were the equivalent of children and their folklore was a form of children's literature. Because the film did so well, Imperial decided to commission Crawley to do a film on

Newfoundland, which had just entered Confederation, as a way of introducing Canadians to Canada's newest province and thereby promoting national pride. *Newfoundland Scenes* was a thirty-nine-minute film produced and directed by Budge that was named the 1952 Film of the Year at the fourth annual Canadian Film Awards. By this time, Crawley Films was the major competitor to the NFB in these awards. In 1952 the Canadian film industry made $3 million worth of films, including those of the NFB. Of this total, Crawley Films made an impressive one-sixth.[5]

The corporate sector appreciated having a private enterprise component to turn to when it needed film propaganda, especially in the Cold War fifties, when the NFB was sometimes denounced as being too left-wing. Crawley Films was kept in business by the hundreds of business-sponsored films like the 1952 award-winning *Packaged Power* made for the aluminum industry. 'Your gang,' stated Munroe Scott, 'trampled the Hydro tunnels under Niagara, wandered the Arctic tundra, watched the developments at Churchill Falls ... the building of the Seaway ... recreated the last Ice Age on the prairies and explored the action at Chalk River.'[6] Film-makers who didn't work at the NFB worked at Crawley Films or other independents. Curiously, an important source of contracts was the NFB itself, which farmed out a small percentage of its government work to these film-makers. A law had been passed that all federal government film contracts should go to the NFB, but then the NFB subcontracted some of them or declined to do others, which were picked up by Crawley. Like the NFB, Crawley Films also worked in French, with French productions accounting for up to a third of their annual production. Because, in the words of a 1954 government report on the film industry, Crawley 'will make a film exactly as the sponsor wishes,' the company grew rapidly.[7] Crawley's cooperative approach to the corporate sector and its film successes were recognized in 1957 by a special award given to Budge and Judy at the Canadian Film Awards for 'their unique contribution' to Canada's film industry.

Then came the age of television and Crawley, seeing a great business opportunity, jumped feet first into a thirty-nine-episode series on the RCMP, which was co-produced with the CBC and Britain's BBC. This was Canada's first television series that was also made for export. By the end of the decade, Crawley Films had made a thousand films and garnered over a hundred awards.[8] It was time to try something more daring. Budge Crawley turned his hand to feature films. The first, *Amanita Pestilens* (1963), was the second Canadian colour feature to be shot simultaneously in French and English (the first was *Etienne Brûlé, gibier de potence / The Immortal Scoundrel*, in 1952). The story of a man and his mushroom-sprouting lawn was a financial disaster. Directed by Quebecker René Bonnière, it was screened at some European film festivals and reflected the Crawley connection with French-language production. Its only notable feature was an inaugural film role for Montrealer Geneviève Bujold, who went on to have a major international film career. Undeterred by the film's failure, Budge moved to a more identifiable subject with *The Luck of Ginger Coffey* (1964). Adapted from the 1960 novel of the same name by Canadian writer Brian Moore, the film won best feature at the Canadian Film Awards (the novel had won the Governor General's Award for fiction). It was the story of an Irish immigrant who comes to Montreal and struggles to adapt to an alien culture. British stage actor Robert Shaw played the lead. The film got passing reviews and modest sales.

One-third of the funding had come from the owner of a small New York film theatre chain, who also did the U.S. distribution. Even though Crawley lost hundreds of thousands on *Amanita Pestilens* and barely broke even with *The Luck of Ginger Coffey*, the company was grossing one to two million dollars of work annually, and so Budge felt the company could afford to take the risk.[9] Operations were split into the profitable documentary and television commercial section (including animation) and the as yet unprofitable feature film section. This was not the only split that occurred at Crawley Films. Early in the 1960s, Budge renewed his acquaintance with his first love. Although both had families, they began an affair that led to divorce and remarriage for Budge in 1968. Although Judy continued to work for Crawley Films, the situation was no longer as collaborative. At the same time, the situation for feature films was changing because the Canadian government had established the Canadian Film Development Corporation (CFDC) with a mandate to fund a feature film industry.

Budge continued his quixotic quest to find the Holy Grail of Canadian feature films. His next feature project was *The Rowdyman* (1971), a Newfoundland story based on a screenplay by Canadian actor Gordon Pinsent, who played the lead role. The film lost out to *Wedding in White* for best feature at the Canadian Film Awards. *The Rowdyman* cost $350,000 (about the same as *Amanita Pestilens*) but did not make money because it couldn't find American distribution.[10] This was now the third feature film for Crawley, and not one had made money. Perhaps it was the choice of stories about Canadian male anti-heroes that was the problem, or perhaps it was just part of the general negative atmosphere that existed at the time toward Canadian features, both in terms of distribution and critical response. Meanwhile, on the non-feature side of the business, the company had made by the mid-1970s several thousand films, of which 450 were in French.[11] 'It's a tough business,' Budge is quoted as saying, 'but it develops your character.'[12] His next major project, a feature documentary, was to prove a real test of character.

Janis Joplin, a documentary on the famous American rock star, was made with independent funds because he couldn't get CFDC backing for a non-Canadian subject. Because it was an American subject, he signed a deal with Universal Studios for theatrical and television distribution. It was a bad deal. Universal sold the U.S. television rights for a generous $450,000 and didn't care to do much for theatrical distribution.[13] Crawley sued and also bought back the Canadian rights from Universal for more money than he was able to make on the film in Canada. 'The loyalists at Crawley Films,' writes Barbara Wade Rose, 'increasingly considered Budge not as a larger-than-life man who led them fearlessly into the future, but as a loose cannon with whom they had to cope.'[14] The next feature project, a rock opera version of *Hamlet*, was precisely the kind of idea that they dreaded, and which Budge pursued with a vengeance. It is obvious that Budge had an artistic streak. Although he had long ago given up directing films, he wanted to make a cultural statement that couldn't be made in the documentary mode or through corporately sponsored film. And he wanted to make that statement primarily in a Canadian way, using Canadian material. Graeme Fraser, the company's vice-president for sales, mused on what was going wrong. 'Budge changed a lot in later years and I never quite knew why,' Fraser is quoted as saying. 'He fell in love with features. We were not designed for features. None of them paid off. All of them lost money.'[15] From the point of view of the profitable commercial side of the business, it was sheer folly, but from the point of view of a gallant, if hopeless, attempt to foster a feature film industry in Canada, it was the mark of a brave pioneer who may have just been bored with the formulaic success of decades of documentaries and television commercials. Since the 1970s was a period when hundreds of mostly hopeless feature films were made in Canada in response to tax law, Crawley's small body of feature films (five over twenty years) is not a monstrous extravagance. He chose what he was close to, and at this stage the Don Quixote in him, or the Hamlet in him, or the Janis Joplin in him, leaned

Budge Crawley, documentary film producer (1976).

toward the insurmountable. It also led to his greatest documentary success late in his career.

The Man Who Skied down Everest (1975) was a salvage operation. A Japanese film crew had produced a film titled *Everest Symphony* about Yuchiro Miura's attempt to ski Everest. Originally shown at the World's Fair in Osaka, the film failed to garner international distribution. Crawley bought the film and got Judy Crawley to write a narrative and a Hollywood editor and cinematographer to complete the work with new shots and re-editing. The editor and Budge had a falling out (the edited version was lost after being left in a cab), and it took some time to get the film right again, ending up with 30 per cent taken from the original and 70 per cent new material.[16] The film won the feature documentary Oscar in 1976 and quickly made its money back because of the global publicity and the international appeal of its adventure-some subject matter. The images of Miura careening down an Everest slope at one hundred miles per hour, his parachute flapping haplessly behind him, then falling and tumbling helplessly toward what seemed like certain death, left world audiences gasping with amazement and distress. But for Crawley Films it was too little, too late.

In 1982, when the company's debt had reached over one million dollars, it was sold for assumption of the debt. Budge got a small stipend and the right to carry on his own feature projects under a different name. For some years, he had been interested in a literary property he had optioned called *The Strange One*, based on a 1959 novel by Fred Bodsworth about a biologist who falls in love with a Native woman. Their love story is paralleled by that of a Barnacle Goose from Atlantic Canada who ends up mating with a Canada Goose. It had been this project and the other feature films that had contributed to the firm's financial demise.

Crawley Films had flourished on the creative talent and business acumen of Budge and Judy and Budge's father. When Budge became lost in his fantasies of feature film success, and also lacked the help and guiding hand of either Arthur or Judy, the end was inevitable. By the 1980s, Budge Crawley was a film icon rather than a going concern. He was awarded honorary degrees for his past achievements, and in 1986 he and Judy received a Special Achievement Award at the Canadian Film Awards, now renamed the Genies. She died soon after, and he passed away the next year. The firm disappeared as well.

What does the Crawley Films saga signify? Was Budge the sensitive director of documentary romances about people's close ties to the land and the sea, as he was in *Newfoundland Scenes*? Was he the hard-nosed producer of tough feature documentaries such as *Janis Joplin* and *The Man Who Skied down Everest*? Or was he a dreamer, whose feature film escapades came to naught? He was all three and more. In a 1951 *Saturday Night* article, Budge argued that it would be 'in the public interest to increase materially the percentage of creative production work done outside the National Film Board' because it would encourage private companies to compete with the NFB thereby making the film board more efficient and creative.[17] Budge Crawley believed in the private sector approach to film-making in Canada. He had staked his whole career on it and had won, but he had won in the documentary mode alone. It was a pyrrhic victory. When he stepped into the non-sponsored realm of Canadian features, he had become bogged down. Even when the Capital Cost Allowance scheme of the 1970s and 1980s brought vast amounts of tax-sheltered investment into feature film production, Budge struggled because he had artistic integrity. In a 1981 article in *Maclean's*, he criticized the negative effects of the scheme because it encouraged film producers to inflate budgets at the taxpayers' expense, and he offered some solutions that might improve quality by increasing risk.[18] He believed that great art could not come from either the security of state-funded enterprise or an unscrupulous private sector.

The NFB continues and it remains a part of contemporary film production, although much diminished, while Crawley is part of history. In a sense, Crawley Films suffered from the problems facing many family-owned businesses that are created on the charisma of one or two founders. They can only have a continued role if they are sold to another successful firm or passed on within the family. Neither scenario happened in the case of Crawley Films. Budge Crawley was a Central Canadian visionary whose cultural view of Canadian identity was tied closely to the landscape and people of Ontario and Quebec. Although he worked across Canada and in both languages, and made international subjects, he was fundamentally caught up in the mystification associated with the canoe, the sparkling lakes, and lonely forests of the North, and Canada geese. His cinematic eye belonged to the world enshrined by the art of the Group of Seven. Like them, Crawley's work represented a stage in national history.

CHAPTER SEVEN

Goin' down the Road:
The Resurrection of
Anglo-Canadian Feature Films

From 1954 to 1963 there were no awards made to feature films at the annual Canadian Film Awards. What is even more disturbing was that from 1958 to 1963 there were no entries at all in this category! Canadian feature film production had hit this new low because of the closure of the Quebec feature film industry in 1954 and the lack of any production worth noting in English Canada as a result of the infamous Canadian Co-operation Project. It was the National Film Board and its sister organ of state, the Canadian Broadcasting Corporation, that pulled most film talent into its orbit. Gerald Pratley, a film critic and writer, described this sorry state of affairs in a 1955 *Queen's Quarterly* article in which he lamented:

> Unhappily, most Canadian film-makers lack individuality ... have no ideas or opinions to express and seem devoid of feeling ... the annual Canadian Film Awards ... [uphold] downright mediocrity.
>
> The Canadian film is the one art which does not enjoy, in this country, the support of an enthusiastic and vocal group of sophisticated admirers, such as may be found for Canadian painting, music, ballet, theatre, and literature ... And among our 'intellectuals' the film-maker must feel like a pariah ...[1]

With no feature film production to speak of in English Canada after the Second World War, and none in Quebec after 1954, what was there for Canadian intellectuals to discuss in the late 1950s other than foreign films? In 1963 the National Film Board tried to interest the Canadian Broadcasting Corporation in co-producing a dramatic feature titled *Drylanders*, to be used as a one-hour television special. The CBC was not interested in this pioneering story set in Saskatchewan, and so the NFB, after twenty-five years of avoiding feature films, decided to produce it on its own. The film cost $200,000, a vast sum for the NFB to spend on a single production. It recovered only about a third of its costs in theatrical bookings.[2] Nevertheless, in typical style, the NFB later went on to circulate the slow-moving drama as 'a four-part primer for teaching English as a Second Language.'[3] There was also a French-language version titled *Un autre pays*. As a Canadian historical topic about the settling of the prairie, it fitted the NFB's established mandate, but as a work of fiction it was a departure and a precedent, even though the NFB had previously done a number of dramatized short films on social issues.[4]

It was not an auspicious time to be branching out into feature films. By the early 1960s, television had completed its domination of film. An indication of the quick rise to power of television is evident in these grim film statistics: in 1963 there were only 88 million tickets sold in film theatres, compared with 247 million in 1952, when television first came to Canada.[5] For film to make a comeback would require a special set of circumstances. The NFB's second foray into English-language feature film-making began as a documentary on juvenile delinquency and ended up as *the* hallmark film in the resurrection of Anglo-Canadian cinema in the 1960s – Don Owen's *Nobody Waved Good-Bye* (1964).

Owen was a thirty-year-old Torontonian who had directed a few documentaries at the NFB's famous Unit B, where the major award-winning documentary work was then being done.[6] Originally intended as a typical NFB half-hour docudrama on the social issue of juvenile delinquency, the film grew exponentially as Owen kept ordering and receiving more film stock. He shot ten times as much footage as he finally used, shooting in an ad hoc documentary style in which the actors and director improvised dialogue and scenes.[7] When a young film-maker extracts a feature film from the jaws of a documentary, the potential for something novel is high. The story of Peter and Julie, two young Torontonians dissatisfied with their parents' conventional suburban lifestyle, is a fine example of youth rebellion films. At a cost of a mere $75,000, the film had a much greater impact than the pedestrian *Drylanders*.[8] Film scholar Peter Harcourt went so far as to say that 'it achieves greatness' in its 'understanding of the feeling of futurelessness experienced by the moneyed kids from the suburbs.'[9] Shot in 16 mm, and then begrudgingly blown up to 35 mm by the NFB, the film became a kind of *cause célèbre*. Initially panned by Canadian critics, it was praised in New York. Brendan Gill, the *New Yorker*'s film critic, compared the film to the great American coming-of-age novel *Catcher in the Rye*.[10] He wrote that it was 'an almost unbearably just depiction of the pitfalls of family life' and that it had a special quality in which 'not a word of the dialogue sounds invented and in nearly every scene one would swear that the camera ... [was] unbeknownst to the actors.'[11] The improvisational nature of the production actually helped create this illusionary authenticity.

The American praise, based on the film's non-Hollywood style and its documentary-like authenticity, was a welcome antidote to Canadian critics such as Germaine Warkentin, who, writing in the *Canadian Forum*, described the work as 'intensely provincial.'[12] The raw energy of Owen's film appealed to urban American intellectuals attuned to the emerging power of youth culture. It was difficult for Canadian critics, so unaccustomed to seeing Canadian films, to be objective about a home-made product. While Canada had just gone through the stodgy conservatism of the Western populist regime of John Diefenbaker, the United States had enjoyed a youth-oriented mythological 'Camelot' personified by John F. Kennedy, the assassinated president. It was only after New York critics praised the film that it was dutifully and belatedly acknowledged in Canada.

The main protagonist in the film is a young man who is not only in an argumentative rebellion against the bourgeois values of his family, but also seems unable to achieve anything through this rebellion. Later Canadian critics have claimed that the film's main theme is 'the quest for freedom from the materialistic prison ... so closely identified with the American way of life.'[13] When Peter is accused by a Quebecker of not being distinct from Americans, his response is sadly lame. The other important observation about the spirit of *Nobody Waved Good-Bye* concerns the failure of the anti-hero to find his own voice because his pronouncements are always proven wrong.[14] It is a film about an exuberant but failed attempt to break free.

At a press conference held at the Montreal Film Festival, Owen is quoted as saying gloomily that 'there is no English-speaking filmmaking' in Canada.[15] And he was right. He was leading the rebirth. What Harcourt described as the film's 'spontaneity, vitality, transparency' occurred because of the very lack of a feature film tradition.[16] The NFB in the late 1950s had developed the *cinéma direct* style of documentary that encouraged the use of hand-held cameras shooting in the midst of the action. It was this new style that was adopted by Owen in his feature film. The style (discussed more fully in chapter 9) coincided with technological developments in film-making that allowed mobile camera units to film spontaneously without much set-up.

The youth factor was fundamental. Owen was himself barely thirty years old when he made the film. The subject was the angry attitude of youth that caused them to reject an imposed world and to come into conflict with parental authority and the law. One must remember that already the provocative, anti-establishment rock 'n roll music of Elvis Presley was shaking up North American youth culture, that Beatlemania was just around the corner, that the Vietnam War was generating its first opponents, that Bob Dylan was inaugurating protest songs, and that, in a few short years, the whole continent would be aflame with the counterculture, drugs, and youths fleeing from every suburb.

Nobody Waved Good-Bye was in the vanguard of the as yet unnamed radical sixties. That this film should be Canadian is not so much an anomaly as a reflection of the fundamental historical power of this new cultural movement. That the film's plot did not resolve the matter of who wins in this battle between the future and the past is indicative of its being in the forefront, uncertain where the whole journey would lead. Owen's success led to another feature film in 1968. *The Ernie Game*, about an alienated young man, was produced again by the NFB and won the feature film award at the Canadian Film Awards.

Another youthful, aspiring Torontonian film-maker, David Secter, made a 16 mm film at the University of Toronto titled *Winter Kept Us Warm*. This 1965 film was shown at Cannes in 1966, where it received a special jury prize. The story of two male students who grow attached to each other until social forces cause a break-up continued the provocative themes of youth culture inaugurated by Owen. Anglo-Canadian film-making consolidated its identity around stark realism when the talented Canadian film-maker Allan King made *Warrendale* (1967), his explosive and controversial feature documentary on disturbed children.

Allan King was born in Vancouver in 1930, where he was educated and began working in television. He was commissioned by the CBC to do a film about a treatment centre for emotionally disturbed adolescents. When the film was completed, the CBC refused to show it because of the coarse language used by the children. So it was screened in theatres. *Warrendale* had certain similarities with *Nobody Waved Good-Bye*. It was a tough film in the documentary mode that contained emotional outbursts by young people. In a 1988 interview, twenty years after having made the film, King was quoted as saying: 'I turned to filmmaking [from philosophy] in the equally naïve belief that if we could capture life on film exactly as it happened perhaps we could see through the misunderstandings ...'[17] Obviously, it was the conventional social limits placed on television as 'family entertainment' that closed the door to films about rage, swearing, and emotional outbursts. Movie theatres could afford to screen controversial material because obscenity was a local police matter, while screening controversial or offensive material on television was always a parliamentary issue because the CBC was an arm of government.

The Canadian Film Awards named *Warrendale* 'film of the year' in recognition of its power, as well as giving it the feature film award. The film also won the New York Critics' Award for best documentary and shared both the Critics' Prize at Cannes with Antonioni's *Blow Up* and the British Academy's Best Foreign Film Award with Buñuel's *Belle de jour*.[18] That it shared prizes with two outstanding foreign feature films was indicative of its stature in the film world at the time. When a feature-length documentary is considered equal to outstanding feature films, one can reasonably conclude that Canadian film-makers of the 1960s had uncovered the secret potential for innovation hidden in the documentary tradition.

Two years later, King had another hit. *A Married Couple* (1969) was 'King's most dramatic achievement.'[19] This ninety-six-minute colour film had an independently funded budget of $203,000.[20] '*A Married Couple* ... followed *Warrendale* directly and naturally from my central obsession,' King explained. 'If problems of childhood come from problems in parenting these in turn often come from a conflict in marriage.'[21] He found a couple who were willing to have their domestic life filmed as it happened, and he used a very small, documentary-like crew, with Vancouver's Richard Leiterman on camera. In an interview, Leiterman described the making of the film, including the selection of the couple, whom he knew, and the agreement that the crew and the couple would not communicate while filming. 'The first two or three weeks are not in the final cut,' Leiterman explained, because of the couple's obvious self-consciousness, which disappeared over time.[22] The film included bedroom scenes, animated arguments, and a party. It was a hit because of the novelty of watching a marriage coming apart. 'So we made films about real people and told a story about them ...' King said later. 'The fact that they're documentaries, for me, has always been coincidental.'[23] King created a dramatic fictional feel within the

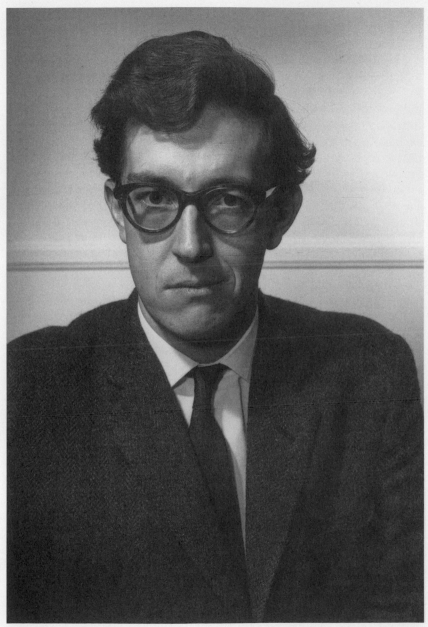

Allan King, film director (1961).

documentary mode of direct cinema. Knowing that this was a real life, real people, and a real marriage heightened the impact for viewing audiences.

The final version was created out of many hours of film, most of which was quickly discarded. The film was neither a chronological treatment of the couple's life nor a re-enactment. The story was created in the editing room using the same dramatic values any fictional feature film would have. The vitality of the two non-actors and the intimacy of each moment in an ordinary life provided the energy that propelled the film's structure and captivated audiences. 'My most humbling discovery as a director,' King revealed, 'was that my best scenes occurred when I was out of the room and for the last three weeks I was rarely on the set at all ...'[24] Clearly, this was a new kind of 'directing,' in which the director seldom intervened once the principal elements were in place. He created a story crafted from actuality. He was forced to make some cuts for foul language to satisfy the Ontario censor, but otherwise the film was screened as it was.

'A Married Couple is a highly distinctive film,' wrote Peter Harcourt. 'There is nothing quite like it anywhere in the world.'[25] This distinctiveness has remained in film culture because King eventually moved more into television production and, after the mid-1970s, into feature films. His experiment became part of Canadian film history. It represented the main spirit of Anglo-Canadian films in the 1960s – a spirit rooted in the documentary experience but wanting to break free of its traditional mould, to be something more innovative and theatrical than educational and informative. Seth Feldman considers King a 'visionary' filmmaker, who 'displayed an acute consciousness' of the new cinematic era that English Canada had embarked upon and to which he made a fundamental contribution.[26] In his intimate exploration of real-life human experience, King created a non-fictional work with the full fictional attributes of narrative film. The enthusiastic reception of King's films became part of a resurgent desire to create a national feature film industry, a desire noticed by the Liberal government of Lester Pearson, which moved to bolster feature film production now that newspaper critics and the public were taking notice of the fact that Canadians were creating an exciting and controversial cinema.

The year 1967 was Canada's centennial year. A world's fair was held in Montreal to coincide with the event. Generous funding of patriotic activities and a general enthusiasm for all things Canadian became the norm. This spirit of renewed nationalism lasted well into the 1970s under the leadership of the charismatic Liberal prime minister, Pierre Elliott Trudeau. Film production was not untouched. In 1967 there were 1,400 movie theatres and drive-ins in Canada, with a gross box office of $103 million.[27] This was down from 1,635 theatres in 1962.[28] At a time of declining venues for film, the federal government passed Bill C-204, which created the Canadian Film Development Corporation (CFDC) with a $10-million budget to fund feature film production. The idea was to have a revolving fund that would provide investment, grants, and loans to producers of films that met certain Canadian content rules. Money from the CFDC would not be forthcoming until at least 50 per cent of a film's budget was guaranteed by a distributor. Canada had not put any restrictions on Hollywood films or their profits. Nor had the Canadian government challenged the increasingly monopolistic structure of theatre ownership and distribution. It simply provided money to create product. What happened to the product in the market place was more of a hope and a prayer than a legislated reality. The end result of this major innovation is described in the next chapter, appropriately titled 'The Escapist Seventies.'

The model for the CFDC was taken from Great Britain, which had a similar film agency in place – the National Film Finance Corporation. However, unlike Canada, Britain had also placed restrictions on American films. Considering that Canada had been hoodwinked by Hollywood with the Canadian Co-operation Project of the 1950s, the CFDC was such a major step forward that it was to become the foundation of an ongoing feature film industry, an industry that continued to be dependent on the state. The rationale for the funding policy was the belief that the state must intervene to give Canada a rich cultural life. It was the same rationale used by the government when it formed the CBC in the 1930s, also using a British model, and later the Canada Council in the 1950s. It would seem that without state intervention there could be no major national institutions of cultural dissemination in the country. Since Canada was suffering from cultural colonialism in film, the state was being called upon to subsidize Canadian production.[29] The government's goal was as much the development of foreign audiences as Canadian ones because the market in Canada was considered rather small.[30]

Up to 1967 the feature films of that decade were being made by the NFB, both its English and French sides, and by independent producers like Crawley Films and Cooperatio in Quebec. The birth of the CFDC meant that the NFB, which had been dragged reluctantly into feature film production in the 1960s, could move aside as the private sector took over. This it did a few years later. By the end of 1971, the CFDC had used up its $10-million fund on sixty-four films with budgets totalling $17.7 million, of which the CFDC's contribution was $6.7 million.[31] One would imagine that such a gush of film production in such a short period would result in a chorus of applause from guardians of the public purse. On the contrary, the CFDC had recovered only $600,000 up to that point, and of the sixty-four films, only three had made money![32] This Canadianization of popular culture did not automatically result in a superlative film product. Funding is only one part of a very complex artistic equation, and the fact that there had not been a Canadian feature film industry for some time meant that the talent and cinematic vision required to articulate a national cinema were not readily available. Even so, English Canada was doing well, considering that most long-established national cinemas at the time had less than a half-dozen accomplished film directors with international reputations, and most countries had only one or two big names. As a newcomer, English Canada was making waves.

France was leading the way with its 'New Wave' of directors: François Truffault, Jean-Luc Godard, Claude Chabrol, and Louis Malle. Reminiscent of the direct cinema movement (see chapter 9) in Canada, these directors 'took to shooting in the streets with handheld cameras and a very small team, using jump cuts, improvisation ... and quotes from literature and other films.'[33] England had Tony Richardson's breakthrough story of working-class life, *The Loneliness of the Long Distance Runner* (1962). English director David Lean was taking the world by storm (via Hollywood) with historical epics such as *Bridge on the River Kwai*, *Lawrence of Arabia*, and *Doctor Zhivago*. Czechoslovakia had Milos Forman, who also used minimal plots and *cinéma vérité* techniques for his smart social commentaries. The Italians had Michelangelo Antonioni and Federico Fellini, with their penchant for the surreal. The Japanese had Akira Kurosawa, and the Swedes, Ingmar Bergman. Even the Americans had singular talents such as the master of suspense, Alfred Hitchcock, and the comedian Woody Allen, who created an unforgettable cinematic persona in the films he directed and starred in. In fact, it was an amazing decade for film around the world as fresh voices appeared from all quarters. That Canada did not have a director of world stature in the 1960s was inevitable, considering its starting point. It was literally building on nothing except its documentary tradition.

This is most evident in Don Shebib's masterpiece *Goin' down the Road*

(1970). Shebib was a Torontonian with Nova Scotia roots. He was born in 1938 and was in his early thirties when he made this landmark film. Shebib's grandfather was a Lebanese immigrant who settled in Cape Breton, Nova Scotia, a region of coal mines and steel mills. His mother came from Newfoundland, and his Nova Scotia father was a barber. Shebib studied cinematography at UCLA after graduating from the University of Toronto. He won a $19,000 grant from the Canadian Film Development Corporation to make his film. The script had been written by William Fruet, and the film was shot by Richard Leiterman, who had just finished working with Allan King on *A Married Couple*. *Goin' down the Road* had been originally conceived as a television drama titled 'The Maritimers,' but the CBC turned it down (echoes of *Drylanders*). So it became Shebib's first feature film and has remained his greatest contribution to Canadian cinema.

Even today the film appears so profoundly Canadian in its form and its content that its authenticity is almost painful. The all-Canadian cast and production crew, as well as Canadian locations, provide it with an at-home genuineness that has seldom been surpassed. Not only were the script, the cinematographer, and the director Canadian, but even the music was Canadian, in the person of the folk singer Bruce Cockburn! It was a film wrapped tightly in the Canadian identity of the time. The film critic Robert Fothergill stated unequivocally that '... Canadian filmmaking has been artistically most successful when it has sailed close to the winds of realism.'[34] No other comment could be more apt than this about *Goin' down the Road*, Canada's original road movie.

The film begins with a collection of images of derelict scenes from Cape Breton – dilapidated row housing, auto junk yards, impoverished kids – and a documentary-like 'voice-over' song about 'goin' down the road' as two young men get into a beat-up, ten-year-old Chevy convertible with 'My Nova Scotia Home' painted on the side. Pete and Joey are the two adventurers leaving behind the hopelessness and restricted possibilities of this economic backwater for the bright lights, good jobs, and sophisticated young women of Toronto. They're going to find a new life, or so they dream. 'Look out, Toronto, here we come,' they yell triumphantly as they approach the city. Having arrived with a mere $30 in their pockets, they end up in the Salvation Army hostel, but eventually they find work in a bottling factory. One of them marries, and we see the young hopefuls enjoying the neon pleasures of Toronto's once-famous downtown Yonge Street strip. Pete has high aspirations, while goofy Joey is content with a colour TV. As can be expected, their jobs come to an end, the marriage starts to unravel, and the two losers have to steal groceries to eat. Homeless and penniless, they respond by 'goin down the road' in their only remaining possession – the Chevy convertible.

Don Quixote and Pancho Sanchez are the classic models for this road/buddy movie of two characters tilting at imaginary windmills in a fruitless quest for fame and fortune. The film attracted critical response, approving audiences, and interested scholars. Not only was it a critical success, it was also a commercial one because its costs were so low.[35] It was 'Feature Film of the Year' at the Canadian Film Awards, and its two male leads, Doug McGrath and Paul Bradley, shared the best actor award. *Maclean's* told readers that the film

> had received more acclaim than any Canadian film, with the possible exception of Allan King's documentaries *Warrendale* and *A Married Couple*. Certainly no feature film since Don Owen's *Nobody Waved Good-bye* (1964) has generated so much optimism about the future of Canada's sputtering film industry.'[36]

Such enthusiastic comments helped the film gross $150,000 in its first two months, a good result on an original budget of $85,000.[37] Of course, the film was set in Toronto, and so Torontonians flocked to see their city and its characters on the big screen. The *New Yorker* termed *Goin' down the Road* 'an honest story,' while the *New York Times* judged it to be 'the most impressive new work of realist cinema in years.'[38] In a *New Yorker* interview, Shebib compared his own film to John Steinbeck's renowned novel *The Grapes of Wrath*.[39] Later in life Shebib described himself as 'a commercial filmmaker' who wanted to appeal to audiences on an emotional level, and decried his decision to stay and make films in Canada.[40] 'I should have left after *Goin' down the Road*,' he said in an interview. 'I should have gone to California.'[41] This sense of disillusionment with Canadian cinema (by this time, he had made another five features) parallels the theme of *Goin' down the Road*, with its Canadian quest for the bright lights and limitless possibilities of Hollywood. Shebib never went down that road. He struggled on in Canada and so ended up with the short end of the stick, feeling that he had lost or failed. This is a fictional theme in Canadian films that scholars have explored intensely, especially in regard to *Goin' down the Road*, which has come to represent an archetype of national sensibility, in which long-term success is impossible. The theme also resonates in real life.

Robert Fothergill began the discussion of this theme with 'Coward, Bully or Clown,' a 1973 article which delineated the main Canadian male types in Canadian cinema and their inadequacy.[42] Instead of the transcendent figures that have come to epitomize the male American role model – the handsome, gallant sheriff fighting nasty outlaws, the heroic GI leading his men to victory, the hard-boiled cop or detective who triumphs over crime – Canada has the pathetic and defeated characters of *Goin' down the Road.* The title of Leonard Cohen's 1966 novel, *Beautiful Losers*, sums up this perception. Fothergill described it as a spirit of 'collective debility.'[43] Geoff Pevere attempted a reassessment a decade later with his 1985 'Images of Men' article, which ended up confirming Fothergill's earlier analysis. Referring to *Nobody Waved Good-Bye, The Luck of Ginger Coffey, The Rowdyman*, and *Goin' down the Road*, he spoke of a 'veritable legacy of losers, creeps and thoughtless heels.'[44] Pevere pushes the Freudian envelope even further by sourcing this prototypical image in the 'psycho-cultural humiliation' brought on by the Canadian film industry's failure in competing with 'big brother at what the big guy does best: making movies.'[45]

Christine Ramsay has done the most extensive and complex analysis of the 'loser' image in reference to *Goin' down the Road.* She links gender, region, class, and culture in the film and concludes that the film is primarily a study in the tension that exists between margin and centre in Canada and how this tension plays out in socio-economic terms. The 'victim metaphor' of Fothergill's time, popularized by Margaret Atwood's seminal theoretical work *Survival: A Thematic Guide to Canadian Literature* (1972), is basic but, according to Ramsay, 'incomplete.'[46] For Ramsay, a postmodernist thinker, it is too simple and too modernistic to be adequate. She believes that *'Goin' down the Road* is about the problem of national definition in English Canada: in particular, the problem created by Toronto's status at the centre of Canada's social and personal identity and economic prosperity as seen from the peripheral perspective of two marginalized Canadian men.'[47] She points out that not all Canadian males are 'losers,' especially those of the ruling elite in Toronto. Toronto is a winner, not a loser, in the Canadian context. The 'losers' are the poor, uneducated, working class from have-not regions that are exploited by capitalism. Extrapolating this very real identity to all Canadians is false. It hides the class and regional divisions that are integral to Canada. The popularity of the film with audiences could have resulted from its subliminal glorification of the working man or from the city slicker's tendency to enjoy a condescending laugh at the expense of his naïve country bumpkin cousins. Pete and Joey's quest had a redeeming quality because the two were able to escape, not from their own delusions, but from the physical prison of the Maritimes and then Toronto. They couldn't win in life's battle, but they could run away. Maybe there is a need in the Canadian psyche to identify with ordinary struggles. Canadian consciousness may be colonized, victimized, and debilitated, but it still dreams of some kind of liberation, of an escape from its colonial status and the vagaries of the metropolitan-hinterland thesis that defines life in the regions. *Goin' down the Road* gave Canadians their first beautiful losers.

In spite of the theme, *Goin' down the Road* ended the remarkable decade of the 1960s on a high note, with its crossover from documentary to feature film realism. The realism came from unknown Canadian actors, very low budgets, Canadian scenes, and youthful directors from Owen to King to Shebib. Their films were an exciting novelty. They had reached out beyond the confines of the traditional documentary mode to the fictional story, where the irrational was as powerful as the rational. The period from *Nobody Waved Good-Bye* to *Goin' down the Road* marked a promising new beginning for Anglo-Canadian feature film. It displayed indigenous qualities that set Canadian cinema apart from all others. This would not last long. The rush into feature film production that followed these pioneering works was spurred by the enticements of the Canadian Film Development Corporation, and later by the tax-avoidance Capital Cost Allowance program of the 1970s. It was a surfeit of money that was to push Canadian cinema from a promising beginning into a problematic future.

CHAPTER EIGHT

The Escapist Seventies

There are people who spend more money at cocktail parties for Canadian movies than at screenings of Canadian movies, [directors] ... who spend more time among financiers than among artists ... who know ... how to cheat on their taxes by investing in Canadian movies, but haven't any idea what is a good movie ...

Robert Fulford, in *Saturday Night*, January 1974

Robert Fulford, in his film critic role as Marshall Delaney, was making a harsh, though valid, judgment about the state of Canadian cinema at a time when the volume of feature film production in the country was unprecedented, but whose quality was generally abysmal.[1] During the decade of the 1970s, Canada (including Quebec) produced an incredible 708 feature films,[2] more than twice as many as had been produced in the previous fifty years. What had happened to turn Canada's state-driven, documentary-dominated film world upside down? Certainly the Canadian Film Development Corporation (CFDC), which had come into play at the very end of the 1960s, was a factor, but its resources were limited and rapidly consumed. Although the CFDC invested almost $20 million in over one hundred films between 1969 and 1975, the funding of an annual average production of seventy feature films was far beyond its capacity.[3] Something else was making this prodigious productivity real, and that something else, as is so often the case in the film industry, was money, easy money.

For some years, the Canadian government had offered a tax incentive to those who wished to invest in Canadian films. The Capital Cost Allowance (CCA), as it was termed, allowed investors to write off 60 per cent of their investment in a film against their personal income taxes, a much better proposition than the limited write-off most Canadians took for donations to charitable institutions. But few investors took advantage of this prior to the 1970s. There was very little product to invest in. The Canadian Film Development Corporation's financial contribution to Canadian cinema legitimized the film industry by giving it state subsidies and commercial credibility. This credibility was used by producers to attract private funding, something the CFDC wanted. The general media buzz concerning a new wave of English-Canadian films such as *Goin' down the Road* suggested to investors that something was happening that might make money.[4] In 1975 the CCA was increased to 100 per cent, and creative accounting went into high gear by taking advantage of loopholes. For example, investors had been allowed to use the total cost of a film in calculating their write-off, rather than simply their share of the investment.[5] Although this practice was eventually stopped, the new 100 per-cent deduction was a magnet for high-income, tax-deduction-hungry professionals, like doctors and dentists, who were enticed to invest in movies as an easy way to save on taxes. What was particularly attractive about the CCA was the investor's ability to write off 100 per cent of a $100,000 investment in any one year, while putting up only $20,000 and taking up to four years to pay out the balance.[6] And it wasn't just the film industry that cashed in. Similar capital cost allowances were established for the oil and gas industry to encourage exploration and development. It was an age of tax-shelter frenzy, and thousands bought multiples of $5,000 units in multi-million dollar productions certified as Canadian. In 1975 there were eighteen features made under the old 60 per-cent CCA, while in 1979 under the new 100 per-cent CCA there were sixty-six.[7] In 1982 the figure was down to thirty features because the CCA had ended.

The tax-shelter scheme certainly took the pressure off the CFDC to provide funding. By 1980 less than 1 per cent of the equity financing of Canadian films was coming from the CFDC, and most film budgets were in the $3-million range.[8] From this one might conclude that the tax incentive idea was a brilliant way of not using taxpayers' money (other than money lost to the system through the deduction) to kick-start an industry. At its peak, the CCA resulted in almost $200 million in annual production, a truly mind-boggling figure. The quality of the films was equally mind-boggling. Film critic Martin Knelman described the general quality of this gush of films as 'a national scandal.'[9] Commercial interest had taken all precedence over art. An example of what this era's average film producer was striving to achieve is the 1979 smash hit *Meatballs*. It was a certified Canadian film made on a $1.6-million budget. The producers of the wacky comedy received $3.3 million from Paramount for U.S. distribution rights and another $300,000 for Canadian rights. The film grossed $40 million in 1979, and its Canadian director, Ivan Reitman, promptly trotted off to Hollywood for fame and fortune.[10]

Nevertheless, the decade was not a total disaster. Of the hundreds of films made (only about half were ever released) there were a dozen or so that are worth mentioning. Pierre Pageau, in his 'Survey of the Commercial Cinema, 1963–1977,' describes the early 1970s as a period when English-Canadian films were developing 'a very original rhetoric between the landscape ... and the Canadian "hero," who almost always exists on the fringe.'[11] *Goin' down the Road* was the ur-text of this genre because it spoke to Canadian audiences without using big budgets, known stars, and Hollywood-style scripts. Two, slightly later, examples of Canadian films set in Newfoundland and the Maritimes were *The Rowdyman* (1972) and *Wedding in White* (1972), both of which dealt with failed male personalities. *The Rowdyman* was a film that attracted a great deal of critical attention because it was so clearly 'down home.' Robert Fothergill, a university professor and the film critic for the *Canadian Forum*, used the film as one example of the then current cinematic portrayal of Canadian males as suffering from 'collective debility.'[12] The script was written by Gordon Pinsent, who also played the lead, a character named Will Cole. Cole is a Newfoundlander whose devil-may-care attitude toward life results in a friend's death and the loss of his girlfriend. Cole is the 'tragic-comic misfit,' the 'clown' figure that Fothergill identifies as one of the main fictional figures of Canadian cinema of the time (the other two are the bully and the coward).[13] Fothergill, in praising *The Rowdyman's* sense of place, claims the film is able 'to bottle the spirit of that community [Corner Brook] with at least as much fidelity as a sober documentary could do.'[14] It was this humorous fictional realism that seemed to make films like *Goin' down the Road* and *The Rowdyman* so appealing to Canadians. When a film was obviously about one of 'us' there was a Canadian audience for it, and when it was about a distinct regional community of seemingly unusual characters its appeal was only heightened. Characters from fringe regions of the country, whose population had escaped urbanization and its dominant culture of success, appeared as entertaining and likeable male misfits. Fothergill attributes the appeal of this character to what he calls the younger brother syndrome in Canadians.[15] The United States is Canada's overachieving older brother, which results in the Canadian male having an inferiority complex.

In spite of its supposedly quintessential Canadianism, *The Rowdyman* lost out at the Canadian Film Awards that year in the category of best picture to *Wedding in White,* another film set in the Atlantic region. William Fruet wrote the script and directed *Wedding in White* in his auteur debut. Fruet, the writer of *Goin' down the Road,* based the script on an earlier play he had written and drew on the cinematographic talents of Richard Leiterman, who had worked on *Goin' down the Road* and on Allan King's documentary features. The film had an overpowering sense of realism and face-to-face conflict. The lead male character was the British actor Donald Pleasance, playing an overbearing father who marries off his daughter to an aging friend in order to preserve patriarchal control and social decorum. The forced wedding of the ill-matched and unloving couple is arranged by the father primarily to protect his own reputation. 'I don't think there's anyone in *Wedding in White* with whom you can sympathize,' Pleasance commented in an interview. 'Maybe the girl.'[16] Fruet himself, considered the film an exposé of the chattel-like attitude of Maritime men toward women.[17] The continued production of stories set on Canada's East Coast, especially in its working-class manifestation, provided a lopsided view of Canadian society because it was so heavily weighted toward one region and one class. Hector Ross, a booking agent for various western Canadian theatre chains at the time, described *Wedding in White* as 'a good picture' but 'a bust,' meaning it didn't attract audiences the way American films did.[18] 'Canadians have got such a downbeat, goddamn attitude to everything they make,' he offered as an explanation for its commercial failure. 'Everything's got to be a tragedy. Everybody's got to suffer in the picture.'[19] He was saying that the story of a forced marriage of an oppressed young woman to a much older man does not attract line-ups at the cashier's window.

The Canadian actor Carol Kane played the scrawny, hollow-eyed young woman who personifies victimhood. The men in the film may be 'selfish, cruel or hypocritical,' but she is limp, completely apathetic to her fate.[20] The film critic for *Maclean's,* John Hofsess, claimed that in films like *The Rowdyman* and *Wedding in White,* 'you know you haven't been lied to, brow beaten, or shoddily entertained,' implying that is what Hollywood films do.[21] While films like *Wedding in White* offered unusual, dramatic, socially challenging, in-your-face realism, they did not create success at the box office, where public taste had been moulded for so long by American escapist fantasy.

An equally powerful film about marginalization, *Fortune and Men's Eyes*, was released in June 1971. Based on John Herbert's play of the same name, which had been produced to great international acclaim in the 1960s, the film was, in the words of John Hofsess, 'a searing indictment of the dehumanizing process of our prisons.'[22] This story of homosexual prison rape was encapsulated by a review in New York's *Village Voice* as 'Gay, yes, but proud it's not.'[23] Made on a modest $700,000 budget, the film was a raw and disturbing social document that reflected the seamier side of Canadian life, and it contributed to the victim theme that was developing strongly in Canadian cultural consciousness in the 1970s.

The following year, the regional focus shifted from the East to the West with two films, *Paperback Hero*, set in Saskatchewan, and *Slipstream*, set in Alberta. Jim Leach, an academic film critic, discussed the two films as examples of how Canadians were struggling 'to evolve a film language capable of responding to the Canadian experience' that was not just a straightforward adoption of 'the ready-made language of the American genres.'[24] Most of the tax-shelter films were of the latter sort. What interested Leach in *Paperback Hero* was the film's direct reference to American imagery and cultural icons. A drab little town in Saskatchewan has a local stud, 'Marshall' Dillon, who affects the swagger of the Marlboro Man as he portrays himself as a John Wayne western movie hero. The story is full of pathos as the laughable anti-hero and his friends end up on the wrong side of a high-noon shoot-out – lying in the dust rather than standing up.

Slipstream also has a rural setting. In this film, American fantasies and realities are finally overthrown by an incorruptible Canadian who turns his back on cultural imperialism. At long last, Canadian cinema had a kind of male hero, an anti-American one, who may not be able to overthrow the grip of his older brother but deprives him of a small part of his turf. The protagonist is a disc jockey operating a radio station out of a farmhouse, who resists the temptations of his girlfriend to settle down when he torches the station to prevent the broadcast of the canned music desired by its American owner. He is jailed but escapes. Robert Fulford saw the film as being full of 'transcendental Canadianism.'[25] Robert Fothergill found in it 'a credible assertion of sovereign identity by a Canadian [male] character who is neither Coward, Bully or Clown.'[26] The film won both best picture and best director awards at the Canadian Film Awards. Since the talented William Fruet (1935–) wrote the script of *Slipstream*, one can say that the Alberta-born director and screenwriter broke out of the Maritime mould (*Goin' down the Road* and *Wedding in White*) and used the western setting as a territory of social liberation, where a Canadian-style 'western' hero could at long last be realized. Fruet used the West as a site of self-realization, something that he felt was lacking in the tradition-bound and impoverished East Coast.

The fixation with issues of male achievement reached its peak in *The Apprenticeship of Duddy Kravitz* (1974). Based on the 1959 novel by renowned Canadian writer Mordecai Richler, the film tells the story of a young Jewish man from Montreal who is on the make, seeking fame and fortune by filming bar mitzvahs. Played by the American actor Richard Dreyfus, the character of Duddy fills the screen with his street-wise philosophizing and his frenetic energy. The *New Yorker*'s film critic, Penelope Gilliat, called it 'a drive-in movie,' referring to its entertainment value.[27] But for Canadians it seemed a certain kind of 'coming-of-age' in cinema because it was based on one of the century's great Canadian novels by one of the country's most popular writers. Its director, Ted Kotcheff (1931–), was a Canadian who worked extensively in film. He turned the comic tale of ethnic rivalry and cultural assimilation in then Anglo-dominated, multi-ethnic Montreal into a nationally recognizable story of immigrant cultures.

'*Kravitz* established itself in three short months,' wrote James McLarty in *Motion*, 'as the most successful English Canadian film yet shown in this country.'[28] About half the original budget came from the CFDC.[29] The film was not only accessible to a broad audience in Canada, but it could draw on the interest of the wider North American Jewish community because of its portrayal of Jewish urban life. It travelled well in the United States. John Hofsess found the film so typical of the Jewish community anywhere in North America that he concluded the film was 'Canadian only in a legal and technical sense.'[30] To which one might reply that all ethnic immigrant communities have trans-border characteristics because of certain commonalities in their construction. A film that dealt transparently with the Jewish community in Montreal carried the codes, language, and attitudes found in the same ethnic community in other North American cities.

One important aspect of the success of the film was the long relationship that had existed between its director, Ted Kotcheff, and its screenwriter, Mordecai Richler. The two men had roomed in London together as expatriates during the 1950s, and Kotcheff had been the first to read the novel in manuscript. Both men were members of White ethnic minorities and were seeking successful careers in the arts. John Kemeny, the film's producer, was of Hungarian background. Obviously, the major players in this cinematic episode had a certain rapport that provided cohesion, understanding, and purpose to the project. Together they created a film statement that went beyond the 'failed male' Anglo-Canadian figure of earlier films. Although Fothergill's bully, coward, and clown figures were all represented in the character of Duddy Kravitz, there is a gained wisdom at the end, situated in the requirements of a poignant, coming-of-age novel, that provides a redemption. The film portrayed the ethnic drive to climb up the 'vertical mosaic' of Canadian society and become a winner. This challenge to the restrictive characterization of the 'loser' found in the earlier working-class, East Coast, Anglo-Canadian films allowed the film to do well in the U.S. market. The Duddy character may be an outsider, but he is integral to the North American urban environment. *The Apprenticeship of Duddy Kravitz* confirms Christopher Gittings's cogent argument in *Canadian National Cinema* that the construction of nationality in Canadian films has been stereotypical and biased. A film portraying a minority in Canada based on the writing of a novelist from that community was a breakthrough that signalled the coming age of multiculturalism. While this multiculturalism was Euro-centric in its conception, it laid the groundwork for the emerging multiracial multiculturalism of the 1980s and its new non-White immigrant minorities.

The new ethnic orientation introduced by *Duddy Kravitz* continued the next year with *Lies My Father Told Me*. The film was based on a script by Ted Allan (1916–95) and was set in the Jewish district of Montreal in the 1920s. Allan had written the original short story in 1949 and then adapted the story for radio. The film was directed by Jan Kadar, the Czech Jewish director who had won the best foreign film Oscar for *The Shop on Main Street* in 1965. It's a sentimental film about a grandfather's relationship with his grandson in an immigrant community. The film's director had come to Canada after the Soviet invasion of Czechoslovakia in 1968. He found making films here 'a bit of an adventure' because, as he said in an interview, 'Canada is not a place where filmmaking has a big and longtime tradition.'[31] Kadar lived until 1979, making TV movies and serving as film-maker-in-residence at the American Film

Institute in Los Angeles. His brief sojourn in Canadian film-making was just one of many episodes during the 1970s that contributed to a vital non-Anglo, non-French voice in the medium.

The search for Canadian material that could be adopted for film continued after the success of *The Apprenticeship of Duddy Kravitz*. In 1977 Allan King directed *Who Has Seen the Wind*, based on W.O. Mitchell's classic novel of a Prairie boy's coming-of-age. The film was shot in Arcola, Saskatchewan. Toronto film reviewer Martin Knelman visited Arcola for the premiere and concluded: 'Canadians believe that their salvation lies in being true to the plain, simple ways of towns like Arcola, where life is lived without adornment or pretension ... *Who Has Seen the Wind* [the book] epitomizes this ... Canadian ideal.'[32] The film had a budget of over a million dollars, of which $300,000 was contributed by the Saskatchewan government in exchange for having King take on a platoon of local trainees. Out of that budget, the novelist W.O. Mitchell, whose script had been passed over by King, received $11,000 for the film rights.[33] The film, based on a script by Allan King's wife, was not as successful as the novel had been and gently faded into the historical woodwork. Although a great Canadian classic as a novel, the film lacked the drive or emotional rapport with the audience that propelled films like *Duddy Kravitz*.

In contrast to this family-oriented agrarian pastoral (it was originally conceived as a TV mini-series), Canada produced two urbane films at the same time – *Outrageous* (1977) and *In Praise of Older Women* (1978). *Outrageous* is the endearing story of a Toronto transvestite and the schizophrenic female he befriends as they both struggle for a meaningful place in society. Made for only $167,000 and starring Craig Russell as the female impersonator, the film attracted both attention and accolades for its content and its style. Based on a short story by Canadian writer Margaret Gibson, the film succeeded in cities like New York, where a large gay community enjoyed the film's portrayal of gay culture in much the same way as *Duddy Kravitz* had succeeded in New York's Jewish community. Doug Fetherling, writing in the intellectual *Canadian Forum*, described the film as 'très New York.'[34]

In Praise of Older Women also had a sexual theme. Based on Stephen Vizinczey's best-selling 1965 novel of the same name (2 million copies in print worldwide), the film told the story of a young stud's amorous adventures with older women, beginning with his life in communist Hungary and concluding with his immigrant existence in Saskatoon.[35] The film ran afoul of the censor in Ontario, which caused a stir, so that, in the words of *Saturday Night*'s prudish Robert Fulford, it came to appeal to a 'soft-core porn audience.'[36] In a sense, *In Praise of Older Women* concluded the rise of the White ethnic male voice of the 1970s, which had begun with *The Apprenticeship of Duddy Kravitz*.

In 1981 the CCA tax shelter was shut down. The whole episode had been a source of cultural embarrassment to the government and to the industry. Writing in *Cinema Canada* in 1982, John Harkness summed up the experience with this stern assessment: 'Canadian producers attempted to mimic an industry ... [without] the knowledge nor the production infrastructure in place. It is like trying to compete with Ford by building cars in your basement.'[37] While the analogy was a bit stretched, Harkness's complaint about the overall failure of the decade of the 1970s to create 'an expression of a nation's soul' was justified if one felt there was such a thing as a unified, singular national soul.[38] For him, 'most of the films created under the shelter ... seem like movies from nowhere.'[39] The prevailing mimicry of American film values resulted in hundreds of unseen and third-rate products. This criticism must be balanced with the amazing amount of film production that occurred – a vast training ground where innumerable people toiled in happy obscurity, and hucksters and wheeler-dealers plied their subterfuges. Under the tax shelter, a 'real' feature film industry was reborn in English Canada for the first time since the short-lived and failed attempt of the silent movies in the 1920s and the quickie quota films of the 1930s. The tax-shelter approach certainly had serious drawbacks, but it was a start and the government of Canada, ever the player, wanted to keep the momentum going, but with less public criticism.

In 1982 the Liberal government's Applebaum-Hébert Report on cultural policy recognized the importance of the film industry with a recommendation that led to the creation of Telefilm Canada, the successor to the Canadian Film Development Corporation. The CFDC had become discredited with the poor reception for most of the films it supported. The government was also interested in assisting private television networks to make Canadian material, and so it moved to combine film and television support in one envelope. In 1982–3 the CFDC had a final year budget of only $4.5 million, while its successor, Telefilm Canada, had a first year budget in 1983–4 of $35 million, which rose to $60 million by 1988.[40] By funding both feature film and independent television production from a single source, the government was linking the two media and using the wealthier and more popular medium of television as a vehicle for the development and promotion of film. With the tax-shelter scheme gone by the wayside, feature film producers of that period quickly shifted into television production with various award-winning series. In 1974 the country had 1,116 movie theatres; ten years later, that number was down to 899 and box office revenue was stagnant.[41] Twenty-five per cent of Canadian households had VCRs by 1984, and the film industry was moving to a stage in which home viewing, either via VCRs or television movie channels, was a major source of its revenue. The emerging world of media in the 1980s was very different from that of the 1970s. When Wyndham Wise, editor of the Canadian film magazine *Take One*, titled his article on the 1970s as 'Canadian Cinema from Boom to Bust: The Tax-Shelter Years' there was a widespread feeling that the decade as a whole was a failure for film.[42] The reaction of popular film reviewer Jay Scott was typical. All he could see was 'a deluge of disappointment.'[43]

Perhaps expectations were simply too high, and Canadian film critics and reviewers, now more influential than ever before, were making unrealistic demands as they tried to shame the industry into producing a cinema with depth. Obviously, there was a kind of wild-west frontier mentality in Canadian film at the time because money was flowing freely and all kinds of people were cashing in. A copious amount of shoddy work was being sold to the gullible and the greedy. Yet this was the way Canadian film came to be populated, first with hundreds and then thousands of new workers, who became the backbone of the evolving and maturing industry of future decades.

Two films were released in the early 1980s that reflected the transition to a more mature and sustainable film culture. The first appealed to the concerns of film critics, and the latter appealed to the general population. *The Grey Fox* (1983) and *The Terry Fox Story* (1983) were two examples of mainstream Canadian film-making that expressed the best of artistic and commercial values that came out of the escapist seventies. Twenty-seven-year-old documentary film-maker Phillip Borsos (1953–95) from Vancouver directed *The Grey Fox* as his first feature film. The film told the story of Bill Miner, an American stage coach robber, who took to robbing trains in Canada in his old age. Shot on a $3.5-million budget and using American actor Richard Farnsworth as the lead, the film created a romanticized and affectionate treatment of the mountainous landscape of southern British Columbia, where the historical events had actually occurred. The doyen of American film critics, Pauline Kael, writing in the *New Yorker*, described the cinematography of the trains chugging through the forest as 'exultant.'[44] The film had been shot in 1980, after concluding the sale to investors of 696 units at $5,000 apiece.[45] It was then edited in 1981 and sat in a vault until the producers could get distribution for it. When it was finally released in 1983, it won best picture and best director at the Genies, the successor to the Canadian Film Awards. Although the film grossed over $6 million in its first year, little made its way back to the producers.[46] Borsos, who had been paid $45,000 to work on the film, was so short of money while waiting for another assignment that he went to Hollywood, where he received a quarter of a million to direct a forgettable film.[47] When he died in 1995 at the age of forty-one, the typical assessment of his career was 'unfulfilled promise.'[48]

The Grey Fox was one of those 'small, enjoyable and successful [in an artistic sense] films ... that are,' in the words of Canadian film producer Fil Fraser, 'moving and fun to watch.'[49] But it didn't make money because it was a period piece with a relatively high budget for a Canadian film. To recoup its costs, it would have had to gross more than double what it took in. While *The Grey Fox* may have met the standards for expressing a nation's soul that some critics wanted, it couldn't keep its talented director in Canada. The tax-shelter years were over and there wasn't any work.

The situation with *The Terry Fox Story* was completely different. It was pre-sold to the CTV network and the American HBO (Home Box Office) pay-per-view channel. Astral Films of Montreal and Twentieth-Century Fox were co-producers. Terry Fox, a cancer victim, had become a national hero for his dramatic and then tragic one-legged run across Canada for cancer research. His was a household name, and the $4-million film opened in 130 theatres across Canada in May 1983. This was not an art house film, but a film close to the hearts of Canadians, inspired by a young man's heroic determination. It spoke to the nation and it made money. Taken together, the two films wrote a closing chapter on life in the escapist seventies.

While film critics may have felt that Canada had been soiled by the experience of tax-shelter films, the tax-shelter era was not a complete disaster. Perhaps the pedantic categorization involved in the certification criteria (and the resultant creative interpretations of its terms) or the mediocrity of state funding processes encouraged the tax-shelter method of funding to seek the lowest common denominator. Or perhaps it was the gleam of fame and fortune in men's eyes as they sought to make 'international' hits (a.k.a. Hollywood imitations) that brought on a tidal wave of ghastly productions. But any large-scale industry has its share of charlatans and rip-off artists, and one cannot expect a film industry to represent only highbrow values. The dozen or so films from the 1970s that made a mark in their day were generally middlebrow films like *The Apprenticeship of Duddy Kravitz*, which was a fair reflection of Canadian film audience tastes. Canada may have been a colonial backwater in terms of film, but its resident deal-makers worked hard to give it some kind of independent stature. The industry's relative immaturity in comparison to other national cinemas and the hot-house atmosphere around the tax-shelter process of film-making meant that philistinism prevailed. In contrast to the experience of English Canada, the Quebec film industry during the same period took a more satisfying turn because it had a longer, better-established tradition and was part of a great cultural and political awakening around the issue of national identity.

CHAPTER NINE

The Quebec Auteur: From Perrault to Arcand

Quebec cinema burst forth with a new spirit in the early 1960s. It was following the lead of the new interventionist Liberal government of Quebec, which wanted Quebeckers to become 'maîtres chez nous.' For film this meant the end of a decade-long drought in feature film production. It is impossible to discuss all the work of the new generation of young film-makers that came into its own in the 1960s within the mandate of a book covering a century of cinema. What is possible is an informed discussion of one or two key films made by each director, the importance of these films to Quebec cultural life, and the interconnections among the various directorial visions and how these visions represented a unique society.

The careers of the half-dozen directors discussed in this chapter are only a sampling of the directorial talent that Quebec experienced in the 1960s and 1970s. The challenge of providing a narrow sample recognizes the incredible artistic bounty that the Quebec film industry developed after 1960. Some of these directors became auteurs – film-makers who wrote, produced, directed, and sometimes acted in their own films. The auteur spirit springs from an individual artist's roots in, and expression of, a society and its cultures. Auteurism theorizes artistic control of a cinematic product similar to an author's control of a book. Auteur films are films with a distinct vision. They contribute to the formation of a national cultural identity because they tend to reflect the film-maker's shared preoccupations with others of the same generation and milieu.

The following film-makers are representative of the highest achievements in Quebec film-making from 1960 to 1990: Pierre Perrault (1927–99) played the role of the documentarist who brought rural traditions into Quebec's current identity; Michel Brault (1928–) is the cinematographer and director who excelled in creating the visual moods that came to distinguish recent Quebec cinema; Jean Pierre Lefebvre (1941–) is the film critic and poet turned revolutionary film-maker; Gilles Carle (1929–) is the cultural *animateur*, whose humour, irony, and social caricature created a cinematic sociology of ordinary life; Claude Jutra (1930–86) was the shy genius who gave Canada the enduring classic *Mon Oncle Antoine*; while Denys Arcand (1941–) concluded this generation's best work with two award-winning and internationally lauded films, *Le Déclin de l'empire américain* (1986) and *Jésus de Montréal* (1989). Together these directors created a major body of work that was the second wave of Quebec's feature film industry.[1]

In 1960 francophone Montreal had 64 cinemas, of which 54 showed only English-language films.[2] That year there were 558 feature films screened in Canada, none of which was Canadian.[3] Canada's population at the time was 18 million, of which 5 million lived in Quebec. Anyone aspiring to create Quebec feature films had to face these daunting statistics and the reality of representing a minority culture in a state that was not making any feature films and had not done so for some time. Not surprising, it was the young who took on the challenge. The new Liberal government had launched a 'Quiet Revolution' after its election in 1960, which called for a secularization of society and the nationalization of industry, so that Quebeckers could control their own economy for the first time and have the educational skills to do it. The future belonged to those who would overthrow the conservative past. A sign of this new spirit was the 1961 law that allowed children to attend matinees for the first time since 1927. Within this atmosphere of encouragement and affirmation, French-language features began to appear, both from the National Film Board (Office Nationale du Film – ONF) and from independent producers. By the end of the decade, almost 50 feature films in French had been released, more than double the number made during the first wave (1944–53).[4] Quebec film historians have associated Quebec's cinema of the 1960s with political change by calling it 'le cinéma de la révolution tranquille.'[5] It was a period when cultural creativity joined hands with political concerns in a veritable epiphany of social renewal.

There were three main factors that coalesced to give Quebec a new start in film. First, there was the rise of the 'cinéma d'auteur,' which claimed that the best in film came from the vision of individual film-makers.[6] It was a concept initiated in the French cinematic culture of the

1950s, which propagated an approach opposed to the industrial model of the American studio system.[7] The French were valorizing the individual director, an appealing prospect for Quebec film-makers, who turned to France for inspiration. Auteurism was integral to what was termed the 'New Wave' cinema of France. 'La Nouvelle Vague française' led Quebec film-makers to seek their own direction and to have confidence that their vision had validity. The young Quebec rebels admired the work of the new French directors Truffault, Godard, Chabrol, and Rohmer, whose approach was heralded in 1959 in Truffault's *Les Quatre Cents Coups* (The 400 Blows), which won the Critics' Prize at Cannes. France's 'Nouvelle Vague' directors distinguished themselves by working improvisationally from an idea, casting friends and lovers in starring roles, and using their own apartments as sets. They rejected typical melodramatic scenarios in favour of exploring the relationship of young heterosexual couples, and they gave their films a certain unstaged 'documentary' feel.[8] These influences quickly surfaced in the work of young Quebeckers, for whom this style and content were seen as a liberation from tradition. Rejecting the values of the older generation allows a new generation to make their own statements, which serve to define their moment in the history of a society.

The whole theme of liberation was a second factor that was important in the 1960s. It provided the post-war generation with a sense of self and a sense of mission. In terms of film work, the social and political issues engaging the young were crucial. What began as an introspective look at young love ended up as a call to revolutionary change. While film may be categorized in numerous ways – by genre, nationality, gender, region, and language – the issue of French as an oppressed language in Canada became paramount to this new generation of Quebec film-makers. The struggle between the English and French languages was rooted in European imperialism from the sixteenth to the twentieth centuries, when colonies around the world were forced to adopt either of these languages, thereby creating both a metropolitan anglophone and a metropolitan francophone universe. Since English was the leading imperial language, and French the secondary imperial language, the francophone linguistic universe was much smaller than the anglophone. The issue of language was tied to a major global movement to topple colonialism. The end of the Second World War launched an intense period of anti-colonial struggle. Among the colonies that the French lost were Algeria and Vietnam. The British lost their African colonies as well as India. The liberation struggles of the

1950s and 1960s were socialist-influenced and appealed to the young idealists of Quebec, who saw Quebec as part of the worldwide anti-colonialist struggle. The theme of national liberation, with its glorification of a people, its emphasis on indigenous language, and its demand for state control to oppose foreign ownership was the ideological atmosphere in which the new films were made. Affirmation of a new Quebec national identity beyond the hyphenated concept of the French-Canadian was the ultimate goal. In 1971, the Association professionnelle des cinéastes du Québec captured the spirit of the times when it issued a manifesto that stated: 'Nous voulons que la collectivité Québécoise retrouve au cinéma un reflet d'elle-même qui soit juste, dynamique et stimulant.'[9]

The third factor that influenced Quebec film-makers was the theory and practice of *cinéma direct*, a concept that was revolutionizing documentary film-making in Britain and the United States. Michel Brault quipped that direct cinema was 'une camera qui écoute' (a cinema that eavesdrops). The National Film Board had launched a series titled 'Candid Eye,' which represented the work of documentarists who used hand-held cameras and portable synchronized sound recorders to reach deeply into the recesses of human activities. The French title of 'Candid Eye' was 'Panoramique.' Direct cinema techniques gave film-makers a sense of vitality, of being involved in daily life. Their films seemed to be in 'direct' contact with their subjects. Rather than be interpreted by a voice-over narrative, people in the films spoke for themselves. The technique gave the viewer a sense of the camera's presence and the involvement of the cinematic eye.[10] Rather than use images to bolster a scripted narrative, direct cinema allowed people to script their own film.

When direct cinema ideas were transferred to feature films in the mid-1960s, the results were startling. Like the New Wave directors in France, the Quebec directors preferred improvised dialogue. They emphasized the importance of what was being expressed in a scene by using non-professional actors to offer a sense of authenticity. They also drew on their own lives and stories for inspiration. The projection of the film-maker's subjective self conveyed a mood of a spontaneous contemporary actuality.

In the early 1950s, the NFB was an assimilationist organization that did not value Quebec culture.[11] After the NFB moved to Montreal in 1956, it became a target of Quebec nationalist accusations of discrimination. An article in *Le Devoir*, Montreal's leading French newspaper, stated that of the 1,109 films the NFB made between 1952 and 1956 only 69 (6%) were in French.[12] Considering the English roots of the NFB, the new spirit of national awakening in Quebec would lead inevitably to clashes. The first expression of direct cinema for Quebec film-makers was the 1958 film *Les Raquetteurs / The Snowshoers*, by Michel Brault and Gilles Groulx, which was made at a convention of showshoers in Sherbrooke. Why did the breakthrough happen first in the documentary? Film scholar and critic Bruno Cornellier believes that Quebec literary fiction of the times was unable to capture the 'gravity of the real' or provide a language for contemporary concerns.[13] To tell *their* stories, the new generation had to turn to their own immediate experiences rather than external sources. Up to this point, Quebec literature was highly traditional and filled with 'folkloric authenticity.'[14] It was not until the 1940s that urban settings appeared in fiction. So the young Quebec documentarists working at the NFB/ONF not only challenged English control, they also revolted against Quebec society's traditional French-Canadianism. It was the way in which they presented traditional activities through *cinéma direct* that challenged older meanings. They imbued what had been seen as ordinary activities with a special energy and significance that they had previously lacked. The films affirmed the validity and distinctness of Quebec society.

At the same time, one can also argue that the new wave in Quebec cinema had to begin in the documentary because this was the only site of training and work for aspiring film-makers in Canada. The NFB, situated in Montreal, was the pre-eminent source of film-making credibility. It was accessible and it was well funded. The person who best personifies the connection between the *cinéma direct* documentary and the new feature film industry that was about to emerge is Pierre Perrault (1927–99). A lawyer by training, a published poet, and a former broadcaster, Perrault represented the introspective, self-examining spirit of the Quebec intellectual. He coined the expression 'le cinéma vécu' (living cinema) as a description of what he was trying to achieve in film. He felt that the idea of a living cinema went further than the earlier *cinéma vérité* concept or even the NFB's direct cinema. Living cinema was meant 'to present cultural nuances' in a very self-conscious way.[15] Perrault wanted to go 'to the people' to capture the essence of their lives and through them the essential spirit of Quebec identity, and to do so in a way in which it had never been done before.

'... Quebec artists have seen the vastness of *la côte nord*, the coldness of the winter, and the centrality of the St. Lawrence River as the sign-

Pierre Perrault (1927–99), film-maker.

posts of their civilization, as the formative symbols of their imagination,' writes Peter Harcourt.[16] Understandably it would be here, on the
St Lawrence, that Perrault would find what he was looking for. It was to
the great river that he went for inspiration. In 1963 he released the fruits
of his journey, the ONF's *Pour la suite du monde*, the first Quebec film to
be entered in competition at Cannes. It was named 'Film of the Year' at
the 1964 Canadian Film Awards and inaugurated a new age in Quebec
film-making. That same year, Claude Jutra's *À tout prendre* was named
best feature film.

Pour la suite du monde (literally 'so the world may continue,' but titled
Moontrap in the NFB's subtitled version) told the story of a community
on Île-aux-Coudres in the Gulf of St Lawrence and its attempt to revive
the tradition of hunting beluga whales.[17] Perrault knew Alexis Tremblay,
the patriarch of the family, personally and selected the Tremblay family
to express his sense of who the Québécois were and what they represented. *Pour la suite du monde* was the first of a trilogy of films about the

Pour la suite du monde (1962), directed by Michel Brault and Pierre Perrault; produced by Fernand Dansereau.

Île-aux-Coudres community, with the second titled *Le Règne du jour* (1967), and the third, *Les Voitures d'eau* (1969). The tiny film crew of Perrault, his co-director and cameraman, Michel Brault, and soundman, Marcel Carrière, went to this far-away region of Quebec to let the people speak for themselves, so that their worldview could express what it meant to be Québécois. 'Un cinéma de la parole' captured the speech and personalities of rustic Quebec using nothing more than a hand-held camera, a microphone, and cultural sensitivity and under-standing. '*Le cinéma vécu* représentait pour moi la possibilité de pratiquer une sorte d'écriture orale ...' wrote Stéphane-Albert Boulais, who worked with Perrault.[18] This folkloric and ethnographic interest in and focus on 'ordinary' speech and the lives of marginalized people was a way for the urban intelligentsia to find a distinct national identity in the lan-guage of the street and the farm. When Quebec critic Michel Marie described Perrault's trilogy as 'a kind of archaeology,' he was acknowl-edging the mutual rediscovery of what was happening to a culture that the new film-makers were engaged in creating.[19] The methodology of this 'archaeology' was a meeting between an urban culture and a rural one, which asked the question on both sides of the camera 'whether the community can survive in recognizable form the changes that threaten its identity.'[20]

After the success of the first film, Perrault continued to dig into the importance of the past when he followed the Tremblay family, including Alexis's wife, Marie (mother of sixteen), to France, where the Tremblays look for a resemblance between themselves and the people of their distant ancestral home. *Le Règne du jour* (The Realm of Time) was followed by the concluding film, *Les Voitures d'eau* (River Schooners), which had the island community build an old-fashioned wooden fishing schooner of the kind that had once been the mainstay of the economy, but which is no longer used.

Perrault's approach won as much criticism as it did praise. Film historian David Clandfield considered this going out and filming ordinary people and making something special of them as a form of 'liberal paternalism.'[21] The idea that film-makers are elitists when they engage with simple people was also propounded by Yves Picard, a Quebec film writer, who considered the whole project of creating a distinct Quebec cinema to be the project of 'une élite francophone.'[22] He saw the filming of a communal identity that was to serve as the basis of a distinct nationality as the project of an ideologically motivated elite who wanted to validate their project of independence. But there were other Quebec critics, like Paul Warren, who were sympathetic to the work and believed that Perrault's films were 'the fullest expression of Quebec cinema and the clearest line of demarcation from the cinema of English Canada.'[23]

Perrault's rather sombre style and hauntingly austere cinematography imbued with elegiac reverence was something that Quebec audiences and others found engaging, even entrancing. Janis Pallister, an American historian of Quebec film, considered *Pour la suite du monde* to have 'some of the most beautiful photography [by Michel Brault] *in all cinema*.'[24] But the beauty had a purpose. It was an expression of an aesthetic that sought to create a beguiling artistry that would give this francophone ancestral heritage a mythological, and therefore a political, power.[25] In an early book on Quebec film, prominent Quebec film historian Yves Lever wrote a chapter on Perrault in which he cast Perrault as the creator of a new sense of Quebec identity that fitted with the project of independence.[26] When Perrault and Brault teamed up again to make a political documentary about a francophone student struggle in New Brunswick, *L'Acadie, l'Acadie* (1971), this underlying political dimension came to the forefront. The film was a statement recognized for its pro-French stance. But later on, when Perrault did a tetralogy of films on the Abitibi region of Quebec, it was less enthusiastically received, an indication that cinematic and political taste had moved beyond this stage.

Perrault's collaborator, Michel Brault (1928–), was the creator of the evocative cinematography of *Pour la suite du monde* and a practitioner of direct cinema, who brought the independence project to the very forefront of Quebec cinema with his controversial film *Les Ordres* (1974). Brault had been part of the Quebec film scene since the 1950s, when he worked with Gilles Groulx on *Les Raquetteurs* (1958) and later with Claude Jutra on his award-winning feature *À tout prendre* (1964). Brault epitomized the unity of aesthetic genius and political commitment that gave Quebec cinema its energy.

Les Ordres is a film about the imposition of the War Measures Act in October 1970, when the British trade commissioner was kidnapped by the FLQ (Front de Libération du Québec) and Quebec's labour minister, Pierre Laporte, was killed. Hundreds were rounded up and jailed without trial or warrant because the federal government claimed there was an apprehended insurrection. None of those arrested was ever charged. Simply being associated with the cause of Quebec independence was sufficient to be a target for the police and the military that occupied Montreal. Brault's film, using documentary techniques, brought the whole event to the screen. An important French film of a few years earlier, *Battle of Algiers* (1966), served as an inspirational precursor. It had been nominated for an Academy Award for best foreign film. Its realistic treatment of the independence struggle of the Algerians against French colonial occupation in the 1950s made the documentary mode the technique of choice for fictionalizing political struggles. The Greek film-maker Costa-Gravas used the same approach in dealing with South American revolutionary movements in *State of Siege* (1974).

Brault was the auteur director of *Les Ordres*, whose script presented his interpretation of what was happening to Quebec society. The Canadian Film Awards named it film of the year and best feature film, and it was honoured at Cannes. Brault's stark treatment of what happened to five characters in Montreal when the War Measures Act was proclaimed expressed his opposition to the federal government's actions. 'I wanted to give a voice to the people who had suffered the horror of this,' he

Claude Gauthier and Geneviève Bujold in Michel Brault's *Entre la mer et l'eau douce* (1966).

said in an interview many years after the event.[27] The political nature of the film was evident when the NFB commissioner, a political appointee of the Cabinet, vetoed the initial making of the film, even though the French program committee had approved it.[28] A few years later, Brault was able to get CFDC funding to make the film independently. While English Canadians found the film controversial, committed *indépendantistes* like Pierre Vallières considered it 'untruthful' because it did not portray the resistance to Anglo occupation, instead focusing on the passivity of the victims.[29]

Brault has been called 'the finest cinematographer Canada has produced,' and while he did make other feature films in the 1990s (to little acclaim), his auteur reputation is based on *Les Ordres*.[30] When he was interviewed by the *Globe and Mail* in 1999 at the age of seventy-two, he came across as a man from the past, a figure associated with the 'cinema of contestation' that was no longer relevant to Quebec politics, as it had been thirty years earlier, or to Quebec cinema in general, which had by the 1980s moved beyond the independence theme. In a sense, the documentary mode and direct cinema, which fitted so well with the spirit of national liberation that had enflamed much of the world at the time, had rightly become a victim of historical passage. *Les Ordres*, which the *Globe and Mail* reporter who interviewed Brault ranked as 'one of the two or three greatest movies made in Canada,' was no longer available in any video rental store in Canada's largest city. At the same time, Perrault's nostalgic classic *Pour la suite du monde* was about to be re-released by the NFB.[31]

Jean Pierre Lefebvre (1941–) was barely twenty years old when the 1960s began. In 1965 he made three low-budget full-length films, the beginning of what would amount to a total of nineteen features within twenty years. Lefebvre did not go through the documentary phase that the other Quebec directors had, though he did do the occasional NFB production after his reputation was established. Instead he was baptized directly into the mysteries of feature film, which allowed him to develop his own style of film-making. *Le Révolutionnaire* (1965) was his inaugural feature. It mocks a group of Quebeckers wanting to create a Cuban-style insurrection in Quebec. A later film, *Le Vieux Pays où Rimbaud est mort* (The Old Country Where Rimbaud Died), which he made in 1977, deals with a Quebecker who goes to France (like Perrault's Tremblays) in search of his identity. In both cases, Lefebvre's sense of politics is challenging and disquieting because he is sarcastic about and critical of his own society's aspirations. Reflecting in 2001 on his early films, Lefebvre stated: 'Even 35 years ago I thought we had to be careful not to become our own colonizers.'[32]

He was a social critic of his own society, and his film style went against the grain of most of the film-making of his compatriots. He favoured the long shot and had the camera dwell for extended periods on a single situation with very little action in the frame. People found his films very slow. His films never had a theatrical release in English Canada, though his ability to make films on next to nothing allowed him to make new ones in spite of their challenging style. For example, *Q-bec My Love* (1970) cost a mere $25,000 to produce and grossed $140,000, of which Lefebvre was paid $7,000.[33]

Peter Harcourt, the English-Canadian film scholar and critic, who has spent a great deal of time coming to understand Lefebvre's work, believes that his films are primarily about people's relationship to the environment they inhabit – be it a room, a city, or a marriage. 'The environment is as much a part of the content of the film as anything the characters do or say.' he writes.[34] This is more than just the figure in the landscape concept. It refers to the way a person or a people inhabit their many spaces and the influences in that environment that mould them into what they have become. Harcourt believes that Lefebvre's films insist that the audience enter into the momentary life of his characters no matter how simple, casual, and uneventful it may be, because every human moment is worthy of contemplation and compassion.[35] This aesthetic may appeal to cinephiles, but it has great difficulty pricking the Hollywood film and American television bubble that most Canadians inhabit. When Canadian film scholar Seth Feldman described Lefebvre as being 'amongst the most foreign of foreign directors' for English-Canadian audiences, he was right because Lefebvre was never viewed outside of Quebec in any meaningful way.[36]

When Lefebvre addressed the limitations of Quebec's nationalist project in his films, he spoke directly to Quebeckers, but when he expressed the need to slow down and appreciate what really matters in a life, he was making a universal statement. If the end result was rather melancholic, this was simply the flip side of the fervent hopes for a new Quebec, which later turned out to be nothing more than a secular antithesis to its religious past. The materialism and commercialism of the post-conservative Quebec were to trouble other film-makers as well, but there were some who indulged both in their profitable films.

Gilles Carle was 'the only Canadian director to consistently produce money-making commercial films.'[37] He began in 1965 with *La Vie heureuse de Léopold Z* (The Happy Life of Leopold Z) and went on to make another fifteen features before 2000. In self-recognition, he directed and co-wrote an autobiographical documentary about his career titled *Moi, j'me fais mon cinéma* (1998). As Carle was thirty-seven when he made *Leopold Z*, he was not the child prodigy that Lefebvre was, but he was very aware of what made for a popular film. *Leopold Z* is the Christmas story of a hapless Montreal snowplough driver who struggles valiantly to fulfil all his pressing duties, from clearing streets to shopping and going to church. Although influenced by a personal need for social caricature or satire, Carle was usually a tender humourist who loved irony. People went to his movies to laugh and enjoy themselves, and Carle knew what kind of comedy worked for Quebec audiences. Films like *Les Mâles* (1971) were filled with buffoonery and farce. Carle described his ability to reach Quebeckers with his films as coming from his 'obedient compliance to the deeply rooted logic of our sub-culture,' which meant he had to identify with John Wayne and the Pope simultaneously.[38] He was so attuned to Quebec's popular culture that he made a feature film about Quebec's most famous fictional family, the Plouffes.

Originally a 1940s radio serial, the Plouffe saga was moved to a television series in the 1960s, including an English version that played nationally on the CBC. The absurdities of the traditional extended francophone family with all its dysfunctions, which the Plouffes epitomized, were a natural for the witty Carle.

The creation of a popular cinema was not just the work of populists like Carle. It was also the work of pornographers. The Canadian Film Development Corporation funded a half-dozen sex films in its first few years. Termed 'Maple Leaf Porno' by *Variety* magazine, these films attracted Quebeckers in droves![39] Denis Heroux and Claude Fournier were the main instigators. Heroux's first excursion into soft-core porn was *Valérie* (1969), which was a black and white film made for under $100,000 that grossed $2 million after screenings in forty countries.[40] The story of a twenty-year-old orphan raised in a convent who becomes a topless dancer and then a prostitute was the vehicle for the audience's prurient desire for nudity. It was the best-attended Quebec film since the shocking *La Petite Aurore, l'enfant martyre* of the early '50s. Heroux then made *L'Initiation* for $180,000, which grossed $2.5 million.[41] Fournier's *Deux Femmes en or* was made for $218,000 and grossed $4 million.[42] These films displayed a European sense of sexual explicitness, which was now tolerated in Quebec's new uncensored environment.

It was in this diverse and hurly-burly atmosphere, where political and art films competed with soft-core porn, that two directors whose work has come to signify Quebec cinema to the rest of Canada came into their own. Between 1970 and 1990, Claude Jutra (1930–86) and Denys Arcand (1941–) created works of Quebec cinema applauded in the rest of Canada. Jutra had been a feature film-maker for five years when his masterpiece, *Mon Oncle Antoine* (1971), was made at the NFB. His first feature, an independent production titled *À tout prendre* (Take It All), had won the Grand Prize at the Montreal Film Festival in 1963 and the Feature Film of the Year Award at the sixteenth annual Canadian Film Awards in 1964. *À tout prendre* was an autobiographical study in the spirit and style of direct cinema and French New Wave, in which Jutra and his former girlfriend play themselves. Prior to this, he had been active in documentary film production at the NFB.

Film critic Martin Knelman described Jutra as a film-maker of ambivalence, complex irony, and a sly, understated humour.[43] It was this personality that Knelman felt allowed Jutra to tackle 'the psychological claustrophobia of a rigid society that defeats people.'[44] Jutra gained international experience between 1957 and 1961 when he went to France and associated with various French film personalities and worked on their projects. His aesthetic was formed first by the NFB and then the new cinema of France. In this he reflected an essential Quebec cultural position – a relationship with two dominating, yet opposed, cultures, with Quebec standing nervously in the middle and seeking its own voice.

Jutra was acknowledged as part of the new wave of Quebec filmmaking of the 1960s because his early films dealt with contemporary topics, but when he moved away from that edginess, he ran into criticism in Quebec. The criticism started with *Mon Oncle Antoine* and reached a crescendo with his film adaptation of Anne Hébert's 1970 gothic novel, *Kamouraska*, set in nineteenth-century rural Quebec. Local critics, wedded to the idea of a new progressive Quebec identity, considered cinematic examinations of the past either nostalgic or reactionary. What relevance, they asked, could a film about an asbestos-mining community of the 1940s (when Quebec was living in the 'dark ages' of Duplessis's Union Nationale government) have to the new Quebec? A film that highlighted past failings was suspect, especially by intellectuals who were still suffering from the trauma of the October Crisis.

In contrast, English-Canadian critics were delighted with this light comedy that seemed to reveal the soul of Quebec. Was this just a replay of the colonial mentality in which English Canada feasted on the antiquated French-Canadian image that pictured Quebeckers as constructs of family, farm, church, and the French language? Or was it relief at finding a Quebec film that wasn't an in-your-face political statement of Canadian oppression? Was the new Quebec so hard to take that the old Quebec was comfortable and soothing? Bruce Elder, an insightful Canadian film commentator with deep aesthetic concerns, views *Mon Oncle Antoine* as a film of political significance.[45] Since the asbestos miners' strikes of 1949 and 1952 were a reflection of the new post-war spirit that eventually became the Quiet Revolution, a film about that period, while not overtly about the strikes, is a way of presenting the confused and uncertain birth of a new age.

Mon Oncle Antoine was based on a screenplay by Clément Perron, a Quebec playwright, film-maker, and screenwriter, who knew the asbestos region personally and who remembered the incidents depicted in the film. The film was shot by the master cinematographer Michel Brault. It is a coming-of-age story of a boy (Benoit), who works in his Uncle Antoine's general store in a Quebec town in the asbestos region. It is winter and Christmas is at hand. Through the eyes of Benoit, we see the life of his insular society unfold in a way that exposes both its personal hypocrisy and its exploitative social structure, including the English ruling class. Religion, sex, and death are the main themes. The climax of the film comes when Benoit accompanies his inebriated uncle to pick up the corpse of another boy, who has died in the countryside. The film is rich in metaphor and symbol (coffins, barrels of nails, trampled wedding gowns, Nativity scenes, etc.). In fact, a major study of the film and its director claims it is an excellent example of the 'cinema of fable.'[46] In *Mon Oncle Antoine* not only is a particular historical period in Quebec history described, but there is a real attempt to expose the essential features of Quebec culture and its identity. Jutra understood this when he said the film was a statement of his own 'sociological and cultural reality.'[47] It was a film about a particular historical moment and how that moment reflected on Quebec's identity.

In the film, the older generation is presented as one that is either trapped in its oppression (Jos Poulin, the asbestos worker, finds no escape in winter logging work) or feeding off its progeny (the father who has indentured his own daughter to work in Antoine's store). The film is saying that the old Quebec is only good for replicating an endless subordination to English Canada. But Benoit, who represents the new generation, offers hope that a new consciousness exists and that one day, when it matures, it will create the kind of Quebec that Jutra was experiencing in the 1960s.

Because the film is presented in an affectionate, delicate, and old-fashioned way, it became the perfect interpretive vehicle for English-Canadian audiences trying to understand what was happening in Quebec.[48] It provided them with the charming depiction of rural life that fitted their stereotype of Quebec, but with enough symbolic resonance to show that the stereotype was completely irrelevant to today's Quebec.[49] What makes *Mon Oncle Antoine* so endearing is its universal aspect, rather than its historical accuracy. The theme of growing up and realizing one's sexual nature, the revelation of adult hypocrisy and misdemeanours, and the constant struggle between life and death make sense to all people, regardless of their culture.

Most Canadians who saw *Mon Oncle Antoine* viewed it when it was broadcast by CBC television.[50] That the film was considered suitable for a television audience was a sign of its acceptability. Even though some might conclude that Jutra was not fully appreciated in Quebec (for a while, he exiled himself to English Canada to make films), it was only a matter of time before his contribution was acknowledged in a major way. In 1999 the Quebec movie industry broke with the Toronto-based Academy of Canadian Cinema and Television, which operates the Genie Awards (successor to the Canadian Film Awards), to create its own Oscar-style awards show in which the awards are named in honour of Claude Jutra – the Jutra Awards.

Denys Arcand was to the 1980s what Jutra had been to the 1970s – an interpreter of Quebec who was embraced by all of Canada and beyond. He began his career at the NFB in the mid-1960s but ran into difficulty with his 1970 documentary on the textile industry in Quebec. *On est au coton* was to be released in 1970, but this did not happen until 1976 because of industry objections over the film's revelation of exploitation of garment workers. Meanwhile Arcand directed his first feature in 1972 (*La Maudite Galette*), which he co-wrote. His auteur debut came with *Gina* in 1974. He continued as an auteur with *Le Crime d'Ovide Plouffe* in 1984. The next two films created his reputation as Quebec's leading director of the 1980s. The 1986 *Le Déclin de l'empire américain* (The Decline of the American Empire) was an international success, which was followed three years later by *Jésus de Montréal*. *The Decline of the American Empire* won the International Critics Prize at Cannes in 1987 and was nominated for an Academy Award in the best foreign film category. The film garnered nine Genies, including best director and best screenplay. It had a decent budget of $1.85 million, with Canadian and Quebec government agencies putting up the bulk of the money.[51] Because of its profile (and provocative title), it received international distribution in three versions – original French, a version subtitled in English, and a version dubbed into English.

The film is a simple story of a group of middle-class academics and their spouses who gather in the countryside one weekend. The setting is contemporary and the film is, on the surface, a discussion of middle-age issues of sexuality and fidelity. Arcand used his documentary experience to heighten the underlying tensions in the dialogue. Some have considered the film to be modelled after the 1983 American film *The Big Chill*, in which a group of friends are reunited for a funeral of one of their own, during which they replay their past relations.[52] *Decline* is a meditation on the direction of Quebec society after the successes of the Quiet Revolution, but it is not a positive interpretation of those successes. 'I was taught at the university to take a very gloomy view of French-Canadian history,' admits Arcand.[53] This sense of gloom pervades *Decline*, and it provides what might be considered a very Catholic view of human affairs – that human nature is unchangeable and

permanently flawed, and that historical progress is an illusion, especially in terms of spirituality. Ben-Z. Shek confirms Arcand's pessimism
by viewing the film as a dialogue on history in which Arcand strips
away 'the economic and political veneer of contemporary capitalist
society in Quebec.'[54] The world as it was is the world as it is.

Martin Knelman believes that Arcand has a highly developed sense
of social justice and that, while he may 'express a revolutionary rage
and sense of betrayal by the established order,' he does not have the
revolutionary's conviction that things can be changed.'[55] This sensibility is best expressed in *Jésus de Montréal*. The film was written, directed,
and co-edited by Arcand, and so is surely the deepest expression of his
Catholic consciousness (he was raised in a strict Catholic home and
educated by Jesuits). At Cannes, *Jésus* won the Jury Prize and an Oscar
nomination in the best foreign film category. At the Genies, it was
awarded the best motion picture award, best director, best original
screenplay, plus acting and cinematography awards. The story was
inspired by an actor who had auditioned for *Decline* and told Arcand of
the degrading life he and his fellow actors had to lead in commercials
and porno films, while at the same time performing in the Passion Play
for tourists.

Because this story spoke to Arcand's Catholic upbringing, he took it
and created a masterpiece, using the slender body, piercing eyes, and
soft-spokenness of Lothaire Bluteau to play Jesus as an actor in an
Easter pageant and as a Christ-figure in contemporary Montreal. The
artificiality of the Passion Play is contrasted with the searing reality of
the actor's contemporary life. Various events that engage the actor in
the streets, homes, and commercial towers of the new Quebec are
contemporary versions of events described in the Gospels, climaxing
with an organ-transplant that is meant to mimic the Resurrection. The
film is suffused with Christian imagery and metaphor, which make the
actor's life parallel that of the biblical Jesus. Only someone steeped in
Christian mythology could produce such a critical yet sensitive portrayal. For some the film was a scandalous, anti-clerical provocation.[56]
Arcand responded by claiming his film was a critique of contemporary
Quebec society and its religious institutions.[57] Informed critics like
Pierre Véronneau astutely consider *Jésus de Montréal*, with its emphasis
on multivocality, a triumph of postmodernism.[58]

Because of his new international fame, Arcand was enticed to make
English-language films. The first of these was *Love and Human Remains*
(1993), a dark portrayal of urban life based on a provocative and dis-

turbing play by Brad Fraser, a gay Alberta playwright whose work was considered sexually explicit and full of tough language and attitudes. The film failed at the box office. Arcand then signed a deal with Canada's leading film production house, Alliance Atlantis, where he wrote and directed his second English feature, *Stardom* (2000), a satire on the television and fashion industries. It also did poorly. The 1990s proved as much a failure for Arcand as the 1980s had been a decade of success. His vision seemed to have lost its edge, or perhaps he was simply spinning his wheels in a milieu that he no longer spoke for. The new internationalist and continentalist Quebec of the 1990s was somehow out of tune with his Catholic sensibility. He rebounded in the new century with *Les Invasions barbares* (2003), a film billed as a sequel to *Decline*, which was awarded best screenplay and best actress (Marie-Josée Croze) at Cannes. The story of a young female heroin addict who helps a dying man and his son opened on 127 screens in Quebec in May 2003.[59] The response was overwhelmingly positive.

Les Invasions barbares was selected as Canada's official entry for the 2004 Academy Awards. It won the Oscar for best foreign film. The film revisits the same characters developed in *The Decline of the American Empire*, using the same actors, but situating them seventeen years later. The impending death of one of the group brings the aging friends together in a spirit of remembrance and self-criticism. The themes of euthanasia, drug use, and the post-9/11 fragility of Western culture and economics place the film in the same trajectory as *Decline* and *Jésus de Montréal*. It may even be argued that the three films form a trilogy in which the hallmarks of Quebec's distinct identity – language, religion, land and family – are explored in both a poignant and devastating manner. While *Les Invasions barbares* is a study of the angst of middle age, it is also an attempt at reconciliation between generations. It provides a surprisingly powerful portrait of young professionals caught in a post-separatist era, in which a globally connected and North Americanized Quebec contrasts with yesterday's fervent nationalist Quebec created by their parents. The success of the film indicates that Arcand remains capable of continuing his cutting social exploration of an evolving Quebec. It would not be surprising if in future films he took this new generation of actors, whose personalities have such a magnetic screen presence, and created stories around them.

The rise of the Quebec auteur and the birth of a viable feature film industry in Quebec are rooted in Quebec's obsession with, and concern about, independence. Films that explored Quebec's identity paralleled what was happening in the other arts. The joual-loaded urban plays of Michel Tremblay, the folksy novels of Roch Carrier, or the dark visions of Anne Hébert (*Kamouraska*) or Marie Claire Blais (*Une saison dans la vie d'Emmanuel*) were the literary equivalent of *Les Ordres* or *Mon Oncle Antoine*. In music, the evolution from the 1960s popularity of old-fashioned *chansonniers* like Gilles Vigneault to that of 1970s Quebec pop star Charlebois marked a new content for Quebec culture that eventually found its North American fulfilment in the 1990s world of singing sensation Celine Dion and her American fame. After the Parti Québécois's electoral victory in 1976 there was a renewed emphasis on the French language as the language of life and work. This legitimized francophone cinema as a medium of popular culture. Not only did the CFDC and its successor, Telefilm Canada, provide financial support to Quebec film-makers, but so did the Quebec government. The political project of a distinct identity and sovereignty put francophone artists of all kinds on a pedestal. Nor was Hollywood threatened by Quebec cinema. After 1974, Canada provided about 10 per cent of the world market for Hollywood products, and Quebec represented 20 per cent of 10 per cent or 2 per cent.[60] Of course, Quebec cinema's share of the Quebec market was much less than Hollywood's, and its films hardly ever made it to English Canada.[61] Quebeckers continued to view Hollywood movies as their prime film resource.

Because of television and home video viewing, movie theatre capacity fell dramatically from 1970 to 1992.[62] Yet the Quebec industry's products were reaching a wide enough audience to be a cultural influence of some importance. Film historian Yves Lever believes that Quebec cinema of this period was overly preoccupied with a kind of cultural solipsism that sought to dig into Quebec's collective psyche with a merciless judgmental honesty.[63] The result was a national cinema with its own distinctive features. Although Quebec audiences had been subjected to 'une colonisation systématique de son imaginaire,' they still wanted to see expressions of their life on the screen.[64] After 1960, Quebec developed a viable industry that produced everything from avant-garde art house films to mainstream comedies because it wanted cinematic self-expression to parallel the growth in its political self-confidence.

Nevertheless, one can argue that what had been born in Quebec in the 1960s could be considered more as a *quasi-national* cinema because the independence project had not been realized in spite of two referenda – 1980 and 1996. This argument would claim that the achievement of sovereignty in Quebec is a precondition for a distinct national cinema on a par with that of France or Chile or Iran. However, it may also be validly argued that Quebec has a greater claim to possessing a national cinema than English Canada because Quebec films express a coherent cinematic idiom in a variety of genres appreciated by its population, while the English-Canadian public has little if any appreciation of English-Canadian films. This view was expressed by William Beard and Jerry White in a recent anthology on English-Canadian cinema, in which they excluded essays on Quebec film because 'Québec has its own national cinema' even if it does not have its own nation state.[65] Operating in a North American context and influenced by French, American, and English-Canadian cinema (via Telefilm), the cinema of Quebec retains a certain ambivalence about itself in spite of its triumphs.[66] It would not be far off the mark to conclude that Quebec cinema in the period 1960 to 1990, while initially influenced by France's New Wave and direct cinema, developed sufficient critical mass to go in its own direction. French or American or even English-Canadian feature films of the same period are so dissimilar from the Quebec product that Quebec's claim to a national cinema is very strong, at least as strong as its claim to national political independence.

Like other newer national cinemas, Quebec film culture suffers from a healthy internal questioning that can be expected in an age when nationality is under attack and the international market place for cinema is American-dominated.[67] The cultural offensive that post-Duplessis Quebec launched in 1960 did succeed in creating a powerful cinematic entity, but the failure of the Parti Québécois to create a sovereign Quebec has left Quebec cinema in a state of limbo, awaiting the next great historical leap. Or could it be that in a post-nationalist universe of increasingly irrelevant nation-state boundaries and symbols, cinema can be more interesting in its sub–nation-state manifestation, and that the period from 1960 to 1990 was a golden age of Quebec cinema? This possibility exists because the framework of a contested nationality inside a nation state may have a more complicated and challenging structure than that offered by simple independence.[68]

The great achievement of Quebec society between 1960 and 1990 in creating a cadre of auteur directors who received Canada-wide and even international recognition, benefited the whole Canadian industry because it helped to elevate Canada's film identity to a completely new level of international recognition beyond the documentary. The difference between what was happening in English Canada and Quebec at this time was to prove more than just cosmetic. It was a difference of major proportions in which the voices from the one culture either clashed with or completely bypassed the voices of the other. As the next chapter will show, the directors of English-Canadian cinema during this period had very little in common with those in Quebec, except for their male gender.

CHAPTER TEN

English-Canadian Auteurs: David Cronenberg and Atom Egoyan

It is problematic that all the film-makers discussed in the previous chapter were men. Whether one is discussing French auteur directors of the 1960s and 1970s (Truffault to Godard) or Quebec auteur directors (Lefebvre to Arcand), the cinematic universe of the period is a male preserve. This serious gender imbalance created a one-sided orientation in film imagery that replicated the male universe of Hollywood directors and scriptwriters in other national cinemas. The representations of women and women's issues in the films made by men ranged from the progressive to the stereotypical to the reactionary, but in all cases the gaze was male. It was not until the 1980s that female directors in English Canada and Quebec, who are discussed in the next chapter, became known for their feature film work. In discussing the work of auteur directors in English Canada, the limits of male imagining is soon self-evident.

In Quebec the nationalist project provided the intellectual glue for the articulation of a national cinema. The linguistic unity of this autonomous society created a strong connectivity in Quebec cinema, but in English Canada the task of creating an identifiable, vaguely unified, and distinct cinematic voice was much more difficult. Not only were English Canadians opposed to Quebec independence internally, they lacked their own project of political independence, preferring to maintain their long-running ambiguity with, and acquiescence to, American power. While Quebec society and culture gathered an internalizing centripetal strength in the first two decades of the independence movement, cultural and economic forces in English Canada tended to be centrifugal, throwing people outward in differing directions. A producer and director like Ivan Reitman (1947–), who began as a film-maker in Canada in the early 1970s, ended up in Hollywood making commercial entertainment. Ted Kotcheff, who directed Canadian literary-based films – *The Apprenticeship of Duddy Kravitz* (1974) and *Joshua Then and Now* (1985) – moved in and out of Canadian material and ended up in the 1990s making TV series.

The reality for a Canadian-born director working in a North American context is best exemplified by the career of Norman Jewison (1926–), who in 1999 was awarded the Irving C. Thalberg Award at the Academy Awards for 'the most consistently high level of production achievement by an individual producer.' Jewison's directorial style spoke to the masses and was generally indistinguishable from other well-made mainstream American cinema. As a young man, he left Canada to work in American television, where he won three Emmys before heading to Hollywood to become a film director. His big breakthrough came with *In the Heat of the Night* (1967), which won an Oscar for best picture. It is a film about the racism of the southern United States and starred the leading African-American actor of the day, Sidney Poitier. Jewison consistently worked with American actors and themes. As an all-purpose director, he made musicals like *Fiddler on the Roof* (1971) and *Jesus Christ Superstar* (1973) as well as romantic comedies (*Moonstruck* 1987) and dramas of various kinds, such as *A Soldier's Story* (1984), which was set in the United States. In 1988, when he was at the height of his fame, Jewison established the Canadian Film Centre in Toronto to help developing Canadian writers, directors, and producers.

In spite of this magnanimous gesture toward Canadian feature film development, Jewison's legacy for Canadian cinema is one of partnership with American cinematic taste and a focus on directorial skills. It was his lack of auteurial vision and his connection to Hollywood that kept him out of the loop in building a distinct national cinema in Canada, especially when so many of the stories he told were American-based. Some commentators have stated that his liberalism, which they attributed to his Canadian roots, made him a 'pinko' in Hollywood, but in the end this left-of-centre label made more sense 'there' than 'here.'[1] It worked in differentiating him in a Hollywood context, not a Canadian one. His film *Hurricane* (2000) seemed to repeat his 1960s interest in American racial prejudice. It is the true story of 'Hurricane' Carter, an African-American boxer unjustly convicted of a crime, who is saved by Canadians.

In contrast to Norman Jewison's middle-of-the-road career and its dependence on American material and mainstream film language, the work of David Cronenberg (1943–) has been on the edge, provocative and controversial. Born in Toronto during the Second World War, Cronenberg was a science student before majoring in English and then turning to film as his métier. Cronenberg possessed a quirky and unusual imagination, to which he added a studied directorial eye, a strong philosophical bent, and a talent as a scriptwriter that made him the epitome of auteurism. His defining role in Canadian cinema went far beyond the norm of any other English-Canadian or Quebec director, before or since. He was able to turn his natural inclination to the physical sciences and their techniques into disturbing cinematic drama.

'David Cronenberg's films are looked upon as aberrations in the cinematic landscape of this country,' writes Piers Handling, because they are 'totally alien to our artistic tradition.'[2] The 'body-horror' genre, which he developed and which characterizes most of his films, is far from the realism tradition of most Canadian cinema. In a major study of Cronenberg's oeuvre, film critic and scholar William Beard used terms such as 'deliberate provocativeness and transgressiveness' and 'emotionally and psychologically dysfunctional status' to describe the spirit of his films.[3] While working as an independent film-maker in Canada, Cronenberg made films that seemed radically un-Canadian. Cronenberg's desire to 'show the unshowable' and thereby shock and even disgust film audiences is rooted in his belief that the twisted monstrosities of dream life should be put on the screen.[4] In a statement for the Toronto International Film Festival in 2000, he wrote about the inspiration for the film short that he had just done for the occasion:

> I had a dream a long time ago, before I had achieved anything professionally. I dreamt I was in a cinema watching a movie with an audience. And suddenly I realized I was aging rapidly, growing horribly old as I sat there, and it was the movie that was doing it. I had caught some kind of disease from the movie and it was making me grow old, bringing me closer and closer to death. I woke up terrified.[5]

Cronenberg's exploitation of nightmares became his doorway to inner artistic truth by drawing on the imagery of dream life that fitted with three different film genres. He used pornography to arouse, horror to terrify, and science fiction to create disturbing technological fantasies. He fused these three elements into a consistent vision that was so singular and powerful that it brought him both acclaim and denunciation. The Toronto International Film Festival's director, Piers Handling, claimed with justification that Cronenberg's films are either 'adored or reviled.'[6] No one in English Canada has ever created such a consistent challenge to the very concept of a defining national cinema as Cronenberg has. If Cronenberg is arguably Canada's most famous film director of the twentieth century, then what does his work say about Canadian film and its characterization? Is he an eccentric phenomenon working in marginal genres, or is his vision central to the Canadian imagination, no matter how bizarre or excessive it may seem? The answers to these questions continue to be debated.

Cronenberg began his career as a film-maker in the 1960s when he made three films while still in his mid-twenties. They represent his student apprenticeship period. *Transfer* (1966) and *From the Drain* (1967) were anxious art statements, while the third film, *Stereo* (1969), became his first feature-length film, with a miniscule budget of $8,500.[7] *Crimes of the Future* (1970), his first colour feature, was shot for $15,000 (including CFDC money) and moved him toward the world of commercial possibilities.[8] Typical Cronenberg subjects that appear in these early works are pseudo-scientific organizations (e.g., Institute for Neo-Venereal Disease), and mad doctors who create bizarre experiments or perform procedures that go awry, resulting in bodies and organs that are put to bizarre uses. Each film was packaged with female nudity and sexual tension. Even at this early stage as a film-maker, Cronenberg spoke to and for the dark side of human desire, knowledge, and relationships, creating an ugly, chaos-strewn universe, whose only escape is death.

In the early 1970s, the youthful Cronenberg took a break from film and then surfaced in the commercial cinema five years later with a work that is still considered to be his most audacious personal statement and the forerunner of contemporary body-horror films, whose goal is to get 'under-the-skin' of its audiences. It was the first of five films that formed a distinct phase in his career. *Shivers* (also released under the titles *Frissons* [French], *They Came from Within*, and *The Parasite Murders*) was his first commercial success. It was made for a mere $180,000 and grossed $5 million,[9] making it the CFDC's most successful investment! Inspired by a dream that Cronenberg had about a spider that emerged from a sleeping woman's mouth, the plot involves a scientific experiment gone wrong that results in a sexually transmitted parasite infecting an apartment complex with sexual orgy, murder, and mayhem.[10] In one particularly offensive scene, a parasite climbs up a drain while a woman is taking a bath and then enters her vagina. The film was denounced by film critic Robert Fulford as utterly repulsive and an insult to taxpayers because it received CFDC's support.[11] In fact, it had taken Cinepix, the Quebec soft-core porn film producer and distributor and the film's backer, three years to get the CFDC to put up some money ($75,000) because Cronenberg's script was considered too offensive.[12] Scenes had to be cut for the American release, so that it would avoid an X-rating, which would have precluded its screening in mainstream theatres.[13] The controversy only encouraged Cronenberg and Cinepix to continue, though the CFDC had to find ways to get around the political outcry. In a 1992 interview, Cronenberg stated that *Shivers* was 'the beginning of my career as a movie-maker, and the end of my career as a film-maker.'[14] Beard confirms this analysis when he describes *Shivers* as a 'low-budget horror movie, whose characteristics include graphic, sensational depictions of violence and sex-plus-violence.'[15] *Shivers* proved that Cronenberg's films could make money and garner him a particular, even cult, following. The movie-maker stage had begun.

Rabid (1976) was the second in this 'exploitation film' phase of his career, when he made low-budget films to appeal to audiences wanting female nudity, grotesque violence, and thrills.[16] *Rabid* cost $350,000 to make and returned a gross of $7 million.[17] The female lead is played by a well-known porno star of the time, Marilyn Chambers, who receives surgery after a motorcycle accident that generates a phallus-like organ in her armpit, which she uses to suck blood, the only nourishment she can digest. This vampire then spreads a rabies-like disease to all her victims, who, in turn, unleash a maniacal violence on Montreal in which thousands die. Cronenberg wrote and directed both *Shivers* and *Rabid*, and they expressed his view that human beings are 'little pockets of private and personal chaos brewing in the interstices in the structure of society, which likes to stress its order and control.'[18] Eventually this personal chaos explodes and becomes public, engulfing everyone. Cronenberg's response to the negative public criticism of the time was defiant: 'I have something that has been lacking in Canada, a real artistic vision.'[19] Now in his thirties, he presented himself as a serious artist with a serious message. As Canadian directors had not worked in the horror genre so there were no immediate reference points to serve Canadian critics as 'national' comparisons. What Cronenberg was competing with at the time was established American product that included such highly popular horror films as *The Exorcist* (1973) and *Texas Chainsaw Massacre* (1974).

Cronenberg took advantage of the tax-shelter provisions of the 1970s to make his films in Canada. At least he could get financing. His third film, *The Brood* (1979), had a $1.4-million budget. It was followed the next year by *Scanners*, with an impressive $4.1-million budget.[20] *Scanners* had a sci-fi theme about warring groups of mutant telepaths, and it was considered more of an action film than the previous three. The 'exploitation film' phase of his career ended with a fifth film, *Videodrome*, in 1982. As well as marking the end of his auteurist phase, it was his last tax-shelter film. The next year, he directed *The Dead Zone*, based on a novel by the American horror writer Stephen King. *Videodrome* and *The Dead Zone* are a study in contrasts.

Videodrome tells the story of a television producer who is seeking to expand his audience by moving from soft-core to hard-core pornography. He gets seduced by a 'snuff' TV show called 'Videodrome' and the group that is using it to control people's minds.[21] The television producer Max Renn (played by James Wood) is subjected to hallucinations of violence in which his body becomes a womb for video cassettes, his hand is transformed into a ghoulish gun, and he ends up killing his partners and himself while trying to merge with television technology in a mad attempt to unite body and machine to create an immortal 'new flesh.' The film is set in a hard and unforgiving concrete jungle filled with distasteful colours. William Beard describes the film as a study in 'sadism ... sinfulness ... [and] compulsion.'[22] Only an intense, highly personal vision is able to make such a bizarre plot convincing.

In contrast, *The Dead Zone* is set in a pleasant small town with supposedly respectable people who face an evil presence in their midst. This presence is successfully challenged by the hero, whose ability to envisage the future saves the world, though he has to sacrifice his own life. In the Canadian-authored *Videodrome*, the main character is an unappealing megalomaniac who pays dearly for his arrogant belief that he can control technology, while in the American-authored *Dead Zone* the main character, wholesomely named Johnny Smith (played by American actor Christopher Walken), makes the ultimate sacrifice for the good of the community. In *Videodrome* the world is unredeemed, while in *The Dead Zone* the hero receives the parting kiss of his true love, a perfect testament to narrative closure. No wonder *The Dead Zone*'s author described himself as the 'Big Mac' of the horror genre – to be consumed by millions who follow the best-seller charts.[23]

Cronenberg's flirtation with Hollywood values began when Universal Pictures decided to distribute *Videodrome* while insisting that the film meet Motion Picture Association of America standards. When it did, Universal released nine hundred prints! The film did not do well commercially because it was neither exploitation nor art.[24] *The Dead Zone*, which Cronenberg said he made to get away from the energy-draining auteurism of *Videodrome*, did not sell in spite of the King name.[25] 'It is certainly the least offensive film I've made,' Cronenberg admitted in retrospect.[26] The renowned Italian producer Dino De Laurentis headed the project, and it had the largest cast of American stars in any of Cronenberg's films to that date.

With *The Dead Zone*, Cronenberg had turned thirty-nine, and he used the film to signal the end of the second phase of his career and the turn to a new third phase – the films of his maturity. In this stage, he worked with budgets that could generate Hollywood-level production values while still adhering to his idiosyncratic vision. This phase included three major works – *The Fly* (1986), *Dead Ringers* (1988), and *Naked Lunch* (1991). He co-authored the screenplays and directed each film in Canada, even though the original sources for the material were not his. *The Fly* cost $10 million and was a remake of a 1958 horror film. It grossed $100 million.[27] With figures like these, Cronenberg was definitely playing in the major leagues. *The Fly*, the story of a scientist who is gradually transformed into a fly, became Cronenberg's 'biggest financial success' because it made more money than all the previous films combined.[28] The next film, *Dead Ringers*, was based on a true story of identical twin gynaecologists who died in mysterious circumstances. Cronenberg took the story and transformed it into a ghoulish love triangle, in which the British actor Jeremy Irons plays both men and Geneviève Bujold plays the unfortunate woman with three entrances to her womb. Although Dino De Laurentis was to produce the film, his company collapsed before principal shooting and Cronenberg had to act as his own producer to salvage the situation. *Dead Ringers* had a larger budget ($13 million) than *The Fly*. In turn, this amount was surpassed by the $17 million spent on the making of William S. Burroughs's *Naked Lunch*.[29]

The American author William S. Burroughs had a special place in Cronenberg's literary pantheon, along with Russian émigré novelist Vladimir Nabokov, both of whose work Cronenberg admired greatly. Burroughs's *Naked Lunch* is a phantasmagoric universe created by the distorted minds of junkies who fall prey to a bizarre addiction and its antidote. At one point in this delusional universe, a typewriter becomes a giant cockroach on which the narrator writes his reports from 'Interzone.' In fact, Cronenberg's screenplay is really an invention about the writing of Burroughs's novel rather than a strict adaptation.[30] In this way, Cronenberg paid homage to a work he held in esteem and still played with his own sense of the outrageous. Even so, he was working with another genius's vision. Nevertheless, the film represents a climactic point in the third phase of his career. All the imbalance of the psyche is placed totally within the mind, whose reality is represented by special effects.[31]

When he made *M. Butterfly* two years later, one could sense that he was signalling a new phase was at hand, just as he had with *The Dead Zone* a decade earlier. *M. Butterfly* was originally a play about a female impersonator, and Cronenberg simply directed the film version. It was a transitional film that allowed him to escape from the intensity of the climactic moment of the previous phase. He was now fifty and a world-famous film-maker. What was the next phase – phase four – going to be about?

The fourth phase was inaugurated by *Crash* in 1996. The film was adapted, produced, and directed by Cronenberg. It was based on a 1973 cult novel by J.G. Ballard, which fantasized the sexual lives of women and men who are aroused by automobile crashes. Although the film won a Special Jury Prize at Cannes for its audacity (the film begins with three different sex scenes in a row), its focus on sexual explicitness (anal sex and sexual penetration of a wound) meant that it was considered X-rated in certain jurisdictions. For example, there was a campaign in Britain to have it banned from public cinemas, and the video version of the film was only available in British Columbia 'under the counter.' Cronenberg considered the film a study in 'techno-sex,' which would move it toward science fiction, while most viewers considered it sliding toward the pornographic.[32] Chris Rodley, who has studied Cronenberg's oeuvre, describes the film as being 'very stark and very bleak.'[33] Some might view the film as Cronenberg's ultimate statement on the binary unity of sex and death in the context of crushed steel and plastic. Others may see it as a personal reaction to the kind of studio films he had been doing from *The Fly* to *M. Butterfly*, which created an antithetical desire to return to a more comfortable grade-B format. For example, *M. Butterfly* was a relatively lavish $22-million feature, while *Crash* cost less than half that amount.[34] Now that he was in his fifties and had been making feature films for two decades, Cronenberg may have felt that he had to prove that he could still shock, offend, and create controversy, which is exactly what he did with *Crash*.

eXistenZ (1999) was termed 'Cronenberg's slap-happiest movie' and an antidote to the bleakness and controversy of *Crash*.[35] This $30-million production about virtual reality games with a science fiction theme was not a commercial success (it was competing with the runaway hit *The Matrix* in the same genre), even though it was aimed at a broad audience.[36] In the film, Cronenberg returned to his tried and true pool of imagery while exploiting his considerable reputation to garner large budgets, which in the case of *eXistenZ* was ten times a typical Canadian feature film budget. Hollywood-level budgets demanded Hollywood-level returns, a risky venture for a Cronenberg film.

In 2001 Cronenberg completed filming *Spider*, based on a novel and script by British writer Patrick McGrath about a mentally disturbed young man named 'Spider,' who is played by Ralph Fiennes. The film, released in the spring of 2003, had a much smaller budget than *eXistenZ* and was a drama. It would seem that Cronenberg was developing a new pattern of going back and forth by creating a lower budget film that was controversial in reaction to a big-budget mainstream film (*Crash* versus eXistenZ versus *Spider*). Unlike the earlier phases that reached a progressive high point and then made an about-face, this fourth phase may not have a simple trajectory, as the director tries to find a new point of focus for his vision.

Cronenberg turned sixty in 2003, and *Spider* was his fifteenth feature, a record for any Canadian feature film-maker. In talking about *Spider* before it was edited, Cronenberg dealt with a theme that was becoming pervasive in this phase of his career: 'You wouldn't see this film and say that I've mellowed ... because it is pretty uncompromised.'[37] Ever since *Crash*, he has been out to prove that he is not *passé* and that he is capable of expanding the range of the allowable. At age thirty, vision is such a bright revelation, but at age sixty originality is more difficult because cinema and its audiences have evolved and the auteur film-maker, who has been bold in his earlier work, has a diminished capacity for being new and different. *Spider* is an excellent example of the quandary facing maturing auteur directors. Calling it 'a chilly masterpiece of Freudian psychodrama,' Brian D. Johnson, film critic for *Maclean's*, considers the film 'the most austere and restrained film' of Cronenberg's career.[38] It is a departure from the 'body grotesque' with which he is commonly associated, but it retains the frightfulness and delusionary nature of the human mind/soul that has preoccupied Cronenberg.[39] The film was in official competition at Cannes. Cronenberg received the best director award for the film at the Genies in 2002 (Egoyan's *Ararat* won best film), but few other accolades. It was not a long-running, popular film on the art-house circuit.

Judging the Cronenberg legacy, its relationship to Canadian cinema and its contribution to the horror genre, is not an easy task. The range of critical comment over the years has been varied and contradictory. There continues to be a perception that Cronenberg is basically a packager of racy material whose movies sell because of their offensive content, while the opposite view holds that he is an artistic genius with a profound message about technology and the human condition. Academic assessments have been generally positive. Peter Morris concluded that 'his film worlds reflected the shifting interface of mind and body, the rational and the irrational, the conscious and subconscious. They explored our often problematic relationship with science and technology.'[40] The distrust of technology and fear of its transforming power is considered a Canadian theme because so much of the Canadian technological universe is not a self-generated reality but an imposed one. It is as if the threatening and destructive monster that is at the base of the horror genre is particularly well suited to the Canadian psyche, where the monstrous is an untamed natural world or its antithesis, overpowering human technology.[41]

Piers Handling finds another Canadian theme in the frequent presence of emasculated males in Cronenberg films, in a similar vein to *Goin' down the Road* and *The Rowdyman*. The doctors/scientists in his films are destroyed by their own hubris, rather than reigning supreme as do the clichéd heroes of American cinema, though it is important to point out that the theme of hubris is a mainstay of the horror genre going back to German expressionist cinema of the 1920s.[42] Even so, it is not beyond speculation to conceive of the Canadian imagining of monstrous evil as more likely to succeed than its human adversaries.[43] This approach flows into another distinctive Canadian feature that Handling finds in Cronenberg films – the lack of narrative closure. At the end of Cronenberg films, little is resolved. The problem of evil that Hollywood always banishes with its feel-good-and-safe endings is absent in Cronenberg, except when he adapts American material, as was the case in *The Dead Zone*.[44] These 'endings without resolution,' as Handling terms them, indicate a view of the world in which evil is a fundamental structure of society and the individual human psyche, rather than some external aberration that challenges a basically good world.[45] The 'body-horror' idea presented a-coming-from-within idea of evil that made the human condition permanently problematic. Vanquishing evil means self-destruction.

Bart Testa links Cronenberg as a genre director to national cinema when he claims that Cronenberg is an innovator in the science fiction genre with his own 'discourse on technology springing from the Canadian ethos,' which another Canadian critic, Robin Wood, considers to be a 'joyless' and 'reactionary' discourse when viewed in the context of horror genre traditions.[46] In other words, the negativity inherent in the Cronenberg vision is a challenge to the conventions of horror films, but a good fit with the conventions of dystopias of the Canadian imagination.

In the 1980s, Canadian feminist critics attacked the Cronenberg vision as misogynist because of its treatment and portrayal of women. A film like *Dead Ringers*, with its invasive male gynaecological approach to the female body, was considered particularly offensive.[47] Cronenberg's traditional heterosexual view of the female body was only increased by his use of horror and pornography. Feminist theories of the male gaze exposed patriarchal power.[48] The typical objectivization of the female body as a site of desire and control found in Cronenberg's films made them susceptible to this criticism.

Fitting the Cronenberg legacy into the context of Canadian 'national' cinema is problematic because his work is such a departure from the mainstream of Canadian feature film production of the last thirty years. William Beard, who produced a major tome on Cronenberg's work, thinks that an account of 'Cronenberg's place in Canadian cinematic culture' is yet to be written.[49] In a subsequent essay titled 'Thirty-Two Paragraphs about David Cronenberg,' Beard rejected the view that Cronenberg was outside the canon when he concluded that 'Cronenberg's essential bleakness and defeatedness ... are more traditionally Canadian than anything else.'[50] This leads one to believe that there must be some kind of fit between his work and his nationality because he is Canadian and has worked for a long time in Canada, but defining or explaining that fit is another matter. Cronenberg has created a tension among the genres he uses, which allows space for an auteur vision. By picking and choosing, mixing and matching standard elements and approaches from a variety of genres, he has blended distinct streams into a single visionary river. This distinctness has been aided by the continued marginality of English-Canadian cinema, in general, which has created a little corner for itself where the unusual can exist. Geoff

Pevere points out how 'Cronenberg's films suggest that the accommo-
dating, thoughtful Canadian exterior is a veneer that has been maintained only at the cost of a great and ever-increasing repression of
psycho-sexual impulses.'[51] What Cronenberg has done for English-
Canadian cinema is to lift the lid on this social and cultural repression
and throw its hidden imagery into the face of the audience from which
it came.

Cronenberg's portrayal of libidinal trauma has served as a pathway
that allowed other English-Canadian film-makers to break out of the
restrictions of realism.[52] His fame and financial success confirmed that
films which dealt forcefully and unabashedly with the inner life of the
individual psyche at war with the external life of the collectivity would
be heralded. It was Cronenberg, more than any other director, who
liberated English-Canadian cinema. By twisting the conventions of
several genres into an overlapping creation, he constructed a space
alive with nightmare and symbol. It was by embracing marginalized
film genres that he brought English-Canadian cinema to a higher artistic level. Without a serious political project like Quebec's, which provided a compelling narrative, English-Canadian cinema turned to
dreams and fantasies as a way beyond the encrusted modalities of
realism. Those who followed after Cronenberg would do radically different films, but always within the space of strangeness, angst, and
torment that he established. His films allowed the weird to be equated
with being Canadian. When the leading representative of the next
generation of feature film-makers, Atom Egoyan, said, 'I'm really attracted to patterns of behaviour which seem delusional and bordering
on the pathological but society has embraced as quite normal,' the
echoes of Cronenberg are loud and clear.[53]

Atom Egoyan (1960–) became the leading film-maker to branch off
the path prepared by Cronenberg. Both men were from ethnic minorities – Cronenberg is Jewish and Egoyan, Armenian – which suggests
the important role of the outsider in refreshing a national culture. Born
in Egypt, Egoyan immigrated to Canada with his parents when he was
only a baby. Raised in Victoria, British Columbia, and educated, like
Cronenberg, at the University of Toronto, Egoyan began making films,
again like Cronenberg, as an undergraduate. For both film-makers
there is a continuity between early work and later years.

Howard in Particular (1979), made when he was still a teenager, was a
fourteen-minute short about a pressured retiree. The next year, he
expanded to a twenty-five-minute short, *After Grad with Dad*, followed

by *Open House* in 1982, also twenty-five minutes. For each of these shorts, he wrote the screenplay, directed the cast, and edited. After *Open House* was broadcast by the CBC, Egoyan made his first auteur feature-length film, *Next of Kin* (1984). The film deals with ethnic relations. A young WASP male presents himself to an Armenian family as their lost son. Obviously a metaphor for his own life as an acculturated Canadian trying to relate to ethnic immigrant parents, the 16 mm colour film was funded by the Canada Council and the Ontario Arts Council. Egoyan was only twenty-four when he tackled the complex narrative structure of a feature film. Three years later, he premiered his second feature, *Family Viewing*, a rather dark exploration of family identity found in a father's videos. He then made *Speaking Parts* (1989), his first Telefilm Canada–funded feature, followed by *The Adjuster* (1991), both of which were 35 mm productions. *Speaking Parts* is the story of 'three people [who] become fatally entangled in a web of psycho-sexual desire.'[54] *The Adjuster* was described by Egoyan as a film 'about believable [read ordinary] people doing believable things in an unbelievable [read abnormal] way.'[55] One scholar of his films has observed that his films do not contain the social reality 'found in tourist brochures.'[56]

Exposing familial and individual dysfunction has become his trademark in a way that seems to parallel Cronenberg's exploration of the dark recesses of the mind and technology. Egoyan's juxtaposing of the bizarre with the ordinary cuts through the surface of human relations to some hidden darkness, as do Cronenberg's films, except that in Egoyan's films there are no special effects and no twisted manifestations of the living. It is the very ordinariness of his characters that is frightening. Not taking anything for granted is suggested in the eeriness of the music, by the introspective faces of the actors, whose eyes (and dialogue) do not quite connect with the world, by the dark colours that bathe his scenes, and in the events whose rationality is constructed in such a way as to disturb the viewer. The actors in his films present their characters in a cold and distant manner that is unsettling to filmgoers accustomed to the emotional releases of melodrama. While Cronenberg let the excesses of the id spill out in a perverse and grotesque world of rampant parasites, exploding heads, and ghoulish medical instruments, Egoyan holds the instinctual inside firmly under artistic control, so that psychological perversion only emerges gradually.

The best example of his approach may be found in *Exotica* (1994), which won the International Critics' Prize at Cannes and best motion picture at the Genies, along with best original screenplay and best achievement in direction. *Exotica* represents Egoyan, then aged thirty-four, as having reached the same stage as Cronenberg had reached with *Videodrome* when he was thirty-nine. It can be argued that these two films represent the high point of both directors' English-Canadian auteurism. While Cronenberg's sense of the 'grotesque and pathological' is quickly visualized for audiences, in Egoyan's world it remains deep inside, requiring the audience to probe the film and their own understanding.[57]

Exotica's importance as a landmark comes from the film's 'deliberate summation of the formal and thematic interests that preceded it.'[58] Like *Videodrome* for Cronenberg, *Exotica* provided aficionados of Canadian cinema with a masterly statement of the director's approach to film and his interpretation of the human condition. The story involves a gay pet-store owner and smuggler, a tax inspector with a dark secret and a morbid interest in a stripper who dresses in a schoolgirl's uniform, and the Exotica strip club's emcee, whose personal history and desires conflict with his role as the club's announcer. Their lives intertwine as each pressures the other to fulfil certain hard-to-determine needs. Whether it is the dark false-front exoticism of the club's lavish interior, where male fantasies are indulged in mentally (not physically), or the sallow purple-green light filtered through fish tanks in the strange pet store, where no one ever shops, the worlds of deception and normality are not separated, but united. The only escape from the pervasive tension that permeates this netherworld is the brightly lit flashbacks to another time, when nature's sunny outdoors seem innocent and the dark characters from the club Exotica reappear fresh and lively. Only later is it revealed that they are searching for a body. The distraught and implicated father of so many of Egoyan's films; the violated innocence that is the traumatic burden of young women; and the focus on the mental construction of sexuality rather than its physical indulgence are some of the major themes. Egoyan's moody and evocative treatment of sexual transgression must be considered a tremendous accomplishment for a director in his mid-thirties. It was *Exotica* that opened the door to international celebrity status for its auteur director.

The Sweet Hereafter (1997) was the film that reflected this new stage. The film received a nomination for best director at the Academy Awards and won eight Genies, including best picture and best director. However, it was not an auteur film. Based on the novel of the same name by American writer Russell Banks, the film uses an adapted screenplay by

Egoyan. Set in a small town that has undergone the trauma of a school-bus crash and its tragic impact, the film begins an emotional unravelling of the façade of clean living associated with rural existence. The townsfolk are visited by a city lawyer who seeks to build a case on their behalf against whomever has deep pockets, but is thwarted by a young accident victim who gives false testimony in order to sabotage the scheme. The young woman's triumph over the wiles of adults includes retribution on her incestuous father. Because the film contains the narrative closure of mainstream American cinema, in which good triumphs over evil and audiences go away feeling some sort of justice has been done, it is unlike his own (and Cronenberg's) Canadian vision of the world, in which evil is not vanquished but carries on. *The Sweet Hereafter* played the same role for Egoyan as *The Dead Zone* played for Cronenberg – a diversion from auteurial intensity. For mainstream North American audiences who had never seen his earlier work, including *Exotica*, *The Sweet Hereafter*'s sombre imagery, peculiar lighting effects, and the uncomfortable secrets of the slightly off-centre characters served as a sanitized introduction to the core of Egoyan's sensibility. *Cineaste* magazine interviewed Egoyan after *The Sweet Hereafter* won awards at Cannes and asked him to explain the goal of the film. 'Since I had complete authorship for all of my previous films,' Egoyan said, 'I wanted to feel that I was true to what Russell [Banks] intended.'[59] Egoyan was using literary material by others to help him express the issue that continued to fascinate him, while using that 'other' material to liberate his vision so as to make his work more accessible to a wider audience. Curiously, *Exotica* actually grossed more money than *The Sweet Hereafter*, even with its major awards and Oscar nomination. Most likely the reason was the sexual content of the strip club in *Exotica*, rather than the early film's artistic merit.[60]

The Sweet Hereafter, because of its mainstream popularity, encouraged Egoyan to continue the practice of adaptation. *Felicia's Journey* (1999) is based on Irish author William Trevor's 1994 novel of the same name, in which a disturbed man befriends a pregnant teenager, who is destined to be the latest in a string of female victims of his neurosis. The author insisted that Egoyan situate the story in Ireland and England. The film was not as well received as *The Sweet Hereafter*, though it had a substantially larger budget. It would seem that the audience appeal of Egoyan's persistent theme of young female innocence corrupted by obsessive and abusive older men may have run its course. In a 1999 article on Egoyan, Brian D. Johnson, film critic for *Maclean's*, asked what was at the bottom of Egoyan's obsession with father figures and teenage women. Egoyan responded candidly:

There was a young woman whom I adored from a very young age, and who was inaccessible to me for the longest time. Later on, it was revealed that there was an abusive relationship with her father. All the clues were there. But it wasn't a society at that point that could read them or respond to them, and I felt kind of helpless about it. So rather than address it, I went into denial over it, like everybody else.[61]

The denial eventually surfaced in his films. Themes of voyeurism and isolation, images of bleakness, and feelings of permanent entrapment and unrelenting alienation are just some of the ways this youthful trauma has formed the basis of his auteur vision. With *The Sweet Hereafter*, followed by *Felicia's Journey*, one might think that a new, post-auteur stage had begun in Egoyan's oeuvre, but he returned to auteurism with *Ararat*, a contemporary drama dealing with the genocide of Armenians in Turkey during the First World War.

Ararat (2002) can be considered a departure from Egoyan's previous father obsession, though the film has a number of father figures in it (a customs inspector, a film director, and a dead father whose death propels one of the narratives). It is a film about the making of a contemporary film about the Armenian genocide as viewed through the eyes of several generations of Armenians in Toronto, in particular, a single mother, who is an art historian, her son, who is caught carrying drugs from Turkey, and a stepdaughter who hates her art historian stepmother and sleeps with her stepbrother. This all seems like vintage Egoyan, especially the use of his actor wife, Arsinée Khanjian, to play the Armenian-Canadian historian. She had previously appeared in *Exotica* and *The Sweet Hereafter*. But engagement with a historical topic is new for Egoyan, and very challenging. When one considers that his body of work to this point has always dealt with contemporary characters in urban settings, it is evident why he decided not to make a straight historical melodrama set in 1915. It would have been too radical a departure from his basic interests.

Critical reaction to the film has been generally negative, even though the film received the 2002 Genie for best film. Brian D. Johnson, of *Maclean's*, termed the structure of the film frustrating and unconvincing.[62] Roger Ebert called it 'a needlessly confusing film' because the visual interplay between sequences depicting staged historical scenes viewed through the movie set's camera (a primary perspective) and sequences showing the filming of the film scenes and what happens around the stage (a secondary perspective) requires an unusual level of audience concentration in order to comprehend what is going on.[63] At various points, the film is edited in such a way as to lead the audience to identify with the historical re-creation at face value, but then the audience is presented with all the apparatus of film staging in order to make it question what it has just seen and believed. The audience's traditional suspension of disbelief is challenged, creating a lack of identification. Egoyan defended the film's fragmented structure by admitting that 'it does require a degree of effort on the part of the viewer,' but that this is necessary because the viewer needs to understand how the issue of the Armenian genocide fits into current consciousness.[64] Egoyan's approach is postmodernist in that he forces the viewer in and out of several different time frames and in and out of different viewpoints, resulting in a planned confusion and uncertainty about what is real. The story of the genocide that is being filmed is based on a real, first-hand account by an American physician, and it serves as the basis for the narrative of the film within the film. This cinematically reworked historical narrative presented from the Armenian perspective then clashes with the narrative of the contemporary Armenian family that is involved in the film, whose issues are much deeper than ones of nationality. There are two parallel narratives in the film dealing with how the truth of the past is constructed in our minds. The conflicting interpretations of the cause of a contemporary father's death are juxtaposed with the conflicting narratives of the historical genocide, the certainty of its having happened, and the role of 'witnesses' in both. Egoyan's convoluted exploration of the multiple levels of meaning we attach to history, depending on who we are and the reason for our attachment, is a genuine attempt to deal with a complex problem. His coming to grips with the meaning of history, memory, and the rhetoric of accusation and denial may not have succeeded fully in this case, but it is a worthy attempt. Having his audience engage with the problem of what it is doing when it grasps for the 'truth' of the past through numerous modes of presentation (a film, a book, storytelling) is an indication of Egoyan's tendency to privilege consciousness over facts. The 'facts' of the genocide are an ongoing debate because of their link to morality, culpability, and the construction of the past, the real issues that Egoyan is facing.[65] One critic has termed this aspect of his work as dealing with 'the crisis of representation.'[66]

For several reasons, critical response to Egoyan's work has not been as extensive as the response to Cronenberg's work. First, Cronenberg's work has been around for three decades, and it is a much more extensive filmography. Second, Egoyan works specifically in the crowded field of drama, rather than in a genre like horror, which has an international following, and numerous interpreters and commentators outside of Canada. Geoff Pevere points out that Egoyan's refusal (until *The Sweet Hereafter*) 'to employ two of the most secure toeholds to the suspension of disbelief in the commercial cinema – expository dialogue and a coherent psychological point of view' has made the 'enjoyment' of his films problematic for audiences.[67] As *Ararat* clearly indicates, they are not consumable in the Hollywood sense. Peter Harcourt describes the 'uncertain sense of self' and 'exile' in Egoyan's films as part of the moodiness of his work.[68] He considers the unusual and disarming manner in which Egoyan constructs his film images as 'distinctly Canadian' because his approach seeks to challenge a North American culture 'supersaturated' with imagery that has blurred the line between the real and the created.[69] Throughout Egoyan's films, the issues of viewing and spectacle reappear in various guises.

In a collection of essays on Egoyan published in France there is an emphasis on how the European model of *cinéma d'auteur* 'allows the Canadians to turn their backs on Hollywood and set out on their own.'[70] Canadian audiences attuned to Hollywood films experience a 'foreign' sense of emotionality and sensuality, both visual and aural, in his films. One could argue that Egoyan sought to escape this 'foreignness' through the adaptation of other-authored material much as Cronenberg did in several of his key films. At the beginning of the twenty-first century, the forty-two-year-old Egoyan is positioned at about the same stage in his career as Cronenberg was in the mid-to-late 1980s. Egoyan has built on his earlier auteur films to develop a $10-million project like *Felicia's Journey* and a $15-million project like *Ararat*.[71] In entering this level of production, Egoyan has reached a competitive plateau with Cronenberg, who many consider Canada's pre-eminent auteur.[72] *Spider*, which was shown at the same time as *Ararat*, cost a comparable $18 million.[73] These figures put both men at the top of Canadian feature-film production budgets. The increasing competitiveness between the two men is evident in comments that Cronenberg made about how the Canadian film community was 'denied the drama' of *Spider* versus *Ararat* at the 2002 Genies because *Spider* was not nominated in the best film category.[74]

On the surface, the work of Cronenberg and Egoyan seems so mutually exclusive in terms of genre and style that it becomes very difficult to characterize Anglo-Canadian cinema in general using them as a basis, even though there are critics and scholars like Beard who draw parallels.[75] Although auteur theory had its heyday decades ago and has since been replaced by various waves of academic schools of criticism, it can serve as a starting point for understanding the impact of individual creativity on Canadian film. It has been through auteurism and its similarity to literary authorship that a distinct sensibility in English-Canadian film has been able to emerge. While talented Canadian directors like Norman Jewison can direct American stars and subjects that appeal to Hollywood-accustomed audiences, it is Canadian auteur film directors that have given Canadian and international audiences something different.

Stephen Crofts, in an overview of the authorial concept and how other theories have superceded it, claims that auteur theory 'still has enormous influence within cultural discourse' because it 'has become a central means of marketing and product differentiation.'[76] Media headlines such as 'Powered by David Cronenberg and Atom Egoyan, Canada delivers a double whammy at Cannes' are meant to foster individual name recognition and so sell films.[77] The marketing device of name-recognition is one thing, but the film artist needs to create a saleable product that is heralded before receiving the benefit of corporate hype. Both Cronenberg and Egoyan have individually created bodies of work that display their own thematic and stylistic unity. Each of their discernible and analysable texts carries the imprint of its creator. The construction of a relationship between the individual psyche of the film-maker and the cultural milieu from which he or she arose is made easier by auteur theory. As a result, one can talk about the 'Canadian' elements in a film by Egoyan or Cronenberg that may be rooted in a personal imagination, but which also reflect the national or regional universe that the film-maker inhabits. Through the concept of authorship, the work of an individual artist can engage a critical response that draws on the experiences, concepts, and language of the auteur, while situating the auteur in a broader context defined by gender, class, race, nationality or ideology, and the structure of the industry in which he or she works. In the case of Cronenberg and Egoyan, their status as contemporary icons of Canadian cinema means it is possible to formulate a statement on what passes as 'mainstream' Canadian cinema. It is through their celebrity status that the un-American 'weirdness' of Canadian cinema finds cultural vindication and international validity. Even though Canadian cinema in the age of Cronenberg and Egoyan has remained for the most part 'art,' and as 'art' has been marginalized from the majority of the Canadian public, it nonetheless offers an insight into the cultural agendas of the Canadian intelligentsia of the past few decades.

That agenda has four main characteristics. The first agenda is the valorization of individual artistic achievement as the fountain of cultural progress. From the perspective of marketing someone or something in a capitalist economy, what management theory terms 'brand recognition' is crucial. It is the same for painters and novelists. The focus on individual achievement has been a pillar of modern capitalist societies for centuries. The second agenda believes in the necessity of public-private partnership in the inauguration and sustaining of film careers. Beginning with Canada Council support for young artists and culminating with Telefilm Canada funding to private film producers, film work in Canada is tied to this specific public-private model. The third agenda comprehends the Canadian film project as contributing somehow to a 'national' definition of creative material, seeking to distinguish its form and content from other influences, while encouraging creators to remain in Canada. The defining system of 'nationality' in Canadian film production with its quotas and subsidies both protects and restricts film-makers. The fourth agenda requires Canadian film-makers to achieve some level of international, preferably American, recognition. When a Canadian film-maker receives either Cannes or Oscar recognition, Canadian cinema is viewed as 'world class.'

In contrast to auteur theory, structuralism and semiotics treat film as a work of art influenced far beyond the intentions and organizing power of the author/director, with the author simply the product of the ideological and institutional/corporate context in which a film is made.[78] Both these approaches would construe Cronenberg's innovations in the horror genre and Egoyan's in dramatic subjects as tied to wider cultural and commercial transformations in Canadian society that favoured the emergence of English-Canadian directors after the founding of the Canadian Film Development Corporation in 1968. Cronenberg and Egoyan, according to this viewpoint, are simply the favoured products of a new system begun by the CFDC, followed by the tax-shelter era of the 1970s and continued by Telefilm Canada funding. The strange, bizarre, and even grotesque imaginings of these two outstanding directors may have been realized because of these structural realities, but the imaginings themselves are not the product of state initiative, or new forms of corporate concentration, or the manipulation of cultural taste by the market. Shocking audiences and challenging the conventionality and complacency of filmgoers is a statement about how English-Canadian film has created a non-Hollywood discourse for itself.

This discourse is tied inordinately to the male gaze. In the case of Cronenberg's repeated theme of bodily violation, the impact on female viewers is justifiably disturbing, considering how sexual violence has been a hallmark of patriarchy. In the case of Egoyan, the male gaze has been moderated through its damning exposure of the male psyche, but even so it has made the male psyche, especially that of the father, its prime interest. These gender limitations have laid one-sided foundations for an original feature-film national cinema in English Canada as conceived by male auteur film-makers. In contrast, Anglo-Canadian, Quebec, and Aboriginal women film-makers have brought a radically different sensibility to their work and challenged the presumptions of this male gaze.

CHAPTER ELEVEN

English-Canadian, Quebec, and Aboriginal Women Film-Makers

The work of women film-makers has been less visible in Anglo-Canadian and Quebec cinema because of the prominence given to male film-makers. The cinematic construction of the female persona was conditioned until the 1970s by patriarchal attitudes toward women and the feminine. It was not until the impact of the second wave of feminism in the 1960s (the first was the movement for women's suffrage in the early twentieth century) that gender issues returned to the forefront of movements for social change. 'Women's liberation,' as it was initially referred to, sought equality in the workplace by challenging the limitations of 'pink-collar' careers and insisting on pay equity. Post-1960s feminism sought improvements to the treatment of women in family law with regard to divorce and child support, access to abortion and contraception, and, later, a heightened awareness and condemnation of violence against women and children. Second-wave feminism was very effective in providing a new focus on women, their issues, and their historical absence from major decision-making roles in society. The field of women's studies, a new discipline, emerged in the 1970s to become a generator of feminist theory, history, and ideology. Together, these factors created a sphere in which women film-makers could speak with authenticity and power in a new and original way.

The women's movement, whose goals reflected the aspirations of White middle-class women, was a popular social movement that brought about major legal and social changes to the status of women in Canada. It was inevitable that the demands of the movement should have an impact on the film industry and the role of women in it. The first area where the new feminism made its mark was at the National Film Board. In 1974, Kathleen Shannon (1935–98) was appointed executive producer of Studio D, a new women's studio, at the NFB. It was the first government-sponsored all-women's feminist film initiative in the world. Shannon had been working since 1956 at the NFB, where she had risen through the ranks to the position of director and producer and was very conscious of the 'glass ceiling' that faced women film-makers.[1] At the inception of Studio D, she had been directing and producing a series of eleven films titled *Working Mothers* for the NFB's 'Challenge for Change' program. She remained Studio D's executive producer until 1986. The studio itself continued for another ten years after her retirement.

Shannon's goal was to use Studio D to train women to make films and then have these professionals focus on subjects of interest to women, presented from a feminist perspective. The studio emphasized the concept of 'community film-making,' which had three distinct components: it encouraged a group approach to film work as opposed to auteur individualism; it took as a focal point communities of ordinary women and how they supported one another in their struggles; and it highlighted the practical successes of the women's movement. During Shannon's tenure, Studio D won several Academy Awards for its documentaries. The first was Beverly Shaffer's *I'll Find a Way* (1978), about a plucky girl with spina bifida. The second was Terre Nash's anti-nuclear *If You Love This Planet* (1983), which was deemed 'political propaganda' by the U.S. Justice Department. The third film that made a major impact was Bonnie Sherr Klein's *Not a Love Story: A Film about Pornography* (1981), which was banned by the Ontario Censor Board because of its topic and images.

At its height, Studio D was getting a modest 10 per cent of the English-language budget, and by the time Shannon left, it was down to 7 per cent.[2] Even so, the popularity, and even the notoriety, of some of the films ensured that they generated up to 50 per cent more revenue than NFB films in general.[3] When third-wave feminism, with its emphasis on women of colour, working-class women, and lesbian rights became increasingly prominent in the 1990s, films like *Forbidden Love: The Unashamed Stories of Lesbian Lives* (1993) expressed this new sensibility, continuing the tradition of provocative feminist material.[4] Studio D did not survive the massive government cutbacks to the NFB budget of the mid-1990s.[5] It left a legacy of over 125 feminist documentaries done in a 'social realist' style.[6] But this legacy was primarily the product of a middle-class feminist ideology, which was subsequently criticized for its links to 'the NFB's liberal humanist discourse' and its failure to address more forcefully the demands of female diversity and multiculturalism in Canada.[7] By the time it had begun to address these concerns, it was closed down.

In the early 1980s, Canadian women's cinema was found mainly in the documentary (Studio D) or in the experimental and avant-garde (e.g., the work of Joyce Wieland; see ch. 12). Neither was sufficient to bring women's perspective before mainstream audiences.[8] Hundreds of 'escapist seventies' tax-shelter films attested to the lack of feminist consciousness on the silver screen. Even the CBC was reluctant to show Studio D documentaries because their feminist approach was considered too controversial for television. Only with the rise of women's directorial power was the feature film industry liberated from its culture of male domination. What feminist theorists wanted was a new representation of the female, a critique of an audience's relationship to the cinematic text, a deconstruction of patriarchal film ideology and language, and a focus on the female gaze as opposed to the male gaze.[9] Since feature films were such a powerful force in cultural formation, role modelling, and aspiration, feminists wanted films to reflect their egalitarian ideology and its increasing role in public discourse. Feminists wanted female leads to be characterized as independent and self-defining. They also hoped for a realistic portrayal of women's lives in Canada at the end of the twentieth century.[10]

The first of the prominent women directors was Anne Wheeler (1946–), a western Canadian who began making feature films in the 1980s. Wheeler started as a documentary film-maker in Edmonton working with an independent group of young film-makers (Filmwest) and then moved to the NFB's North West Studio, also based in Edmonton. Her feminist documentary *Great Grand Mother* (1976) explored the lives of pioneer women in the West, their culture of mutual aid, and the relationship between this historical sense of women's community and contemporary needs. She then moved toward feature films with a docudrama titled *A War Story* (1981), about her father's experiences as a Japanese prisoner of war during the Scond World War. Her debut feature was *Loyalties* (1986), made on a budget of $2.5 million.[11] The screenwriter was Sharon Riis, who then lived in Lac La Biche, Alberta. The town served as a set for the film, which tells the story of two women, one a Metis, who has difficulty making ends meet, and the other a recent immigrant from England and wife of a successful doctor. Their paths cross and the drama unfolds. The film explores the racial, ethnic, and class nature of the community, and the dark secrets hidden behind a veil of propriety. The film was a co-production with a U.K. company and had the CBC as a partner. Reflecting her own western roots and feminist interests, Wheeler is quoted in an interview during the film's production as wanting 'to make some sort of statement on the history of women in the west.'[12]

Although the story is contemporary, the interplay in the film between White and Aboriginal men, and between White and Aboriginal women, captures the spirit of the long history of colonizing White-Aboriginal relations. An Alberta-born and -raised novelist of Wheeler's generation, Katherine Govier, explored the same vein of historical and contemporary violence toward Native women with her 1989 Calgary-based novel Between Men. Wheeler's film's feminist ideology leads to a reconciliation between the two female protagonists when the wife of the doctor decides to speak out about his sexual assault on their Native babysitter. The film's choice of Alberta as a suitable site for a human drama dealing with feminist issues is a reflection of Wheeler's regionalism, while her use of the melodrama displayed her desire to make mainstream films. The combination of feminism, regionalism, and melodrama is the mix that defined Wheeler's Alberta-based work. Of the three elements, the most significant and permanent has proven to be her feminism.

Susan Lord claims Wheeler's work of this period is anchored in 'her critique of colonial patriarchy.'[13] The Quebec cinema scholar Denyse Therrien has commented on how Loyalties and Wheeler's later film Bye Bye Blues (1989) are not about the world of women as such but about women's situation in a patriarchal world.[14] In Loyalties the interaction between the female universe and the male universe is fraught with violence and abuse. The feminist ideology of the film acknowledges that there may be a tension between women on one level (class and ethnicity), but it is resolvable on another, deeper level (gender) because women's experience in a male-dominated universe is similar and more fundamental than other determinants of their lives. After Loyalties, Wheeler made a detour from overt feminist interests to direct Cowboys Don't Cry (1988), a film that is based on a novel by Alberta writer Marilyn Halvorson and deals with a dysfunctional relationship between a rural father and his son. But it is her 1989 film Bye Bye Blues that brought her commercial recognition in Canadian cinema.

Again it was a film set in Alberta, but it was an auteur piece. Take One magazine described Bye Bye Blues as 'an unapologetically old-fashioned weepie.'[15] The story is rooted in her own mother's life during the

Ron White and Anne Wheeler, euphoric after bull rider is pulled to safety. St Albert, Alberta, during the filming of *Cowboys Don't Cry* (1988).

Second World War, while her husband (Wheeler's father) was a prisoner of war. The film had a budget of $4.5 million and told the story of a woman's experiences as a singer in a swing band and the complications it causes.[16] Like *Loyalties*, it spoke from a woman's perspective. Rebecca Jenkins, who played the lead, received the Best Actress Award at the 1990 Genies for her performance, but the film itself was in competition with Denys Arcand's outstanding *Jésus de Montréal*, which garnered the major awards.

Daisy Cooper (Rebecca Jenkins) and wartime suitor Max Gramley (Luke Reilly) are drawn together far away from the front line in *Bye Bye Blues* (1989).

Wheeler's identification with Alberta stories came to an end when she moved to British Columbia in the 1990s. Although films like *A War Story* and *Bye Bye Blues* are her 'sentimental favourites' because they reflect her personal family history, the Alberta feature film industry lacked sufficient critical mass to keep her.[17] The province was primarily a location for Hollywood films dealing with northern themes or westerns. British Columbia, by contrast, was the scene of a major film industry thanks to the shooting of large numbers of American made-for-TV films. Wheeler's regional focus simply switched from Alberta to British Columbia. What followed was a trying period of adjustment to her new environment, resulting in some dry years of directing episodes of television drama, but she eventually resurfaced in 1999 with *Better Than Chocolate*, a film which reflected her new locale perfectly.

Made for a modest $1.6 million, *Better Than Chocolate* was a romantic comedy that was specifically aimed at the lesbian market, where it did very well and made more money than any of her previous films.[18] Scripted by a Vancouver woman writer and set in Vancouver, the film reflected the city's large gay and lesbian community. While the film was a departure for Wheeler because of its lesbian themes, it brought her back into the feature film industry with a renewed profile. Her next film, based on a novel by Vancouverite Linda Svendsen, was also set in Vancouver. *Marine Life* (2000) told the story of a middle-aged female lounge singer with a dysfunctional family and a young male lover. The theme of an older woman / young male lover was taken up in the next film, *Suddenly Naked* (2001), which was another romantic comedy, a genre Wheeler was now inhabiting with professional confidence.

Wheeler may not be an auteur director with a singular vision and cinematic style, or a film-maker who can garner large budgets, but her track record in using women-authored material and creating strong female characters for her films is outstanding. Most recently, she has directed adaptations of the works of two leading Canadian writers – Alice Munro and Barbara Gowdy. Her gender and her regional roots have given her a trajectory that has escaped the metropolitan-centred, male-oriented world of Toronto and Hollywood. By working primarily with female characterization in a commercially oriented genre like romantic comedy, far from the cinematic heartland of central Canada, she has faced a certain degree of marginalization. Her overall body of work has served as a prelude to that of Canadian women directors with stronger visions, greater cinematic intensity, and avant-garde artistic concerns.

The first of these is Patricia Rozema (1958–), whose debut feature, *I've Heard the Mermaids Singing* (1987), became a classic of Canadian cinema. The film was selected for the Directors' Fortnight at Cannes, along with Jean-Claude Lauzon's debut feature, *Un zoo la nuit* (see chapter 13). *Mermaids* won the Prix de Jeunesse at Cannes and was released in thirty-four countries. Rozema wrote, directed, and co-produced the film in 16 mm on a budget of $350,000, all of which came from Ontario and federal government sources.[19] The plot centres on Polly, a young single woman with limited skills who lands a job in an art gallery, where she is treated poorly. The character of Polly is played by Sheila McCarthy, whose performance garnered her the Best Actress Award at the 1988 Genies. The naïve Polly, plain in appearance and awkward in manner, is nonetheless intense in her self-conscious feelings and, through her photography, displays an interest in art in a goofy, imaginative way. She becomes entranced by the art gallery's curator, who seems to be everything she is not – sophisticated, urbane, and gay.

The film has a populist comic appeal. The editor of the American cinema magazine *Cineaste* captured this populism when she described the Polly character as 'very Canadian ... unassuming, polite and subservient, but secretly fantasizing about superhuman feats.'[20] Polly is the universal everywoman in the way that Charlie Chaplin's silent film character was so popular because he represented the little guy's battle with authority. This everywoman figure ultimately triumphs over the wiles of the world and the know-it-alls who are full of intellectual and cultural snobbery.

The feminist aspect of the film relates to the female-empowered universe of Polly's life and to the importance of careers as essential vehicles of women's self-expression. How feminist ideology is expressed in the film was dealt with in some detail in a 1988 article in *Cinema Canada* by George Godwin. He argued that *Mermaids* turns the female from a male sexual object to a psychological subject. First, Rozema collapses the normal distance between the spectator and the text by having Polly document her views on videotape and so adopts a confessional stance; and, secondly, Polly's 'probing look' throughout the film allows her to see with a piercing female gaze into the false constructs of authority.[21] The gallery's curator represents, according to Godwin, a woman who has internalized the values of the patriarchal society.[22]

The film's feminist credentials were challenged by another critic, who claims that the Polly character is 'trite and offensive to women' and that a true feminist film would have engaged the lesbian themes more fully than the titillating way the film did.[23] Rozema had admitted earlier that she created Polly as a non-sexual character so that the film would appeal to men.[24] What was found lacking in the film, according to a stricter feminist interpretation, was a 'positive image' of women.[25] But as a comedy which makes awkwardness a virtue and urbanity a vice, the film's conceit works for a wide audience, as Rozema intended. The film's financial success (by 1992 the film had grossed $2.5 million in the United States and over $600,000 in Canada) was a powerful indicator of its appeal.[26] The lesbian orientation in the film was dealt with discreetly because of its intended market, but having that basic tension in the film's story and in the characters was a bold breakthrough for a film with mainstream aspirations. The use of comedy to make the subject palatable was a stroke of genius.

Patricia Rozema was raised in a strict Dutch Calvinist home in small-town Ontario, educated at a Calvinist college in the United States, and was only twenty-nine years old when she earned instant fame for her debut feature. Her next film, *White Room* (1990), was about a young man's breakdown and did poorly. She then returned to lesbian themes with her auteur film *When Night Is Falling* (1995), the story of a professor who falls in love with a circus performer. The film did well on the lesbian art-house circuit. As she entered her forties, she wrote and directed an adaptation of Jane Austen's *Mansfield Park* (1999), again aiming for a wide audience. She was approached to do the film by Miramax, the company that had distributed *Mermaids* in the United States. Rozema included suggested lesbianism in the film, but its most controversial aspect was the pominence of slavery.[27] The fact that Rozema dealt openly with lesbianism in her feature films was a sign of how feminist ideology was creating a safe environment for its portrayal. In reaching for a mainstream audience, Rozema has rejected being viewed solely as 'a lesbian auteur,' a position which fits with contemporary queer theory about the fluidity of identities.[28] The subject of lesbianism reached its apogee with the works of Quebec film-maker Léa Pool.

Pool was born in Switzerland in 1950, worked as a teacher in Geneva, and moved to Montreal in 1975 when she was twenty-five. Her European immigrant background and her resettlement in Quebec created a certain transatlantic élan in Quebec cinema. Her sexual orientation, and the fact that female auteurs are a distinct minority in Quebec cinema, also moved her in her own direction. The American scholar of Quebec films Janis Pallister claims that Pool's 'use of Quebec cultural materials is ... slight.'[29] Not only is Pool steeped in, and expressive of, the French art-house tradition, but her approach, according to Pallister, 'marks the entrance of the Quebec cinema into worldwide feminist iconography.'[30] Pool's creative life in Quebec resulted in films that had a 'feeling of foreignness,' according to one critic.[31]

Her first film was an experimental black and white short titled *Strass Café* (1980), which depicted a woman and a man living separately as they try to find their own identities after having been in love. It was her debut feature, *La Femme de l'hôtel* (A Woman in Transit, 1984), which brought her to critical attention when it won best Canadian film at the Toronto Festival of Festivals and the International Critics' Prize at the Montreal World Film Festival. Then thirty-four, Pool both wrote the screenplay and directed the $500,000 feature. The film revolves around three women, one of whom is a film-maker, and their relationship. Pool considers the film 'more or less autobiographical.'[32] Yet it is the moodiness of her film that is so subversive of typical Hollywood narrative. 'I'm more concerned with communicating emotions in a film,' Pool is quoted as saying, 'as opposed to telling a story.'[33] The moods she creates are those of alienation and displacement, with her characters existing 'on the edge' in a cityscape that is 'cold and anonymous.'[34] It is 'a women's world of dark feelings and dark passages,' is the way one reviewer described the film.[35] Her characters seem to be adrift, their lives filled with isolation, uncertainty, and a desire to find love.

Her next film, *Anne Trister* (1986), again has a personal, autobiographical element. A woman, whose father has died, abandons her male lover and her country (Israel) for Quebec, where she falls in love with a woman who refuses to enter into a lesbian relationship. The title is a play on the French word *tristesse*, meaning sadness. But, after doing three auteur films, Pool decided to go in a new direction, adapting the 1977 novel *Kurwenal*, by Yves Navarre, a prominent gay writer in France.

This time the central character is a bisexual male photographer who returns from an assignment in a war-torn Central American country to find that both the woman and the man with whom he lived have disappeared. He is left to deal with his pain. The film did not do as well as her previous features, but it maintained a continuity with them because of its self-reflective engagement with issues of art and the life of the artist. In *La Femme de l'hôtel* the key character is a female film-maker; in *Anne Trister* it is a painter; and in *À corps perdu* (Straight to the Heart), a photojournalist. In each case, the director reflected on the meaning of visual art creation for both the creator and the viewer. One critic described these characters as 'anguished art-figures' with whom, no doubt, the director had more than slight identification.[36]

Her first film of the 1990s, *Mouvements du désir* (Desire and Motion, 1994), had two characters on a train travelling from Montreal to Vancouver who remain lost in their individual selves. Then in 1998 she was the auteur director of *Emporte-moi* (Set Me Free), a return to an autobiographical portrait, which she described as 'my life from a distance.'[37] It was the story of a thirteen-year-old girl (the year is 1963) struggling with her religious, ethnic, and sexual identity who uses a Godard film that she sees as a guide to life and discovers this is a mistake. Again, Pool used the theme of art and its power.

Léa Pool's cinema expresses a European sense of feminism that is removed from the American-influenced Canadian feminism of English Canada and its social pre-occupations. In the case of *Emporte-moi*, this European spirit was expressed first in the subject, second in the fact of its being a Canadian-Swiss-French co-production, and thirdly, in the screenplay itself, co-written with Nancy Huston, a Paris-based novelist, who had lived for a while in Alberta.[38] Pool's films have spoken out of the French literary tradition, with its avant-garde, aesthetic, and introspective view of sexuality, a sense of existential angst pervading human life, and an understanding of the crises that face professional women operating in the dislocating universe of contemporary urban life, where the struggle between creativity and the self is vital but problematic. Pool's style of film-making, which feels 'exiled' in the Quebec context (even more so in the Anglo-Canadian context), betrays the inevitable tension between diverse cultural traditions and how they intersect in the immigrant psyche. What is most powerful in her work is her rejection of 'traditional cinematic stereotypes' of women, which has a strong international appeal.[39]

In 2001, Pool released her first English-language film, *Lost and Delirious*, which returned to her theme of sexual awakening, this time in a private girls' school. She then began work on a major budget English-language film called *The Blue Butterfly*, about a Québécois boy who goes to Mexico in search of a rare butterfly.[40] The move into English-language films marks a new stage in her career. It will be interesting to see whether her career is paralleling Rozema's shift in *Mansfield Park* and whether she can cross the linguistic divide successfully, as Denys Arcand was not able to do in the 1990s with *Love and Human Remains*.

The gaze of the outsider and the theme of diaspora found in Pool's films are also central to the work of Deepa Mehta (1949–), a film-maker who lives in Canada but is best known for her films about India, a nation with a large, well-developed, and popular cinema industry known as 'Bollywood' because it is located in Bombay. Mehta's debut film, *Sam and Me* (1991), deals with inter-ethnic relations in Toronto and has been described as a film about 'cultural schizophrenia.'[41] Not only is it a film about the immigrant experience, but it is also a statement of post-colonial identity. The plot deals with a young East Indian immigrant who takes care of a cranky Jewish grandfather in a tragicomedy filled with stereotypical characters. The film is a humorous multicultural mosaic reminiscent of *The Apprenticeship of Duddy Kravitz*, except that it takes place a half-century later, and in Toronto rather than Montreal.

Born in Amritsar and educated at the University of New Delhi (philosophy), Deepa Mehta came to Canada in 1973, after marrying a Canadian whom she met while he was filming a documentary in India. After *Sam and Me*, she did some work in Hollywood, directing *Camilla* (1994), which starred Jessica Tandy and Bridget Fonda. She then launched into her auteur trilogy, *Fire* (1996), *Earth* (1999), and the as yet uncompleted *Water*. *Fire* generated controversy for its depiction of a lesbian relationship between married Indian women. The film was made after the break-up of her own marriage. She wrote the screenplay in order to express her own critical views of social mores that do not allow choices.[42] Self-identifying as 'an Indian-Canadian,' she works in an international context, where she wins praise for her feminist views in First World countries, while being condemned and vilified by traditionalists in India.[43]

Fire is an English-language film shot in India with Indian actors; it cost only $800,000 to make, with the crew deferring salaries of $450,000 and the financing coming from private investment.[44] Because of its foreign content, the film was not eligible for the usual Canadian government funding. Ignoring her Canadian identity, an Australian film magazine described Mehta as 'one of India's most controversial and taboo-breaking film makers.'[45] Canada's *Take One* magazine described her as 'a woman not to be trifled with.'[46] This rather serious and determined persona is reflected in her own description of how she saw *Fire*: 'I wanted to make a film about contemporary, middle-class India ... More than 350 million Indians belong to the burgeoning middle-class and lead lives not unlike the Kapur family in *Fire*.'[47] She used the film to oppose arranged marriages and the isolation of Indian women in traditional roles, as well as to point out the contradiction between the Hindu portrayal of Indian women as 'pious, dutiful, self-sacrificing [and how] Indian popular cinema, a.k.a. "Bollywood" portrays women as sex objects.'[48] Her rejections of both these viewpoints resulted in protest and scandal in India.

Her engagement with issues of Indian culture from the perspective of Canada – where her viewpoint is not viewed as extreme – indicates how life in one culture can encourage criticism of another. Indian cinema is as influential in India as Hollywood is in the United States. It is a star-based system which engages the Indian masses with endless formulaic fantasies in a variety of regional and ethnic languages. Considered 'a purely escapist form of mass entertainment' that appeals primarily to the rural and urban poor, Indian cinema is an influential part of Indian culture, the complete opposite of the situation of Canadian cinema in Canada.[49] Mehta's work is generally restricted to the art house film circuit in Canada, where it is applauded, while its impact in India, where cinema is both revered and despised, is limited to English-speaking educated audiences. Because she chooses to attack the mores of Indian society in her films, an approach uncommon in Indian cinema, her work is best understood as a product of her cross-cultural sensibility in which her Canadian experience has strengthened her criticism of traditional societies.

The second film in the trilogy, *Earth,* was released in 1999. Mehta adapted an Indian novel that dealt with the partition of India after independence and the bloody communal strife that ensued. While *Earth* was tolerated because the history it portrayed was well known, *Water*, her subsequent film, created even more of a reaction in India than *Fire* had. *Water* was to be filmed in India in 2000, but the main set was destroyed by a mob when the film was denounced by religious political parties. Reacting to this political pressure, the local government refused to issue permits, fearing more violence, and filming stopped. The international film community was outraged.[50] The Mehta-authored story of a teenage widow who has an affair with a teenage priest was simply too offensive to fundamentalist sensibilities in Indian society to be allowed to go ahead.

After her frustrating experiences in India, Mehta returned to Toronto, where she wrote a screenplay whose lead character is an Indo-Canadian drag queen. Filmed on location in Toronto, *Hollywood/Bollywood* is a return to the ethnic world of *Sam and Me* that launched her career. The film is a romantic comedy set in Toronto's immigrant Indian community, which is criticized for embracing the conventional Bollywood film as a statement of its own diasporic cultural identity.[51] While the violence that confronted her work in India may not exist in the multicultural universe of contemporary Canada, her embracing of the comic to deal with issues of nationality and gender in Canada is a turn to the more easily digestible. Her films about Canada are a Mehta 'lite' version of her vision, while India gets the full brunt of her personal crusade. The situation in India is very serious for her, while Canada and its ethnic communities can be dealt with humorously. She must raise funding for her films about India privately, while Telefilm Canada is there for her Canadian locations and subjects.

In 2003 Mehta's *Republic of Love*, a film based on the novel of the same name by celebrated Canadian writer Carol Shields, was released on the film festival circuit. The project had gone through a number of earlier permutations, with others involved, until Mehta took an interest and completed the project using her own script.[52] The film was a departure from both her usual Indo-Canadian comedies and her serious Indian films. Writing her own screenplay and directing a story with non-Indian leads signalled a new versatility, even as using Toronto for the location of the Winnipeg story affirmed her attachment to the familiar.

Mehta represents a new kind of immigrant film-maker in Canada, who is comfortable working in two radically distinct societies, Indian and Canadian, while using the new universality of the English language as her bridge between the two worlds. She epitomizes a transnational postcolonialism in which two former British colonies, one of which has a sizeable immigrant population from the other, create the interlocking dynamics of commonality and difference which signal a globalized twenty-first-century identity. In India, Mehta is viewed as an artist formed by Canada, while in Canada she is viewed as an artist formed by an Indian sensibility. Because of her English-language films, Deepa Mehta is now English Canada's pre-eminent immigrant female director, just as Léa Pool is Quebec's pre-eminent immigrant female director. They are not the only ones.

Hong Kong–born Mina Shum (1966–) is the first Chinese Canadian to have directed a feature film in Canada. *Double Happiness* (1994) is a story of inter-generational conflict between a young daughter and her immigrant father. Described as a semi-autobiographical work of 'self-ethnography' that seeks to explore the Chinese immigrant culture and its issues, *Double Happiness* uses its contemporary urban domestic setting to picture a non-typical Canadian family.[53] The film reflects the growing demographic importance of Chinese immigration to Canada in the 1990s, first from Hong Kong prior to the reversion of that city to Chinese sovereignty, then from Taiwan, and finally from China itself. The issues raised by Shum are those that affected the lives of many Chinese adapting to life in Vancouver and Toronto during the 1990s.

Alanis Obomsawin, film-maker.

While the role of immigrant women film directors has become an important element of Anglo-Canadian and Quebec film-making, the role of Aboriginal women film-makers has also become a noticeable factor for the first time. Curiously, Alanis Obomsawin (1932–), Canada's leading Aboriginal (Abenaki) female film-maker, was born in the United States and is technically an immigrant like the previous three film-makers. She has been a documentary film-maker since the 1970s, working for the NFB on films concerning First Nations peoples and issues. Her most famous work, *Kanehsatake: 270 Years of Resistance* (1993), is a feature-length documentary about the 1990 armed stand-off at Oka between the Mohawks of Kanehsatake in Quebec, on one side, and the Quebec police and the Canadian army, on the other. Obomsawin spent seventy-eight days filming from behind ever shrinking Mohawk lines, until the final day when the remaining Mohawk men, women, and children broke free. The film, produced, directed, written, and narrated by Obomsawin, was named best Canadian feature at the Toronto International Film Festival. Gittings summarizes the film as 'counter-cinema resisting the hegemonic colonial discourses of Quebec and Anglo-Canadian nations.'[54] Just as Pool's films engaged the universality and otherness of gay women, Mehta the otherness of India and the Indian community in Canada, and Shum the otherness of Chinese Canadians, so Obomsawin takes the point of view of the First Nations in their persona as the Other. 'I wanted to show what the Mohawk people were like and why they took the stand they did,' she explained in the film's press kit.[55] By adopting a single point of view in her documentary, she can be criticized for being one-sided, which puts the film firmly in the Griersonian tradition of documentary propaganda and social education.[56]

The crisis at Oka was a major event in the history of Canadian and Quebec racism toward the Aboriginal peoples. Obomsawin's courageous film work (she was alone filming in the final days) was a statement of how revived national identities among First Nations peoples were challenging the dominant national discourse of the two 'founding' peoples of Canada. Her film serves as a 'biting critique of the way in which nationhood is defined.'[57] The role of the documentary film has proven crucial in providing a visual record of major events in recent Aboriginal-White relations, as First Nations demand self-government. As a film-maker, Obomsawin participated in historical events that made her films 'validate [Aboriginal] culture as an experience of history.'[58] Through her, the Aboriginal side of Canadian history has finally found its cinematic spokesperson.

There are several factors that become evident from this overview of Canadian women directors of the past two decades. First is the presence of lesbian themes. The prevalence of lesbian subject matter is a distinct characteristic of Canadian feminist film-makers. The subject appears more frequently than gay material in Canadian films, even though the gay male community has a larger sociological presence.[59] It would seem that both second-wave feminism and contemporary third-wave feminism, which emphasizes the class, cultural, racial, and sexual diversity of women, have created a feminist consciousness in Canadian cinema that validates this subject. That this has not happened in Hollywood cinema, which influences audience tastes in Canada, has meant that Canadian feminist cinema remains ghettoized, like most Canadian films, within the universe of art-house films and their limited audiences. That 'the lesbian postmodern,' as one critic terms it, has found a home in Canadian feminist film-making is indicative of the alternative sensibilities that film-making offers in a national industry that finds itself free of Hollywood restraints.[60]

The other aspect of women's feature film-making is its diversity of genres, including Wheeler's melodrama *Bye Bye Blues*, Rozema's comedy *I've Heard the Mermaids Singing*, dramas such as Pool's *La Femme de l'hôtel* and Mehta's *Fire*, and the documentary success of Obomsawin. Feminist perspectives in Canadian cinema are presented in diverse forms and with influences from ethnicity, regional life, and sexual orientation, which create an individuality for each director within the overall context of feminist consciousness. The creation of 'new Canadian heroines who maintain control of their own inner space,' as Katherine Monk describes them, occurs most frequently in the auteur works of Rozema, Pool, and Mehta.[61] Because of their feminist perspectives, none of these directors has yet achieved the mainstream stature of Cronenberg or Egoyan. Even so, their visions represent a broad spectrum of innovative film-making that seeks to balance the dominance of the male imagination with the voice and gaze of engaged women with a sense of urgency and mission.

The final aspect that should be noted is the budgets of films made by women film-makers. Although they have worked in feature films with budgets from under $1 million (*Fire*) to almost $5 million (*Bye Bye Blues*), none of them has worked consistently with the large budgets commanded by their well-known and well-connected male counterparts. An important exception is Patricia Rozema, whose *Mansfield Park* had a budget of $16 million. While some might argue that lower budgets represent a ghettoization of women film-makers based on gender, subject matter, and approach, it is also true that these recognized and respected women film-makers are viewed as having played a fundamental role in redefining and expanding the content of Canada's national cinemas. As a body of work, their films represent a diverse, engaged, and uncompromising perspective on human relations that is the equal of women film-makers in other national cinemas and a challenge to the vision of their male colleagues.

CHAPTER TWELVE

Experimental and Cult Films: Snow, Wieland, and Maddin

Canada's contribution to world cinema has extended into the area of experimental and cult films, which has given Canada an international audience, while reducing that audience to a specific niche. Avant-garde films can create an international reputation for a film-maker, but only among a very select group of people. Experimental films are usually associated with art galleries rather than movie theatres. The films are not created for entertainment purposes; nor do they contain traditional narrative structures. Their goal is to push the boundaries of the cinematic form in a highly self-reflective manner. The concepts used in experimental film-making flow out of art theories about colour, the techniques of representation, and the meaning of space, time, etc., which are the intellectual preserve of artists, critics, and academics concerned with innovation. In experimental film-making, aesthetic ideas and unusual imagery are the primary currencies.

Cult films, by contrast, have a sizeable, albeit distinct, market. Cult films are usually low-budget films screened in art-house cinemas that generate a following among those who value the films' eccentric representation of reality. Cult films have a quality that connects them to their movie audience outside the envelope of mainstream consumerism. Because of their subject matter or their style, cult films create a tribal identification for social subcultures that reaches deep into the psyche of their followers. The audience returns to the same film over and over again as a form of communal celebration. While experimental films tend to have audiences walk out on them, cult films are imprinted on those who believe in them.

Two Canadian film-makers who have been most prominently associated with experimental films are Ontario artists Michael Snow (1929–)

and Joyce Wieland (1931–98), while the Manitoba film-maker Guy
Maddin (1957–) is Canada's leading creator of cult films. While there
are other artists working in film and video/digital formats, especially
the latest wave of 'new media' artists (see chapter 17), whose gallery
and internet 'installations' are the norm in avant-garde art circles, the
work of this older generation captures the essence of the movement
that sought to challenge the orthodoxies of celluloid.

It is Michael Snow who brought a new stature to experimental film in
Canada, and the story of his work in the field both exemplifies the
nature of experimental film and points to its limitations. Historically,
the roots of experimental film are centred in the European surrealist art
movement of the 1920s and 1930s. Surrealists rejected faithful representation of reality as a goal of art, or even the impressionistic interpretation of external reality centred on light and colour. They were more
interested in internal mental space, where the psyche and the senses
created symbolic meaning and imagery through the contrast and juxta-
position of objects. For surrealist artists, the world was very much
psychoanalytical. They also tried to be anti-conventional by turning
media like photography and film into statements of art. Man Ray, for
example, watched films through his fingers, focusing on various parts
of the image so that he could dissect its construction and at the same
time lose himself in an unintended aspect of the image.[1] A prominent
surrealist was the French painter Marcel Duchamp, who moved to New
York in the mid-twentieth century. Michael Snow acknowledged him as
an inspiration for his own work. R. Bruce Elder, a Canadian avant-
garde film-maker and critic, believes that the origins of experimental-
ism in film in Europe meant that Canada was very much a latecomer to
the field.[2] Being late, however, did not mean being derivative. In fact, a
whole new era in art had surfaced in New York after the Second World
War with abstract expressionism, a movement that turned New York
into the new capital of the avant-garde art world, replacing the pre-war
primacy of Paris. This change worked well for Snow, who, as a Torontonian, was geographically close to New York's dynamic art scene.

Educated at Toronto's elite Upper Canada College and the Ontario
College of Art, Snow began exhibiting as an artist in the early 1950s
while playing as a jazz musician. He (along with his wife, Joyce Wieland)
moved to New York in 1962, where they spent the rest of the decade
before returning to Canada. It was in New York that they were wel-
comed into the American film avant-garde because of Snow's much-
admired experimental film (A to Z). The mid-1960s were a time of

political radicalism in the streets and widespread experimentation with drugs by the young. It was an explosive environment that worked for Snow's and Wieland's creativity.[3]

The film *Wavelength* (1967) is often considered Snow's major work. It was shot in his loft in New York in 1966. It is a forty-five-minute-long zoom that ends on a photo of waves on a wall. Accompanying the visual element is a soundtrack, which Snow called 'an ear equivalent to what a zoom was.'[4] He used a sine wave generator during the film to decrease the wavelength (ergo the title of the film) of its sound from that of a low pitch of 60 cycles per second to a high pitch of 12,000 cycles per second, thereby imitating the gradual reduction of the field of vision and its focus. As a visual artist, Snow valued the aesthetics championed by Duchamp, in which small changes in the image produce large perceptual results.[5] Snow had already given sound and image an equal presence in *New York Eye and Ear* (1964).[6] His desire to treat the medium and its elements in a way that was completely different from their normal function in regular cinema made his films experimental and provocative.

Snow was focusing on 'the exploitation of various modes of cinematic experience,' meaning he was actively commenting on what film does to its audience, an appealing prospect for critics but not necessarily for audiences.[7] *Wavelength* has no real plot, though the odd human presence appears. The lack of diverse camera angles or any narrative action that can be followed results in a mesmerizing attachment to the sound rather than the image that is generated. Snow believed that his films were made for 'attention, contemplation, meditation.'[8] The film was meant to quiet the viewer. During the long zoom, different colour filters, changes in aperture, and so forth, are applied in order to make the audience focus on the apparatus of film-making and its effects rather than on some sequence of human activity with which we identify. Elder termed *Wavelength* 'a kind of cinematic deconstruction' because it looked primarily at what the camera was doing in framing the audience's perception and talked about the operation of human consciousness, rather than encouraging the typical suspension of disbelief that storytelling entails.[9] The preoccupations of the artist and the musician triumph over those of typical narrative structure and its use in documentary and fiction.

During his time in New York, Snow was part of what was later termed 'structural film,' a name given to the avant-garde films being made in New York during that period. These cinematic works of art

Michael Snow, experimental film-maker and artist (1962).

were concerned with the structure of film itself and so eliminated reference to 'symbol, allegory and metaphor.'[10] On several occasions, Snow spoke of how he was stripping film to absolute purity. 'I am trying to do something very pure,' he said of *Wavelength,* 'and about the kinds of realities involved.'[11] For Snow a film can be used to express an abstraction of its own operating principles.

His second significant film came several years later. *La Région centrale* (1971) moved from indoors to Canada's dramatic wilderness landscape. In describing the film prior to its production, he explained that it was meant to be 'a kind of absolute record of a piece of wilderness.'[12] He didn't want to use landscape as a backdrop for human action but as a thing in itself, and he wanted to present it the way it might be viewed for the first time. In fact, he had to use a helicopter to locate a suitably hostile terrain in northern Quebec, and he had an engineer design a machine on which to mount the camera so that it could move spherically in all directions and also be remotely controlled. The camera, in effect, operated like 'an eye floating in space.'[13] Snow made the film with $28,000 from the Canadian Film Development Corporation.[14] He considered *La Région centrale* (a term taken from physics, not geography) as his cinematic answer to the Group of Seven's obsession with interpreting the Canadian wilderness.[15]

In 1974, Snow made a four-and-a-half-hour film titled *Rameau's Nephew by Diderot (Thanx to Dennis Young).* It contained twenty-five sequences separated by twenty-seven abstract colour compositions. Snow's desire to challenge viewers by exposing the techniques of cinema is evident in his categorization of film as a 'hallucination of representation' in which 'lips are ghost lips and the voice is not a voice but a ghost voice, a *used* voice, a memory of a voice, a *recorded* voice.'[16] R. Bruce Elder saw Snow's films as epistemological deconstructions, which they certainly are, but their 'exploration of illusionism' created grist mainly for the academic mills eager to expound on his insights.[17]

Snow continued his work, both as an artist and a film-maker, right into the twenty-first century with *Corpus Callosum,* a limited budget film with digital special effects. He released a portion of the film as *The Living Room* in 2001. In it three human figures remained fixed, while their images and the objects in the room they inhabit change.[18] In 2000, Snow was awarded the first Governor General's Award for visual and media arts (along with six other artists in other related media) specifically for his work in film. The jury noted that 'his films are legendary. They have been shown throughout North America, Europe and the Far

East and are included in the curricula of film schools around the globe.'[19] Other critics share an enthusiasm for his achievement. Jim Shedden, the editor of a compilation of essays on Michael Snow's films, writes that 'Snow's work has been written about as much, if not more, than any other visual artist working with the film medium.'[20] Bart Testa of the University of Toronto concludes that Snow has become a 'canonical experimental film-maker for cinema academics.'[21] R. Bruce Elder, the most philosophical interpreter of Snow's films, considers him a great film-maker of vigorous originality who probed to the very depths of the nature of film.[22]

All these accolades beg the question of what significance experimental film and its creators have in the overall thrust of the cinematic medium. Snow himself acknowledged that his films have had a limited audience, but small audiences, he claims, do not mean that the films aren't important for our understanding of the art form.[23] One could argue that there could be a 'trickle-down' effect that may see some of these insights reach mainstream film-making through the film education process. But it may be equally true that avant-garde insights are so critical of the medium and its illusions that they threaten the commercial goals of mainstream cinema or, in the words of Atom Egoyan, 'defy the conventional rules of industrial cinema.'[24] The problem is the distance between experimental film and the world of feature film-making. It may be too great for the possibility of cross-fertilization because 'fringe film' is fundamentally anti-conventional. The intellectualization of experimental film appeals primarily to highly specialized critics and scholars, while its realization appeals to the artistic avant-garde. Snow considered experimental film 'accessible to anyone who can see and think,' and he condemned 'the training people get with narrative films' as the cause of resistance to the experimental.[25] His wife, Joyce Wieland, tried to cross the gulf between the two with tragic results.

Joyce Wieland has been called 'the mother of Canadian experimental cinema,' an epithet that seems to imply Snow was the father.[26] They were both from Toronto, of the same generation, and known primarily as avant-garde visual artists rather than film-makers. Snow came from money; Wieland came from poverty. Their marriage and their art made them the first couple of the Canadian art scene in the 1970s, after they returned from New York. While in New York, Wieland took up experimental film-making in a serious way, although she had, like Snow, made several shorts during the 1950s while still in Toronto.

She made thirteen experimental films between 1963 and 1969, with the shortest running three minutes and the longest eighty-two. Among the shorter films are *Water Sark* (1965), *Handtinting* (1968), and *Sailboat* (1968). Each expresses an aspect of her approach to art and film. *Water Sark* is read today as a feminist statement because it deals with paper-cuts placed over a white lampshade, signifying the celebration of domestic life. Wieland introduced her own body into the scene, as well as various objects such as rubber gloves and toy boats.[27] The general mood of this fourteen-minute colour film is joyful discovery of a world near at hand. In *Handtinting* she used ordinary fabric dyes on sections of the film to turn black and white photos she had taken earlier of American women factory workers into an artistic and political statement. In this film, she expresses the social critique and political commentary that distinguished her work from that of Snow. *Sailboat* consists of a single scene of a sailboat crossing the screen under a large title that reads 'Sailboat.' The use of written text, thereby creating a visual poem, is a hallmark that appeared in subsequent films.

Two other films from the 1960s that expressed her approach to politics were *Rat Life and Diet in North America* (1968), in which she used her pet gerbils as a metaphor for American war resisters fleeing to Canada during the Vietnam War, and *Reason over Passion / La Raison avant la passion* (1967–9), which was a commentary on Canadian prime minister Pierre Trudeau's famous quip about what he believed was essential for Canadian politics. *Reason over Passion* is a faux documentary road movie that consists of eighty-two minutes of viewing the Canadian landscape through a car window (Cape Breton to Vancouver) interspersed with the national anthem, Trudeau's dictum and his portrait, as well as a French lesson. Wieland used the visual aspect to challenge male rationality and its desire to impose itself on nature. In a sense, it was her response to the nationalist fervour that accompanied the country's centennial in 1967. Nationalist rhetoric was at a peak, and Wieland placed the vastness of the landscape against the patriotic construction favoured by the state. At the same time, she produced an etching and two quilts using the same slogan. Placing the prime minister's slogan in a film and other art media subverted its power by transforming it into critical art.

Her interest in matters Canadian and her New York reputation resulted in her being the first woman artist to have a solo exhibition at the National Gallery during her lifetime. Titled *True Patriot Love*, this 1971 show included animals and home-made perfume titled 'Sweet Beaver.' A small bronze titled 'The Spirit of Canada Suckles the French and

Film-maker and multimedia artist Joyce Wieland in her studio (circa 1960).

English Beaver' was composed of a reclining female nude, representing Canada, with a beaver at each breast. It was this mix of implied irreverence and serious commentary that made people take notice. No other artist at the time was so engaged in political commentary using well-recognized national symbols. She continued this political orientation with a thirty-minute film of Pierre Vallières, the famous ideologue of Quebec independence, which shows only his mouth as he speaks about the state of Quebec and women. This film was followed by *Solidarity*, which showed the shoes of walking strikers with the word 'solidarity' printed over the image.

At this point, Wieland decided to make a feature film that would combine her national interests, her feminism, and her experimental aesthetic. It proved to be a bad decision. Experimental film-making tries to deny its viewers 'easy access to information.'[28] Avant-garde films are filled with the unexpected, the difficult to understand, and theoretical concerns. When this sensibility is transferred to a feature film that seeks a mainstream audience, disaster looms. After struggling for several years to raise the necessary funds, Wieland was able to get $435,000 from the CFDC. The film, originally titled *True Patriot Love* and then renamed *The Far Shore*, is loosely modelled on the life of the Group of Seven painter Tom Thomson, who drowned while canoeing in northern Ontario during the First World War. The film was described by *Saturday Night* film critic Robert Fulford as full of 'blatant symbolism.'[29] The attractive heroine from Quebec marries an ambitious engineer from Ontario but falls in love with an artist who takes her to the north woods for love, peace, and natural beauty. Feminist critics put a brave face on the project, calling it a response to patriarchal values. Feminist critic Brenda Longfellow called the film 'an allegory of colonization' that challenged the technological project of subjugating nature.[30] Intellectual allegory is fine if it connects with its audience, which didn't happen in a film that most critics considered nothing more than an excess of melodrama. They measured it against the common standards of narrative film and found it wanting. In this film, Canada may have been intellectually more like a painting of a female body than an engineer's railroad, but the metaphor did not translate into the public's conventional mindset.

Wieland's attempt to transfer her feminist, environmentalist, and nationalist perspectives, which had brought her fame in the experimental realm, to the norms of the feature film, resulted in *The Far Shore* being 'laughed off the screen.'[31] Wieland was devastated by the experience and turned away from film altogether until the 1980s, when she returned to some of her earlier material.[32] In a 1971 interview, Wieland said: 'All the art I've been doing or will be doing is about Canada. I may tend to overly identify with Canada.'[33] But the legacy of nationalist content in her art was a challenge to the 'patriarchal representations of Canadian national identity.'[34] Her questioning of how Canada was being constructed for Canadians by the dominant discourse meant that the vision of the artist inevitably stood against the vision of the politician. Canada in the 1970s was going through a dramatic nationalist revival, with much talk about national identity in literature (Margaret Atwood's *Survival* and Northrop Frye's *The Bush Garden*) and a dismal prognosis for Canadian independence (George Grant's *Lament for a Nation*). Wieland's work was an integral part of this intellectual and cultural milieu, which was centred in Ontario, a province used to dominating national dialogue but at the time threatened by the Quebec independence movement. However, it was not only the artist's naturally critical observation of society that fostered her novel way of viewing the Canadian situation in film. 'Drugs opened the door to film,' she admitted, indicating that the use of LSD was 'very important' for her creativity in the 1960s and that she edited her political masterpiece *Reason over Passion* using marijuana, because it allowed her to 'pick out everything that was wrong.'[35]

In a review of two biographies of Wieland published in 2001, the Canadian art critic Adele Freedman concluded that 'Wieland's life, with its highs and heartbreaks, had come to symbolize women's defiant struggle for self-expression ...'[36] Wieland is now a feminist/nationalist icon, a curious yet provocative mix of what has been termed 'female aesthetic' and self-conscious Canadianism.[37] That she attempted, however unsuccessfully, to cross the gulf between experimental and narrative films is a sign of her artistic courage to reach out to a larger and less sophisticated audience. Bridging the gap between unconventional and conventional cinema requires a level of eccentric genius that she may have lacked, but that eccentricity is evident in the work of Guy Maddin, who was able to attain cult status for his films before returning to the experimental *à la* Snow and Wieland.

Guy Maddin is a Winnipeg film-maker of Icelandic descent who has done for the cult genre what Cronenberg has done for horror. His first feature, *Tales from the Gimli Hospital* (1988), is the story of two men lying ill in a hospital during a smallpox epidemic in a turn-of-the-century Icelandic settlement in Manitoba and all the strange things that are done to them. The film has a Norse saga structure and is shot in a form that resembles the sound films of the late 1920s, when differing techniques of synchronized sound (so-called 'part-talkies') were attempted. That an ultra-low budget black and white film became 'Canada's first cult sensation' is indicative of Maddin's originality and the power of his unlikely source of inspiration – a small ethnic rural culture (Icelandic) situated in a province with a limited film history.[38] The story of the film's rise to cult status parallels other off-beat Canadian success stories, such as those of *Goin' down the Road* and *I've Heard the Mermaids Singing*.

Officially the production cost $22,000, most of it coming from the Manitoba Arts Council.[39] Then Maddin's friend, Greg Klymkiw, raised $40,000 from the Winnipeg Film Group to market this strange entity filled with silent young actors.[40] It was screened at the Montreal Film Festival and other Canadian and European film festivals, eventually doing 'a round of midnight madness showings in most major U.S. cities.'[41] By 1992 the film had grossed $116,000 in Canada in various venues and had played for a year in New York. As well, Maddin had a career and a formula that worked – a weird film that takes its inspiration from a visual language rooted in the silent cinema, made on next-to-nothing, but aggressively marketed to a particular audience that prefers its films after midnight, when black and white absurdity is best appreciated. By taking his audience into a cinematic world that was long dead, he created what one critic termed 'confounding, disturbing and visually brilliant cinema that repels and fascinates in equal measure.'[42] This equal measure of appeal and distaste may be based in what one critic calls 'Maddin's (mis)appropriation of past genres,' in which anachronistic forms such as silent-film melodrama are reburied and made to feel even more 'past' than the originals because they are made in the present.[43]

Because of their roots in a recognizable archaic cinema tradition, Maddin's films had a certain outside-of-Canada appeal, described by the eminent *New Yorker* magazine in the following trendy language:

NORDIC NETHERWORLDS – Winnipeg native Guy Maddin's trippy films are a movie lover's dream (sometimes literally) photographed in the surreal style of early silent features. Two of his best dark fairy tales – 'Careful' and 'Tales from the Gimli Hospital' – will be shown at BAM ... along with his masterly five-minute short, 'Heart of the World,' a melodrama that combines elements of archaic horror films and propaganda reels, science-fiction imagery, and a passion play.[44]

Angela Heck and Michael Gottli with fish in *Tales from the Gimli Hospital* (1988).

What is most interesting about this categorization is its failure to situate Maddin in any sort of Canadian context, which is what also happened to Michael Snow's experimental films made in New York in the 1960s when they were heralded as an important part of the city's structural film movement. The work is viewed as purely avant-garde, whose references are to cinema history itself and not to any national context.

If one takes Maddin's second feature, *Archangel* (1990), as a film located solely in the history of cinema, one can easily forget Winnipeg's multicultural mosaic, out of which works like *Archangel* are contrived. *Archangel* is set in a northern Russian town at the end of the First World War. Its major character is a one-legged Canadian soldier who has lost his memory and lives in a delusional world of battles, while his mind searches for his lost love. One has to be acquainted with Winnipeg's Slavic North End, with its legacy of communist sympathies, to perceive the significance of a film about the Allied intervention against the Russian Revolution. While the avant-garde focuses on how Maddin tips his hat to Russian cinema in this film, Canadians may find a

Guy Maddin at his Gimli cottage during the filming of *Tales from the Gimli Hospital* (circa 1988).

different subtext in the film, associated more with the political divisions of his native city. *Archangel*, with a budget of $340,000 (fifteen times that of *Gimli Hospital*), won the best experimental film award from the National Society of Film Critics in the United States in 1991. Maddin himself called it 'my favorite disfigured secret child.'[45]

But *Archangel* did not do as well financially as *Gimli Hospital*. Even so, Maddin did receive significant funding from Telefilm Canada for his next historical throw-back, *Careful* (1992), a spoof on the pre–Second World War German 'mountain-film' genre.[46] Once again, the film is set in Europe. This time it is an alpine village whose inhabitants speak in whispers to avoid starting an avalanche. The colour film is a tale of obsession, incest, and suicide shot with title cards, lots of static, and cardboard sets. Critical acclaim for *Careful* allowed Maddin to retreat into making shorts until he came up with a new idea. In 1995 he was given a lifetime achievement award at the Telluride Film Festival when he was only thirty-eight, an award also given to the likes of Francis Ford Coppola, Andrei Tarkovsky, and Clint Eastwood.

Twilight of the Ice Nymphs (1997), his third feature, was also shot in colour. A political prisoner returns to his native island where the sun never sets and the air is full of falling ostrich feathers. The plot ensues with unrequited love and murder, all shot in washed-out hues of peculiar blues, pinks, and greens, in which the actors seem to float. The film is probably the closest his work has come to being camp. In a 1999 interview, Maddin claimed that he would like 'to rise out of the cult movie status eventually.'[47] In 2002 the CBC fulfilled his wish by broadcasting *Dracula – Pages from a Virgin's Diary*, on which he collaborated with the Royal Winnipeg Ballet. When Maddin told the documentarist who was filming the filming of *Twilight* that he was 'sick of the twenties,' he was saying he wanted to move on. With a budget of $1.6 million and a CBC telelvision debut, Maddin was in the mainstream, although a very arty one.[48] Instead of the 'midnight madness' circuit he was accustomed to, he was now playing to a prime time television audience.[49] Perhaps his winning a 2001 Genie for his classic short *The Heart of the World* signalled a coming of age.

In 2003, forty-seven-year-old Maddin released a new feature, *The Saddest Music in the World*, adapted from a script by English novelist Kazuo Ishiguro. With a budget reported to be $3 million, it was shot in a 'willfully primitive' way.[50] While working on this film, Maddin released an experimental film titled *Cowards Bend the Knee*, a series of short films presented consecutively on monitors in a darkened room. This art gallery presentation was a 'creative cross-pollinization' because it was also shown at the Rotterdam International Film Festival several months earlier.[51] The 'catalogue' for the show is actually a book with a scenario for each film.[52] Maddin's ability to play with genres, venues, and meaning (he termed the film 'an autobiography') is probably the closest any avant-garde Canadian film-maker has come to bridging the gap between experimental film and conventional narrative.

When *The Saddest Music in the World* began doing the rounds of the film festival circuit in 2003, it drew full houses because of Maddin's reputation. Audiences were not disappointed. With his usual bravado, he made icy Winnipeg, or 'Winterpeg' as it has been nicknamed, the snow-encapsulated locale for a Depression-era black and white talkie in which a beer company sponsors a worldwide contest whose winner must produce the saddest music in the world. The Canadian military theme from *Archangel* resurfaces in the figure of a leg-amputating alcoholic doctor, while the inbred sexual confusions of *Careful* reappear in the strange liaisons of his two sons. A doe-eyed, angelic female figure, who will sleep with just about anyone, is reminiscent of *Twilight of the Ice Nymphs*. Together this self-reflection makes *The Saddest Music in the World* a summation of his previous imagery, while spoofing various 1930s film genres such as the musical and the newsreel. Dressed up as a musical Olympics, the film ends with the Serb contestant defeating the American contestant, who has bought up various other contestants with false promises. This small triumph for little nations is an absurdity since both the Serbian representative and the American are rival sons of the same Canadian doctor. With its newsreel-style stereotyping of peoples in ethnic costume, *The Saddest Music in the World* continues Maddin's over-the-top treatment of nationality and global identity. In spite of situating the film in the 1930s, his representation of identity issues is postmodernist to the extreme.

Critical interpretation of Maddin's achievement ranges from complimenting him on his disavowal of the 'social-realist tendency in much of Canadian film' to recognizing his unique commitment to the 'painstaking reconstruction of lost or minor filmic styles.'[53] *Maclean's* film critic Brian Bergman termed Maddin's approach 'confounding, disturbing and visually brilliant cinema that repels and fascinates in equal measure.'[54]

When someone accustomed to mainstream feature films watches a Maddin film, either in black and white or colour, that person is made to reflect on the role of cinema in culture and how society normally constructs its social imagery through an emphasis on realism, of which there is precious little in Maddin's work. Surrealistic lunacy is a way of challenging audiences, which is why Maddin's work from the 1980s and 1990s attracted both critical attention and a niche audience. Pevere indicates that bringing out-of-date art forms into the present is a wake-up call for film audiences accustomed to sleep-walking through commercial features. Maddin's excursions into the beleaguered psyche and the torments of the subconscious are something that resonate more than the theory-driven world of most avant-garde productions.

The Winnipeg Film Group, to which Maddin belongs, has turned low budgets, cheesy sets, amateur acting, and an isolated cinematic location into a springboard for a troubled distinctness. What would seem to be a drawback has become an asset as its film-makers evolved a particular style in the 1980s.[55] 'Prairie postmodernism' is the term most often used to describe the Group's style and that of its most famous director.[56] Perhaps because the majority of its membership is composed of mainstream White males, Winnipeg Film Group films are populated by 'men inflicted with various psychological conditions' reflected in their physical (mainly facial) aberrations.[57] The end result from the Canadian perspective is 'one of the most fertile and idiosyncratic movements in the history of so-called regional filmmaking in Canada.'[58] That this out-of-the-way city found within its cultural self the origins of a whole new cinematic style is a tribute to the explosive power inherent in the intersection between isolation, multiculturalism, and individual creativity. If the metropolitan culture of Toronto could revel in its role as a welcoming platform for experimental film, so Winnipeg, with its contemporary sense of economic obscurity and faded architectural glory (the city's heyday was 1920–50), could serve as an inspiration for the faded cinematic glory of the silent era. If a culturally and cinematically marginalized country like Sweden could give the world a culture-specific cinematic genius like Ingmar Bergman, it is not surprising that a similarly marginalized Canada could give the world the idiosyncratic genius of Guy Maddin.

The distance between the experimental and the cult is not as great as one might think, especially if we relate the works of Snow and Maddin to the history of experimental film and the art movements that influenced it. Surrealist film-making in the 1920s, when silent cinema peaked, was a direct inspiration for Snow. This was the same period that has fascinated and inspired Maddin. During the 1920s, art movements such as German expressionism, Russian futurism, and surrealism influenced various national European cinemas. Maddin's films can be discussed in terms of the imagery and editing of Luis Buñuel, while Snow's can be related to Buñuel's colleague, Marcel Duchamp.[59] There is a joint legacy of inspiration for both artists.

As well, Canada's experimental film-makers, in rejecting the commercial, have followed the trajectory begun by Grierson at the NFB, when he sought to raise the documentary to an equal partnership with commercial cinema and in the process created a vital direction for Canadian film. For Snow, Wieland, and Maddin there are significant Canadian influences that inform and distinguish their work, be they the iconography of the Group of Seven or the ethnic mix of Winnipeg. In his introduction to contemporary Canadian experimental film-makers, Mike Hoolboom described the experimental as 'the minor literature of cinema, the poetry, the fringe, the underground.'[60] This may well be the case, but, even as a minor form, experimental film is a rejuvenating cinematic anti-force, a gravitational black hole that sucks the viewing audience into its bizarre worlds. Through Snow, Wieland, and Maddin, Canada has played a role in the international experimental and cult film traditions. This is a sign of the country's cinematic maturity and evidence of how excluded cinematic cultures can make a mark for themselves in minor forms such as the documentary, animation, and the experimental. Because of the inherent playfulness of Maddin's vision and its postmodern appeal, there is a chance that it may yet leave a mark on feature film-making. Maddin's escape from the gravitational pull of cult sensibility is not assured, but it is possible. Maddin has turned what was once conventional film-making (the silent film) into a new avant-garde. Turning approaches resurrected from the depths of film history into a contemporary art form is no mean feat.

CHAPTER THIRTEEN

Quebec's Next Generation: Lauzon to Turpin

The work of Quebec's film-makers that began in the mid-1960s climaxed with Arcand's masterful portrayal of the new secularized Quebec in *Déclin de l'empire américain* (1986). The founding generation encouraged the worldview of a new generation that had not grown up in the Duplessis era, but rather in the open world of the Quiet Revolution and the sovereignty-oriented rhetoric of the Parti Québécois. After sixteen years of modernizing Liberal rule (1960–76) and a decade of Parti Québécois transformation, Quebec was assured in its francophone identity and its distinctness. It was inevitable that the new generation would speak differently.

Interpreting Quebec society from the new, liberated perspective of collective confidence and self-assurance meant that Quebec history, its symbolic tradition, and its iconography could be challenged. Jean-Claude Lauzon (1953–97) was the intermediary, the herald of transition from the earlier period to the world of the 1990s and beyond. He pointed the way to the new generation represented by Robert Lepage (1958–), Denis Villeneuve (1967–), and André Turpin (1965–), none of whom knew anything else except the secularism of the post-Duplessis world and francophone dominance.

Lauzon was a working-class high-school drop-out whose father was a labourer with a grade two education. He returned to university, where he became an award-winning student film-maker and was offered $70,000 to turn his screenplay 'Piwi' into a film, which he did in 1982.[1] The film caused a political stir in Quebec because of its sexual violence. His second film, *Un zoo la nuit* (Night Zoo), won thirteen Genies in 1988, the largest number of Genies ever won by a single film. Initially he had been unable to get the film funded, but his reward was its opening of the Directors' Fortnight at Cannes. Sadly, Lauzon was to create only one other film, *Léolo* (1992), which was his masterpiece. He died tragically in 1997 in the crash of the bush plane he was flying in northern Quebec. He was thirty-five when *Un Zoo* became a sensation and not yet forty when *Léolo* challenged the popular imagination with its incredible imagery and style.

Un zoo won the best motion picture, best director, best original screenplay, best music, best editing, and best acting awards at the Genies, plus seven other categories. Stylistically, it was conceived as 'a complete subversion of the Hollywood action flick.'[2] The film tells the story of a criminal released from jail who is pursued by corrupt and sadistic cops who want the money he has stashed away. His father is dying, and the two men reconnect and then try to pursue their mutual love of hunting and fishing, activities dear to Lauzon himself. In the end, the son steals his dying father from his hospital bed to go to the city zoo to shoot an elephant. The final scene in the film has the son ritually purify his father's naked body by washing it and then lying down beside it. This scene is meant to balance the opening scene of the movie, in which the son is being raped in prison. During the course of the film, the cop that ordered the rape is dutifully hunted down by his victim.

Bill Marshall, a European scholar of Quebec cinema, has pointed out how *Un zoo* uses the two male leads (the young man and the old man) to symbolize a continuity between the urban working class and Quebec's rural/pastoral and wilderness past.[3] The theme of continuity is essential. As a child, Lauzon knew the introspective Quebec world of the 1950s, and then as an adult he knew the contemporary Quebec world of 'cultural globalization and the detraditionalization of identity,' and he created a natural bridge between the two worlds.[4] When Montreal film critic Jean Marcel wrote about *Un zoo* in *Le Devoir*, his article was titled 'Un cinéma qui reflète le Québec d'aujourd'hui.'[5] This 'Quebec of to-day' was still imbued with its Catholic identity, which is evident in the description of the film offered by *Le Droit*: 'une version moderne de la parabole de l'enfant prodigue' – the biblical parable of the prodigal son.[6]

After Lauzon's untimely death, Jean Marcel wrote a tribute in which he remarked on Lauzon's innate ability to combine tenderness and violence.[7] The power of *Un zoo* was such that it had grossed $1 million in Quebec within three months of its release.[8] But in typical Lauzon style, the auteur refused a $100,000 Quebec film prize to fund his next film because of his criticism of how funding worked in Quebec. Lauzon was constantly in a battle with Quebec's cultural bureaucracy and, in fact, made his living directing television commercials, which may very well have given him the surrealistic sensibility that frames his masterpiece, *Léolo*.

Léolo is a difficult film to characterize or to summarize. On one level, it is a coming-of-age story of twelve-year-old Léo Lozeau, a son of a francophone working-class family. Léo keeps a diary, in which he insists that his name is Léolo, Italian for Leo. He creates a fantasy world in which his own conception is semi-immaculate (his mother was impregnated by falling in a Montreal market on a tomato on which a peasant in Sicily had masturbated during its harvesting). Léo lusts after a neighbouring Italian girl, who prostitutes herself for his grandfather. In revenge, Léo tries to murder his grandfather in an amazing scene which the syndicated American film critic Roger Ebert called 'one of the most astonishing I have seen.'[9] In fact, Ebert stated that 'Lauzon's film contains images no other film would dare to show.'[10] For example, Léolo's father and mother are obsessed with bowel movements, with the father dispensing laxatives weekly in a ritual parody of Holy Communion in order to maintain family health. Léolo's sisters are insane, and his bodybuilder brother lets himself be bullied by the local Anglo thug, even though he has the physical power to thrash the fellow. The madness and dysfunction are reflected in a tension-filled scene of bestiality that one critic described as 'almost unwatchable.'[11] Lauzon's Quebec is a place of unredeemed psychopathological angst.

American critics were enthralled with the film. *Time* magazine named it one of the top ten movies of 1993, claiming that there is 'no movie bolder in fashioning domestic tragedy into art.'[12] In Canada, *Maclean's* magazine ranked it as the number one movie of 1992.[13] Brian D. Johnson's review of the film in *Maclean's* was titled 'Rebel Masterpiece.'[14] He claimed that the film 'elevates Canadian cinema to new heights of creative ambition and achievement' and compared Lauzon to Fellini and Truffaut in their prime.[15] Such exuberant praise was not matched in that year's Genies, where the film won only the original screenplay award. It was Cronenberg's year to be lauded for *Naked Lunch*.

Lauzon is quoted as saying this about his masterpiece: 'This is really a movie on the edge. If we hadn't taken the time to film it properly with the right music and ambience, it could have been really crass and ugly.'[16] Scenes with Léolo masturbating with a piece of liver, which his brother later eats at dinner, or the rape of a cat by one of a gang of adolescents are disgusting, and yet Lauzon is able to infuse both events with symbolic meaning while retaining their offensiveness. One of the key elements in his redemption of the ugly is the amazing music he chose for the film, including hypnotic Arabic drumming, choral dirges, the throaty blues of Tom Waits, and even the Rolling Stones. The film has a strong autobiographical undercurrent, with the use of the Lozeau name to parallel Lauzon and the extensive mental illness in the film taken from Lauzon's own family experience.

Originally, Lauzon had tried to get the film done in English but was rebuffed. He then attempted to escape the boundaries of his national identity by making the majority of the film in English, the language in which Léolo speaks to himself and to us. His casting the charismatic Pierre Bourgault, a leading separatist orator and founder of the Rassemblement pour l'Indépendance Nationale in the late 1960s and one of Lauzon's professors in university, in the role of a silent reader of Léo's diary (in one scene, he walks through a candle-lit sanctuary as if he were some kind of priest reading a sacred text or a breviary) could not but arouse commentary and speculation among Quebec audiences. Bourgault, who died to reverential acclaim in 2003, and whose oratory was excessive and passionate, was the most outspoken of early Quebec separatists. That his role should be mostly a silent one is not an accident, in spite of Lauzon's protestations that the film has no political connotations. As well, the whole issue of assimilation of immigrants into francophone society is played up in the relationship between Léolo and his Italian neighbour, Bianca. The young Quebec boy who is confused about his identity lusts after the unattainable other, which he wishes to be. The metaphor is obvious, as is the film's strong critique of Quebec's uni-lingual and uni-cultural francophone goals.

A film in which Quebec's leading separatist is silenced, a muscular brother cowers before an Anglo half his size, most of the francophones are insane, the music is non-Quebec, and the film itself is narrated primarily in English cannot be anything else but an allegory of a national identity crisis. Only Léolo's nurturing, tolerant, and hugely present mother is characterized somewhat sympathetically. She is the non-judgmental source of life that exists beyond politically constructed identities.[17] Marshall describes the film as enunciating Quebec's two most basic myths – the primordial mother and a lost paradise.[18] Unable to take on the dominant society to prove his manhood, Léolo can only escape his Quebec mother through a fantasy of paradise, a totally different and 'other' identity which becomes an idyllic landscape in the final scene.[19]

That Lauzon did not make another film during the five years before his death was a statement of his alienation from the cinematic world as it existed in Quebec, but it may also have been an expression of a silence resulting from an auteur's having poured so much of himself into his creation.[20] When one is, in the words of Marcel Jean, 'un cinéaste sauvage, qui n'avait pas été domestiqué par le système,' one awaits the right, fulfilling, and deep moment for the next act of provocation.[21] 'I think my work as a director,' Lauzon said in an interview in Cannes at the screening of *Léolo*, 'is to be able to show our deepest fears.'[22] But rather than create pure horror or total revulsion, he put those fears within an envelope of preposterous unreality. In this way, that which is most threatening is made palatable (such as hanging one's grandfather through an amazing system of ropes and pulleys). *Léolo* is a work of genius, the most outstanding Quebec film of the 1990s.

Lauzon showed that there were things to say and images to create about Quebec that could surpass a masterpiece like Arcand's *Jésus de Montréal*, while still articulating basic paradigms in the culture. Lauzon proved that not all was said and done about contemporary Quebec. Its ongoing subconscious traumas had come to roost in the street-smart kids of the working class.[23] This was the challenge his work laid before Lepage, Villeneuve, and Turpin. Could they surpass the brutal energy and honesty of Lauzon, as he had surpassed Arcand?

Lepage was born only four years after Lauzon, but he already belonged to a different world. Although he is officially classified as belonging to the 'baby boomer' generation like Lauzon, his sensibility is closer to that of Villeneuve and Turpin than to Lauzon because he did not know 'the fifties' that belonged to the old Quebec and he did not begin making films till the mid-1990s. He was born in a poor family in Quebec City (similar to Lauzon's working-class roots), which had adopted two English-Canadian children. Because of alopecia, an immune disease that caused him to lose all his hair, he had to deal with his unusual appearance at an early age. He found salvation in theatre and its world of adopted identities and masks. Here he became a playwright and the director of his own theatre company, Ex Machina, both of which roles eventually provided him with an international reputation and an entrée into the esoteric world of opera, which he has also directed. After his success as a theatre director and playwright he turned to film. His first film, *Le Confessional*, dealt with the mysteries of Quebec City, the city he was born in and in which he continues to live.[24]

The film was an international co-production with a budget of $4 million.[25] Lepage wrote the script with a goal of showing how the past haunts the present by using a historical incident as his framing event.[26] In 1952 Alfred Hitchcock had made a film in Quebec City titled *I Confess*, the story of a priest dealing with the confession of a murderer. Lepage creates fictional scenes about the production of *I Confess* that suggest that a taxi driver (the father of the main character in the film), who is driving Hitchcock around town, is the man who fathered the cousin/brother of the main character in *Le Confessional*. Like *I Confess*, *Le Confessional* probes the dark secrets that underlie the illusions and false identities that we are offered by family and society and ultimately film itself. The main metaphor in the film is Quebec City's Pont de Québec, where the brother's mother committed suicide and the main character symbolically carries a young child on his shoulders. One important 'bridge' is the lead, played by the actor Lothaire Bluteau, who also played 'Jesus' in Arcand's *Jésus de Montréal*, a film in which Lepage also acted. It is as if Lepage was using the script he wrote, the locale he chose, and the actors' credits to have his debut film become inextricably bound to the history of film in Quebec. Likewise it is a spanning of generations, a linking of two distant shores (the brothers) into a single paternal unity, and finally, it is a bridge between historical periods. The film asks how different is the world of 1990s Quebec, with its secularism, diversity, and sexual tolerance, from that of the Duplessis era, in which the earlier film was made? He suggests that human issues don't change much from era to era. Each era lives within its own illusions, and self-distancing from the past may very well be the fundamental illusion of 1990s Quebec.

Le Confessional triumphed at the Genies in 1995, winning best motion picture and best director. This success led Lepage to make *Le Polygraphe* the next year. The film was based on Lepage's stage play and explored the difficult nuances of a mysterious murder, inspired in part by Lepage's own knowledge of a real murder case. Again there is a 'film-within-a-film' motif in which the auditioning for a part in a film based on a real murder ends up in murder itself. The film was not accorded much recognition. Two years later, Lepage rebounded with *Nô*, a comedy about the FLQ crisis of 1970 that received more attention and better reviews. *Take One* termed it a 'jaunty follow-up to his dourly Kafkaesque *Le Polygraphe*.'[27] The scene is the Osaka World's Fair of 1970, where a

Quebec actress is performing a French farce at the Canadian pavilion. On discovering that she is pregnant, she contacts her boyfriend in Quebec, who is part of a farcical FLQ cell. The title of the film comes from traditional Japanese Nôh theatre, with its stylized conventions of dialogue, costuming, and staging. The film cost a mere $1 million, about a quarter of the budget for the previous two Lepage films.[28]

The multi-layered meaning in Nôh drama is reflected in the meaning of the film, with its subtle nod toward the 1995 independence referendum and the close Yes/No vote. Obviously Lepage preferred the 'No' side. In a 1999 interview, he argued that Quebec was more than its francophone roots.[29] A film like *Nô* would appeal to the anti-sovereignty crowd and to anglophones because it made fun of separatism. One Toronto film magazine called it 'wickedly hilarious.'[30] An article in the English daily *Montreal Gazette* concluded that Lepage had made *Le Confessional* for the producers because it was so well received, *Le Polygraphe* for the critics because it was so difficult, and *Nô* for the people because it was a comedy and popular.[31]

It was inevitable that Lepage's lifestyle as an international jet-setting playwright and stage director and his desire to make Quebec's culture expansive and extroverted would lead to his making an English-language feature.[32] Arcand had tried this in the mid-1990s with his failed *Love and Human Remains*, a film version of a gritty urban play by then Alberta playwright Brad Fraser. Lepage did much better with *Possible Worlds* (2000). He adapted a play by John Mighton, whose plot 'verges on the indescribable.'[33]

The main character lives simultaneously in a variety of parallel universes. He remains the same, but the universes change as he appears in one and then the other and returns to previous ones. The continuity in this strange world is provided by the woman he loves, who herself appears in different roles and identities. This bizarre narrative is framed by an investigation into his murder and the theft of his brain. Part science fiction, part philosophical treatise, part *policier* (the investigating cop is played by Sean McCann), *Possible Worlds* is equally confusing and enthralling. The independent American murder-thriller *Memento* (2001), which succeeds in the difficult task of narrating its chronological events linearly, but backwards, comes closest to the spirit of *Possible Worlds*.

Lepage's directorial versatility and his prolific creativity on stage and screen have made him a Quebec wunderkind. With *Le Confessional*, he mirrored his own birth family – a bilingual taxi-driver father and adopted siblings – and his own sexual orientation, while in *Possible Worlds* he reached toward his own multiplicity of identities, which the film suggests infects us all. Although Lepage has his share of critics, the achievements of his theatre and film careers indicate a major talent.[34] Making four features in six years sets him apart from anyone else of the new generation.

The next most prolific director is Denis Villeneuve (1967–), who has made two feature films – *Un 32 août sur terre* (August 32nd on Earth) in 1998 and *Maelström* in 2000. The first film never received commercial theatrical release in either English Canada or the United States, even though most of the film is set in an American desert.[35] A young model has a car accident, which results in her deciding to change her life by having a baby. She turns to her friend to fulfil her wish. The two characters basically fill the screen with their light-hearted yet edgy story. *Take One* termed it 'an existential road movie with a Generation X relationship,' which suggests a certain alienated hopelessness.[36] Although it had a typical undercurrent of anxiety over life's aimlessness that some consider a hallmark of Generation X sensibility, it also seemed to echo the introspective universe of the 1960s generation of Quebec film-makers, who began their careers with then popular New Wave introspection about the lives of the young and urbane. In fact, Villeneuve, who was just thirty when he made the film, referred to the film as encapsulating 'the French New Wave's liberty, freedom and breath.'[37] But the mood of this new generation's films is a more playful self-parody. The rather curious but understandable marriage of early 1960s sensibility with that of the late 1990s represented a generational make-over, which took the same subject but expressed it in a different spirit.

Although *Un 32 août sur terre* was screened at Cannes and was Canada's official entry for that year's Academy Awards, it was Villeneuve's second feature, *Maelström*, that marked his inauguration into celebrity status. That film won the Best Canadian Film Award at the Montreal World Film Festival. The film is best known for its narrator – a talking fish whose head is chopped off repeatedly throughout the film. Again the lead is a young woman. This time she is a disillusioned boutique owner who has recently had an abortion (graphic opening scene) and like the previous film has an accident which changes her life. She strikes a middle-aged working-class man while driving. He dies soon afterward, and the woman enters a journey of self-understanding and healing involving the man's son. The father was a fishmonger, whose job it was to kill fish, ergo the irony of the narrating fish.

We see the world from an underwater perspective. If the singular metaphor of the empty desert framed the first film, then its opposite, the ocean, is the key one in the second. One American reviewer considered Villeneuve as moving in the same circles as 'David Lynch's brand of bizarre cinema.'[38] Another American review played on the fish pun in its title: 'Quirky "Maelstrom" Ultimately Flounders.'[39]

If American reviewers found the film bizarre, the Canadian film establishment was captivated. The film won best picture, best director, best original screenplay, and best cinematography at the Genies in 2001.[40] Admittedly, Villeneuve is considered to have an 'oddball style ... reflecting the angst of a generation,' but the awards were a recognition that Quebec continued to set the standard for alluring imagery, innovative narratives, and introspective characterization.[41] In an interview after the release of *Maelström*, Villeneuve indicated that, whether he liked it or not, his films tended to be more and more European.[42] The fish, the ocean, the immigrant fishmonger who dies, and his Norwegian oceanographer son are all echoes of Europe and the fishery that first brought Europeans to North America. But the ocean is more than a historical or even an aesthetic concept; the ocean is the source of life itself, which harks back to the abortion image that launches the film.[43]

Villeneuve's work is still too limited in quantity and it is too early in his career to be making any definitive judgment or interpretation. Nevertheless, it is obvious that he is a major auteur talent who has the backing of Quebec's leading producer, Roger Frappier of Max Films. Villeneuve sees himself as part of a new generation. 'J'aime travailler avec des réalisateurs de mon âge,' he said.[44] His closest collaborator is André Turpin (1965–), who was the cinematographer on *Maelström* as well as *Un 32 août sur terre*. Friends as well as collaborators, the two film-makers are often viewed as expressing a youthful Montreal milieu and the 'loft-dwelling, latte-guzzling people they know best.'[45]

Turpin's feature, *Un crabe dans la tête* (A Crab in the Head) came out in 2001 and was titled *Soft Shell Man* in English. Turpin wrote, directed, and filmed the movie, and so appropriately won Quebec's Jutra Award in 2002 for best screenplay, best director, and best cinematography. It is the story of a thirty-year-old underwater photographer who lives life on the surface, as it were, lying about everything and displaying a primary interest in seducing women. Turpin says the story begins with himself, who 'was one of these compulsive charmers who couldn't say no.'[46] Already lauded for his cinematography in other films, Turpin was able to use this extraordinary talent to make a visually appealing film on a budget of only $400,000.[47] In an interview about *Un crabe*, Turpin admitted that he was getting tired of the kind of films he and Villeneuve had been making about his generation and that he expected they would move beyond what the interviewer called 'the generational identity slot.'[48]

Of course, Lauzon, Lepage, Villeneuve, and Turpin do not exhaust the new directorial talent pool in Quebec cinema. Among the contenders are Louis Bélanger, with his 1999 film *Post Mortem*, and Catherine Martin, with *Mariages* (2001). Both are first features. Writer/director Bélanger won the Jutra for best first feature, and then the best screenplay at the Genies. But these serious film-makers are very much part of the art-house cinema circuit and its confines. In contrast, Quebeckers flock to clichéd comedies such as *Les Boys* (1998), *Les Boys 2* (1999), and *Les Boys 3* (2001), with low-level locker and bar-room humour. The first two films in the series grossed over $11 million in box-office sales in Quebec, entitling them to the Golden Reel Award, which goes to the highest box-office grossing Canadian film of the year.[49] Then there are action films like Michel Jetté's *Hochelaga* (2000), about Montreal's motorcycle gang wars. Charles Binamé released in 2002 an auteur remake of the 1950s film *Séraphin*, which also had a run as a television series. The film grossed $8 million in Quebec, indicative of the power of classic Quebec themes.[50] This diversity of genres indicates an industry that continues to generate everything from schlock to high art. For some, it creates profit; for others, it builds reputations; and for film critics and historians, it generates a steady stream of products requiring commentary and analysis.

The existence of a Quebec national cinema is confirmed by the new generation of film-makers, who have added freshness to tradition. Bill Marshall recognized the new wave when he lauded recent Quebec cinema for its 'pluralizing, anti-hegemonic potential.'[51] The next generation, which began with Lauzon's critique of Quebec's francophone identity, continues to move toward a multicultural understanding of Quebec's role in the global community and its continental anglophone American reality. The identity which the previous generation had fought to create as the new Québécois is precisely the identity that this new generation is deconstructing.

CHAPTER FOURTEEN

English Canada's Next Generation: McDonald to Burns

In the 1990s the language of English-Canadian cinema changed dramatically. The range of films and styles generated by the tax-shelter 1970s was so disparate that one could say that there was no united cinematic culture or expression characterizing English-Canadian film in comparison to Quebec cinema, which was highly introspective about its own society and its changes. The work of Torontonians Bruce McDonald (1954–) and Don McKellar (1962–), the most prominent practitioners of the so-called 'Toronto new wave,' created a more unified statement for English-Canadian cinema. Added to this wave was the urban spirit of Vancouver's Lynne Stopkewich (1968–) and Calgary's Gary Burns (1960–). They are the Anglo-Canadian counterparts to Lauzon, Lepage, Villeneuve, and Turpin, and together they gave a certain unity to the world of English-Canadian feature films.

Toronto-born Bruce McDonald can be viewed as the equivalent of Jean-Claude Lauzon. Although McDonald has made five feature films, compared to the two that Lauzon made before his tragic death, the same spirit of anti-establishment rebellion that characterized Lauzon is evident in McDonald. Don McKellar is a multi-talented scriptwriter, actor, and director, a renaissance man who began his career in theatre. He parallels the equally multi-talented scriptwriter, director, actor, and playwright Robert Lepage. Lynne Stopkewich, who comes originally from Montreal's anglophone community, is English Canada's equivalent of Denis Villeneuve because of her focus on female characters. Gary Burns, while older than André Turpin, shares with him a cynical Generation-X mentality with its sour view of human relationships and its sympathy for his generation's struggle to make sense of an alienating urban (and suburban) environment.

Bruce McDonald, who is best known for his rock music / road movie trilogy of *Roadkill* (1990), *Highway 61* (1992), and *Hard Core Logo* (1996), is the oldest of this generation of film-makers. Originally, his films spoke to a whole new audience of young Anglo-Canadian cinephiles, who felt their lives, attitudes, and interests had been finally discovered. They could see themselves on the screeen for the first time. Pop music's rough and tumble universe of failed expectations and its relationship to the American cultural juggernaut was something the young inhabited in their imaginations, and McDonald expressed that imagination with humour, sex, drugs, and lots of edgy music. The fact that his trilogy had roots in a generational reality gave it a certain cult status and opened English-Canadian cinema to a younger audience.

McDonald was one of the of founding figures of what quickly came to be called the 'Toronto new wave.'[1] He was a graduate of Toronto's Ryerson Polytechnic University film program and was instrumental in creating the Liaison of Independent Filmmakers of Toronto (LIFT), a film co-op, to which aspiring young Toronto film-makers gravitated. This generation had 'virtually no contact with the documentary tradi-tion' of the NFB.[2] McDonald served as an 'intellectual' spokesperson for this new generation when he edited a famous issue of *Cinema Canada*, titled the 'Outlaw Issue' (October 1988, no. 156), devoted to the views of the new generation. He had started creating an intellectual space for this new film community as early as 1985, when he wrote a provocative public letter titled 'Dear Norman, What Is to Be Done?' which he addressed to Norman Jewison as the titular head of the English-Canadian directorial establishment. The article described how McDonald was Jewison's driver on the making of *Agnes of God* and what he learned in that role. 'Toronto independent film is beginning to dance ...' he announced to Jewison. 'We need to get our work shown ...' he informed the master boldly and then denounced 'a system that is hesitant, if not resistant in its support for artists, and a cultural identity as nebulous and elusive as the American Goliath is overwhelming.'[3] McDonald cast his new generation as the heroic David, who would work in Canada on Canadian subjects and not sell out to the Holly-wood philistines, represented by Jewison.

McDonald's first feature began as a documentary about a Toronto rock band, but when the band disbanded, McDonald hired Don McKellar, then in his mid-twenties, to create a fictional story on the same theme. With a crew of nine, an eventual budget of $250,000, and a fifteen-day shoot with black and white film stock, McDonald created a film that announced to a whole new generation of English Canadians that their era had begun.[4] Maybe distant echoes of fellow Torontonian Shebib's *Goin' down the Road* were resonating in McDonald's mind when he shot Don McKellar's script using the punk sound of Nash the Slash and the soulful Cowboy Junkies, but the spirit was radically different. Instead of country hicks coming to the big city to be tormented by their lack of sophistication, it was city slickers heading to the country that created the satirical drama. The end result was a mixed bag – in the words of one critic, 'badly acted, sophomoric and ... funny, high-spirited ... heavy-handed satire.'[5] The story of Ramona (Valerie Buhagiar), a rock promoter's assistant sent to northern Ontario to find a lost band and get them back on track, has her meeting an aspiring serial killer (Don McKellar) and assorted other weirdos and losers. '*Roadkill* was the first Canadian film ...,' according to Katherine Monk, to express, 'hipster chic.'[6] The film won the prize for the best Canadian feature film at Toronto's International Film Festival. The road theme, the music theme, and the anti-bourgeois absurdist situations and characters (McDonald admires Jean-Luc Godard's films) were all combined with a Group of Seven backdrop to forge a *nouveau* Anglo-Canadian identity on the screen.

With his reputation enhanced by *Roadkill*, McDonald moved quickly to do his second feature, *Highway 61*, which had a budget of $1 million.[7] Again McDonald had McKellar write the script and star in the film. Valerie Buhagiar appears as a *femme fatale*, and McKellar plays the naïve Pokey Jones, a northern Ontario small-town barber, who is gladly seduced into living out his New Orlean's music fantasies via a secret stash of drugs, a corpse, and a quintessential 1961 mint-condition black Ford Fairlane. As the odd couple set out on Highway 61, which will take them from Thunder Bay to New Orleans, they are pursued by a satanic American figure called Mr Skin, who wants the soul of the corpse in the coffin. Along the way, American society is presented as a psychotic, fame-obsessed, and gun-crazy culture in which money and drugs destroy happiness. The only genuine American characters in the film are the downtrodden and oppressed black minority, and it is with them that Pokey finds revelation and salvation.

The film is filled with role reversals that make the satire work. For example, the virginal Pokey is deflowered against his will by the flaming red-haired Jackie Bangs in a church graveyard during a downpour. Satan turns out to be a suburbanite with a fire and photo obsession who turns America's barbecue heaven into a suburban hell. The neighbours watch the pyrotechnics from their lawn chairs as if they were watching a show put on by a television evangelist. A mansion owned by paranoid and self-glorifying rock stars, where guests shoot live chickens for supper, serves as a metaphor for American culture. One analysis of *Highway 61* considers the film to be an expression of the Canadian national psyche's dreams of escape to warmer climes.[8] It also points out how the film parodies the American 'Bonnie and Clyde' road movie because it ends in the peaceful stillness of a bayou, representing serenity, paradise, and redemption, instead of a hail of bullets.[9] The Americans go to hell, while Canadians go to heaven is the patriotic moral of the story, at least, after English Canadians realize how illusory and false their dreams of America are (a similar theme appears in the contemporaneous Quebec comedy *La Florida*). For these reasons, the film can be considered a radical 'decolonizing of Canadian cinema' and of the English-Canadian film audience, which is so attuned to American cinematic discourse.[10] No other English-Canadian film of the 1990s spoke so critically of the-escape-from-Canada mindset, so favourably of its down-home Canadian naïveté, and so confidently of the importance of being un-American.

When American critics viewed this Canadian portrayal of the United States, they drew two conclusions. Internationally syndicated film columnist Roger Ebert commented on how McKellar and Buhagiar 'look surprisingly like real people.'[11] For the *Washington Post* the film was 'offbeat' and a 'masterpiece.'[12] In other words, the film was a delightful Altmanesque portrayal of American life as seen through characters whose Canadianness fitted the peculiarity attached to them by Americans. Unlike American actors, these unknown performers seemed 'real.' This theme was taken up again when the *San Francisco Chronicle* asked rhetorically of a later McDonald film: 'Is this chaotic band of whacked-out geniuses really being played by actors?'[13] There was so much apparent reality to McDonald's films that they seemed more like documentaries than features, which is a curious yet fascinating conclusion considering that he was not trained in the documentary mode. The documentary feel of his fiction is rooted in the 'reality' of his characters, his locations, and his self-mocking, unorthodox portrayal of human desires. By working outside the constructed world of American imagery and star idolatry, his films seemed refreshingly 'real,' that is, different.

McDonald took a break from the road movie scenario with *Dance Me Outside* (1995), based on W.P. Kinsella's 1977 book of Native stories. Although McDonald and McKellar wrote the script, it was an adaptation of another writer's sensibility, one that was controversial in its day when arguments over 'cultural appropriation' raged in literary circles and Kinsella's non-Aboriginal heritage was considered by some as an inappropriate background for the writing of spoofs on Aboriginal characters. 'The conventional (and disappointing) Hollywood storytelling techniques of executive producer Norman Jewison are clearly evident' is *Take One*'s accurate assessment of McDonald's diversion into a mainstream format.[14] It would seem that turning this film into a 'real' story with a conventional narrative was a regression. So it was a relief that McDonald completed his trilogy with *Hard Core Logo* the following year.

Hard Core Logo is based on a 1993 book by Canadian writer Michael Turner.[15] It tells the story of a reunited punk band that is making its last tour across western Canada in a beat-up delivery van. The now empty and dilapidated milk van serves as a metaphor for the passengers' lost innocence. McDonald claimed the film 'pulls the rug from under the male bravado, poser thing.'[16] The lead in the film is played by Hugh Dillon, himself a singer in Toronto's Headstones band. Like so many other portrayals of naïve, failing, happy-go-lucky male losers in English-Canadian buddy films, beginning with *Goin' down the Road*, this one captures the inevitable tensions between dreams and reality. For McDonald, a Canadian performer's unhappiness with a national horizon for success leads only to tragedy (this is pre–Celine Dion divahood). The rockers live in a fantasyland of their own self-importance, and when reality hits them hard, their egos collapse. 'The right chord of insolence and wit' was a valid assessment of the film's spirit.[17] The director's doleful creation of a Canadian attempt to emulate American-style on-the-road freedom and macho individualism is refreshing and playful. McDonald himself spoke mockingly to this *Easy Rider* fantasy when he had a publicity photo of himself – on a Harley with scruffy hair, in leather and jeans, with a cigarette hanging from his mouth – accompany an article on his films. The caption reads teasingly: 'Canada's outlaw filmmaker.'[18] *Hard Core Logo* itself came to be viewed as a 'mockumentary' because it was shot with hand-held cameras and its supposed subject matter was a 'real' band. McDonald had shown that satire, parody, and irreverence were a generational specialty. The absurdist magical realism of his mockumentary acted as a liberation from traditional documentary realism.

With the completion of the trilogy, McDonald turned to television with a highly successful Canadian comedy series titled 'Twitch City,' which he produced and directed and which starred Don McKellar. The series was shot in Toronto's Kensington Market area, where both McDonald and McKellar live. After a five-year hiatus from film, McDonald returned to shoot *Claire's Hat*, a film that has never been released. He was now forty-one. With a budget of over $10 million from Canada's media and film giant Alliance Atlantis (via Robert Lantos's company Serendipity Point Films), McDonald could afford to use American stars in this story of a 'hapless *jeune fille* (Juliette Lewis) from Montreal's east end, who winds up in Toronto, linguistically challenged, chased by thugs and wanted by the police.'[19] In hyping the film before its release, McDonald said, 'This one looks like a movie. It's beautiful. It's got good actors in it. It's fun. It's a good caper movie ...'[20] But the experience turned out to be a disaster. Making a conventional movie, first attempted with *Dance Me Outside*, was not something McDonald could do successfully. In a revealing and candid interview after *Claire* was not released, McDonald repudiated the film, calling it 'a shit movie.'[21] He blamed Robert Lantos, Canada's premier film producer, for talking him into a movie using known American stars. In response to this self-judged inauthenticity, McDonald did a private movie using outs from the original editing to comment on the film's mistakes. 'The big corporate machine,' with which McDonald had made his movie pact, did not respond.[22] In a very real way, McDonald became one of his own flawed characters from the trilogy – a Canadian who thought he could make a deal with the American approach and win. He lost just as his fictional characters did, but his acknowledgment of this failure only enhanced his nationalist commitment. McDonald was a rebel with a cause – the cause of anti-corporate Canadian nationalism, in the tradition of Joyce Wieland. When a director makes his reputation as a young rebel making youth-oriented rock and roll films, the challenge of speaking for a middle-aging generation is significant. Hopefully, it will not be insurmountable.

His original partner in the film arts, Don McKellar, has a less problematic history. Originally an actor and writer for collective theatre, McKellar has become a Canadian celebrity with a 'prickly, nebbish persona' comparable with that of the American comic writer, actor, and film director Woody Allen.[23] His scriptwriting for McDonald's first two comedies has been overshadowed by his performances in both films, and in others such as Atom Egoyan's *Exotica*. The thin, wimpy-faced, soft-spoken, and wiry-voiced McKellar is now a recognized entity in the country, not so much because of his film roles, but because of his television appearances in *Twitch City* and other youth-oriented productions. He is offered up as the Anglo-Canadian voice of his generation. In 1994 he co-wrote *Thirty-Two Short Films about Glenn Gould*, a feature film that won a number of Genies. The producer was Toronto's Rhombus Media, which went on to produce McKellar's directorial film debut, *Last Night*, in 1999. McKellar was the auteur, who wrote the story set in Toronto dealing with the last night before the end of the world. Everyone knows the end is coming, and the film follows the frantic activities of a number of Torontonians as they prepare for the end, each in his or her own bizarre way. Of course, McKellar plays his usual emotionally withdrawn persona. The cast for the film included Canadian actors Sarah Polley, Sandra Oh, Geneviève Bujold, Callum Keith Rennie, and even David Cronenberg.

McKellar was only in his mid-thirties when *Last Night* won the Prix de la Jeunesse at Cannes in 1998 and the Jutra at the Genies for his directorial debut. That same year, McKellar shared the best screenplay Genie for his scriptwriting on *The Red Violin*, that year's best motion picture and an internationally distributed co-production. *Last Night* was positively reviewed in the foreign press as 'the perfect antidote to ... [American] fire-and-fury apocalypse.'[24] With the millennium approaching, the U.S. film industry was producing the usual disaster films, such as the special-effects driven, top-grossing *Armageddon*, so that little *Last Night* came across as a breath of normality and freshness. 'Only in Canada can you get away with a film like this,' wrote one British reviewer.[25] The film had much in common with the McDonald trilogy. First, it was made for a mere $2 million, while Cronenberg's contemporaneous sci-fi extravaganza *eXistenZ* cost $31 million.[26] Second, *Last Night* was filled with an 'awkward charm' that made comic heroes and villains ordinary mortals with common emotions and attitudes.[27] It was a celebration of the ordinary rather than an expedition into the psychic deep. When discussing his influences, McKellar listed his own generation – Bruce McDonald, Atom Egoyan, Patricia Rozema, and François Girard (his co-writer on *Thirty-Two Short Films about Glenn Gould* and *The Red Violin*) – as a complete Canadian context of his film work.[28] Because McKellar has situated himself as a recognizable Canadian figure in numerous films and become a symbol of this male generation's overwhelmed psyche, he is among the first Canadian actors, along with Molly Parker, to serve as a draw for contemporary Canadian films. Canada's *Take One* film magazine presented McKellar as a team player whose multifaceted career has real potential when it speculated, 'Time will tell whether McKellar will prove himself to be a stand-alone auteur or continue on his well-trodden path of being a fine film collaborator.'[29]

The most important woman film director of this new generation is Lynne Stopkewich, whose film *Kissed* (1997) 'cemented our national image as sexual deviants abroad.'[30] She co-wrote the screenplay and directed the film, thereby launching her auteur career. *Kissed* is the disturbing story of a young woman necrophile who gets a job in a funeral home in order to have sex with the corpses of young men. The film is based on a 1990s short story from Canadian writer Barbara Gowdy's collection *We So Seldom Look on Love*, a story which is itself based on a real-life incident in the United States in which a woman was apprehended for having sex with a body in a hearse. While the premise of the film is bizarre, Stopkewich's treatment of the subject is impressive. 'The original story was very poetic,' Stopkewich explained in an interview. 'I was trying to find, as much as possible, the cinematic equivalent for the experience I had when I was reading the story.'[31] What Stopkewich was trying to do was to get 'over the shock and horror of the necrophilia.'[32] She succeeded. Brian D. Johnson concluded that she had created in the character of Sandra (played by twenty-four-year-old Vancouver actor Molly Parker) 'a tender, graceful and empathetic portrait of a woman who has sex with corpses.'[33] The film cost under $1 million to make.[34]

The achievement of turning a taboo subject into an understandable (if not acceptable) activity is certainly a credit to such a young director. Roger Ebert described the portrayal of the sex scene in this way: 'The dead are so lonely. When she comforts them with a farewell touch from the living, the room fills with light, and an angelic choir sings in orgasmic female voices.'[35] The film is basically a portrayal of spirituality because Sandra approaches the dead reverentially as if necrophilia was a 'sacred ceremony.'[36] She seeks to 'cross over' to the land of the dead through reverential sex with the bodies, and so either enter their 'lives' or bring them back to her life. For Sandra, the dead are alive, more so than the living. In fact, she finds sex with a live male unappealing. Molly Parker's convincing performance as the freckle-faced, green-eyed necrophile has turned her into the female equivalent of Don McKellar – a quirky hero so unlike American stars. She won a Genie for the part and then went on to act in the *Twitch City* series. Canadian audiences value the unusual screen presence that seems to characterize these young Canadian stars precisely because they lack conventional Hollywood sex appeal.[37]

While on the surface the conclusion of one American reviewer seems valid ('... our neighbors to the north, despite their dowdy reputation, are being swept by a plague of psychosexual pathology ... or just plain silliness'),[38] underneath there is a feminist and nationalist statement. In feminist terms, the film celebrates the hero's female sexuality, while condemning the male funeral director's implied necrophilia. In nationalist terms, the film expresses the overcoming of 'the guilt that sex has historically carried in Canadian culture.'[39] While American sexual culture can approach necrophilia either as a disgusting and perverted crime or as a joke (two extremes), only a Canadian director would dare make such a repulsive act a source of spiritual redemption or enlightenment. Geoff Pevere, a critic imbued with Canadian film values, described Molly Parker's portrayal as 'virtually luminescent,' while the previously quoted American critic completely ignored the characterization and focused solely on the sordidness of necrophilia.[40] There is even a Romeo and Juliet aspect to the story because Sandra's living lover must kill himself to be united with her in love. As well there are echoes of the Greek myth of Eurydice and Orpheus and the one-way crossing of the River Styx to the land of the shades. The multiple literary allusions of the film are a tribute to a young director's surprisingly mature engagement with her material. Like Cronenberg, she can play with the horror genre and overcome its conventions, thereby creating something new.

After this stunning debut, Stopkewich wrote and directed a second feature starring Molly Parker. *Suspicious River* premiered on the Canadian film festival circuit in 2000, where it was dismissed as a failure. 'Stopkewich does not succeed' was *Take One*'s initial assessment.[41] A later review in the *Globe and Mail* concluded that 'this movie ends up duplicating the emotional void it means to explore.'[42] Basically the story is set in a small town (Suspicious River) where a female hotel clerk supplements her income with prostitution and ends up attracted to the sexual abuse and violence of one Gary Jensen (Callum Keith Rennie). While Stopkewich was able to redeem necrophilia through feminism, the deviant sexuality of this film remains suspect. With a debut as powerful as *Kissed*, it is unlikely that a director can surpass such an achievement immediately. *Suspicious River* would have worked better for Stopkewich if it had been her first film and *Kissed* her second, but then Molly Parker would not have been heralded for her performance in *Suspicious River* the way she was in *Kissed*. What is important about Stopkewich's work for this generation is that she brings a female sensibility to the Generation-X milieu, thereby providing gender balance to the predominantly male vision.

The most recent success in this group is that of Calgarian Gary Burns. He began his feature film career with *Suburbanators* in 1995. The film cost a mere $65,000 and was invited to the prestigious Sundance Festival, where it was sold to the Sundance Channel.[43] Described as 'a tale of three Calgary losers combing the streets for dope and women,' the film was aimed specifically at the 'male Gen-X demographic.'[44] 'The way Burns catches the drab locality of the suburban West,' wrote one Canadian reviewer, '– a slacker's repudiation of the nearby Rockies and their postcard grandeur, was, arguably, the best thing about *The Suburbanators*.'[45] He gave the world a contemporary, unromanticized West, in all its urban pettiness. Gary Burns was working in a film environment (Calgary) that was not conducive to indigenous feature film production. Besides the inevitable sense of hinterland isolation, the province was soon to close down tax incentives for local production.[46] But Burns pressed on with his second film, *Kitchen Party* (1998), again filmed in Alberta. It was the story of college-aged kids who are restricted to having a party in their parents' kitchen. Burns both wrote and directed the film. His exploration of suburban dysfunction is based on an interest in getting people 'to interact in odd ways.'[47] By limiting the young crowd to a kitchen as his *mise-en-scène*, he was able to generate humorous and absurd situations.

What could be considered a trilogy was concluded with *Waydowntown* (2000), which won best Canadian feature at the Toronto International Film Festival (beating out Denis Villeneuve's *Maelström*), and most popular Canadian film at the Vancouver International Film Festival. *Waydowntown* is a delightful story of four office workers who make a bet on who can stay indoors at work for the longest period of time. It is a satire on Calgary's Plus-15 network of enclosed above-ground walkways by which most of the city's downtown core is connected. 'My films are anywhere in North America,' says Burns. 'If you're Canadian, there's the odd clue ... [the Calgary Tower, for example].'[48] This is Burns's secret of success – while using his own native environment, he creates a metaphor for urban/suburban life in all of North America. The film was shot inexpensively on digital video and then blown up to 35 mm. Don McKellar is one of the performers, whose presence links Burns's film to others of his generation.

As an auteur director from a non-film centre, he has developed a special style that reflects 'the lives of millions of people everywhere.'[49] The use of Canadian actors imparts an every-person aura to the film, while its satire of urban life gives it an inherent continentalism. Living

Gary Burns on the set of *A Problem with Fear* in 2002.

in Canada's most Americanized city gives his films 'an independence of spirit, a freshness, a freedom ... that seems like it couldn't come from anywhere else.'[50] In all three films there is a claustrophobic sense of being trapped – in a car, in a kitchen, or in an office – and wanting to get out into something different, but there isn't anything different out there. There is a certain parallel to McDonald's trilogy in the Burns trilogy, with its youthful actors and generational imagery, and its portrayal of absurdity and acerbic social commentary, but whereas the McDonald/McKellar characters live in the flow of music and the illusory freedom of the road, Burns's characters live inside boxes with walls of inevitability. While Burns satirizes North American urban life beyond national boundaries, McDonald retains a stubborn emphasis on the difference in national character. The tension between an Americanized Alberta vision of contemporary life and a Canadianized Ontario version represents an important and healthy internal cultural dialectic for this generation of film-makers.

At the Toronto International Film Festival in fall 2003, Burns premiered *A Problem with Fear*, a quirky cross-genre film (science fiction / romantic comedy / horror) that played to a variety of conflicting emotions. Co-written with his wife, Donna Brunsdale, the film utilizes the same youthful characters as his previous films and is meant to appeal to an audience whose demographics attract film distributors. It can be considered Burns's post-9/11 film since it deals with a technological society driven by a consumerist paranoia about disaster. It is a difficult film to appreciate because of its multi-layered imagery and unsympathetic characters, who either wear their brashness in loud-coloured lipstick or their exaggerated timidity in furtive glances, hunched-over faces, and skinny pursed lips. The film continues the Burns commentary on contemporary society, combining self-deprecating humour with sardonic analysis. Shot in 35 mm, the film displays cinematographic values resembling those found in Hollywood, but with an idiosyncratic character, whose social satire could only come from Burns.

The competing and complementary sensibilities of McKellar, McDonald, and Burns may have given contemporary English-Canadian cinema a lift, but it has not inaugurated any world-class talent comparable to the earlier reputations of Egoyan and Cronenberg. The 1990s were a time when computer-generated digital special effects became the mainstay of Hollywood appeal, with global audiences lining up for the latest innovation from lifelike dinosaurs to humanoid robots that pass through solid doors. Directors like the American Quentin Tarantino (*Pulp Fiction*) were called the new wave, while Britain won international acclaim for comedies like *Four Weddings and a Funeral* and *The Full Monty*. In the late 1990s, the international art-house circuit began to resonate with a revived Asian cinema that included Chinese directors from Hong Kong, Taiwan, and China. But the general trend in global cinema (except in Asia) continued toward ever greater monopolization by Hollywood.[51]

In the twenty years after McDonald's 1985 call for the recognition of his contemporaries, the established structural barriers remain, with state funding being a prerequisite for new Canadian cinema. The Canadian audience for Canadian film remained mired in the low single digits. But what had changed was the importance of the television market, which allowed investment to flow from the needs of a diffuse, many channel universe into film production. Most documentary films were now being made for private television channels. Feature films, if they were low-budget enough, could survive on DVD and television sales in the global market place. Screen time was no longer essential. But even in this area there was growth. In 1990, Calgary – then an already substantial city of 700,000 – had one single-screen art-house cinema. By 2000, when its population was 850,000, the city had three art-house cinemas with five screens where Canadian films were likely to be shown. Not every city could show such growth, but the general impact of film festivals, Canadian film awards, the growing national distribution power of such prominent Canadian companies as Alliance Atlantis, and funding from Telefilm Canada meant that at home and abroad the new generation of film-makers were not denied a chance. By 2003 it could be claimed with some evidence that to be a new Canadian film-maker could be rewarding for one's ego if not one's pocketbook.

Canadian cultural identity fostered by this new generation of auteurs reflected, first, the tricky interplay of global and local influences; second, the tightrope of NAFTA continentalism played against continued national loyalty; and finally, the diverse postmodernist sensibility of First World economies based on the technological hedonism associated with emerging digital culture. English-Canadian cinema of the 1990s had a spirit reflecting the concerns and aspirations of its own generation. With the passage of time, this subject became dated. What would youthful self-centredness become in English Canada, as Turpin and Villeneuve asked of youth and their own Quebec films? It is too early to tell whether the new cinema of the 1990s should be considered a building-block for a new stage, a second act of importance, or an era that came, produced a momentary mark, and disappeared.

CHAPTER FIFTEEN

The Anguished Critic

Three distinct categories of writers provide the intellectual framework for understanding English-Canadian and Quebec films. First there are the journalists, who provide film reviews for daily newspapers and popular magazines. These film critics range from those writing in single-city entertainment weeklies to those who write for national and sometimes international readerships numbering in the millions. The media film review represents the most common 'literature' on film because of its frequency and popularity.

Second there are the academics, usually in the discipline of film studies, who specialize in the meaning of a particular film, the work of a specific director, or the study a film genre. Their numbers are augmented by those in the new field of cultural studies, who appropriate categories from sociological to linguistic theories to understand how film operates in society. The scholarly interpretation of the cinematic arts (in the form of books and articles in scholarly journals) has a smaller impact on the public because its readership is limited, on the whole, to university audiences. Even so, scholarly writing is highly influential among those who take cinema seriously as an art form.

Finally there are the film historians, who may be academics or journalists whose distinct interest is the evolution of film over time, usually in a particular national context. What distinguishes their work from the other two categories is their framing of cinema as a historical phenomenon rather than as an immediate aesthetic or cultural one. Although the major contribution of film historians is the provision of a chronological overview of a particular subject, that overview has roots in the opinions and evaluations created by writers in the previous two categories. While film historians may study the political economy of a film-related subject, such as government policy, their interests are guided ultimately by a canon of films and film-makers first articulated by film critics and scholars.

Together these three distinct groups of writers provide various understandings, explanations, and interpretations that compete with one another for attention and approval. In turn, the three strands of criticism operate within their own cultural and linguistic milieu. Because English Canada and Quebec have their distinct personalities and hierarchies in both journalism and academia, this chapter will examine them separately. These interpreters provide information primarily for their own societies. It is safe to say that the work of journalists, film scholars, and film historians in either society is not readily available in the other, and is not considered in the other society except by a few specialists.

Journalism, whether low- or high-brow, provides a daily, weekly, or monthly commentary for the film-going public based on value judgments presented in ordinary language in which common sense attitudes prevail about what is good and what is bad and what the public ought to spend its money on. Superficially, the role of the journalist-reviewer is viewed as a check on the hyperbole of the film industry's ad copy as it seeks to attract an audience for a particular film, but at a deeper level film reviews are a way of bringing attention and credibility to a particular film, film director, or actor. Reviewing is part and parcel of the capitalist system of promoting consumption of cultural products. Film journalism directs consumers to various products and makes readers think about film and its importance to them. Every review and news item cries out to its readers to 'pay attention' to the importance of film and its personalities, while negative reviewing usually has little impact on the box office. Some have criticized film journalism for its promotional nature and its simplistic ratings that result in a certain 'institutional glibness.'[1]

In contrast, academic writing, with its own special jargon, has an aura of what the public might consider obscurantist scholarly discourse. Scholarship offers a theoretically constructed terminology that seeks to raise the subject beyond the mundane language of the newspaper film reviewer, thereby claiming to see in film and its effects secret aspects that ordinary mortals are blind to. Originally, theoretical understanding of film was based in aesthetic theories derived from Russian Formalism or montage (editing) theory, which showed how film was an art form with its own technical and artistic language. Then came auteur theory, which created the concept of the film director as the individual artist/god of cinema with a private vision that made his or her work distinctive and valuable. This, in turn, was followed by various adaptations from other disciplines, such as philosophy, with its Marxist proponents and its structuralist interpreters. An earlier school based its views on Freudian theories of psychoanalysis, but most recently the semiotically based theories of Saussure and Lacan have provided a grand theory of how film works, which, of course, is attacked by other thinkers. A simple example of how this debate enjoys its own terminology is this sentence from a recent academic text on the subject of film theory:

> Deleuze deploys Peirce's theory of signs against Metzian filmolinguistics and against the Lacanian system which makes cinematic desire orbit around the 'lack' rooted in the gap between an imaginary signifier and its signified.[2]

This peacock-like display of virtuoso expertise and name-dropping has no role in public discourse. Instead it is reserved for the intellectual sphere. In general there are two fundamental academic camps – those who seek to explain film *from within* as a distinct art form with its own language and those who seek to explain it *from without*, using theories borrowed from other disciplines.

Those who use borrowed ideas for academic readings of cinema can draw on a variety of ideologies embedded in the contemporary postmodern intellectual universe. Feminism has been very active in the past two decades in deconstructing the patriarchal nature of the industry, its creators, and their conventional narratives, and replacing them with a valorization of the work of women film-makers. This has been augmented by gay and lesbian criticism and the development of queer theory, which promotes 'non-normative expressions of gender' in the arts.[3] All of these global intellectual trends have found a home among English-Canadian and Quebec academics. But the influence on film-makers of these theories varies a great deal. However, the role of film journalism, in a financial sense if not a critical one, is crucial to success.

Engaged film journalism in English Canada began with Nathan Cohen of the *Toronto Star*, who was primarily a theatre critic but who wrote about film from time to time. Prior to the 1960s, when English-Canadian feature films emerged, the documentary and animation production of the National Film Board with its educational mandate was irrelevant to newspaper reviewers because it was not part of the commercial universe of feature films that the public flocked to for weekend entertainment. Gerald Pratley, an early radio critic of film on CBC, had little Canadian material to review. Later came Marshall Delaney (Robert Fulford) writing in *Saturday Night* magazine, Martin Knelman and Jay Scott writing in Toronto's *Globe and Mail*, and John Hofsess and Brian D. Johnson in *Maclean's* magazine. These journalists had a national audience for their views, but they were all based in Toronto. The symbiosis between English-Canadian film and Toronto, the media and cultural capital of English Canada, was reflected in the fact that every major magazine about English-Canadian film (*Cinema Canada*, *Take One*) came out of that city. Although these magazines covered the national scene, they did so with a Toronto perspective that ordinarily relegated non-Toronto film production to hinterland status.

The more important of the English-Canadian film reviewers/critics published books of their reviews. Beginning with Robert Fulford's *Marshall Delaney at the Movies: The Contemporary World As Seen on Film* (1974) there appeared a steady stream of books over the next two decades. In 1975 John Hofsess published the first book exclusively devoted to Canadian directors, *Inner Views: Ten Canadian Filmmakers*. Then Martin Knelman came out with *This Is Where We Came In* (1977), a competing look at the industry, which was then deep in the throes of the tax-shelter follies. A decade later, Knelman came out with a second volume, *Home Movies: Tales from the Canadian Film World* (1987). A few years earlier, Jay Scott had collected his film reviews in *Midnight Matinées* (1985), which contained his tax-shelter critique, 'Burnout Factory: Canada's Hollywood.' After his death, a volume of his best movie reviews (*Great Scott: The Best of Jay Scott's Movie Reviews* [1994]) was edited by Karen York, which contained only a half-dozen reviews of Canadian films.

What is valuable about these books is their portrayal of Canadian cinema by leading reviewers. Robert Fulford's *Marshall Delaney at the Movies* contained reviews written between 1965 and 1974. The first third of the book is taken up by the Canadian scene, which was a sign that there was sufficient product to examine by the mid-1970s. His observations focused on the concept of 'success.' He called *Valérie* (1969) 'the first successful Canadian dirty movie,' and he concluded his review of the 1974 film *The Apprenticeship of Duddy Kravitz* with the comment that 'it's pleasant to report on *Duddy Kravitz* as a success.'[4] The great desire of the moment was to have the fledgling film industry of the day produce films that were 'successful,' meaning popular and profitable. By the mid-1980s Fulford's view of Canadian cinema had become less sanguine when he wrote: 'The Canadian feature film has been seen as a problem, an issue to be worried over rather than an accomplishment to be celebrated. In the world movie business it exists as at best a marginal element; in the consciousness of Canadian movie-goers it lives a kind of shadowy half-life, neither quite present nor altogether absent ...'[5]

The theme of the absent audience had already been made a central point by John Hofsess a decade earlier. Using the idea of Canadians as a minority culture (comparable to African Americans), Hofsess had con-cluded in 1975 that what Canada had was 'an unpopular and prema-ture' national cinema that still awaited a national consciousness to appear.[6] He claimed that print culture (Canlit) had an easier time reach-ing a wide audience, while film culture (Canfilm) was weak in Canada because of the disinterested audience.[7] 'One can hardly expect English-Canadian film,' he wrote, 'to rise above all the cultural ambiguities and compromises of English Canada itself.'[8] For him, Canfilm was trapped in a confused consciousness, while Canlit was free of American mythol-ogy. One factor that may have contributed to this confused identity was the lack of a historical tradition in Canadian feature films comparable to the novels of Canadian literature. Whereas there were thousands of books by Canadians on Canada, there were very few films.

Martin Knelman used his 1977 book to attack 'Canada's Hollywood' and the whole tax-shelter film phenomenon that was more interested in making money than making meaning.[9] His pessimistic view of Cana-dian cinema in general (he was a fan of Quebec cinema) continued long after the 1970s. Writing in the latter 1980s he said: 'The Canadian psyche is better suited to information programming than to drama, partly because of the documentary tradition established in this country by John Grierson, founder of the National Film Board. The essence of drama is conflict, and Canadians historically and by temperament tend to avoid conflict.'[10]

In contrast, Jay Scott, the *Globe and Mail*'s film reviewer from 1978 to 1993, believed that 'Canadian stories were important and that Canadi-ans could tell them beautifully if given a chance.'[11] Scott often wrote emotionally about films made in Canada. For example, he described *Jésus de Montréal* as filling 'the eyes with rapture, the mind with energy and the heart with love.'[12] In the introduction to Scott's posthumous collection of essays and reviews, his colleague Robert Fulford wrote how a reviewer of Scott's calibre creates 'a centre of discourse' about Canadian films, which an audience shares.[13] 'For years,' Fulford wrote of Scott, 'he saw every Canadian feature made; he played a large role in the careers of directors ranging from Denys Arcand (*Jésus de Montréal*) to Atom Egoyan (*Family Viewing*).'[14]

The most recent book-length work by a Canadian journalist about Canadian films is Katherine Monk's *Weird Sex and Snowshoes and Other Canadian Film Phenomena* (2001). Writing a quarter-century after initial texts by Fulford, Hofsess, and Knelman, she was still able to repeat the same sense of disillusionment that they had to deal with – the lack of popular acceptance of Canadian cinema within Canada. 'Canadians have grown to respect the rhetoric of self-loathing more than self-love,' she groaned, '... the way we've tended to view Canadian film as some poor, maladjusted backwoods cousin to Chiclet-toothed Tinseltown.'[15] Her feel-good book was meant to be, in her own words, 'a little chicken soup for our neglected Canadian psyche.'[16] This uplifting and promotion-toned narrative of Canadian film, filled with biographic sketches of contemporary directors, was meant to remedy the general ignorance of the Canadian public about its cinematic stars. She also pointed out some distinguishing features of Canadian cinema, including its liberal sexual content (compared to that of Hollywood), its gender-bending proclivities, and its creation of 'the strong-willed, highly competent and generally intellectually superior female character.'[17] In short, she liked what Canadian cinema offered, but she admitted sadly that cinema was still banging its fragile head against the wall of Canadian popularity long hardened by a century of American cinema. The review of Monk's book in the *Canadian Journal of Film Studies* placed the book squarely in the nationalist tradition represented by earlier writers like Martin Knelman, who found common features and themes in many Canadian films.[18]

In the same year the Monk book came out, an article appeared in the *Toronto Star* titled 'Why Canadian Movies Suck.' The writer boldly claimed that 'English Canada in the past 30 years has not produced a single small- or large-budget movie that gives adequate expression to facets of the nation's life, history and character and that also appeals to English-speaking Canadians in significant numbers.'[19] This typical curmudgeonly attitude was bolstered by statistics on how poorly English-Canadian films did at the box office, with few making over $1 million. Quebec was offered to readers as a much better market for its domestic films, with the implication that English Canada was a hopeless cause.

The article concluded with a variety of experts pointing fingers at who and what was responsible for the problem, which included everything from Telefilm's 'Byzantine bureaucratic processes' to the allure of television programming.[20] It is truly fascinating and slightly disheartening to read, after almost thirty-five years of English-Canadian feature film cinema, how journalists were still treating it as an abject failure. The gold bar of consummate popularity, which is what journalism seems most interested in, remains too high for English-Canadian cinema to reach, though it has been crossed from time to time in Quebec.

There have been several major magazines dealing exclusively with Canadian cinema. The first was *Cinema Canada*, an industry monthly that began publication in 1961 under the auspices of the Canadian Society of Cinematographers. It provided a synopsis of events in the industry, creating an on-going historical account of who was doing what, when, and for how much. It also ran interviews with leading personalities and reviews of every Canadian feature film. The second significant magazine is *Take One*, which began as a bi-monthly in 1968. Initially the magazine was internationally oriented, describing itself as a 'Magazine of the Movies,' but in the 1990s it moved to deal exclusively with Canadian cinema and by the end of the decade had added Canadian television to its mandate. It provided a more critical analysis of Canadian cinema, with a greater emphasis on aesthetic concerns. In 2001 its editor and publisher, Wyndham Wise, created *Take One's Essential Guide to Canadian Film*, an encyclopedia of short articles on Canadian films and film-makers. If *Cinema Canada* was workaday and comprehensive, *Take One* was selective and glossy.

Another magazine, *Motion*, which was launched in 1971, dealt with 'Canadian film, Theatre and TV.' It did not have the same stature as the previous two and was short-lived. More recently, the Directors Guild of Canada has produced its own magazine, *Montage*, which features interviews with its members. There have also been Canadian film magazines, such as *Ciné Tracts*, a quarterly out of Montreal, which, while predominantly oriented toward international cinema, also did special issues on Canadian film, as has *CinéAction*, published in Toronto since 1985. While these journals are available on the news-stand, they are generally considered part of the arts niche and do not have a general readership.

In contrast to the journalistic universe of newspapers and monthly magazines, the academic universe has a narrower audience. In 1977, only a decade after film courses began to be taught in Canada, Cana-

Left to right: Jim Kitses, Jean Renoir, and Peter Harcourt, circa 1970.

dian academics formed the Film Studies Association of Canada. Among the founding members were a number of Ontario university professors who set the intellectual agenda for Canadian cinema, including Peter Harcourt, Peter Morris, Seth Feldman, Jim Leach, and Bill Wees. FSAC eventually established Canada's only scholarly journal devoted exclusively to film – the *Canadian Journal of Film Studies / Revue canadienne d'études cinématographiques*. Although it dealt with film globally, it naturally gave Canadian subjects more coverage than did scholarly film journals published in other countries, and while it was bilingual, the majority of its contributions were in English. The whole field of film studies caused one observer to write: 'The rapidity with which academic film study developed and promulgated its own jargon undoubtedly had a lot to do with the impatience of pioneers in the field to establish their own sphere of expertise.'[21]

Academic discourse is geared to defining a discipline and then creating a hierarchy of intellectual accomplishment in that field. This makes it seem hermetically sealed, which allows precision and seriousness, but also adds to its isolation from the general public.[22] Eventually, Canadian film studies took its theoretical cues from film theories articulated elsewhere, from other disciplines in Canada like literature, and from ideological movements of one kind or another. While journalists sought to address the masses, academics sought to address their peers.

'My work was part of the essentialist nationalist movement of the 1970s,' explains Peter Harcourt, who was the first to teach film in Canada in the late 1960s. 'It endorsed the two solitudes mythology.'[23] As an English Canadian, he was interested in the achievements of Quebec cinema in the 1960s and 1970s, when it far surpassed what was happening in English Canada. His specialty was the work of Jean Pierre Lefebvre. In 1988 he published a provocative essay in *Cinema Canada* titled 'Canadian Film Studies and Canadian Film: The Education We Need,' in which he argued that it was art-house cinema that created 'a distinctly national flavour' through the 'controlling consciousness' of the film-maker.[24] He lamented the lack of influence on Canadian cinema that the academic community in Canada has and observed that 'Canada must be the only country in the world that does not put its own achievement at the centre of its educational systems.'[25] In particular, he was concerned that Canadian experimental film from Norman McLaren to Michael Snow, be incorporated 'in a meaningful way' into Canadian culture.[26]

The debate over the nature and future direction of Canadian film had been sparked several years earlier by an article in the *Canadian Forum* by experimental film-maker and theorist Bruce Elder.[27] In the article, Elder, who later published an erudite book outlining his theory of Canadian cinema (*Image and Identity: Reflections on Canadian Film and Culture* [1989]), attacked Harcourt and others for their encouragement of a sociologically and psychologically realistic cinema. He claimed this was wrong because 'narratives misrepresent experience [by eliminating] the unmanaged ambiguities and the painful contradictions inherent in experience.'[28] Realism was a simplistic construct that was ideologically motivated. Elder's attack garnered an immediate response. Bart Testa, who teaches film at the Unversity of Toronto and is an expert on the films of David Cronenberg, complained that Elder's putting experimental cinema at the centre of Canadian film would lead to an extreme anti-populism.[29] Piers Handling, who had written extensively and edited books on Canadian cinema before he became director of the Toronto International Film Festival, took up the populist cry when he stated that cinema 'is a mass medium and it has to address itself to the general public.'[30] Basically, this approach argued that nothing should distract Canadian feature films from their fundamental (and as yet unachieved) goal of penetrating the Americanized popular psyche of Canadian filmgoers.

Geoff Pevere, who became an advocate of Canadian pop culture with his 1996 book *Mondo Canuck*, was a postgraduate student at Carleton University's film program (where Harcourt taught) when he got into the fray by attacking the whole idea of academics providing prescriptive remedies for Canadian film, which, he believed, would only bring the patient closer to death's door.[31] Elder responded by saying that the struggle for Canadian identity was lost. He had concluded that technological domination over public consciousness mitigated against a distinct national cinema, an argument that was made again by others when the Internet became culturally pervasive fifteen years later.[32]

The preoccupation over a viable national cinema in English Canada had begun during the 1970s when academics decided that there was a body of work called Canadian cinema that was worth discussing and interpreting. *The Canadian Film Reader*, co-edited by Seth Feldman and Joyce Nelson, came out in 1973. It was followed a decade later by *Take Two*, again edited by Feldman. In this second volume of essays, James Leach of Brock University wrote an article in which he outlined two basic characteristics of Canadian feature films. The first was 'the quest for freedom from the materialistic prism that has become closely identified with the "American way of life."'[33] He concluded that this was a painful search because English-Canadian and Quebec cinemas lacked the 'reassurance and affirmation' common in other national cinemas.[34] The end result was an overriding theme of failure and collective victimhood.[35] The second was the basic division into two national cinemas. In 1999 Leach wrote a study of the Quebec film-maker Claude Jutra, in which Leach presented the Quebec intelligentsia's view of English Canada as a colony of the United States, which made Quebec (a colony of English Canada) twice colonized.[36] This hierarchy of colonization (similar to the victimhood theme of his earlier analysis) resulted in his concluding that Canada had 'one national cinema fragmented and divided like all national cinemas, with linguistic difference as the most significant but far from impregnable boundary line.'[37] In other words, colonization brought both cinemas into an uneasy unity. An academic attempt at dialogue between the two colonized cinemas occurred in 1987 with the publication of *Dialogue: Canadian and Quebec Cinemas*, a bilingual book that combined essays on both cinemas by their resident critics and scholars.

The national cinema(s) debate has also been engaged by Michael

Dorland of Carleton University. He argues that English-Canadian cinema draws its sense of identity more from state-sponsored nationalism than does Quebec cinema, which has a 'greater sense of singular identity belonging to the people.'[38] The existence of two 'national' cinemas in two languages within one nation-state entity has allowed distinctions and comparisons to be made between them. As a result, Dorland raised the thorny problem of why English Canada lacked a significant film industry, while Quebec had such an industry, and how scholarship might explain the differences between English Canada and Quebec. He questions the 'prescriptive and moralistic' role of scholar-critics who keep pointing out how Canadian film has failed to reach an ideal.[39] He identifies four basic interpretations of this failure – nationalist inadequacy, dependent capitalism (Pendakur), negotiated dependency (Madger) and an alternative one (Elder).[40] He himself describes Canadian cinema, beginning with the NFB, as dependent on an 'administrative rationality' that made the Canadian state the bedrock of cultural production in a fiscal and legislative way.[41] Whatever the state did, from creating the NFB to the CFDC to Telefilm Canada, became the framework through which creativity had to flow. The end result was a film industry of sorts, but it was an industry rooted in state-initiated mandates rather than a popular cinematic language of the kind Americans had. 'The makers of feature films ... invented an aesthetic of uncoded, refractory visual experience,' Dorland concluded, which, outside the films they had made, 'had no place.'[42] Canadian cinema is a displaced cinema because it has no place in the hearts and minds of Canadians, or, as Charles Acland said, it is a cinema for an 'absent audience.'[43] The end result is a kind of 'pseudo-communication' between Canadians and their films.[44]

While Dorland's work on the state and film in Canada was closer to that of a film historian than a film critic, Seth Feldman's 2001 Robarts Lecture at York University summarized mainstream Canadian academic thinking to date. In an earlier essay on Canadian cinema, Feldman had described the 'pantheistic silence' of the landscape as attracting Canadian film-makers opposed to the standard 'imperial voice' of the documentary voiceover.[45] Discussing the contemporary situation, Feldman concluded that the current 'triumph of Canadian cinema' in quantitative terms was 'entirely invisible' to most Canadians, thereby harking back to the Dorland/Acland analysis.[46] After three decades of observing the industry, Feldman stated firmly, 'We don't have a national cinema.'[47] While Canadian cinema continues to be embraced solely by the art-house cinema universe, it remains marginalized. 'We fund the less lucrative, more artistic films, through a combination of industry subsidies and arts council grants,' said Feldman, thereby keeping the commercial space for Hollywood films as the state once did through funding of documentaries.[48]

Bart Testa, a professor of cinema studies at the University of Toronto, took up the issue of Canadian national cinema in a major review essay published in the *Literary Review of Canada* in 2003.[49] He claims that 'the last two decades [1980–2000] have not been a period to encourage scholars to develop frameworks for a national-cultural cinema.'[50] Postmodernist/postcolonialist issues of race, gender, class, and ethnic identity have dominated the discourse in academe during this period, effectively pushing the national question aside. As well, he states that state funding of feature film production has served only 'to maintain a phantasmatically faint Canadian cultural cinema.'[51] Because Canada lacks 'a national commercial industrial project' there simply isn't much cinema to write about.[52] He places his hope in 'mainstream, middle-brow moviemaking' that attracts what he considers 'enduring Canadian directors' such as Cronenberg, Egoyan, Mehta, and Wheeler because he considers Canada 'an obdurately middle-brow country.'[53] He points to the middle-brow, international success of Canadian literature in the past twenty years, as well as the success of Canadian pop musicians and singers as the direction for Canadian cinema. Of course, his argument is based on the premise that a national identity is somehow deficient if it does not have a substantial national cinema to its credit. There are those who view the quest for a national cinema, especially for English Canada, as quixotic and lacking in critical awareness of the implications of national identity.

A contemporary critique that moves away from valorizing Canadian cinema is offered by Christopher E. Gittings, who deconstructs Canada's 'national cinema' using gender, class, and race in his recent study of those who have been excluded from the dominant 'cinematic images' or represented in a negative and disempowering way.[54] He considers Canada's early films as 'a cinematic genealogy of the racist and sexist foundations of Canadian nation.'[55] His study, *Canadian National Cinema*, explores how Canadian nationality was constructed historically by Canada's feature films to result in certain 'racial and ethnic hierarchies of belonging to the nation' which created an imagined 'national community of white Anglo Canada' to the exclusion on non-White minorities.[56] In analysing various well-known Canadian films, he provides numerous cinematic examples of structural racism and sexism, while, at the same time, providing a detailed description and analysis of alternative voices from ethnic and racial communities who have used film to represent themselves in a non-prejudicial way. This theme was taken up by Brenda Longfellow and Thomas Waugh, who edited a special issue of the *Canadian Journal of Film Studies* on Canadian cinemas. They claimed that their collection expressed 'the necessity of theorizing national cinemas as sites of diversity itself.'[57] Looking at the history of Canadian films from the contemporary perspective of a multicultural universe, Gittings and other contemporary scholars of Canadian cinema find much that is lacking in what previous scholars and journalists had come to conceive of as defining Canadian characteristics. What the new generation of scholars has discovered is the 'limits of bicultural and bilingual fields of vision to represent the complexity, diversity and continued internal colonialism that mark Canadian national cinemas.'[58] They have adopted a critical stance toward these cinemas in order to unmask their exclusionary ideological underpinnings and inaugurate a new discourse of concerns ignored by previous scholarship. One example of this new Canadian *Weltanschauung* is captured in an article on contemporary Canadian literature in the American magazine *Harper's*, which sees Canadian literature as 'the nationality-bending avant garde of the emerging global soul,' rather than the more old-fashioned national roughing-it-in-the-bush identity.[59] Contemporary Canadian film scholarship would prefer such new metaphors because they open nationality to more inclusive redefining, as well as exposing its previous agendas.

Gittings's critique is rooted in the earlier work of Canadian feminist film critics such as Brenda Longfellow and Kay Armatage. To their feminist critiques must be added the postcolonial critique of First Nations writers and writers of colour, as well as the more recent proponents of queer theory, all of whom seek to claim space for their previously marginalized identities against the hegemonic tendencies of a singular patriarchal interpretation of Canadian identity that is now viewed as homophobic, sexist, and racist. It seems that the call for an overriding national cinema, first exposed as false by the presence of a stronger distinct Quebec cinema, is now being challenged forcefully by other communities who want a diversity of identities to be the cornerstone of nationality. The editors of *Gendering the Nation: Canadian Women's Cinema* (1999) challenged 'the struggle for national identity' as 'an enduring framework for a critical examination of Canadian cinema.'[60] They even questioned second-wave feminism as an adequate response to contemporary Canadian film, when they asked: 'In the cultural diaspora of blurred borders and hybrid identities, does the project of gendering the nation bear the marks of an archaic nationalism or a problematic liberal feminism?'[61]

While contemporary academic debates over the meaning of Canadian film continue, the more staid and less theoretical work of film historians is viewed as less central to the debate. Part of this may result from the general reputation of 'history' as *the* place of no return, while another part may result from the view that people in the know only use film history as a stepping stone to what really matters, which is creativity. Curiously, film historians have actually discussed the history of film criticism in Canada as an important topic. For example, Peter Morris, writing in *CinéAction*, claimed that the general negativity toward Canadian film displayed by Canadian film critics in the 1960s actually encouraged the Canadian government to favour an industry model for Canadian features, which gave the public discourse created by journalists credibility.[62] Peter Morris is the father of Canadian film history because he was the first to write a substantive history of film in Canada. When *Embattled Shadows: A History of Canadian Cinema 1895-1939* appeared in 1978, it marked a milestone in the evolution of Canadian cultural history. It was the first work to cover such a long period using detailed primary archival sources as the basis of its narrative. The reason why Canada did not develop a substantial feature film industry of its own, Morris argued, was its commitment to 'classical liberalism with full emphasis on the role of individual initiative.'[63] According to him, the 'Canadian ethos' promoted 'regionalism and possessive individualism,' which worked against the creation of a centralized industry.[64] Besides, when Canadian feature films did get made, they 'rarely spoke using Hollywood forms,' which was both a downfall and a strength.[65] Later, Morris wrote an important article that questioned how Canadian film critics' emphasis 'on the cultural uniqueness of Quebec led to an increasing valorization of Quebec films over English-Canadian ones,' in spite of some critics showing there were more similarities than dissimilarities.[66] In his voice, one can hear the anguished cry of the Central Canadian psyche struggling for a national identity with the energy of Quebec nationalism.

The historian's attempt to explain why Canada did not have a more successful cinema of its own also had a popular interpreter in the figure of Pierre Berton, who has provided the Canadian public with an endless stream of books on Canadian history. *Hollywood's Canada: The Americanization of Our National Image* (1975) showed the inaccuracy and downright silliness of American cinematic portrayals of Canada in hundreds of films up to 1960, most of which tended to follow the clichéd plots and characters of American westerns, which were themselves anti-Aboriginal constructs glorifying White American expansionism. While Berton lamented the lack of an authentic image of Canada in feature films, he provided little insight on why this occurred or how Canadian audiences shared in the racial prejudices and patriarchal attitudes of their American neighbours. He preferred to lampoon Hollywood rather than critique Canadian authorities. In this, he continued a long tradition of Central Canadian nationalism in historical writing, which presented Canadian nationality as being ideologically and morally superior to American nationalism and ideology. When Will Straw of McGill University wrote that 'the debate over cultural identity has moved from the conventional preoccupation with national specificity to embrace the complexities of identity politics and the shifting status of the nation-state,' he was referring to the rejected and superceded status of unified Central Canadian nationalism represented by Pierre Berton.[67]

A different approach to American-Canadian film history was offered by Seth Feldman of York University in the 2001 Robarts Lecture, in which he linked the fortunes of Canadian cinema to developments in the United States. He said that Canada's film history had gone through three distinct stages based on American film history.[68] First, was the factory model of film-making, of which the National Film Board was Canada's sole successful example because it imitated the Hollywood studio system of production. The second stage lasted from the Second World War to 1975. This was a time of Hollywood's de-monopolization through anti-trust rulings. During this period, film became a secondary form of entertainment to television, and this, along with a new post-1960 American interest in foreign feature films, provided Canada with a slim opening to become part of the expanding non-Hollywood film world. Then the post-1975, but pre-digital, period encouraged decentralized film production, with the rise of non-studio independents in the United States, all of which benefited the marginalized Canadian industry, which did not have a studio system. The current stage is one of digitalized film-making, which allows for low-cost feature film production at the same time that Canada has developed its own significant distribution firms such as Alliance Atlantis. While wisely eschewing the national question in his overview, Feldman presents a continentalist understanding of the evolution of Canadian film that is less judgmental than Berton's. It can be argued that this continentalist approach makes sense, considering how Canada moved from being a colony of Great Britain to being a colony of the United States, while Quebec moved from being a cultural colony of France to self-affirmation in the North American context.[69]

External and internal comparisons seem to hang heavily not only over Canadian film itself but also over the scholarship of Canadian film history. Dorland concluded a few years ago that the writing of the film history of Canada was 'underdeveloped' compared to other national cinemas, and that it was 'entangled in conceptual difficulties largely of its own making.'[70] One of the causes for this was 'the utter heterogeneity' of Canadian cinema, which is so diverse that it is difficult to conceptualize in a unified way.[71] This diversity has led to an inevitable 'instability' in Canfilm as a subject of study. The end result is the construction of Canadian cinema by both scholars and critics as a cinema of denied potential that is idealized 'but always deferred.'[72] This deconstruction of 'national' cinema as a concept has occurred of late because national identity as a unified concept, with its traditional subtext of a unified and common reality, is too problematic a category to apply to most Canadian film history: it does not encompass the contradictory realities of what has actually happened. The nationalist interpretation is now seen as being more an ideological than a scientific tool. In his introduction to an anthology of academic essays on Canadian feature films, Eugene Walz of the University of Manitoba confirms the current rejection of 'a film's Canadianness ... because of the wide-ranging idiosyncracies, extreme geographic diversity, and irregularly developed talents of Canadian filmmakers.'[73] Because Canadian film is sited in diverse spaces, communities, and identities, it displays the wide range of approaches associated with independent film-making.

A convincing grand interpretation also seemed to elude Quebec journalists and academics, who, like their English-Canadian counterparts, have struggled to define Quebec cinema as a distinct national cinema. This preoccupation has also attracted non-Quebec and non-Canadian scholars and critics of Quebec cinema. While standing outside the political debates over Quebec sovereignty inside Canada, they face the same issues inherent in the concept of nationality as do critics of English-Canadian cinema.

The University of Glasgow's Bill Marshall has provided the most recent and most extensive treatment in English of Quebec cinema (*Que-*

bec National Cinema [2001]). He argues that '... national cultural elites maintain an interest in polarizing the relationship between their "national" cinema and Hollywood,' so that their project of a distinct national identity is strengthened.[74] In particular, the auteurist approach to film criticism serves these interests by creating 'national' cultural heroes.[75] While anglophone critics hold up Quebec cinema as being so much more popular than English-Canadian cinema, Marshall still considers Quebec cinema 'marginal' in its own market because its annual audience is usually 5 per cent of filmgoers, though it occasionally can rise as high as 10 per cent of the Quebec theatre market.[76] This may be double the English figure, but it is still very small. The main characteristic that Marshall attributes to Quebec cinema since 1960 is 'modernization.'[77] Quebec-made cinema aspired to be part of its contemporary world and so was part of the modernization of Quebec during and after the Quiet Revolution, when Quebec was reinventing itself. The second feature, he notes, is the hybridity underlying Quebec cinema, which comes from an amalgamation of American, French, and Canadian cinematic values. He concludes that it is in comedy that Quebec cinema best reflects its own society and so attains its highest popularity. The popularity of the *Les Boys* series of films in the late 1990s is a perfect example of this intersection of local audience and local material.

A few years earlier, the American scholar Janis L. Pallister (*The Cinema of Quebec* [1995]) concluded that Quebec cinema, while rooted in the *cinéma direct* documentary, was 'often more sociopolitical in nature than is the rest of Canadian film,' mainly because of a sovereignist longing that requires a distinct identity.[78] She also points out that Quebec films have been made almost exclusively by Québécois filmmakers. This has resulted in a body of work primarily by francophone Quebeckers that can be considered representative of the culture and its aspirations. The all-consuming nature of Quebec's francophone nationalist project of the past forty years, and its unwavering promotion of francophone culture, have all but eliminated the voice of non-francophone film-makers in Quebec. In comparison to the range of film-makers representing minority communities in contemporary English-Canadian cinema, Quebec cinema is significantly deficient. Nor is Quebec the only site for francophone film-making in Canada (primarily through French-language television in Ontario.)

A good example of how Quebec cinema has been valorized for the dominant community is offered by Quebec film magazines, which have played an important role in the acculturization of Quebec audiences.

The magazine *Séquences* began in 1955 as part of the Catholic Church's outreach to youth through film clubs. After 1970 the magazine gave prominence to Quebec films, with extensive reviews, as well as interviews with and articles on Quebec film personalities. A short-lived film journal titled *Objectif* (1960–7) represented the new generation of Quebec cinephiles, who sought to break out of the Catholic mould. It was followed briefly by *Champ Libre* (1971–3), which presented a left-wing critique of film, one that was continued by *Format Cinéma* and *24 images*. In 1971, Quebecker Jean-Pierre Tadros, the publisher of *Cinema Canada*, began publishing *Cinéma Québec* as a guide to the industry in the province. The academics followed in 1979 with *Copie Zéro*, a quarterly published by La Cinémathèque Québécoise in Montreal with co-editors Pierre Jutras and Pierre Véronneau. It provided excellent filmographies of current productions. The Cinémathèque also published *Nouveau Cinéma Canadien / New Canadian Film*, which was a comprehensive listing of every Canadian film made that year.

Because Quebec film-makers were considered to be integral to the polemics of national identity, they often wrote on the subject. The film-maker Jean Pierre Lefebvre wrote an essay titled 'Le Concept de cinéma national,' in which he argued that all cinema is 'national' because nationalism is a creative invention and cinema helps create that identity.[79] A volume of Quebec film commentary spanning thirty years (*Cinéma en rouge et noir*) was published in the mid-1990s. The most telling feature of the volume is its focus on the ongoing intellectual debate within the Quebec film community about the nature of film, its social role, and its possibilities. While discussions in English-Canadian cinema focused on legislative, financial, and production issues, Quebec film discussion was much more oriented toward the aesthetic and the ideological.

Quebec has produced two major film historians – Yves Lever and Pierre Véronneau. Lever's *Histoire générale du cinéma au Québec* was published in 1988, with a second edition in 1995. Lever had been writing about Quebec film since 1972 (*Cinéma et société québécoise*). He concluded that Quebec film should not excuse its failings with the argument that it is young and inexperienced because it is, in fact, an established cinema going back half a century.[80] He also rejected the excuse of 'poverty' compared to Hollywood productions. Because Quebec did not have the costs of an international star system like Hollywood's nor a global market for its films, the amounts available to it for film production were more than adequate. In 1985 the Quebec film industry received $50 million in state funding of one kind or another, and this figure had reached $100 million by 1993.[81] Lever claims that a mature film industry is one that makes films that speak to a range of Quebec audiences and that this kind of production should be state-supported.[82] As for his overall assessment of Quebec films, he disagrees with the 1982 observation of Quebec film-maker Fernand Dansereau that so much of Quebec film to date seems like 'one and the same film,' filled with nostalgia and lacking in dramatic conflict.[83] Lever rejects this criticism because of the variety of genres in which Quebec film operates, though he admits that the division between films for cinephiles and films for the masses has been basic since 1960.[84]

The second major figure is Pierre Véronneau. He has published a multi-volume history of Quebec cinema beginning in 1979 (*Le Succès est au film parlant français, Cinéma de l'époque Duplessiste*, and *Résistance et affirmation: La Production francophone à l'ONF, 1939–1964*). As a film scholar, he documents Quebec's prodigious output, housed in the Cinémathèque Québécoise archives in Montreal. Among the Québécois critics is Heinz Weinmann, whose *Cinéma de l'imaginaire québécois* (1991) provided a Freudian interpretation of Quebec feature films. Earlier, the Quebec feminist film critic Louise Carrière provided a counterpoint to the dominant nationalist critique with *Femmes et cinéma québécois* (1983), in which she opened up discussion of feminist challenges to patriarchal construction of women characters in Quebec cinema.

In comparing the work of English critics and scholars with that of their francophone counterparts, one immediately sees a difference. While anglophones are drawn to a discussion of Quebec film because of its seeming singularity and thematic unity, in short its 'nationality,' francophone critics are less interested in English-Canadian film because of its inherent diversity as a national cinema and its identification with a colonizing power. While English-Canadian criticism and scholarship revolved around dissecting the reasons for the lack of a national cinema in Canada, Quebec critics looked at their own cinema and wondered why it contained so much coherence, which seemed to them to be a limiting or suspect factor. While Quebec cinema was praised in English Canada for its relative cultural success and local market penetration, compared to the rest of Canada, in Quebec it was popularly viewed as less important than francophone Quebec literature in articulating nationality. While English-Canadian critics were constantly on the look out for some breakthrough Canadian movie that would say it

all, Quebec critics were busy critiquing Quebec films already considered to be worthy accomplishments elsewhere.

A non-Canadian academic observer of Quebec film has placed issues
of Quebec film in the wider context of *francophonie*, the French-speaking
world, and the struggle of various national and sub-national identities
for a fuller cultural self-expression using cinema. What the films of
former French colonies show is that the cinema of these countries is
individually and collectively '*multicultural* and *multilingual*,' and that it
is this globalized context which ultimately will allow French to remain
a 'language' of cinema.[85] The continued use of the English language in
Quebec films and the presence of non-francophone characters are re-
minders of this multiculturalism. In the case of Quebec, the emphasis
'on the interaction between memory, society and identity' that has been
an integral part of its cinema is now being challenged by 'an emerging
interest in the individual whose personal experience is located outside
Quebec.'[86] In other words, it is by going outside Quebec that contemporary Québécois film-makers express the emerging world order, which
has given legitimacy to their culture. Because the context of their nationalism has changed profoundly, so has their nationalism, its confidence, and expanding perspectives.

The critical debate over cinema, whether popular or scholarly, is part
of the essential literary discourse that supplements and contextualizes
the visual image. The critical task of articulating subtle meanings, clarifying hidden messages, and creating novel interpretations of what one
sees on the screen flows from the evaluative process that has always
accompanied the arts as an aesthetic/social experience. Judgment and
evaluation are part of every person's experience of film. The journalists,
critics, and scholars who do it professionally offer readers the voice of
expertise and the status of the expert, implying greater knowledge,
fuller understanding, and deeper insight than that of the casual observer. These opinions become part of the discourse of people who talk
about the films prior to and after viewing. English-Canadian and Quebec discourse on film was very much tied up with the national question
in the 1970s, with ideologies that challenge public pieties such as feminism in the 1980s, and with postcolonial and postmodernist sensibilities in the 1990s. Any analysis of Canadian film, whether as a review of
a contemporary film or as a historical narrative, is part of shared mythologies about Canadian culture in general. These mythologies struggle
with 'the other,' however defined. In that struggle, they seem forever to

lack a level of accomplishment that critical judgment has awarded to the personages and cinemas of other countries. For example, Brian D. Johnson, film critic for *Maclean's*, wrote in 2002 of the thriving nature of contemporary Canlit and pop music on the world stage in comparison to 'our cinema, the Achilles heel of Canadian culture.'[87] He condemned the system of state support for Canadian film because it nurtures 'an astringent, self-conscious style of cinema – starved of romance, humour and diversity.'[88] So much of Canadian film discourse gives Canadian cinema a secondary status, which in turn limits envisioning some sort of future primacy.

The role of the critical voice is not as central to the dialogue within and about English-Canadian and Quebec film as one might imagine from the rather lengthy list of players discussed here, including non-Canadian critics. Directly between the film artist and his/her audience stand the financier and the state, while the energized critic remains in the wings pointing and gesticulating, sometimes helping and sometimes hindering the main action. As long as Canadian film remains a shadowy and marginal reality in the mind of the public, Canadian film criticism will have a similar status. Not even attention from non-Canadian scholars and critics, which seems to be growing, can bring Canadian film home to its public. The long-time penchant of Canadian critics for caustic prescriptions has circumscribed the Canadian public with either journalistic bromides or the unintelligible results of theory-bound academic dissection. The work of popularizing theoretical insights awaits its practitioners.

CHAPTER SIXTEEN

The Canadian Film Industry and the Digital Revolution

The end result of the cinematic process may be called art or culture or entertainment, but political, economic, and corporate structures are the engines that drive its ultimate realization. Film is part of Canada's cultural industries, and as such it has an 'industrial' base comparable to other cultural industries like publishing, theatre, or music. Those who simply view Canadian films, as well as those who study them intensely, need to be aware of the non-artistic factors that impact the films' creation. Multiple factors, ranging from ownership of theatres to government subsidies, are something every Canadian film-maker has to deal with when trying to reach an audience. Matters of technology, politics, foreign ownership, economic incentives, and industrial concentration are part and parcel of Canada's film history. While journalists and scholars are the verbal intermediaries between film and its audience, they are after-the-fact intermediaries compared to the phalanx of companies, producers, bankers, bureaucrats, tax lawyers, distributors, and equipment rental operators who form the core of decision-making prior to the first day of principal shooting.

In 1998 the Department of Foreign Affairs and International Trade published a comparative study of the Canadian and American film industries, which sought to explain why countries like Canada 'develop regulatory measures, tax incentives and subsidies' to support a domestic film industry in the face of 'the overwhelming presence of the United States in the cultural and entertainment industries.'[1] The U.S. visual media industry (film, video, and television) at the time was generating $18 billion (U.S) in foreign sales, of which $2.4 billion was from film.[2] American-made films accounted for 80 per cent of the world's gross box office revenues.[3] This domination of the world cinema market is only heightened in Canada, where more than 90 per cent of box office revenues are generated by non-Canadian films.[4] The writer of the report, who was viewing Canadian film as a possible export commodity, concluded that 'Canadian production needs to see the world as its market' as a way of solving the national problem of the absent audience.[5] International co-productions, she argued, could link non-American money and expertise to Canadian film productions and then help sell them abroad in those countries which had signed on as co-producers. While 1990s films like *The Red Violin* (1998), with U.S., U.K., and Italian co-producers, or *Margaret's Museum* (1996), which was a U.K.-Canada co-production, did get wider than usual distribution within Canada (i.e., outside the festival circuit), they made no substantive impact on overall Canadian box office revenue for Canadian films when compared to the American percentage.[6] A more typical example is the 1998 science fiction film *Cube*, with a budget under $1 million, which eventually earned U.S. $10 million in France and Japan without any real exposure in Canada.[7]

Of course, box office revenues are a decreasing part of film industry sales, with video/DVD rentals generating more than 52 per cent of American film studio revenues in 1998. That year, Canadians contributed $1 billion to the North American total of $8 billion in video rentals and sales. Estimating a lowly 1 per cent of those Canadian sales to be for Canadian video products, the $10 million in gross income is comparable to the theatrical box office. Television sales of feature films add to this overall income source, as do foreign sales, but even so the income stream for feature films is much lower than the subsidy stream, which totals well over $100 million.[8] As one scholar wrote rather bluntly but accurately, 'only state support can keep feature film alive in Canada.'[9] The nature of that support has waxed and waned over time.

The subsidy stream has existed in various forms since the beginning of the National Film Board (1939) and earlier if we consider various government documentary film-making departments. The traditional form of state involvement was the direct use of tax income to support government departments or arms-length agencies like the National Film Board or the Canadian Broadcasting Corporation in radio and television. The heyday of the NFB was in the 1950s and 1960s, when its budgets reached a post-war high. In its declining years, the budget for documentaries and animation was $60 million (1997–8), with which it produced fifty-three of its own productions and sixty-four co-productions.[10] This was small potatoes compared to the $1.5-billion CBC budget.[11] The Canada Council for the Arts also provides grants (up to $60,000) to film, video, and new media artists. But this kind of state involvement, which prior to 1968 was the only kind available, gradually shifted over to the current model in which the majority of assistance flows to the private sector. A notorious form of early private sector subsidy was the tax shelter used in the 1970s, when the Canadian government was encouraging feature film production through private investment. Eventually every dollar invested in a certified Canadian film was 100 per-cent tax-deductible against one's income. In short, all risk was removed, but the idea lost popularity when the end result was a stream of hundreds of lamentable productions.

The third form of subsidy, and the one most popular with private Canadian film-makers, was direct government investment in a film, which began in 1968 with the Canadian Film Development Corporation and its $10-million budget, and ended up with its successor, Telefilm Canada, with a budget approaching $150 million in 1999/2000, a figure that does not include provisions for Telefilm loan guarantees of up to $25 million.[12] On top of this is a $28-million Cultural Industries Development Fund (CIDF), administered by the Business Development Bank of Canada, which resulted in a total exceeding $200 million of aid in one form or another in 2000. Subsequently, this amount has been increased. While this is not a large sum compared to the money invested in American film production, it is certainly not negligible.

To qualify for funding, a film must have a Canadian citizen as a producer plus earn a minimum of six points out of ten based on use of Canadian key creative people (director / 2 points, screenwriter / 2 points, etc.), as well as being shot and set primarily in Canada. Most of the production and post-production costs must be paid to Canadians. A majority of Telefilm Canada funds provide equity investment in productions for television, including made-for-television movie productions. There is a $20-million feature film fund for films made for theatrical release plus a $11-million feature film distribution fund, as well as monies for dubbing or subtitling and for foreign marketing of these films.[13]

The fourth form of subsidy is the tax credit, which is provided not only by the federal government but also by provincial governments. The largest is the Canadian Film or Video Production Tax Credit (begun in 1995), which replaced the Capital Cost Allowance incentive for certified Canadian productions. It is administered by the Ministry of Canadian Heritage, which in 2002 called for 5 per cent of the total domestic box office to be Canadian films by 2005.[14] Up to 12 per cent of the cost of a production can be saved through this tax credit on salaries. For foreign producers there is another Film or Video Production Services Tax Credit, which provided savings of up to 11 per cent until 2003, when it was increased to 16 per cent. Quebec, Ontario, British Columbia, Manitoba, and Saskatchewan also have tax credit programs to offset provincial taxes and attract film productions. In addition, these provinces offer loan and investment programs for their local film-makers.[15]

Federal and provincial government subsidies are now an integral part of the Canadian film scene. According to Canadian film scholar Ted Madger, these initiatives 'have helped to nurture and consolidate a Hollywood North.'[16] The most noticeable results have appeared in television and video production, especially in the lucrative international market for children's animation, where private Canadian companies have become world leaders. Ontario and Quebec are the prime locations for this kind of work. Recently, Mercury Filmworks, a 120-worker Vancouver animation studio, moved its operations to Toronto because of Ontario's 20 per-cent tax credits for computer animation visual effects work, which enabled it to work with a Canadian industry leader such as Nelvana.[17] The explosion of television cartoon products in the 1980s, based on computer software, fitted Canada well because of the strong NFB animation tradition, which had actually pioneered computer-generated animation in 1968.[18]

The largest private animation company is Nelvana, begun in the 1970s by a trio of Toronto partners who developed half-hour television animations. The company produced a full-length rock musical animation titled *Ring of Fire* in 1983, which was meant for theatrical release but almost bankrupted the company.[19] Two years later, their film *Care Bears: The Movie* became the highest grossing ($25 million) non-Disney animation up to that time.[20] The film was tied to very popular commercial toy products of the day. Much of this work, including bread-and-butter television series, was contracted by American corporations. For example, George Lucas contracted Nelvana to do a Saturday morning cartoon series based on his *Star Wars* series characters. In 1998, Nelvana was producing every single television cartoon on CBS Saturday mornings.[21] As well, Nelvana was producing films and television series in Europe based on popular children's literature – the *Tintin* comic books and *Babar*. In 2000, Nelvana was sold to Corus Entertainment, a Toronto television and radio broadcaster.

The Quebec counterpart to Nelvana is Cinar, founded by the husband-and-wife team of Micheline Charest and Ronald Weinberg, who bought and sold international properties and developed 'Canadian' animation. Eventually the use of the Canadian designation to earn tax credits brought the company into disrepute. The company was investigated for using American scriptwriters, while claiming they were Canadian, and for their founders' use of $120 million of company money for personal investments.[22] The Quebec Securities Commission fined the couple $2 million for their activities. No criminal charges were pursued. But the company had to repay almost $2 million to Canadian and Quebec tax authorities to settle the tax issue plus another $2.6 million to Telefilm Canada.[23] The way in which Canadian animation companies have become such strong players in the international television market is evident in the market capitalization of Cinar Corp., which stood at $1.5 billion in 1999. No wonder shareholder battles over control and direction of the company were fought hard and furiously after this incident.[24]

How did Canada become such a powerhouse in animated film? The talent developed over the years by the NFB, which had an international reputation, was the bedrock. However, it was the computerization of animation, followed by the expanding international market for animation products on television, initially through new cable networks and then the exploding 1990s demand for product in the 500-channel universe with twenty-four-hour designated cartoon channels, that made Canada a significant player. Added to this was the demand for video games played on computer screens around the world, the popularity of adult animations on television, and the lucrative fees paid to creators of computer game software, digitalization, and special effects for films. This new technologically driven international entertainment environment was a new frontier wherein all sorts of new players found success.

This success attracted the attention of American capitalism. For example, Softimage of Montreal, a computer-graphics firm which did the special effects for the *Jurassic Park* films in the 1990s, was bought by Microsoft Corporation in 1994, and Toronto's Alias Research was bought by California's Silicon Graphics in 1995 and merged with an American firm. This orientation toward creative work for big-budget Hollywood features and American television networks created a schizophrenic animation industry in Canada. On the one hand, it played to non-Canadian cultural values because its main commercial role was to adapt non-Canadian subjects; on the other hand, it developed indigenous talent and some original material.

The major source of new Canadian animators is now Sheridan College in Toronto, whose program is one of the most respected in the world.[25] But a substantial portion of the graduates go to the United States.[26] In a sense, the new non-NFB private sector animation industry is a challenge to traditional nationalism, which held that only the Canadian state could maintain Canadian distinctness in the arts. The private sector is part of the globalization phenomenon, with the Canadian industry participating as much through American eyes as it does through its own. The challenge to nationalism comes from the demands of a new computer-based economic system, but also from the universal appeal of animation for children, as the Disney studios learned very early on. Once a story and its characters touch a powerful mythological nerve for children everywhere, its international market is assured through a variety of products from toy figures to books.

Another aspect of Canadian film production that is highly integrated into the American media entertainment industry is the use of Canada as a location for American films. This occurs primarily in Vancouver and Toronto. In British Columbia, for example, $1 billion was spent on two hundred film and television productions in 1999, the majority of which was spent on U.S.-originated productions.[27] The big appeal, especially in the business of made-for-TV movies, was the low value of the Canadian dollar, which was below 70 cents U.S. in the early 2000s (it began to move up in 2003). This meant that American scripts could use Canadian locations to substitute for American ones and thereby cut their budgets by 30 per cent. An American film research institute claimed that by 2000 'more than a third of all major Hollywood feature films [and] nearly two-thirds of all TV movies-of-the-week and mini-series are now filmed in Canada.'[28] In 2001 the U.S. Commerce Department issued a report warning about the negative impact of what Americans call 'runaway productions.'

Not only was the exchange rate an attractive lure to U.S. film producers, but so were the tax credits available from both federal and provincial authorities to foreign companies that shot in Canada. Of Canada's $4.4-billion film and TV industry (mostly television) in 2000, $1.5 billion came from foreign sources, practically all of that amount from the United States.[29] By the millennium, Hollywood was producing over a thousand feature films, almost three per day![30] This was a 40 per cent increase over the 1990 figure, so that although Canada was getting a slice of the American movie-making pie, the pie was growing for all concerned. An accounting study done by PricewaterhouseCoopers showed that Canada was receiving in financial terms only 'two per cent of all Hollywood-based production' in 1998.[31] The justification for encouraging American film production in Canada is the employment it creates in the industry, plus the belief that Canadian films will benefit from this pool of talent and production expertise. Since this pool is dependent on foreign production it is susceptible to decreased demand. In 2002 the value of production in British Columbia dropped, resulting in significant unemployment in an industry whose value had ballooned from $188 million in 1990 to $1.1 billion in 2001.[32] Both federal and provincial governments responded by increasing tax credits for foreign productions.

In 2000 there were only 30 Canadian feature films made (the United States made 1,075), with a value of $330 million compared to Hollywood's $31 billion U.S.[33] In other words, the value of Canadian-originated feature film production (taking the rate of exchange into consideration) was less than 1 per cent of what the Americans invested in their industry! And the average Canadian film budget remained under $3 million, a figure which was steady throughout the 1990s, while American films in the same decade moved up substantially to routine costs of more than U.S. $100 million per film because of the fees paid to film stars. The average cost of a made-in-the-U.S. film in 1998 was over $75 million (Can.)![34]

The large budgets of American films made in Canada made low-budget Canadian films unappealing to Canadian workers in the industry. As one journalist observed, 'Runaway productions, with their big, stable budgets in U.S. dollars, are far more attractive to [Canadian] film crews.'[35] It seems that building a national film culture through being 'hewers of miniseries and drawers of movies-of-the-week' has not been all that successful.[36] The results parallel the recent animation experience, which has built significant Canadian companies and expertise that are more or less dependent on the U.S. market for work. A major scholarly study of the feature film industry in British Columbia, which was published in 2002, concluded that the industry was distinguished by its 'vulnerability' to foreign productions.[37] The author argued that the globalization of locations for the Hollywood industry meant that its productions would be made for the U.S. and international markets wherever it was economically advantageous. This meant that Canada and other countries could end up having an industry that was foreign-oriented.[38]

Even with inherent dependency problems, the Canadian film industry has made a quantum leap forward in terms of corporate structure and power. The largest Canadian producer of films is Alliance Atlantis, a Toronto-based firm with 2002 revenues of almost $1 billion.[39] Alliance Atlantis Communications describes itself as a 'leading vertically integrated broadcaster, creator and distributor of filmed entertainment.'[40] The company came about in a reverse takeover merger in 1998 of Alliance Communications (co-founded by Robert Lantos in the early 1970s) and Michael MacMillan's Atlantis Communications, which created a $750-million entity that was ranked in the 'top 12 film and television studios in North America.'[41] Robert Lantos, the most prominent producer of Canadian feature films, cashed out of 500–employee Alliance and launched Serendipity Point Films with only 12 people to produce films exclusively for Alliance Atlantis for three years.[42] Among his early releases were David Cronenberg's eXistenZ (1999) and Denys Arcand's Stardom (2000).

Lantos's counterpart, Michael MacMillan, started Atlantis in 1978 as a TV and movie production house and later went on to become CEO of Alliance Atlantis. In the 1980s his company moved into distribution by importing films into Canada, and in the 1990s it got involved in Canadian cable television channels. After the merger, Alliance Atlantis–distributed films (mostly non-Canadian) had 18 per cent of the Canadian box office.[43] The firm also began buying up movie theatres to show its films. The company has three main groups – Broadcast, Motion Picture Distribution, and Entertainment – with most of the revenue coming from the production of television series and films. Recently the company has announced a strategy of limiting the number and size of in-house motion picture productions, which may contribute to the narrowing of Canadian film production in the short term.[44] Not that it was a powerhouse of Canadian film production previously. In 1997 Alliance only distributed three Canadian films.[45] A sign of the company's growing interest in the lucrative television industry was its 2001 acquisition of the Halifax production firm of Salter Street Films Ltd, which was well known for its Canadian weekly comedy television program This Hour Has 22 Minutes. In a move to limit production, Alliance Atlantis closed Salter Street in 2004.

The very close integration of Canadian cable television and Canadian film production houses underlines the dependence of the Canadian film industry on the television market for its bread-and-butter profits. In 2000, 53 per cent of Alliance Atlantis revenue came from television, and three-quarters of the television series developed by the company were aimed at export.[46] The next largest chunk, primarily film distribution, accounted for only 30 per cent. A sign of how film is of decreasing interest to the large firms is the 1999 purchase by CanWest Global, a Canadian media giant (Global TV network and the Southam newspaper chain), of 20 per cent voting interest in Alliance Atlantis, making CanWest Global a significant shareholder and an influence on Alliance Atlantis policy as well as a buyer of its television product. When one considers that in 1999 Canadian films took in a paltry $13.8 million in box office, the attachment to television production and specialty channel ownership is necessary from a capitalist standpoint.[47] 'The Alliance corporate-state construct is in direct opposition to the decentered and decentralized network of ... films that have characterized ... Canadian production,' writes one observer. 'As Alliance Atlantis moves up the corporate food chain, it is just a matter of time before it becomes irresistible takeover bait and dissipates into the purification process of the global mega-merger.'[48] In recognition of the growing strength of the Canadian television industry, the $250-million Canadian Television Fund for Canadian productions received a 25 per cent budget cut to its $100 million federal government component in 2003.[49] But the reaction was swift and furious. So entrenched is the private sector's claim to state support that the federal government was forced to reinstate half the amount as an 'advance' against next year's budget.

Because Canadian films continue to exist in the realm of independent productions with only a very small number receiving relatively large budgets (over $10 million) and the promotional clout of a company like Alliance Atlantis, they are seldom heard above the din of Hollywood hype. While Canada is developing some strong players both in television animation production and feature film distribution, current trends in the industry suggest that Canadian feature films will have to find support somewhere else, probably in the marginalized, but sometimes profitable, world of small-time independent boutique film producers and directors. One curious example of this arena is a firm named Cloud Ten Pictures, run by two Ontario brothers, Peter and Paul Lalonde, who began making 'Christian films' in 1998 with the release of *Apocalypse*, a $300,000 film released only on video, which sold 300,000 copies in North America.[50] Their 2001 film, *Left Behind*, sold 3.5 million copies on video and DVD.[51] The film, funded by 'Cloud Ten's own evangelical war chest,' cost $17.4 million.[52] Their prime market, the evangelical Christian community in the United States, numbers almost 100 million adherents.

A technological development that is having a positive impact on lowering the budgets of feature film production is digital filming and computer editing, but the electronic transfer of digital films directly to theatres may be some time in coming. A single 35 mm film print for screening costs $2,000 to make plus another $1,000 to ship and insure.[53] There are 30,000 screens in North America, so that only the largest distributors can afford to make sufficient prints for a continent-wide launch. With digitalization, these distribution costs shrink by 90 per cent. But the cost of new projection equipment is estimated at $2–3 billion for the conversion of North American cinemas, and few movie theatres have made the conversion as of 2002.[54] Today independent film-makers like Gary Burns shoot their features digitally to save money, and then they pay to have them converted to 35 mm, which is still a big saving. Canadian experience has shown that the lower the budget, the greater the chance of recouping costs. Of course, digitally produced films can be screened on the Internet, and this medium may become a popular format, especially when it can be tied to large-format high definition television screens in home entertainment systems. Rather than go to a video store for a DVD or to a movie theatre, one would simply download a movie to one's television screen.

The possibility of a micro-budget film-making wave happened in 1999 when the independent American film *The Blair Witch Project* unexpectedly became an instant success, grossing U.S. $140 million in four months, making it the most profitable film of all time.[55] Apparently the movie's website was innovatively alluring and the film itself so different from the run-of-the-mill Hollywood product, that its no-name actors and film-makers became cult heroes. Of course, the film's horror-movie theme had a built-in audience of youthful thrill-seekers.

What impact technological developments like digital filming, website promotion, and downloadable products will have on Canadian films and their audiences is yet to be determined. Lower budgets for films would mean more films, but that does not necessarily translate into a larger Canadian audience, which may not be as small as box office statistics have suggested. A Leger Marketing poll done in 2002 on Canadian culture asked movie-goers (63 per cent of the 1,500 person sample) what percentage had seen a Canadian film in the past year, and an amazing 30 per cent responded that they had![56] Of the 37 per cent who had gone to a theatre to attend a play, 61 per cent had watched a Canadian production; and of the 73 per cent who had read a book in the past year, 61 per cent had read at least one book by a Canadian author.[57]

Of the total sample, 43 per cent had read a Canadian book; 24 per cent had seen a Canadian play, and 19 per cent had seen a Canadian film. Perhaps the unusually high figure for film came from a strong showing in Quebec or a bias in the sample to those in large metropolitan areas. If the figure held firm for all Canadians of movie-going age, then over 5 million Canadians would have seen at least one Canadian film in the previous year, a figure the box office statistics do not support. It is more likely that the number is under 2 million.

The history of the Canadian film industry indicates that the search for a Canadian audience/market continues to face insurmountable barriers. In 1990 political economist Manjunath Pendakur concluded that 'regardless of the number and quality of films produced in Canada, they remain obscure and inaccessible to moviegoers, and their profitability is severely limited.'[58] Nothing much has changed since then. It would seem that the holy grail of Canadian cinema that requires national audiences to be enamoured of their own creative product is an illusionary one in English Canada. In Quebec, comedies like *Les Boys 3* grossed $5.5 million in 2002 with only Quebec theatrical release.[59] Even with this market-oriented proliferation of genre films, Quebeckers spend less than 10 per cent of every dollar on their own films.

Canadian cinema has always struggled against the American tide that engulfs film in Canada. The occasional piece of talented driftwood may be discovered, but it is invariably a stand-alone experience. No wonder it is television and video/DVD sales that make up the vast bulk of distributors' income from Canadian films. The Hollywood genre film is a Canadian movie theatre's main attraction. 'Today's genre films,' writes American film scholar W.W. Dixon, 'have become the dominant force in motion picture production ... because they are to a large extent a pre-sold, pre-tested quantity whose qualities and limitations are known to the audience ...'[60] The big-budget blockbuster is something that has proved to be beyond the capacity of the Canadian film industry, and it is this type of film that Hollywood excels in making and Canadian audiences enjoy. Seth Feldman in his 1996 Martin Walsh Memorial Lecture at the Film Studies Association of Canada stated that 'these are hard times for the cinematic ideal.'[61] The cinematic ideal may be part of Canadian films because of the view that within small, limited national cinemas far from Hollywood's maddening crowd resides artfulness and a diversity of national spirits. Film critic Rick Groen called this ideal cinema's power to generate 'unending magic,' but, of course, most movie viewers consider magic simply digital special effects.[62] This means that the 'magic' provided by cinema to Canadians throughout their history has come primarily from American ideology and imagination. As a result, the 'Canadian' filmic imagination is always viewed as an upstart in the minds of Canadian film audiences. That does not mean that there is not a 'magic' to Canadian films to be appreciated and admired. It is simply a different magic, seldom viewed.

Because of its ties to the American juggernaut, the industry in Canada has come to be criticized for its dependence on 'the strict logic of commercialism', which influences what is produced and for whom.[63] The state subsidies that allow this to happen are also being questioned because they have failed to generate a self-sustaining national cinema.[64] In contrast, Canadian government (CRTC) music content quotas on radio have actually worked to create an internationally recognized industry with numerous stars. Could it be that the quota system, so feared by Hollywood, and so much avoided by the Canadian state because of American pressure, is an option that needs revisiting?

The tug-of-war over Canadian identity in cinema and the role of private industry and government subsidy have been fundamental aspects of Canada's film history. The business of 'culture and the arts' has always attracted legitimate entrepreneurs as well as those interested in the 'quick-buck.' Both groups have played on the continuing 'need' for subsidies to create a Canadian film industry. In some cases, the Canadian film and television industry has created personal fortunes (Robert Lantos received a reported $60 million for his stake in Alliance).[65] Playing the nationalist card makes economic sense for national elites, who use the state to further their interests under the guise of contributing to national identities (Quebec's or Canada's). 'Canadian discourses on national identity,' Michael Dorland explained, are part and parcel of 'the transition to commodity exchange in the political economies of culture.'[66]

While the United States uses the supposedly value-free concept of 'entertainment' to justify its global cultural penetration, Canada uses the concept of defending 'culture' to justify its right to support national enterprises. That state intervention has resulted in a privately owned industry that is primarily oriented to U.S. television production indicates that the siren song of Canadian nationalism is one that cultural business elites have used effectively to promote their economic self-interest. That Canadian government policy has been simultaneously pro-Canadian and pro-American is not surprising, considering that the main purpose of the Canadian state's interventionist policies is the furtherance of national capitalism in a continental market. If that capitalism chooses to grow through Americanization, then the Canadian state has not, and will not, oppose it.

CHAPTER SEVENTEEN

A History of the Future

In the period from 1991 to 2001, Quebec produced six of the top ten grossing Canadian box office films, all of which were comedies with an average box office per film of about $3.5 million.[1] All of the money came from Quebec because none of the films was screened elsewhere in Canada, except at film festivals. Basically, English Canada did not see (except in video or on television) the country's top-grossing films. The entrenched division into two non-communicating national cinemas should be viewed as a major barrier for building a sustained critical mass for the nation's cinema. When the federal government announced in 2000 that it was increasing the Feature Film Fund to $100 million per year beginning in fiscal year 2001–2 (three-quarters for theatrical releases), it must be understood that Quebec would get a significant portion of that amount and that those films would generally not be seen in the rest of the country.[2]

The popularity in the 1990s of Quebec film comedies like *La Florida* and *Les Boys* was not lost on English-Canadian film producers and directors, especially those with close ties to television. Two English-Canadian films were released in 2002 for general theatrical distribution that sought to reach a wide Canadian audience using the Quebec approach. *Men with Brooms* was created by Paul Gross, known to Canadians for his comic Mountie role in *Due South*, a hit television series of the late 1990s. *Men with Brooms* had a production budget of $7.5 million and a record-breaking promotion budget of $1.75 million.[3] Lantos's Serendipity Point Films was the producer, using $2.5 million from the newly enhanced Canadian Feature Film Fund for the production, while Alliance Atlantis received $1.2 million to subsidize the publicity campaign.[4] Canadian pay-TV rights were estimated to be $400,000, while CBC broadcast rights were estimated at $300,000. There was also an estimated $1 million in tax credits.[5] With the distribution power of Alliance Atlantis, this comedy about curling opened in 207 theatres in Canada in March 2002, and its 'box-office gross of $1.04 million was the highest opening weekend for an English-language feature.'[6] Promoting a product paid off at the start, but the higher initial cost of the film could undermine profits. In a historical context, a Canadian market gross of $5 million would be considered outstanding, but that would still be insufficient to recoup costs. International sales would have to make up the difference.

This example of 'true Canadiana' was matched by a film starring the backwoods comic persona of Red Green, played by Steve Smith.[7] The Toronto comedian had been starring in a highly successful weekly television comedy show called *The Red Green Show*, which was also carried in the United States on the Public Broadcasting System (PBS). The show had been airing since 1997 and had a weekly audience of about 1 million in Canada.[8] Smith used his own production company's funds to make *Duct Tape Forever*, which was released a month after *Men with Brooms*. The film had half the budget of *Men with Brooms* and a lot less publicity, but with a potential American audience for the film (his fan club has 120,000 members), it had a better chance of recouping costs.[9] Neither film received rave reviews from critics, which is typical for comedies.[10]

The comedy route is currently perceived as having real potential because of Canadian comedic success on Canadian television. There were a number of popular sketch-comedy shows (*The Royal Canadian Air Farce*, *This Hour Has 22 Minutes*) with a large Canadian following. Producers view a feature film based on these television characters or actors as having a built-in audience. In fall 2001 *Mambo Italiano*, a play by Steve Gallucio, broke attendance records at Montreal's anglophone Centaur Theatre. The play about a traditional Italian family facing a crisis when a son reveals that he is gay is filled with sitcom clichés, wherein its popularity lay. That money-making popularity generated a film version of the same name, starring Mary Walsh of *22 Minutes* fame. The film received a major release in mainstream theatres across Canada in fall 2003. Its Canadian producers were certainly aware of the previous popularity of the American ethnic film comedy *My Big Fat Greek Wedding*, written by and starring a Canadian, which became in 2002 an extremely profitable independent American film that spawned its own short-lived television sitcom. Their hopes of emulating at least some of that success were based on the large size of the Italian community in North America (Toronto alone has an Italian community of half a million) and on the general public's current appetite for ethnic comedies.

While all three of these comedies were Central Canadian in locale there was a regional Maritime feature film phenomenon that had begun with melodramas like *Margaret's Museum* (1996) and *The Hanging Garden* (1997) but had moved to comedy with such films as *New Waterford Girl* (2000). Since a number of nationally known Canadian television comics come from the Maritimes and the idiosyncrasies of regional culture have proven susceptible to humorous personification, the film industry was attracted to this potential.

But a feature film industry would be very narrow if it depended solely on comedy. An alternative to comedy was the first Inuit-language feature film every produced. *Atanarjuat: The Fast Runner* was released in Canadian art-house cinemas in the spring of 2002. The film had garnered the Caméra d'Or or first-feature-film award at Cannes in 2001, the first time that award had ever been won by a Canadian. The film went on to win other awards, including the Prix du Public at the Montreal International Festival of New Cinema and New Media, best Canadian feature at the Toronto International Film Festival, and the best picture and best director at the Genies. The 172-minute film was not easy to place in theatres because of its length, which allowed for only one screening per evening, but Canadian critics were enthusiastic. Rick Groen of the *Globe and Mail* termed it 'a superb film ... intriguingly exotic and uniquely Canadian.'[11] *Maclean's* called it 'an Arctic masterpiece' and 'a landmark for world cinema.'[12] Even the venerable Margaret Atwood wrote glowingly about the film.[13]

It would seem that the first-ever feature film made almost entirely by Inuit in the Inuktitut language was a novel enough experience to be hailed as a milestone. Like all milestones, it had a distant predecessor. Robert Flaherty's 1922 documentary *Nanook of the North* was a precursor that dramatized the life of Eskimos for people around the world. The challenge of primitive survival in the Arctic's harsh and forbidding climate fascinated audiences everywhere. The same fascination continued eighty years later. *Atanarjuat* was directed by Zacharias Kunuk and filmed by Norman Cohn in digital video. The film cost $1.9 million to produce.[14] The script by Paul Angilirq, which was pieced together from elders' stories, represents the 'first long piece of written literature in the Inuktitut language.'[15] Kunuk had first heard the story as a young boy in the early 1960s, and it remained with him into adulthood.[16] Cohn had moved to the settlement of Igloolik from the South, where he became one of the founders of Igloolik Isuma Productions, established in 1990 to do video training and production in the North. Getting funding for the film was not easy because funding agencies at the time had no category for non-official language films (this was prior to the establishment of Nunavut, whose official language is Inuktitut).

The plot involves two brothers, one of whom is called Atanarjuat. An evil shaman has cast a curse on the area in a rivalry between two family clans. Atanarjuat takes a second wife while on a hunting trip, a woman who has desired him ever since she lost him to another. This second wife eventually seduces Atanarjuat's brother as well and is expelled from the camp. Her expulsion is cause for a revenge killing. In one of the most memorable and bone-chilling scenes in cinema, the naked and barefoot Atanarjuat flees from his brother's murderers across sheet ice, barely escaping with his life. The film's conclusion reflects the mythology, matriarchal power, and group survival ethics of its people.

From the film-maker's point of view, the film represents 'this storytelling tradition – albeit in a different medium.'[17] For Inuit viewers in touch with their cultural heritage, the film becomes a continuation of mythology.[18] But for non-Inuit viewers, it is read more as an insight into pre-contact history. In viewing the three-hour film, one is moved to a place and time and culture that are utterly foreign and yet strangely familiar. 'Greek tragedy' is a term that has come up in seeking a comparison with something similar in the Western tradition.[19] The spirit world that inhabits the daily lives of the characters in *Atanarjuat* may not fit the scientific mind, but it does resonate at a deeper subconscious level with contemporary viewers, for whom the epic battle of vice and virtue makes perfect sense. One critic described the film as 'overwhelming in its meaning' because it speaks with the same power as 'Greek epic poetry and Shakespearean epic tragedy.'[20] Non-Inuit viewers eventually succumb to the film's mythological magic, after first approaching it as a historical or ethnographic insight into a way of life long gone. Because *Atanarjuat* exists in the contemporary idiom of film but derives from an oral story, it combines the historical and the mythological, the contemporary and the traditional.

Kunuk has been working on a sequel in which the arrival of White men is presented from the Inuit perspective. Here history and mythology struggle with each other even more. The same mythological power is present in this new story, which involves dreams, symbols, and magical transformations, but it is based on a real event in the late

1800s.[21] Considering the fame he has garnered with *Atanarjuat*, this new film should take less than the six years his inaugural film took to make. Kunuk's achievement was recognized by columnist Robert Everett-Green, who named Kunuk Canada's 'Nation Builder of the Year' because his film was 'a trumpet blast of vitality' from a marginalized community.[22] The film, the columnist explained, burst onto the Canadian and international film scene with such power that it awakened Canadians and others to 'a wealth of narrative clinging to life in the Far North.'[23] The *Globe and Mail* named Kunuk '2002 Artist of the Year.'[24] This enthusiasm indicates a certain hunger in Canadian film criticism for an alternative to the clichés of a Southern Canadian culture such as beavers in *Men with Brooms* and the Canada Goose in *Duct Tape Forever*. The film, while aimed primarily at an Inuit audience, confirmed the importance of the Aboriginal vision to a non-Eurocentric Canadianism. The publication of a large coffee-table–sized book of the film's script, with hundreds of photos from the production, recognized the film's importance.[25]

The Inuit population of Canada is a mere 45,000 (2001 census), and yet it has created a film of distinct power that announces a new epoch in which Aboriginal voices can take centre stage. In 2001 the combined Aboriginal population of Canada stood at 1.3 million, or 3 per cent of the overall population. The Aboriginal element is a diverse population of many different First Nations peoples, spread primarily from Quebec to British Columbia. Out of this rich mosaic of once repressed cultures is the potential for recreating Canadian identity away from its Eurocentric heritage.

Scott MacKenzie of the University of Glasgow published an article in the *Canadian Aesthetics Journal*'s special issue on art in an age of diversity and globalization that offers a context for understanding the postcolonial and postmodernist importance of *Atanarjuat* and its relationship to the economics of digitalized film-making.[26] He discusses the concept of a 'post-national' identity for Canadian culture and a cinema that reflects a multicultural reality. *Atanarjuat* is exactly the kind of film that challenges the former conventions of Canadian identity represented by *Men with Brooms*. The various competing national identities within Canada (English, Québécois, Aboriginal, etc.) are, according to MacKenzie, 'dialogistic and antagonistic in nature,' meaning they oppose each other and yet remain tied to each other.[27] MacKenzie argues that 'there's no Canadian identity' as such, only a 'conflicted, negotiated identity' dominated by and obsessed with images from the

United States.[28] There is no 'us' as a unified singularity but an 'us' that is multiple. The sense of a singular us comes from contrast with the American other – with the outside not the inside. *Atanarjuat* is completely enclosed in its own idiom: the characters, the language, the environment, and the mythology are totally Inuit, a culture currently belonging to less than half of 1 per cent of the country's population. When non-Inuit Canadians view the film, they experience it as 'foreign' much in the same way, if not more so, as English Canadians view quintessentially Quebec films – with subtitles. Canadian cinema, when viewed from the perspective of *Atanarjuat*, becomes a cinema of translation for its own inhabitants. It also becomes a cinema of minorities in which the languages and cultures, which represent small numbers of people, can be fundamental. Embracing that internal foreignness prevents Canadians from accumulating a simplistic or exclusionary sense of self.

Earlier the National Film Board director Alanis Obomsawin, a veteran of numerous documentaries and the award-winning *Kanehsatake: 270 Years of Resistance* (1993), about the armed stand-off at Oka, Quebec, in 1990, had made films about Aboriginal issues, but in English. It is the centrality of a 'foreign' language that distinguishes *Atanarjuat* and challenges Canadians to accept the vitality and validity of other national identities within one nation-state. Shirley Cheechoo, the first First Nations woman to write, produce, direct, and act in a fiction feature, *Backroads* (1999), used both English and Cree in her film, reflecting the mixed cultural reality of contemporary Cree culture. *Atanarjuat* makes no such cultural compromises. It encourages Canadians to reflect on Canada in its pre-Canadian reality. It provides a narrative that comes from the heart of the formerly colonized peoples to challenge and overthrow the superiority of the colonizer's worldview. At the same time, the film's portrayal of ancient Inuit culture rather than the contemporary one may actually encourage non-Inuit audiences to indulge older images of romanticized primitivism created by outsiders. Should Kunuk's film about the contact era be made, the issue of non-Inuit audience perspective and perception will be crucial. It would not be surprising if identification with Inuit culture by non-Inuit film audiences becomes more problematic when non-Inuit culture is represented for the first time.

The cultural importance of Aboriginal themes in Canadian cinema can be seen in two films made in the early 1990s by non-Aboriginals. *Black Robe* (1991) was a Genie award–winning film about the missionary experience in New France based on a novel by Brian Moore, which, in turn, drew on the accounts recorded by seventeenth-century Jesuit missionaries in *The Jesuit Relations*. The film's point of view is that of the missionary. The film was initially hailed for its authenticity in costuming and sets, use of subtitled non-European dialogue, and magnificent nature cinematography. But Gittings has exposed 'the film's cultural biases' and its emphasis on 'the Aboriginal Other.'[29] He argues convincingly that the discourse of the film remains colonial because of its Eurocentric pedigree (*The Jesuit Relations*), by which the White audience identifies with the priestly project and the construction of Native people as 'savages.'

Clearcut, also released in 1991, is a more interesting case. Based on a Governor General's Award–winning novel, it tells the story of a White city lawyer struggling to stop logging in northern Ontario on behalf of a local band. He loses the legal battle and becomes involved in a kidnapping of the local pulp-mill manager by a strange Native character, whose actions are deeply violent. The film deals primarily with the excruciating suffering that the journey involves. The torturer turns out to be a shamanistic dream character, a projection of the lawyer's own feelings. The film presents the lawyer as undergoing a vision quest in which he sees the limitations of the White world that he had once taken for granted. Graham Greene, an actor born on the Six Nations Reserve in Ontario, plays the strange figure of the kidnapper, Arthur, with 'uncommon intensity.'[30] Both films differ markedly from American films of the same period, such as the Native American–authored *Pow-Wow Highway* and the mainstream *Dances with Wolves*. Their view of White-Aboriginal relations is not predicated on an emphasis on social disparity (*Pow-Wow Highway*) nor the romanticism of the 'noble savage' of *Dances with Wolves*. They present colonization as an internal process for all participants.

Considering that Canada's Aboriginal population numbers only 1.3 million and is composed of numerous First Nations identities, its role in Canadian cinema exceeds its demographic reality.[31] Whether it be the documentary work of Obomsawin or the Inuit-language work of Kunuk, Aboriginal film-making should be considered foremost 'a marriage of art and politics.'[32] In this sense, it follows the path embraced by Quebec film-makers in the 1960s and 1970s, when a profound political project energized the arts. It seems that a renewed affirmation of a historically suppressed nationality, language, or ethnic identity brings forth cinematic innovation. The new voice reinvents its identity from inside, rather than accept an externally imposed identity. While critics may embrace this spirit of innovation as a breakthrough, the meaning of that art to the general Canadian public is not quite so obvious. How the public reads films like *Atanarjuat* depends on the range and depth of its stereotypes, interests, and openness to new approaches. Considering the limited audience for Canadian films in Canada, films like *Clearcut* and *Atanarjuat* do not have a major impact on public consciousness in general, though they play significant roles in their respective communities.

The issue of a diverse cinema for Canada is taken up in a different context by Atom Egoyan's *Ararat*, a film about the Armenian genocide by Turks during the First World War. When a Canadian director of Armenian descent makes a film in Toronto on a $15-million budget that is meant to speak about a historic tragedy to world audiences, he is moving far beyond the norms of Canadian content.[33] Told in English and using the fictional narrative device of the Canadian Armenian community's involvement in making a film about the genocide, the film distances itself from typical historical drama. While it has 'foreign' subject matter like *Atanarjuat*, it has a mainstream Eurocentric feeling. *Atanarjuat* speaks difference, while *Ararat* speaks familiarity, even though the subject may not be familiar. The two films are worlds apart. One is filled with the spirit of an ancient culture contextualized outside the colonized experience, while the other is filled with a sense of urban drama contextualized in a contemporary mode. *Ararat* comes out of the film language and culture that formed Egoyan, while *Atanarjuat* comes from a mythological universe that Canadians have experienced only through the national art (carving, prints, etc.) of a small community. *Ararat* expressed continuity with the mainstream of English-Canadian cinema, while *Atanarjuat* interrupted that continuity. Both Kunuk and Egoyan dealt with issues facing their ethnic communities, and the radical difference between the two films is indicative of the distance between an assimilated White immigrant sensibility and a resistant indigenous one. *Atanarjuat* and *Ararat* symbolize the two fundamental directions that nationality-based cinema in Canada can go. *Atanarjuat* represents a creative force that could revitalize and refresh Canadian difference, while *Ararat* represents a creative force that restates Eurocentric dominance. Egoyan's goal was to bring the genocide issue to world mainstream audiences. If he had done the film in a subtitled form, he would have lessened its impact politically but heightened its artistic contribution. The road suggested by *Atanarjuat* is more daring than that suggested by *Ararat*. If every nationality in Canada were willing to speak in cinema in its own language, the cinematic redefinition of Canada would be profound. Canadian cinema would then be configured as a safe haven for self-affirming cultures that resist the globalizing homogeneity of English. This is already true of Quebec cinema. For a resurgent indigenous consciousness this is a real possibility, while for the immigrant consciousness English remains the language of expression.

A historian is not a futurist. A history of the future is a contradiction. The title of this concluding chapter is meant to highlight the historical problem of how the past is read by the present and how this reading is projected into the future. Historical readings encourage the formulation of a basic identity meant to determine future possibilities. To draw conclusions about what might be, based on the history of English-Canadian and Quebec cinema, is predicated on the contentious belief that what went before has sufficient momentum to carry on into the future. In English-Canadian and Quebec cinema, what went before was the powerful role of the state in defining the nature of cinematic practice, the restrictive impact of a successful documentary and animation tradition on the development of a vibrant feature film industry, and the historical marginalization of Canadian cinema for home audiences despite three decades of on-going feature film production. To these should be added the lack of representation for various elements of the community on the screen. Which of these four elements will define Canadian cinema in the future is a question that only the future can answer.

The four broad aspects of Canadian cinema, highlighted in this history, have combined to create a national cinema of insufficient weight to influence public perceptions of national identities, especially in English Canada. The reasons for that past failure have been widely analysed. Looking at the present moment rather than the past century, one sees immediately a technological revolution created by digitalization, which is liberating but also confining English-Canadian and Quebec film. The explosion in the demand for visual cultural products for television, the screen, and computers has resulted in an increasing demand for creative expression, both artistic and mundane. How this demand ultimately impacts a traditional form like film is uncertain. No doubt there will be both positive and negative results. For those living in the historical present (post-2000) there is a tension between the tradition that has been created by previous technologies and policies and the very real contemporary dynamic pressures that seek to both accommodate and break from what was. One example of this is the current emphasis on 'intellectual' versus 'physical' property, wherein the ownership of ideas and creative innovation are more valued than so-called 'bricks and mortar.' In the digital universe of the present and the immediate future, smaller entities, initially at least, have certain advantages and possibilities for growth.

Jeremy Rifkin, an American analyst of cultural change and social issues, claims that this new digital reality makes culture industries 'the fastest growing sector of the global economy.'[34] The place of national cinemas in the 'Age of Information' and the digital Internet highway may be promising from one perspective and yet be tentative from another. It is promising because of the decentralized nature of digital cultural production and commerce in this early period of its growing dominance, which can offer minority voices a global access. It is tentative because of the growing hegemonic control of cultural creation by the English-language world. Because Canada participates in both English and non-English cultures, its cinemas are caught in the hegemonic battle, as are other national cinemas.

Cyberspace is an interactive site with theatrical dimensions for all its participants.[35] As a synthetic environment, it has ties to our experience of cinema, which like other cultural forms takes us into realms where the imagination has priority. As cyberspace becomes more and more the overriding realm of entertainment, commerce, and human communication, the demands of virtual reality make cultural production 'the high-end sector of the economic value chain.'[36] Film is part of this sector. Critics of economic globalization have sought to defend the independence of national and regional cultural spheres from the homogenization of American cultural production, but their voice is that of a critical minority not of the consuming majority. Will the prevalence of cyberspace environments and the digitalized media of the Internet lead to solving the age-old problem of audiences for Canadian films or will it simply continue the same old story? The answer is in the future.[37]

It would be foolhardy to predict the rise or demise or even plateauing of Canadian cinematic production when a new technological era is being created. A new era is a process over which its creators and promoters have no substantive control. They ride the wave looking for benefits. Those who have studied the nature of film in earlier historical contexts (silent films, 35 mm) do not see the digital universe as anything essentially different. It is simply another technical transformation for delivering the same old imaginary product. The amazing verisimilitude of contemporary computer-generated special effects may be a galaxy away from the cardboard models of a century ago, but they are still special effects dependent on the audience's willing suspension of its disbelief as it watches a screen – theatrical, television, or computer. These critics say that illusion will always be illusion, whether for a medieval audience or a contemporary one.

But some feel that the all-encompassing nature of cyberspace may mean that film and its meaning will be radically transformed.[38] It is the tension between the forces of a dynamic present (the radical) and an inert past (the conservative) that makes understanding of the future difficult and speculative. The process of digitalized film distribution, which, as discussed in the previous chapter, is simply a new technological delivery system, is not the real revolution these critics see.[39] Instead, they view the digitalization of the moving image as part of a new all-encompassing technological culture integral to advanced countries. The distinctness of film as a product, already challenged for half a century by television, will be further compromised in the digital universe, where simulation and reality merge. 'The future of the moving image,' writes one film theorist, 'is ... removing us further and further from our corporeal reality [and toward] ... the mesmeric embrace of the phantom zone ... in which the copy increasingly approaches the verisimilitude of the original.'[40] Cinema, rooted in the physicality of the theatrical stage, may have to find a new home.

The film theorist André Bazin's definition of cinema as 'change mummified' can also be applied to the writing of film history.[41] A history of a cinema mummifies the change inherent in life and society because the words of a history book turn life and work into an *objective* narration – a static object. Reading a history of film delivers a completely different experience from watching a film. Watching a film involves an emotional journey that is visually and aurally controlling, like oral storytelling. A literary text that is read in silence by an individual reader narrates events into words, creating a new event that is qualitatively different from the events described. When a history book turns films and their authors into objects for understanding and rationalization, the historian is performing a post-mortem dissection.

In performing an autopsy and then stitching the body together to make it look whole, a historical text reassembles the persons involved and their art in such a way as to make them look complete and untouched by the truncation of narration. A description of a two-hour film that takes a reader twenty seconds to read approaches neither the visual richness and impact of a film nor a description of the thousands of hours of work and human interaction that went into the film's making. A historical text offers a mummy preserved in a covering of words. Even a contemporary viewing of a film from the past is problematic. The historical context of the film-maker who releases a film in 1975 is not the context of a viewer watching it in 2005. General history and cinematic history have intervened, so that the film cannot be viewed the way it once was or with a similar impact. It is now a mummified historical object taken out of a living context, an intellectual museum to be visited and revisited.

Marshall McLuhan, Canada's leading late twentieth-century thinker on the media (Harold Innis was his counterpart earlier), offered an interpretive framework that he thought explained how electronic media operated and would continue to operate. First, the introduction of a new medium enhances (the law of amplification); second, by enhancing the importance of the medium, the new medium makes an older medium obsolete (law of obsolesence); third, the new medium retrieves something from the obsolescent medium (law of retrieval); and finally, it flips the medium into something else when pushed to its limits (law of reversal).[42]

McLuhan's tetradic movement, when applied to Canadian cinematic culture, turns it into a both/and and a not either/or. The problem with McLuhan's system is that it gives priority to technological imperative. So a film like *Atanarjuat*, while suitable to a tetradic anaylysis of enhancement (oral tradition), obsolescence (oral tradition), retrieval (oral tradition), and reversal (film replaces the storyteller), ends up being viewed more from its cinematic/video construction than from its traditional sources. McLuhan's emphasis on form rather than content makes the Aboriginal content secondary and the filmic form primary. But in the Inuit worldview, technology is simply a new medium for an old message and the message is what is important. McLuhan would give communicative power to the medium, which signals the end of oral storytelling through its transformation into a film, while Inuit culture would give it to the message by claiming fundamental orality remains in the new medium.

The contradictions of Canadian cinema are not simply based in technological innovation. They are social, economic, cultural, and historic. Overcoming contradictory concepts such as the Canadianness of Inuit mythology requires an acknowledgment that Canadian cinema contains within itself an *otherness*, which both challenges and defines it. Canadian cinema is a cinema of *otherness*. The debate concerns the

meaning of this *otherness.* 'Contradictions are self-produced opposi-
tions,' explains a Marxist dialectician, 'in which a cultural given shows
itself to be process instead of thing by traducing the boundary of its
own self-definition and becoming its otherness.'[43] The current contradictions between the spirit of *Atanarjuat* and *Duct Tape Forever* mean
that both display an otherness to each other. From the perspective of
Inuit culture, *Duct Tape Forever* is a statement of Eurocentric culture.
From the perspective of traditional Canadian identity, it is a statement
rooted in the traditional symbols of national identity, while *Atanarjuat*
is an un-Canadian strangeness because of Canada's historic self-definition as a Eurocentric reality. The question is whether postmodern,
postcolonial cultures that are now Canada are becoming identified
more with the resurgent colonized cultures within them (*Atanarjuat*) or
with an overarching globalized technology developed by Anglo-American culture? This is the driving issue/challenge/contradiction of Canadian film today. On the one hand, the industry grows economically by
creating American market products; on the other hand, it produces
works like *Atanarjuat* that speak out of an authenticity that Hollywood
narrative could never approach. This authenticity is seen by few and
understood by even fewer. The Americanization of the Canadian cinematic imagination, an established reality going back a century, has
made the majority of Canadians immune to their own cinematic imagination. Only a small minority of Canadians remain open to their own
cinema.

A cultural revolution could take Canadian film history out of its
present contradictions (the foreignness of its own cinema, for example)
and move it to the next stage. By cultural revolution, I do not mean
technological change. I mean an explosion of creative artistic energy
recognized by the general public as a new voice that it wants to hear
and see. Such an explosion can only come about when a national
entity (like Quebec) embarks on a fundamental redefinition. There is
nothing in the era of continental free trade and the overwhelming
power of the pro-American media that would encourage such a development. At the present moment, Canada does not have a political
context for redefining its identity inwardly and away from continental and global parameters.

A revolution in Canadian and/or Quebec culture is a dream. It is
nothing more than a desire. The countries of the First World have been
in the gradually tightening grip of electronic media ever since the
invention of the telegraph a century and a half ago. Film is just another

manifestation of electricity-based communication. The reality promoted by an electronic universe is one that 'emphasizes seeing and hearing, and is multiperspectival and environmental.'[44] The latest cyberworld engaging the leading edge of human energy is building on a techno-logical culture of which film was an early example.[45] It is also a world seemingly without end, in which the human self is constantly evolving in an ever changing web of digitalized relationships that keep meta-morphosing and expanding.[46] In such a homogenizing world, it is ancient sub–nation-state identities that hold promise for enhanced human values and not traditional nation states, which are the products of a nineteenth- and twentieth-century nationalism. These ancient iden-tities have this power because their cultural symbols have a depth that national identity constructed during modernity does not. In an age of English-language dominance, a film in Inuktitut can be viewed in the heartland of that dominance as 'startling and fresh,' even though its American distributor retitles the film *The Fast Runner*.[47]

Canadian film is operating in a new national and global environment in which Eurocentric culture is technologically powerful, but whose imagery and identities are being challenged. With Canadian literature increasingly defined by non-traditional anglophone immigrant voices and even Quebec culture contacting its allophone and anglophone otherness (*Léolo* is a strong example), national social imagery in Canada is undergoing a profound transformation propelled by these new cul-tures. But as long as English-Canadian and Quebec cinema are primar-ily elitist art cinemas, they will not play the kind of defining and formative role for the Canadian public that American cinema plays for the U.S. public. The search for non-American motifs in Canadian cultures is not a difficult one, but relating these motifs to 'the world of everyday percep-tions' of Canadians is problematic and has been for three decades.[48] For some time, English-Canadian and Quebec film has had an impact in Canada similar to the independent American film in the United States – very limited. Its 'independence' and 'difference' are artistically positive but economically negative, because these narratives are read as 'foreign' by mainstream audiences. Multiculturalism in Canadian cinema will not help overcome the marginalization. The multiculturalism that keeps Ca-nadian film in the realm of art cinema is the same multiculturalism that in literature is *building* an established and popularly accepted literary tradition. It does not do so in Canadian film because Canadian film has been historically inherently 'foreign' to Canadians.

Canadian film remains a secondary cultural influence in Canada, but the characteristics that have come to define this cinema are not in themselves unimportant. They reflect the geopolitical nature of the country – its two national cinemas, which are distinct and complementary, its evolutionary rather than revolutionary path to inclusiveness, its minor role in global cultural dominance, and its occasional flashes of filmic innovation that garner international recognition. Canadian cinema has a multiple identity that is recognized by cinephiles around the world as having validity and distinctness. The issue is how to turn that validity and distinctness into part of a widely appreciated public discourse in Canada. For English-Canadian and Quebec film-makers that has been a never-ending battle. They know the holy grail of national cinema has been a tarnished one, but in the end they would like us to view their creations in a spirit of goodwill, with insight and self-understanding. We owe them at least that much.

Notes

Introduction

1 A summary of the postcolonialist attack on the traditional Canadian nationalist construction of identity may be found in Martin Allor, Danielle Juteau, and John Shepherd, 'Contingencies of Culture: The Space of Culture in Canada and Québec,' *Culture and Policy* 6.1 (1994); http://www.gu.edu.au/centre/cmp/journal/html.

2 For a broad-ranging discussion of today's critical cultural theories, see Shaobo Xie and Fengzhen Wang, eds, *Dialogues on Cultural Studies* (Calgary: University of Calgary Press, 2002).

3 Robert Stam, *Film Theory: An Introduction* (Malden, MA: Blackwell, 2000), 183.

4 For a summary of Canadian film's invisibility, see Charles R. Acland, 'From the Absent Audience to Expo-Mentality: Popular Film in Canada,' in *A Passion for Identity: Canadian Studies for the Twenty-First Century*, ed. David Taras and Beverly Rasporich, 4th ed. (Toronto: Nelson, 2001), 275–91.

5 Christopher E. Gittings, *Canadian National Cinema* (London and New York: Routledge, 2002), 5.

6 For a recent discussion of American military imperialism and its effect on Canada, see George Melnyk, ed., *Canada and the New American Empire: War and Anti-War* (Calgary: University of Calgary Press, 2003).

7 Taras and Rasporich, eds, *A Passion for Identity*, 5.

8 In *Canadian National Cinema*, Gittings shows both Canadian and Quebec national cinemas as being equally guilty of racist and patriarchal stereotyping. He describes both traditions as creating a 'white phallocentric, heterosexual canon' (4).

9 Brian D. Johnson, 'Down by the Bays,' *Maclean's*, 3 Feb. 2003, p. 46.

10 James Leach, 'The Reel Nation: Image and Reality in Contemporary Canadian Cinema,' *Canadian Journal of Film Studies* 11.2 (Fall 2002): 8.

11 An example of such a perspective on a global scale is the postcolonialism found in this typical contemporary academic statement: 'The dominant European/American form of cinema not only inherited and disseminated a hegemonic colonial discourse, but also created a powerful hegemony of its own through monopolistic control of film distribution and exhibition ... Eurocolonial cinema thus mapped history not only for domestic audiences but also for the world ...' (Stam, *Film Theory*, 20).

12 This historian does not claim to have viewed most of the films that he writes about. In a number of cases, these films are not available. Viewing hundreds of films would not make my narrative more accurate historically. It would simply put me on the road to being a critical analyst, which is not my role nor my expertise. The historian accepts his dependency on the textual insights of those who have viewed the films or provided credible interpretations.

13 Interview with Arif Dirlik, in Xie and Wang, eds, *Dialogues on Cultural Studies*, 9.

1. Foundations of the Silver Screen

1 Peter Morris, *Embattled Shadows: A History of Canadian Cinema, 1895–1939* (Montreal and Kingston: McGill-Queen's University Press, 1978), 34.

2 Ibid., 45.

3 See Douglas Fetherling, ed., *Documents in Canadian Film* (Peterborough, ON: Broadview Press, 1988), 7, for a translation of the review in Montreal's *La Presse* of Canada's first screening. It carried the headline 'Animated Photography.'

4 Geoffrey Nowell-Smith, 'Introduction,' in Geoffrey Nowell-Smith, ed., *The Oxford History of World Cinema* (London: Oxford University Press, 1996), 3.

5 Paolo Cherchi Usai, 'Origins and Survival,' in Nowell-Smith, ed., *Oxford History of World Cinema*, 12.

6 Curiously, this competition between individual and public entertainment was replayed a century later when computer video games became all the rage, with individual players viewing a screen. At the same time, impressive digitalized special effects creations in films were turning theatre releases into equally impressive examples of virtual reality. It is conceivable that in the near future the digitalization of theatrical film releases could lead to theatres filled with people interacting with a simulated reality rather than simply individual or dual players as we have currently.

7 Roberta Pearson, 'Early Cinema,' in Nowell-Smith, ed., *Oxford History of World Cinema*, 14.

8 Fetherling, ed., *Documents in Canadian Film*, 9.

9 Ibid., 18.

10 Pam Cook and Mieke Bernink, eds, *The Cinema Book*, 2nd ed. (London: BFI Publishing, 1999), 4.

11 Laurence Nowry, 'The Early Scenario of Ernest Quimet, Grandpère of Film,' in Fetherling, ed., *Documents in Canadian Film*, 15.

12 Roberta Pearson, 'Transitional Cinema,' in Nowell-Smith, ed., *Oxford History of World Cinema*, 28.

13 Usai, 'Origins and Survival,' 14; Pearson, 'Transitional Cinema,' 23–4.

14 In 1910 two-thirds of the movies shown in the world were made in France (Louis Menard, 'Paris, Texas,' *New Yorker*, 17 and 24 Feb. 2003, p. 169).

15 Cinema historians Pam Cook and Mieke Bernink claim that, in 1910, 26 million people were viewing films every week! (*The Cinema Book*, 5).

16 Janis L. Pallister, *The Cinema of Quebec: Masters in Their Own House* (Madison: Associated University Presses, 1995), 18.

17 Fetherling, ed., *Documents in Canadian Film*, 18.

18 The first one-hundred-seat nickelodeon opened in Pittsburgh in 1905.

19 The class nature of the early cinema audience is discussed in Douglas Gomery, 'Hollywood As Industry,' in *The Oxford Guide to Film Studies*, ed. John Hill and Pamela Church Gibson (London: Oxford University Press, 1998), 245.

20 Ibid.

21 Ibid., 258.

22 Ibid., 268.

23 Pearson, 'Transitional Cinema,' 33.

24 Douglas Gomery, 'The Hollywood Studio System,' in Nowell-Smith, ed., *Oxford History of World Cinema*, 43.

25 Cook and Bernink, eds, *The Cinema Book*, 5.

26 David Clandfield, *Canadian Film* (Toronto: Oxford University Press, 1987), 3.

27 For a brief discussion of some of these writers, see G. Melnyk, *The Literary History of Alberta*, Volume One: *From Writing-on-Stone to World War Two* (Edmonton: University of Alberta Press, 1998): 62–72.

28 Clandfield indicates that by 1914 about one hundred dramatic films with Canadian content had been made by American film companies (*Canadian Film*, 3).

29 The Anglo-Protestant majority of turn-of-the-century Canada participated fully in this racism by viewing non-English, non-Nordic peoples, such as the French, Italians, and Eastern Europeans, as 'darker' races. That these

European peoples often came from predominantly Catholic countries only augmented the prejudice.

30 Morris, *Embattled Shadows*, 50.
31 George Blaisdell, 'Review of Evangeline,' in Fetherling, ed., *Documents in Canadian Film*, 10.
32 Robyn Karney, ed., *Cinema Year by Year: 1894–2000* (London: Dorling Kindersley, 2000), 61.
33 Ibid., 100.
34 Stam, *Film Theory*, 19.
35 Karney, ed., *Cinema Year by Year*, 113.
36 Gomery, 'The Hollywood Studio System,' 43.
37 Geoff Pevere and Greig Dymond, *Mondo Canuck: A Canadian Pop Culture Odyssey* (Toronto: Prentice-Hall, 1996), 98.
38 Cook and Bernink, *The Cinema Book*, 34.
39 Karney, ed., *Cinema Year by Year*, 40.

2. Back to God's Country: The Shipman Saga

1 Morris, *Embattled Shadows*, 66.
2 Ibid., 69.
3 Ibid., 101.
4 Ibid., 106.
5 Ibid., 107.
6 Nell Shipman's experience with the film is discussed in detail in Kay Armatage, *The Girl from God's Country: Nell Shipman and the Silent Cinema* (Toronto: University of Toronto Press, 2003), 161–75.
7 Morris, *Embattled Shadows*, 117.
8 Ibid., 95.
9 Allan Dawn, 'Canada Has a Movie Future but Certain Restrictions Must Be Removed,' in Fetherling, ed., *Documents in Canadian Film*, 32.
10 Robert A. Segal, *Joseph Campbell: An Introduction*, rev. ed. (New York: Mentor, 1990), 191.
11 Pierre Berton, *Hollywood's Canada: The Americanization of Our National Image* (Toronto: McClelland and Stewart, 1975).
12 Ibid., 126.
13 Ruth Vasey, 'The World-Wide Spread of Cinema,' in Nowell-Smith, ed., *Oxford History of World Cinema*, 58
14 Ibid., 60.
15 See 'Artaud and the Surrealists Provoke a Riot at the Ursulines,' in Karney, ed., *Cinema Year by Year*, 196.
16 A.L. Rees, 'Cinema and the Avant-Garde,' in Nowell-Smith, ed., *Oxford History of World Cinema*, 99–100.

17 Morris, *Embattled Shadows*, 127.
18 Michael Dorland, *So Close to the State/s: The Emergence of a Canadian Feature Film Policy* (Toronto: University of Toronto Press, 1998), 11.
19 Charles Backhouse, *Canadian Government Motion Picture Bureau* (Ottawa: Canadian Film Institute, 1974), 8.
20 Ibid., 41.
21 Ibid., 13.
22 Ibid., 10.
23 Morris, *Embattled Shadows*, 152.
24 Ibid., 71.
25 Ibid., 79.
26 Bairnsfather's play *The Better 'Ole* was distributed as a film under the title *Carry On!* (Morris, *Embattled Shadows*, 74).
27 Germain Lacasse, *Histoires de scopes: Le Cinéma muet au Québec* (Montreal: Cinémathèque québécoise, 1988), 61.
28 Ibid., 64.
29 Ibid., 84.
30 Yves Lever, *Histoire générale du cinéma au Québec* (Montreal: Boréal, 1995), 75.
31 Ted Madger, *Canada's Hollywood: The Canadian State and Feature Film* (Toronto: University of Toronto Press, 1993), 25.
32 Berton, *Hollywood's Canada*, 230–1.

3. The Dirty Thirties: The British Quota Era

1 Morris, *Embattled Shadows*, 181.
2 Ibid., 182.
3 The fullest treatment to date of the racist construction of the Asian Other in this film is found in Gittings, *Canadian National Cinema*, 54–69. The term 'demonized' is from p. 56.
4 Morris, *Embattled Shadows*, 194.
5 The most extensive treatment of the British Columbia film industry, past and present, is Mike Gasher, *Hollywood North: The Feature Film Industry in British Columbia* (Vancouver: UBC Press, 2002). A table on p. 108 indicates that foreign spending on film production in British Columbia increased sixfold from 1990 to 2000 ($134 million to $761 million).
6 See Greg Gatenby's *The Wild Is Always There: Canada through the Eyes of Foreign Writers* (Toronto: Vintage Books, 1994). It documents a century and a half of travel writing about Canada.
7 Ronald Bergan, 'Movies Find a Voice,' in Karney, ed., *Cinema Year by Year*, 213.
8 Karney, ed., *Cinema Year by Year*, 276.

9 Ibid., 212.
10 Toby Miller, 'Hollywood and the World,' in Hill and Gibson, eds, *The Oxford Guide to Film Studies*, 372.
11 Antonia Lant, 'Britain at the End of Empire,' in Nowell-Smith, ed., *Oxford History of World Cinema*, 362.
12 Bill Routt, 'The Emergence of Australian Film,' in Nowell-Smith, ed., *Oxford History of World Cinema*, 424.
13 Morris, *Embattled Shadows*, 223.
14 Michel Houle, in 'Some Ideological and Thematic Aspects of the Quebec Cinema,' in *Self-Portraits: Essays on the Canadian and Quebec Cinemas*, ed. Pierre Véronneau and Piers Handling (Ottawa: Canadian Film Institute, 1988), claims that there were at least 25,000 clergy and nuns in the province in 1940.
15 Pallister, *The Cinema of Quebec*, 24.
16 Léo Bonneville, ed., *Le Cinéma québécois: Par ceux qui le font* (Montreal: Éditions Paulines, 1979), 9.
17 Montrealer Hugh MacLennan's 1945 novel *Two Solitudes* captures the conflict between the two communities, as does his 1959 sequel, *The Watch That Ends the Night*.

4. The Rise of the NFB: Grierson and McLaren

1 Piers Handling, 'The National Film Board of Canada, 1939–1959,' in Véronneau and Handling, eds, *Self-Portraits*, 42.
2 Elizabeth Sussex, *The Rise and Fall of British Documentary: The Story of the Film Movement Founded by John Grierson* (Berkeley: University of California Press, 1975), 3.
3 Forsyth Hardy, ed., *Grierson on Documentary* (London: Faber and Faber, 1966), 142.
4 Sussex, *The Rise and Fall of British Documentary*, 194.
5 Hardy, ed., *Grierson on Documentary*, 165.
6 Ibid., 36.
7 Ibid., 147.
8 Ibid., 173.
9 Ibid., 174.
10 James Beveridge, *John Grierson: Film Master* (New York: Macmillan, 1978), 46.
11 Forsyth Hardy, *John Grierson: A Documentary Biography* (London: Faber and Faber, 1979), 95.
12 Jack Ellis, 'Grierson's First Years at the NFB,' in *Canadian Film Reader*,

ed. Seth Feldman and Joyce Nelson (Toronto: Peter Martin Associates, 1977), 40.

13 Peter Morris, ed., *The National Film Board of Canada: The War Years* (Ottawa: Canadian Film Institute, 1965), 1.

14 Peter Morris, 'After Grierson: The National Film Board 1945–1953,' in *Take Two: A Tribute to Film in Canada*, ed. Seth Feldman (Toronto: Irwin, 1984), 183.

15 A major collection of essays on the NFB documentary tradition was published in 2003. *Candid Eyes: Essays on Canadian Documentaries* (Toronto: University of Toronto Press, 2003), edited by Jim Leach and Jeannette Sloniowski, provides fourteen studies of individual NFB documentaries from the 1950s to the 1990s.

16 Peter Morris, 'Re-thinking Grierson: The Ideology of John Grierson,' in *Dialogue: Canadian and Quebec Cinema*, ed. Pierre Véronneau, Michael Dorland, and Seth Feldman (Montreal: Mediatexte, 1987), 44.

17 For an overview of McLean's career at the NFB, see Carol Cooper, 'He Filmed the Difficult, Riled the Powerful,' *Globe and Mail*, 11 Jan. 2003, p. F8.

18 Donald W. Buchanan, 'The Projection of Canada,' in Morris, ed., *The National Film Board of Canada*, 16.

19 Hardy, ed., *Grierson on Documentary*, 233.

20 Morris, 'Re-thinking Grierson,' 41.

21 Hardy, *John Grierson: A Documentary Biography*, 37.

22 Sussex, *The Rise and Fall of British Documentary*, 196.

23 Beveridge, *John Grierson: Film Master*, 201.

24 Ibid., 136.

25 Joyce Nelson, *The Colonized Eye: Rethinking the Grierson Legend* (Toronto: Between the Lines, 1988), 13.

26 Ian Aitken, *Film and Reform: John Grierson and the Documentary Film Movement* (London: Routledge, 1990), 4.

27 Ibid., 60.

28 Grierson's style in handling people reflected these values. James Beveridge, in his film-based biography *John Grierson*, refers to Grierson's puritanism (85). Likewise, colleagues like Sydney Newman, who came to head the NFB, considered Grierson's management style 'domineering' (*John Grierson*, 157). Later on in the biography, Grierson is described as 'austere' (253).

29 Morris, 'Re-thinking Grierson,' 43.

30 Ibid., 37.

31 Beveridge, *John Grierson: Film Master*, 220.

32 Aitken, *Film and Reform*, 94.

33 Hardy, ed., *Grierson on Documentary*, 43.
34 Eleanor Beattie's comment in *John Grierson and the NFB* (Toronto: ECW Press, 1984), a selection of papers presented at a 1981 conference at McGill University.
35 Hardy, *John Grierson: A Documentary Biography*, 150.
36 Martin Knelman, *This Is Where We Came In: The Career and Character of Canadian Film* (Toronto: McClelland and Stewart, 1977), 72.
37 His friend Forsyth Hardy says, 'It was politics not technology (tv) that killed documentary and that left Grierson effectively stranded in the 1950s' (*John Grierson: A Documentary Biography*, 257).
38 Aitken, *Film and Reform*, 149.
39 Hardy, ed., *Grierson on Documentary*, 74.
40 Ibid., 89.
41 Peter Morris, 'Backwards to the Future: John Grierson's Film Policy for Canada,' in *Flashback: People and Institutions in Canadian Film History*, ed. Eugene P. Walz (Montreal: Mediatexte, 1986), 31.
42 This famous or infamous – depending on your viewpoint – article was titled 'A Film Policy for Canada' and published in *Canadian Affairs*, 15 June 1944. It is reprinted in Fetherling, ed., *Documents in Canadian Film*, 51–67, and in Hardy, ed., *Grierson on Documentary*.
43 Hardy, ed., *Grierson on Documentary*, 18.
44 Morris, 'Backwards to the Future,' 28–30.
45 Kathryn Kane, *Visions of War: Hollywood Combat Films of World War II* (Ann Arbor, MI: UMI Research Press, 1982), 10.
46 Nelson, *The Colonized Eye*, 161.
47 Jim Leach and Jeannette Sloniowski, 'Introduction,' in Leach and Sloniowski, eds, *Candid Eyes*, 6.
48 Menard, 'Paris, Texas,' 171.
49 Hardy, *John Grierson: A Documentary Biography*, 83.
50 *John Grierson and the NFB*, 144.
51 Hardy, ed., *Grierson on Documentary*, 398.
52 Beveridge, *John Grierson: Film Master*, 180.
53 Derek Elley, 'Rhythm n' Truths: Norman McLaren,' in Feldman and Nelson, eds, *Canadian Film Reader*, 98.
54 Norman McLaren, 'Animated Film,' in Morris, ed., *The National Film Board of Canada: The War Years*, 10.
55 Ibid., 11, 12.
56 Beveridge, *John Grierson: Film Master*, 125.
57 Germaine Warkentin, 'Norman McLaren,' in Fetherling, ed., *Documents in Canadian Film*, 77.

58 Elley, 'Rhythm n' Truths,' 101.
59 Ibid., 102.
60 Warkentin, 'Norman McLaren,' 77.
61 Gary Evans, *In the National Interest: A Chronicle of the National Film Board of Canada from 1949 to 1989* (Toronto: University of Toronto Press, 1991), 317.
62 An example of this earlier attitude is Marjorie McKay's *History of the National Film Board of Canada* (Ottawa: National Film Board, 1964), which calls the NFB 'a valued Canadian institution' (147).
63 John Grierson is quoted as saying in 1970 that 'Canada's only gift to the world has been the Film Board' (in Beveridge, *John Grierson: Film Master*, 152).
64 Peter Morris's, 'Re-thinking Grierson: The Ideology of John Grierson' and 'After Grierson: The National Film Board 1945–1953' are two examples of reappraisal.
65 Quoted in Evans, *In the National Interest*, 4.
66 In 1978 the NFB had a budget of $48 million (*NFB Annual Report 1977–78*, 51). In 1993 it had a budget of $89 million (*NFB Annual Report 1992–93*, 84). In 2000 it had a budget of $70 million (*NFB Annual Report 1999–2000*, 85). Taking into account inflation, a 2000 budget comparable to the 1978 budget would be well over $100 million.
67 Morrison, 'Re-thinking Grierson,' 34–7.
68 Northrop Frye, *The Bush Garden* (Toronto: House of Anansi, 1971).
69 Rodney James, *Film As National Art: The NFB of Canada and the Film Board Idea* (New York: Arno Press, 1977), 661.
70 Jean Pierre Lefebvre, 'Le Concept de cinéma national,' in Véronneau et al., eds, *Dialogue*, 83–96.

5. Quebec Goes to the Movies

1 Pierre Pageau and Yves Leger, *Cinémas canadien et québécois: Notes historiques* (Montreal: College Ahuntsic, 1977), 27. These films are described as wartime morale-boosting animations created for popular Quebec folk songs, with which the audience could sing along.
2 Louise Carrière, 'Historique des collaborateurs cinématographiques,' in *Les Relations cinématographiques France-Québec*, ed. Louise Carrière (Montreal: Cinémathèque québécoise, 1994), 183.
3 Ibid., 13.
4 Pierre Véronneau, 'The First Wave of Quebec Feature Films 1944–1953,' in Véronneau and Handling, eds, *Self-Portraits*, 54.

5 Pierre Véronneau, *Histoire du cinéma au Québec*, Vol.1 (Montreal: Cinéma-thèque québécoise, 1979), 27.

6 Pageau and Lever, *Cinémas canadien et québécois*, 26.

7 Véronneau, *Histoire du cinéma au Québec*, 14.

8 Véronneau, 'The First Wave of Quebec Feature Films,' 56.

9 Pageau and Lever, *Cinémas canadien et québécois*, 28.

10 Véronneau, *Histoire du cinéma au Québec*, 44.

11 Véronneau, 'The First Wave of Quebec Feature Films,' 58; and Pageau and Lever, *Cinémas canadien et québécois*, 29.

12 Yves Lever, in his *Histoire générale du cinéma au Québec*, describes *La Forteresse* as 'un essai de film noir à la manière américaine' (106).

13 Marcel Jean, *Le Cinéma québécois* (Montreal: Boréal, 1991), 22.

14 Louise Carrière, ed., *Les Femmes et cinéma québécois* (Montreal: Boréal Express, 1983), 49.

15 Pierre Véronneau, *Cinéma de l'époque Duplessiste* (Montreal: Cinémathèque québécoise, 1979), 113.

16 Ibid.

17 Véronneau, 'The First Wave of Quebec Feature Films,' 59.

18 Pageau and Lever, *Cinémas canadien et québécois*, 31; and Maria Topalovich, *A Pictorial History of the Canadian Film Awards* (Toronto: Stoddart, 1984), 7.

19 Véronneau, *Histoire du cinéma au Québec*, 71.

20 Lever, in *Histoire générale du cinéma au Québec*, claims that Renaissance went through $3 million during the years it made its three films (106).

21 Ibid., 120–1.

22 Jean, *Le Cinéma québécois*, 24.

23 Heinz Weinmann, *Cinéma de l'imaginaire québécois: De 'La Petite Aurore' à 'Jesus de Montréal'* (Montreal: Hexagone, 1990), 13.

24 Ibid., 21.

25 Pageau and Lever, in *Cinémas canadien et québécois*, state that the film had 750,000 admissions in Quebec and grossed $800,000 for its producers (35).

26 Weinmann, *Cinéma de l'imâginaire québécois*, 43.

27 Véronneau, 'The First Wave of Quebec Feature Films,' 63.

28 Translated in Pallister, *The Cinema of Quebec*, 34; the original is in Lever's *Histoire générale du cinéma au Québec*, 114.

29 Pallister, *The Cinema of Quebec*, 28.

30 Lever, *Histoire générale du cinema au Québec*, 113.

31 Weinmann, *Cinéma de l'imaginaire québécois*, 21.

32 Ibid., 65. Weinmann bolsters his interpretation of the importance of the illegitimate child figure to the social imagination of Quebec by pointing out that in 1952 only 5 per cent of children born in Quebec were 'illegiti-

mate,' while in 1988 the figure had grown to 33 per cent. The latter figure represents common-law relationships as a new norm.

33 Véronneau, *Cinéma de l'époque Duplessiste*, 125.
34 Dorland, *So Close to the State/s*, 122.
35 Madger, *Canada's Hollywood*, 63.
36 Manjunath Pendakur, *Canadian Dreams and American Control: The Political Economy of the Canadian Film Industry* (Detroit: Wayne State University Press, 1990), 141.
37 Lever, *Histoire générale du cinéma au Québéc*, 123.
38 Ibid., 124.
39 Ibid.
40 Stephen Crofts, 'Concepts of National Cinema,' in Hill and Gibson, eds, *The Oxford Guide to Film Studies*, 388.
41 Lever, *Histoire générale du cinema au Québec*, 111.
42 Christiane Tremblay-Daviault, 'Avant la Révolution tranquille: Une Terre-Mère en perdition,' in Carrière, ed., *Les Femmes et cinéma québécois*, 24.
43 Lever, *Histoire générale du cinéma au Québec*, 116.
44 Ibid., 117.
45 Tremblay-Daviault, 'Avant la Révolution tranquille,' 22.
46 Houle, 'Some Ideological and Thematic Aspects of the Quebec Cinema,' 162.
47 Christiane Tremblay-Daviault, *Un cinéma orphelin: Structures mentales et sociales du cinéma québécois (1942–1953)* (Montreal: Québec/Amérique, 1981), 307.
48 Ibid., 290.
49 Geoffrey Nowell-Smith, 'After the War,' in Nowell-Smith, ed., *The Oxford History of World Cinema*, 442.
50 Johanna Schneller, 'Memo to Hollywood,' *Globe and Mail*, 4 May 2001, p. R1.

6. Budge Crawley and the Other Documentary Tradition

1 James A. Forrester, *Budge: F.R. Crawley and Crawley Films, 1939–1982* (Lakefield, ON: Information Research Services, 1988), 41.
2 Barbara Wade Rose, *Budge: What Happened to Canada's King of Film* (Toronto: ECW Press, 1998), 55.
3 Wade Rose says that it cost $10,000 (p. 59), and Forrester quotes Budge Crawley as saying it cost $7,000 (p. 36).
4 Forrester, *Budge*, 36
5 Wade Rose, *Budge*, 71.

6 Forrester, *Budge*, 3.
7 Wade Rose, *Budge*, 91.
8 Ibid., 112.
9 Ibid., 121, 124.
10 Forrester, *Budge*, 65.
11 Wade Rose, *Budge*, 154.
12 Forrester, *Budge*, 72.
13 Wade Rose, *Budge*, 162.
14 Ibid., 165.
15 Ibid., 167.
16 Forrester, *Budge*, 72.
17 F.R. Crawley, 'Have Independent Films a Look-In?' *Saturday Night*, 14 Aug. 1951; reprinted in Fetherling, ed., *Documents in Canadian Film*, 86.
18 F.R. Crawley, 'A Slick Way to Skin the Public,' *Maclean's*, 13 April 1981, p. 10.

7. Goin' down the Road: The Resurrection of Anglo-Canadian Feature Films

1 Gerald Pratley, 'Film in Canada,' in Fetherling, ed., *Documents in Canadian Film*, 100. Gerald Pratley (1923–) was an early movie critic on CBC radio. He founded the Ontario Film Institute, the forerunner of Cinémathèque Ontario. The Film Studies Association of Canada instituted a prize in honour of his pioneering work.
2 James, *Film As a National Art*, 352.
3 Evans, *In the National Interest*, 88.
4 Morris, 'After Grierson: The National Film Board 1945–1953,' in Feldman, ed., *Take Two*, 190.
5 Pageau and Lever, *Cinémas canadien et québécois*, 51.
6 For a discussion of Unit B, see Leach and Sloniowski, 'Introduction,' in Leach and Sloniowski, eds, *Candid Eyes*, 6–7.
7 Peter Harcourt, 'The Beginning of a Beginning,' in Véronneau and Handling, eds, *Self-Portraits*, 70.
8 Ibid., 71.
9 Peter Harcourt, *Movies and Mythologies: Towards a National Cinema* (Toronto: CBC Publications, 1977), 140.
10 Brendan Gill, 'Current Cinema,' *New Yorker*, 24 April 1965, p. 163.
11 Ibid., 164.
12 Germaine Warkentin, 'Comment on Film,' *Canadian Forum*, October 1964, p. 158.
13 James Leach, 'Second Images: Reflections on the Canadian Cinema(s) in the Seventies' in Feldman, ed., *Take Two*, 102.

14 Seth Feldman, 'The Silent Subject in English Canadian Film,' in Feldman, ed., *Take Two*, 52.

15 Wendy Michener, 'Look Who's Looking at the Movies,' *Maclean's*, 17 Oct. 1964; reprinted in Fetherling, ed., *Documents in Canadian Film*, 109.

16 Harcourt, 'The Beginning of a Beginning,' 76.

17 Allan King, 'Pourquoi? Round Two,' *Cinema Canada* 159 (Jan. 1989): 5.

18 Topalovich, *A Pictorial History of the Canadian Film Awards*, 77.

19 Peter Harcourt, 'Allan King: Filmmaker,' in Feldman, ed., *Take Two*, 75.

20 Alan Rosenthal, 'Fiction Documentary: *A Married Couple*,' *Film Quarterly*, 23.4 (Summer 1970): 11.

21 King, 'Pourquoi? Round Two,' 5.

22 Alan Rosenthal, 'Interview with Richard Leiterman,' in Fetherling, ed., *Documents in Canadian Film*, 153.

23 Harcourt, 'Allan King: Filmmaker,' 77.

24 King, 'Pourquoi? Round Two,' 5.

25 Harcourt, 'Allan King: Filmmaker,' 75.

26 Seth Feldman, 'Paradise and Its Discontents,' in *Allan King: Filmmaker*, ed. Seth Feldman (Toronto: Toronto International Film Festival, 2002), 3.

27 *Canadian Film Development Corporation Annual Report, 1967*, reprinted as 'Origins of the Canadian Film Development Corporation,' in Fetherling, ed., *Documents in Canadian Film*, 127.

28 Pageau and Lever, *Cinémas canadien et québécois*, 48.

29 Dorland, *So Close to the State(s)*, 112.

30 Ibid.

31 Madger, *Canada's Hollywood*, 137.

32 Ibid.

33 Karney, ed., *Cinema Year by Year*, 492.

34 Robert Fothergill, 'A Place like Home,' in Feldman and Nelson, eds, *Canadian Film Reader*, 348.

35 Bruce Pittman, 'Shebib Exposes Himself,' *Cinema Canada* 81 (Feb. 1982): 18–21.

36 Kaspar Dzeguze, 'Go and See "Goin' Down the Road,"' *Maclean's*, September 1970, 73.

37 Ibid.

38 *New Yorker*, 21 Nov. 1970, 47–9.

39 Ibid.

40 Pittman, 'Shebib Exposes Himself,' 18.

41 Ibid., 19.

42 Robert Fothergill, 'Coward, Bully or Clown: The Dream-Life of a Younger Brother,' in Feldman and Nelson, eds, *Canadian Film Reader*, 241.

43 Ibid., 242.
44 Geoff Pevere, 'Images of Men,' *Canadian Forum*, February 1985, p. 24.
45 Ibid., 27.
46 Christine Ramsay, 'Canadian Narrative Cinema from the Margins: The "Nation" and Masculinity in *Goin' Down the Road*,' *Canadian Journal of Film Studies* 2.2–3 (1993): 38.
47 Ibid., 39.

8. The Escapist Seventies

1 Marshall Delaney, 'It Makes You See the Value of Corruption,' *Saturday Night*, January 1974, pp. 38–9.
2 Wade Rose, *Budge: What Happened to the Canada's King of Film*, 172.
3 Knelman, *This Is Where We Came In*, 89.
4 The concept of a 'new wave' was taken from the term used to describe avant-garde French film-making of the 1960s and was used by film critic Jay Scott ('Burn Out in the Great White North,' in Feldman, ed., *Take Two*, 31) to describe what was happening at the end of the '60s and early '70s in Toronto cinema.
5 Madger, *Canada's Hollywood*, 150.
6 Robert Fulford, 'The Apprenticeship of Phillip Borsos,' *Saturday Night*, December 1984, p. 32.
7 Madger, *Canada's Hollywood*, 168.
8 Ibid., 184.
9 Knelman, *This Is Where We Came In*, 97.
10 Madger, *Canada's Hollywood*, 188.
11 Pierre Pageau, 'A Survey of the Commercial Cinema, 1963–1977,' in Véronneau and Handling, eds, *Self-Portraits*, 155.
12 Fothergill, 'Coward, Bully or Clown: The Dream-Life of a Younger Brother,' in Feldman and Nelson, eds, *Canadian Film Reader*, 242.
13 Ibid., 238.
14 Fothergill, 'A Place like Home,' in Feldman and Nelson, eds, *Canadian Film Reader*, 351.
15 Fothergill, 'Coward, Bully or Clown,' 244.
16 Laurinda Hartt, 'Interview with Donald Pleasance,' *Cinema Canada* 8 (June/July 1973): 60.
17 George Csaba Koller, 'Bill Fruet's *Wedding in White*,' *Cinema Canada* 3 (July/Aug 1972): 45.
18 P.M. Evanchuk, 'The Outspoken Hector Ross,' *Motion*, September/October 1973, p. 11.

19 Ibid.
20 Piers Handling, 'Two or Three Things "Bill Fruet,"' *Cinema Canada* 40 (Sept. 1977): 45.
21 John Hofsess, 'Films,' *Maclean's*, November 1972, p. 101.
22 John Hofsess, 'Fortune and Men's Eyes – Report from the Set in a Quebec City Prison,' *Maclean's*, December 1970, p. 81.
23 Richard McGuinness, 'Gay, Yes but Proud It's Not,' *Village Voice*, 1 July 1972.
24 Jim Leach, 'The Body Snatchers: Genre and Canadian Cinema,' in *Film Genre Reader*, ed. Barry Keith Grant (Austin: University of Texas Press, 1986), 357.
25 Delaney, 'It Makes You See the Value of Corruption,' 38.
26 Fothergill, 'Coward, Bully or Clown,' 249.
27 Penelope Gilliat, 'Duddy-O,' *New Yorker*, 22 July 1974, p. 65.
28 James McLarty, '1,000,000 – Let's Hear It for Duddy,' *Motion*, July/August 1974, p. 30.
29 Madger, *Canada's Hollywood*, 152.
30 John Hofsess and Robert Fothergill, 'The Rich Get Richler: A Dialogue on Duddy Kravitz,' *Canadian Forum*, October 1974, p. 33.
31 Nicholas Pasquariello, 'Jan Kadar,' *Cinema Canada* 68 (Sept. 1980): 20.
32 Martin Knelman, 'A Night at the Pictures in Arcola,' *Saturday Night*, September 1977, p. 28.
33 David Cobb, 'Day of the Gopher,' *Maclean's*, 1 Nov. 1976, p. 46.
34 Douglas Fetherling, 'Outrageous,' *Canadian Forum*, December–January 1977–8, p. 65.
35 John Hofsess, 'In Praise of Older Women,' *Cinema Canada* 49–50 (Sept.–Oct. 1978): 68.
36 Marshall Delaney, 'Sex Is Not a Spectator Sport,' *Saturday Night*, 19 December 1978, p. 59.
37 John Harkness, 'Notes on a Tax-Sheltered Cinema,' *Cinema Canada* 87 (Aug. 1982): 23.
38 Ibid., 22.
39 Ibid., 23.
40 Madger, *Canada's Hollywood*, 190.
41 Steven Globerman and Aidan Vining, *Foreign Ownership and Canada's Feature Film Distribution Section: An Economic Analysis* (Vancouver: Fraser Institute, 1987), 47.
42 Wyndham Wise, 'Canadian Cinema from Boom to Bust: The Tax-Shelter Years,' *Take One* 7.22 (Winter 1999): 17–24.
43 Scott, 'Burn Out in the Great White North,' 34.

44 Pauline Kael, 'The Current Cinema,' *New Yorker*, 8 Aug. 1983, p. 87.
45 Fulford, 'The Apprenticeship of Phillip Borsos,' 36.
46 Ibid., 37.
47 Ibid.
48 Blaine Allan, 'Directed by Phillip Borsos,' in *North of Everything: English-Canadian Cinema since 1980*, ed. William Beard and Jerry White (Edmonton: University of Alberta Press, 2002), 106.
49 Fil Fraser, 'Monkey See, Monkey Do, Monkey Pay,' *Cinema Canada* 71 (Jan./Feb. 1981): 10.

9. The Quebec Auteur: From Perrault to Arcand

 1 The first wave of Quebec feature films from 1944 to 1953 did not create any auteur directors other than Gratien Gélinas.
 2 Pageau and Lever, *Cinémas canadien et québécois*, 44.
 3 Ibid.
 4 *New Canadian Film* 3.13 (April 1971), as reproduced in Pendakur, *Canadian Dreams and American Control*, 154.
 5 Yves Lever, in *Histoire générale du cinéma au Québec*, discusses this in a lengthy section, pp. 143–238.
 6 Ibid., 148.
 7 The 'Cult of the Auteur' is described in Stam, *Film Theory: An Introduction*, 83–8.
 8 Jill Forbes, 'The French Nouvelle Vague,' in Hill and Gibson, eds, *The Oxford Guide of Film Studies*, 464.
 9 Lever, *Histoire générale du cinéma au Québec*, 345.
10 David Clandfield, 'From the Picturesque to the Familiar: Films of the French Unit at the NFB (1958–1964), in Feldman, ed., *Take Two*, 113.
11 Jean, *Le Cinéma québécois*, 31.
12 Ibid.
13 Bruno Cornellier, 'Hollywood et le cinéma québécois (II),' in *Cadrage: Revue de Cinéma* (www.cadrage.net), p. 1.
14 Hubert Aquin, 'The Cultural Fatigue of French Canada,' in *Contemporary Quebec Criticism*, ed. Larry Shouldice (Toronto: University of Toronto Press, 1979), 74.
15 Peter Harcourt, 'Pierre Perrault and *Le cinéma vécu*,' in Feldman, ed., *Take Two*, 125.
16 Ibid., 130.
17 The film with English subtitles was re-released by the NFB in 2001 under the English title *Of Whales, the Moon and Men*. Originally it was titled *The Moontrap*.

18 Stéphane-Albert Boulais, 'Le Cinéma vécu de l'intérieur: Mon expérience avec Pierre Perrault' in Véronneau, Dorland, and Feldman, eds, *Dialogue: Canadian and Quebec Cinema*, 171.

19 Michel Marie, 'Singularité de l'oeuvre de Perrault,' in Véronneau et al., eds, *Dialogue*, 157.

20 David Clandfield, 'Linking Community Renewal to National Identity: The Filmmakers' Role in *Pour la suite du monde*,' in Leach and Sloniowski, eds, *Candid Eyes*, 83.

21 David Clandfield, 'Ritual and Recital: The Perrault Project,' in Feldman, ed., *Take Two*, 146.

22 Yves Picard, 'Les succès du cinéma québécois,' in Véronneau et al., eds, *Dialogue*, 104.

23 English synopsis of Paul Warren, 'Les Québécois et le cinéma,' in Véronneau et al., eds, *Dialogue*, 110.

24 Pallister, *The Cinema of Quebec: Masters in Their Own House*, 43.

25 Michel Larouche, 'Pierre Perrault et la "parlure" du Québec,' in *L'Aventure du cinéma québécois en France*, ed., Michel Larouche (Montreal: XYZ, 1996), 147.

26 Yves Lever, *Cinéma et société québécoise* (Montreal: Éditions du Jour, 1972), 21–55.

27 Ray Conlogue, 'For Michel Brault, the Era Is Over,' *Globe and Mail*, 19 Nov. 1990, p. R3.

28 Knelman, *This Is Where We Came In*, 31.

29 Pierre Vallières, 'An Account by a Privileged Hostage of *Les Ordres*: Brault Has Missed His Shot,' in Feldman and Nelson, eds, *Canadian Film Reader*, 266.

30 Marshall Delaney, 'Artists in the Shadows: Some Notable Canadian Movies,' in Feldman, ed., *Take Two*, 4.

31 Conlogue, 'For Michel Brault, the Era Is Over,' R3.

32 Ray Conlogue, 'Tilting at the U.S. Film Windmill,' *Globe and Mail*, 21 Sept. 2001, p. R3.

33 Lever, *Histoire générale du cinéma au Québéc*, 287.

34 Peter Harcourt, *Jean Pierre Lefebvre: Vidéaste* (Toronto: Toronto International Film Festival Group, 2001), 21.

35 Ibid., 27.

36 Introduction to Peter Harcourt, 'The Old and the New,' in Feldman, ed., *Take Two*, 169.

37 James Leach, 'The Sins of Gilles Carle,' in Feldman, ed., *Take Two*, 160.

38 Knelman, *This Is Where We Came In*, 70.

39 Madger, *Canada's Hollywood*, 136.

40 Jean, *Le Cinéma québécois*, 69.

41 Lever, *Histoire générale du cinéma au Québec*, 305.
42 Ibid., 306.
43 Martin Knelman, 'Claude Jutra in Exile,' in Fetherling, ed., *Documents in Canadian Film*, 216.
44 Ibid.
45 R. Bruce Elder, 'Claude Jutra's "Mon Oncle Antoine,"' in Feldman and Nelson, eds, *Canadian Film Reader*, 194–9 (originally published in *Descant*, Spring 1973).
46 James Leach, *Claude Jutra: Filmmaker* (Montreal and Kingston: McGill-Queen's University Press, 1999), 124.
47 Ibid., 136.
48 These adjectives are used by Martin Knelman, (*This Is Where We Came In*, 48).
49 Elder, 'Claude Jutra's "Mon Oncle Antoine,"' 199.
50 Knelman ('Claude Jutra in Exile,' 224) mentions a figure of 3 million.
51 Lever, *Histoire générale du cinéma au Québec*, 323.
52 Adrian Van Den Hoven, '*The Decline of the American Empire* in a North-American Perspective,' in *Essays on Quebec Cinema*, ed. Joseph Donohoe, Jr (Lansing: Michigan State University Press, 1991), 145.
53 Judy Wright and Debbie Magidson, 'Making Films for Your Own People: An Interview with Denys Arcand,' in Feldman and Nelson, eds, *Canadian Film Reader*, 219.
54 Ben-Z. Shek, 'History As a Unifying Structure in *Le Déclin de l'empire américain*,' *Quebec Studies* 9 (Fall 1989 / Winter 1990): 13.
55 Knelman, *This Is Where We Came In*, 80.
56 Michèle Garneau et Pierre Véronneau, 'Un cinéma <de genre> révélateur d'une inquiétante américanité québécoise,' in Larouche, ed., *L'Aventure du cinéma québécois en France*, 201.
57 Interview with Denys Arcand, www.sundancechannel.com/focus/arcand/5.html.
58 Garneau et Véronneau, 'Un cinéma < de genre >,' 202.
59 Liam Lacey, 'A Socko Québécois Invasion,' *Globe and Mail*, 22 May 2003, p. R1.
60 Lever, *Histoire générale du cinéma au Québec*, 393.
61 Ibid. Lever claims that in the 1980s, 80 per cent of screen time in Quebec belonged to Hollywood, 10 per cent to French films, and the Quebec portion varied from 4 to 10 per cent. When it was at a high of 10 per cent, 1.5 million tickets were sold in the province to view Quebec films (416).
62 From 189,553 seats in 326 theatres in 1970, to 81,765 seats in 250 theatres in 1992 (ibid., 417).

63 Ibid., 373.

64 Ibid., 475.

65 William Beard and Jerry White, eds, *North of Everything*, xix.

66 Bruno Cornellier, 'Hollywood et le cinéma québécois (I),' *Cadrage: Le magazine du cinéma international*, www.cadrage.net.

67 'In the sixties, European films accounted for five per cent of the American box-office. By the mid-nineties, European films accounted for half of one per cent of the box-office here, and Hollywood movies generated eighty per cent of movie revenue in Europe' (Menard, 'Paris, Texas,' 177).

68 For a discussion of this as a political issue in a global context, see Mathew Horsman and Andrew Marshall, *After the Nation-State: Citizens, Tribalism and the New World Disorder* (New York: Harper Collins, 1994).

10. English-Canadian Auteurs: David Cronenberg and Atom Egoyan

1 Pevere and Dymond, *Mondo Canuck*, 71–3.

2 Piers Handling, 'A Canadian Cronenberg,' in Feldman, ed., *Take Two*, 80.

3 William Beard, *The Artist As Monster: The Cinema of David Cronenberg* (Toronto: University of Toronto Press, 2001), viii, ix.

4 William Beard and Piers Handling, 'The Interview,' in *The Shape of Rage: The Films of David Cronenberg*, ed. Piers Handling (Toronto: General, 1983), 173.

5 http://www.e.bell.ca/filmfest/2000/25anniv/preludes_cronenberg.asp

6 Handling, ed., *The Shape of Rage*, vii.

7 Peter Morris, *David Cronenberg: A Delicate Balance* (Toronto: ECW Press, 1994), 29.

8 Ibid.

9 William Beard, 'The Visceral Mind: The Major Films of David Cronenberg,' in Handling, ed., *The Shape of Rage*, 23; and Chris Rodley, ed., *Cronenberg on Cronenberg* (Toronto: Knopf Canada, 1992), xix.

10 Rodley, ed., *Cronenberg on Cronenberg*, 43.

11 Ibid., 18.

12 Ibid., 39; and Morris, *David Cronenberg*, 64.

13 Morris, *David Cronenberg*, 76.

14 Ibid., 40.

15 Beard, *The Artist As Monster*, 26.

16 Ibid., xix.

17 Beard, 'The Visceral Mind,' 24; and Rodley, ed., *Cronenberg on Cronenberg*, xix. Morris gives a figure of $500,000 as the budget (*David Cronenberg*, 80).

18 Beard and Handling, 'The Interview,' 174.

19 Morris, *David Cronenberg*, 7.
20 Beard, 'The Visceral Mind,' 33, 40.
21 'Snuff' is a colloquial term used about hard-core pornographic films which depict the death of a woman by sexual torture.
22 Beard, *The Artist As Monster*, 164.
23 Rodley, ed., *Cronenberg on Cronenberg*, 115.
24 Ibid., 102.
25 Ibid., 109.
26 Ibid., 114.
27 Morris, *David Cronenberg*, 112.
28 Rodley, ed., *Cronenberg on Cronenberg*, 134.
29 Morris, *David Cronenberg*, 125.
30 Beard, *The Artist As Monster*, 278.
31 Ibid., 303.
32 David Cronenberg, *Crash* (London: Faber and Faber, 1996), xvii.
33 Chris Rodley, 'Introduction: From Novel to Film,' in Cronenberg, *Crash*, ix.
34 Beard, *The Artist As Monster*, 379.
35 Wyndham Wise, ed., *Take One's Essential Guide to Canadian Film* (Toronto: University of Toronto Press, 2001), 72.
36 Brian D. Johnson, 'Virtual Director,' *Maclean's*, 26 April 1999, p. 62; and Alan Freeman, '*eXistenZ* Draws Crowds in Berlin,' *Globe and Mail*, 17 Feb. 1999, p. D1.
37 Brenda Bouw, 'Baron of Blood Meets Beckett,' *Globe and Mail*, 29 Sept. 2001, p. R8.
38 Brian D. Johnson, 'An Exquisite Madness,' *Maclean's*, 3 March 2003, p. 42.
39 Ray Conlogue, 'Inside Cronenberg's Web,' *Globe and Mail*, 27 Feb. 2003, p. R1.
40 Morris, *David Cronenberg*, 9.
41 Margaret Atwood's *Strange Things: The Malevolent North in Canadian Literature* (Oxford: Oxford University Press, 1995) has chronicled this theme quite well in Aboriginal and Euro-Canadian traditions.
42 Handling, 'A Canadian Cronenberg,' 85.
43 The work of Canadian cultural studies critic Arthur Kroker (*Technology and the Canadian Mind* [1984], *Body Invaders* [1987], *Data Trash* [1994]) is a good example of the dystopic mentality pushed to extremes.
44 Handling, 'A Canadian Cronenberg,' 89.
45 Ibid.
46 Bart Testa, 'Technology's Body: Cronenberg, Genre, and the Canadian Ethos' (16 Nov. 1998) www.utoronto.ca/cinema/tests1.htm, p. 3; and Robin Wood, 'Cronenberg: A Dissenting View,' in Handling, ed., *The Shape of Rage*, 126, 131.

47 Florence Jacobowitz and Richard Lippe, 'Dead Ringers: The Joke's on Us,' *CineAction*, Spring 1989, pp. 64–8. The article calls the film 'misogynist,' 'exploitive and denigrating.'

48 For a comprehensive discussion of feminist film criticism, see Maggie Humm, *Feminism and Film* (Bloomington: Edinburgh and Indiana University Presses, 1997). Barbara Creed, *The Monstrous Feminine: Film, Feminism, Psychoanalysis* (London: Routledge, 1993) is particularly relevant to Cronenberg.

49 Beard, *The Artist As Monster*, i.

50 William Beard, 'Thirty-Two Paragraphs about David Cronenberg,' in Beard and White, eds, *North of Everything*, 157.

51 Geoff Pevere, 'Cronenberg Tackles Dominant Videology,' in Handling, ed., *Shape of Rage*, 141.

52 There is even a viewpoint that 'a school of Cronenberg' exists that includes Atom Egoyan and Guy Maddin, a cinema of strangeness (Beard, 'Thirty-Two Paragraphs about David Cronenberg,' 157).

53 Interview with Geoff Pevere, in Atom Egoyan, *Exotica* (Toronto: Coach House Press, 1995), 53.

54 Egoyan, *Exotica*, 154.

55 Ibid., 155.

56 Catherine Russell, 'Role Playing and the White Male Imaginary in Atom Egoyan's *Exotica*,' in *Canada's Best Features: Critical Essays on Fifteen Canadian Films*, ed. Eugene P. Walz (Amsterdam: Rodopi, 2002), 322.

57 Interview with Pevere, in Egoyan, *Exotica*, 57.

58 Ibid., 34.

59 *Cineaste*, 23.2 (Dec. 97): 10.

60 Katherine Monk, *Weird Sex and Snowshoes and Other Canadian Film Phenomena* (Vancouver: Raincoast Books, 2001), 115–16.

61 Brian D. Johnson, 'Atom's Journey,' *Maclean's*, 13 Sept. 1999, p. 56.

62 Brian D. Johnson, 'A Maze of Denial,' *Maclean's*, 18 Nov. 2002, pp. 116, 118.

63 Roger Ebert, 'Truth / Not Truth,' *Calgary Herald*, 6 Dec. 2002, p. D1.

64 Mark Hamilton, 'Atom Egoyan and the Art of Denial,' *FFWD*, 5–11 Dec. 2002, p. 50.

65 For a Turkish academic response to the 'history' in *Ararat*, see Professor Nedret Kuran-Bucoolu's essay on the film at http://www.boun.edu.tr/index_eng.html. Professor Kuran-Bucoolu claims not unexpectedly that 'the film is full of misconceptions, misrepresentations and one-sided interpretations.'

66 Monique Tschofen, 'Repetition, Compulsion, and Representation in Atom Egoyan's Films,' in Beard and White, eds, *North of Everything*, 180.

67 Geoff Pevere, 'No Place like Home: The Films of Atom Egoyan,' in Egoyan, *Exotica*, 40.
68 Peter Harcourt, 'Imaginary Images: An Examination of Atom Egoyan's Films,' *Film Quarterly* 48.3 (Spring 1995): 5.
69 Ibid., 6.
70 Carole Desbarats, 'Conquering What They Tell Us Is "Natural,"' in Carole Desbarats et al., *Atom Egoyan* (Paris: Éditions Dis Voir, 1993), 11.
71 *Globe and Mail*, 19 May 1999, p. R1 and 18 June 2001, p. R7.
72 Egoyan has yet to have a documentary made about him. For Cronenberg, see André S. Labarthe's *David Cronenberg – I Have to Make the Word Be Flesh* (AMIP, 1999).
73 Brian D. Johnson, 'Riviera Rendezvous,' *Maclean's*, 3 June 2002, p. 50.
74 Conlogue, 'Inside Cronenberg's Web,' p. R7.
75 Beard writes that 'Egoyan's cinema is just as strange, twisted, obsessive, and repetitive as Cronenberg's ...' ('Thirty-Two Paragraphs about David Cronenberg,' 145).
76 Stephen Crofts, 'Authorship and Hollywood,' in Hill and Gibson, *The Oxford Guide to Film Studies*, 322.
77 Johnson, 'Riviera Rendezvous,' 47.
78 'Auteurism in the 1990s,' in Cook and Bernink, eds, *The Cinema Book*, 311.

11. English-Canadian, Quebec, and Aboriginal Women Film-Makers

1 Jacqueline Levitin, 'Contrechamp sur les démarches de quelques réalisatrices,' in Carrière, ed., *Femmes et cinéma québécoise*, 226.
2 Scott Lauder, 'A Studio with a View: The NFB's Studio D Is Lifting Women's Filmmaking out of the Basement,' *Canadian Forum*, Aug.–Sept. 1986, p. 14.
3 Ibid.
4 For a discussion of *Forbidden Love* in terms of queer theory, see Jean Bruce, 'Queer Cinema at the NFB: The "Strange Case" of *Forbidden Love*,' in Leach and Sloniowski, eds, *Candid Eyes*, 164–80.
5 See Ray Conlogue, 'NFB: Not Dead Yet,' *Globe and Mail*, 29 Oct. 1999, pp. C1, C6. The budget went from $80 million to $56 million in 1995/6.
6 Elizabeth Anderson, 'Studio D's Imagined Community: From Development (1974) to Realignment (1986–1990),' in *Gendering the Nation: Canadian Women's Cinema*, ed. Kay Armatage et al. (Toronto: University of Toronto Press, 1999), 49.
7 Ibid., 56.

8 Kass Banning, 'Surfacing: Canadian Women's Cinema,' *Cinema Canada* 167 (Oct. 1989): 14.

9 Ibid., 16.

10 Kay Armatage and Linda Beath, 'Women in Film' and 'Canadian Women's Cinema,' in Fetherling, ed., *Documents in Canadian Film*, 171.

11 Linda Kupecek, 'Loyalties: Anne Wheeler's Film Family,' *Cinema Canada* 123 (Oct. 1985): 6.

12 Ibid.

13 Susan Lord, 'States of Emergency in the Films of Anne Wheeler,' in Beard and White, eds, *North of Everything*, 324.

14 Denyse Therrien, 'Petit à petit, le cinéma des prairies fait son nid,' in *À la recherche d'une identité: Renaissance du cinéma d'auteur canadien-anglais*, ed. Pierre Véronneau (Montreal: Cinémathèque québécoise, 1991), 151–2.

15 Wise, ed., *Take One's Essential Guide to Canadian Film*, 32.

16 Matthew Hayes, 'Bye Bye Blues,' *Cinema Canada* 157 (Nov. 1988): 9.

17 Interview with Anne Wheeler, Calgary, 29 September 2000.

18 Ibid.

19 *Cinema Canada* 146 (Nov. 1987): 37.

20 Karen Jaehne, 'I've Heard the Mermaids Singing: An Interview with Patricia Rozema,' *Cineaste* 16.3 (1988): 23.

21 George Godwin, 'Reclaiming the Subject: A Feminist Reading of "I've Heard the Mermaids Singing,"' *Cinema Canada* 152 (May 1988): 23–4.

22 Ibid., 24.

23 Marion Harrison, '*Mermaids* Singing Off Key?' *CineAction* 16 (May 1989): 26–7.

24 Jaehne, 'I've Heard the Mermaids Singing,' 23.

25 Harrison, '*Mermaids* Singing Off Key?' 30. In contrast, Robert L. Cagle considers Polly triumphant at the end of the film because she rejects the snobbery of the art world for her own imaginative creativity (Robert L. Cagle, 'A Minority on Someone Else's Continent: Identity, Difference, and the Media in the Films of Patricia Rozema,' in Armatage et al., eds, *Gendering the Nation*, 188).

26 Michael Posner, *Canadian Dreams: The Making and Marketing of Independent Films* (Vancouver: Douglas and McIntyre, 1993), 19, 21.

27 Brian D. Johnson, 'Austen Powers,' *Maclean's*, 22 Nov. 1999, p. 108.

28 Lee Parpart, 'Political Alignments and the Lure of "More Existential Questions" in the Films of Patricia Rozema,' in Beard and White, eds, *North of Everything*, 298–9.

29 Pallister, *The Cinema of Quebec: Masters in Their Own House*, 121.

30 Ibid.
31 Mary Jean Green, 'Léa Pool's *La Femme de l'Hôtel* and Women's Film in Québec,' *Quebec Studies* 9 (Fall 1989/Winter 90): 59
32 Aaron Bor, 'An Interview with Léa Pool,' *Quebec Studies* 9 (1989/90): 64.
33 Suzanne Gaulin, 'Pool's Splash,' *Cinema Canada* 111 (Oct. 1984): 8.
34 Bor, 'Interview with Léa Pool,' 68; and Gaulin, 'Pool's Splash,' 8.
35 David Winch, 'La Femme de l'hôtel,' *Cinema Canada* 111 (Oct. 1984): 10.
36 Thomas Waugh, 'Léa Pool's *À Corps Perdu* (Straight for the Heart),' *Cinema Canada* 149 (Feb. 1988): 25.
37 Monk, *Weird Sex and Snowshoes and Other Canadian Film Phenomena*, 205.
38 Leach, 'The Reel Nation: Image and Reality in Contemporary Canadian Cinema,' 13.
39 Green, 'Léa Pool's *La Femme de l'Hôtel* and Women's Film in Québec,' 49.
40 Leach, 'The Reel Nation,' 18.
41 Peter Harcourt, 'Faces Changing Colour Changing Canon,' *CineAction* 45 (Feb. 1998): 5.
42 Interview with Deepa Mehta, Calgary, 28 Sept. 2000.
43 Ibid.
44 Ibid.
45 Jayne Margetts, 'Deepa's Doctrine,' www.thei.aust.com/film97/celiindeepah.html (accessible via Google.com 'Deepa Mehta').
46 Wise, *Take One's Essential Guide to Canadian Film*, 143.
47 Margetts, 'Deepa's Doctrine.'
48 Ibid.
49 Sara Dickey, *Cinema and the Urban Poor in South India* (London: Cambridge University Press, 1993), 6.
50 Jasmine Yuen-Carrucan, 'The Politics of Deepa Mehta's *Water*,' *Bright Lights Film Journal* 28 (April 2000) (available at www.brightlightsfilm.com/28/water.html).
51 For a discussion of the film shoot, see Kim Honey, 'Welcome to Bollywood North,' *Globe and Mail*, 17 Nov. 2001, p. R9.
52 The process by which the film got made is described in Ray Conlogue, 'The Bumpy Road to Love,' *Globe and Mail*, 30 Aug. 2003, p. R1.
53 Gittings, *Canadian National Cinema*, 239.
54 Ibid., 218.
55 Ibid., 220.
56 Jerry White, 'Alanis Obomsawin: Documentary Form and the Canadian Nation(s),' *CineAction* 49 (1999): 36.
57 Ibid., 26.

58 Zuzana M. Pick, 'This Land Is Ours – Storytelling and History in *Kanehsatake: 270 Years of Resistance*,' in Leach and Sloniowski, eds, *Candid Eyes*, 195.

59 One discussion of Canadian films with gay themes is Peter Dickinson's 'Critically Queenie: The Lessons of *Fortune and Men's Eyes*,' *Canadian Journal of Film Studies* 11.2 (Fall 2002): 19–42.

60 Jean Bruce, 'Querying/Queering the Nation,' in Armatage et al., eds, *Gendering the Nation*, 275.

61 Monk, *Weird Sex and Snowshoes and Other Canadian Film Phenomena*, 136.

12. Experimental and Cult Films: Snow, Wieland, and Maddin

1 Robert B. Ray, 'Impressionism, Surrealism, and Film Theory: Path Dependence, or How a Tradition in Film Theory Gets Lost,' in Hill and Gibson, eds, *The Oxford Guide to Film Studies*, 69.

2 R. Bruce Elder, 'Image: Representation and Object – the Photographic Image in Canada's Avant-Garde Film,' in Feldman, ed., *Take Two*, 246.

3 Snow relates how he first tried 'acid' (LSD) in 1966 and that the resulting 'trip' had an impact on the film *Wavelength* (Joe Medjuck, 'The Life and Times of Michael Snow,' in Feldman and Nelson, eds, *Canadian Film Reader*, 297).

4 Medjuck, 'Life and Times of Michael Snow,' 299.

5 R. Bruce Elder, 'Michael Snow's Presence' in *Presence and Absence: The Films of Michael Snow 1956–1991*, ed. Jim Shedden (Toronto: Art Gallery of Ontario, 1995), 105.

6 Ibid., 294

7 R. Bruce Elder, 'Michael Snow's *Wavelength*,' in Feldman and Nelson, eds, *Canadian Film Reader*, 309.

8 Medjuck, 'Life and Times of Michael Snow,' 307.

9 Elder, 'Michael Snow's *Wavelength*,' 323.

10 Bart Testa, 'An Axiomatic Cinema: Michael Snow's Films,' in Shedden, ed., *Presence and Absence*, 35.

11 Michael Snow, *The Collected Writings of Michael Snow* (Waterloo, ON: Wilfrid Laurier University Press, 1994), 41.

12 Ibid., 54.

13 Medjuck, 'Life and Times of Michael Snow,' 79.

14 Louis Marcorelles, 'Snow Storms Italy,' *Cinema Canada* 6 (Feb./March 1973): 64.

15 Michael Snow, 'La Région Centrale,' in *Collected Writings of Michael Snow*, 53.

16 Snow, *Collected Writings of Michael Snow*, 206.
17 Elder, 'Michael Snow's *Wavelength*,' 308.
18 Barbara Goslawski, 'Reel Experimental,' *Globe and Mail*, 29 Jan. 2001, p. R3.
19 Program booklet for the first Governor General's Award in visual and media arts (Ottawa: Canada Council, 2000), 38.
20 Shedden, ed., *Presence and Absence*, p.8.
21 Testa, 'An Axiomatic Cinema,' 46.
22 Elder, 'Michael Snow's Presence,' 135.
23 Paul Gessell, 'Snow Reaches the Pinnacle,' *Ottawa Citizen*, 24 March 2000, p. E4.
24 Atom Egoyan, 'Foreword,' in *Inside the Pleasure Dome: Fringe Film in Canada*, 2nd ed., ed. Mike Hoolboom (Toronto: Coach House, 2001), 1.
25 Interview with Michael Snow, in Hoolboom, ed., *Inside the Pleasure Dome*, 21.
26 Wise, ed., *Take One's Essential Guide to Canadian Film*, 223.
27 For a detailed discussion, see Kay Armatage, 'The Feminine Body: Joyce Wieland's *Water Sark*,' in *The Films of Joyce Wieland*, ed. Kathryn Elder (Toronto: Toronto International Film Festival Group, 1999), 135–46.
28 Lianne M. McLarty, 'The Experimental Films of Joyce Wieland,' *Ciné Tracts* 17 (1982): 51.
29 Marshall Delaney, 'Wielandism: A Personal Style in Bloom,' in Feldman and Nelson, eds, *Canadian Film Reader*, 279.
30 Brenda Longfellow, 'Gender, Landscape, and Colonial Allegories in *The Far Shore*, *Loyalties*, and *Mouvements du désir*,' in Kay Armatage et al., eds, *Gendering the Nation*, 165.
31 Kay Armatage, 'Joyce Wieland, Feminist Documentary and the Body of Work,' *Canadian Journal of Political and Social Theory* 13.1 (1989): 93.
32 For a discussion of how Wieland felt drained after the film, see Jane Lind's biography, *Joyce Wieland: Artist on Fire* (Toronto: Lorimer, 2001), 233–5. The biography also mentions she actually tried to do another feature but quickly gave up.
33 Kay Armatage, 'Kay Armatage Interviews Joyce Wieland,' in Elder, ed., *The Films of Joyce Wieland*, 155.
34 Kathryn Elder, 'Foreword,' in Elder, ed., *The Films of Joyce Wieland*, 1.
35 Hollis Frampton and Joyce Wieland, 'I Don't Even Know about the Second Stanza,' in Elder, ed., *The Films of Joyce Wieland*, 172–3.
36 Adele Freedman, 'Goddess, Matriarch, Victim,' *Globe and Mail*, 27 Oct. 2001, p. D12.
37 Iris Nowell, *Joyce Wieland: A Life in Art* (Toronto: ECW Press, 2001), 295.
38 Monk, *Weird Sex and Snowshoes and Other Canadian Film Phenomena*, 42.

39 Posner, *Canadian Dreams: The Making and Marketing of Independent Films*, 175.
40 Ibid., 179.
41 Ibid., 184.
42 Brian Bergman, 'Maddin Madness,' *Maclean's*, 23 Dec. 2002, p. 50.
43 Steven Shaviro, 'Fire and Ice: The Films of Guy Maddin,' in Beard and White, eds, *North of Everything*, 219.
44 *New Yorker*, 6 Aug. 2001, p. 21.
45 Caelum Vatnsdal, *Kino Delirium: The Films of Guy Maddin* (Winnipeg: Arbeiter Ring Publishing, 2000), 69, 70.
46 Ibid., 81.
47 Mike Rubin, 'The Pretty Good Films of Guy Maddin: An Interview,' www.motorbooty.com/maddin, p. 11.
48 Les Perreaux, 'Far from the Maddin Crowd,' *National Post*, 11 Sept. 2001, p. B3.
49 Jaime Frederick, 'Undead Can Dance,' *See* [Edmonton], 21–7 Feb. 2002, p.13.
50 Bergman, 'Maddin Madness,' 51.
51 Sarah Milroy, 'Peeping Guy,' *Globe and Mail*, 29 March 2003, p. R10.
52 Guy Maddin, *Cowards Bend the Knee* (Toronto: The Power Plant, 2003).
53 Darell Varga, 'Desire in Bondage: Guy Maddin's *Careful*,' *Canadian Journal of Film Studies* 8.2 (Fall 1999): 59, 67.
54 Bergman, 'Maddin Madness,' 50.
55 For a history of the Winnipeg Film Group, see Patrick Lowe, 'The Winnipeg Film Group Aesthetic,' in *Dislocations*, ed. Gilles Hébert (Winnipeg: Winnipeg Film Group, 1995), 63–73; and Geoff Pevere, 'Greenland Revisited: The Winnipeg Film Group during the 1980s,' in ibid., 37–52.
56 Victor Barac, 'Dislocation and Postmodern Prairie Film,' in Hébert, ed., *Dislocations*, 25–36.
57 Gilles Hébert, 'Dislocations,' in Hébert, ed., *Dislocations*, 10.
58 Pevere, 'Greenland Revisited,' 41.
59 For a discussion of the history of experimental film from 1920 to 1970, see David Curtis, *Experimental Cinema: A Fifty Year Evolution* (London: Studio Vista, 1971).
60 Hoolboom, ed., *Inside the Pleasure Dome*, 3.

13. Quebec's Next Generation: Lauzon to Turpin

1 José Arroyo, 'Howls from the Asphalt Jungle,' *Cinema Canada* 141 (May 1987): 7.

2 Monk, *Weird Sex and Snowshoes and Other Canadian Film Phenomena*, 321.
3 Bill Marshall, *Quebec National Cinema* (Montreal and Kingston: McGill-Queen's University Press, 2001), 114.
4 Ibid., 115.
5 *Le Devoir*, 7 June 1987, p. C4.
6 *Le Droit*, 12 Sept. 1987, p. 5.
7 Jean Marcel, 'Jean-Claude Lauzon,' *24 images* 90 (1998): 21.
8 *Cinema Canada* 146 (Nov. 1987): 42.
9 Roger Ebert, 'Leolo,' *Chicago Sun-Times,* 9 April 1993.
10 Ibid.
11 George Toles, 'Drowning for Love: Jean-Claude Lauzon's *Léolo*,' in Walz, ed., *Canada's Best Features*, 291.
12 *Time*, 3 Jan. 1994, p. 70.
13 *Maclean's*, 11 Jan. 1993, p. 5.
14 Brian D. Johnson, 'Rebel Masterpiece,' *Maclean's*, 25 May 1992, p. 51.
15 Ibid.
16 Ibid., p. 52.
17 For a discussion of national identity in Quebec, see Marshall, *Quebec National Cinema*, 8–15, where he reviews recent scholarship on the concept of national identity, particularly in cinema.
18 Ibid., 5.
19 Marshall makes reference to Freud's 1909 essay 'On Sexuality,' which discusses how a child seeks a nobler birth once he or she discovers the reality of parental failings (104).
20 Marshall indicates that in 1997 the audience share of Quebec films in Quebec was a mere 3.7 per cent and that there were usually only ten features made annually, with 30 per cent of financing coming from one form or another of state support, (*Quebec National Cinema*, 15–17).
21 Marcel, 'Jean-Claude Lauzon,' 21.
22 Maurie Alioff, 'Childhood Memories,' *Take One* 1.4 (Fall 1992): 18.
23 In the Alioff interview, 'Childhood Memories,' Lauzon is quoted as saying, 'All my relationships were with crooks. Eight people who were close to me then had been shot or stabbed and they're dead.'
24 Taras Grescoe, *Sacré Blues: An Unsentimental Journey through Quebec* (Toronto: Macfarlane Walter & Ross, 2000), 161–2.
25 Brian D. Johnson,'A Festival Zeroes In on Quebec,' *Maclean's*, 7 Sept. 1998, p. 52.
26 Maurice Alioff, 'Haunted by Hitchcock: Robert Lepage's *Le Confessional*,' *Take One* 4.9 (Fall 1995): 14.
27 Wise, ed., *Take One's Essential Guide to Canadian Film*, 153.

28 Johnson, 'A Festival Zeroes In on Quebec,' 52.

29 *Globe and Mail*, 18 March 1999, p. A2.

30 *Take One* 7.23 (Sept. 1999): 46.

31 *Montreal Gazette*, 28 Aug. 1998, pp. D1–D2.

32 See Kate Taylor, 'Daring Lepage Crosses Borders and Breeds in Quebec,' *Globe and Mail*, 23 May 2000, p. R1.

33 Isa Tousignant, 'Fated Possibilities: A Conversation with Robert Lepage,' *Take One* 9.30 (Winter 2001): 15.

34 Matthew Hayes, 'Art in the Danger Zone,' *Globe and Mail*, 11 Oct. 2001, p. R1.

35 Monk, *Weird Sex and Snowshoes and Other Canadian Film Phenomena*, 179.

36 Maurice Alioff, 'Denis Villeneuve's *Un 32 août sur terre*: Lost in the Desert,' *Take One* 7.21 (Fall 1998): 30.

37 Ibid.

38 David Sherritt, 'Quirky Canadian Film Blends Calm, Chaos, and a Talking Fish,' *Christian Science Monitor*, 1 Feb. 2002.

39 Ann Hornaday, 'Quirky "Maelstrom" Ultimately Flounders,' *Washington Post*, 22 March 2002, p. C05.

40 Wise, ed., *Take One's Essential Guide to Canadian Film*, 136.

41 Ibid., 214.

42 http://membres.lycos/travelavant/denisvil.htm, 17 Sept. 2001.

43 In Cynthia Amsdem's 'Denis Villeneuve's *Maelström*: Much Ado about a Fish,' Villeneuve states, 'Water is about ... the beginning of life' (*Take One* 9.30 [Winter 2001]: 24).

44 http://membres.lycos/travelavant/denisvil.htm.

45 Maurice Alioff, 'Andre Turpin: Things That Come from the Deep,' *Take One* 10.35 (Dec. 2001–Feb. 2002): 9.

46 Ray Conlogue, 'In the Head of Andre Turpin,' *Globe and Mail*, 15 Feb. 2002.

47 Ibid.

48 Alioff, 'Andre Turpin,' 12.

49 Matthew Hays, 'The Critics May Groan, but Les Boys Are Back,' *Globe and Mail*, 23 Oct. 2001, p. R5.

50 Ray Conlogue, 'Melodrama at Its Exotic Best,' *Globe and Mail*, 4 April 2003, p. R3.

51 Marshall, *Quebec National Cinema*, x.

14. English Canada's Next Generation: McDonald to Burns

1 'Toronto new wave is a catchy phrase for a spirited generation of English-Canadian filmmakers who came to cinematic maturity during the mid- to late-1980s ... What is remarkable about this group of filmmakers is that

they, unlike previous generations, avoid the easy lure of big money and bigger films in Hollywood' (Wise, ed., *Take One's Essential Guide to Canadian Film*, 208–9).

2   Cameron Bailey 'Standing in the Kitchen All Night: A Secret History of the Toronto New Wave,' *Take One* 9.28 (Summer 2000): 9.

3   Bruce McDonald, 'Dear Norman, What Is to Be Done?' *Cinema Canada* 122 (Sept. 1985): 11.

4   Colin Brunton, 'Roadkill,' *Cinema Canada* 165 (July/August 1989): 5.

5   Brian D. Johnson, 'Rock 'n' Roll Renegades,' *Maclean's*, 26 Feb. 1990, p. 40.

6   Monk, *Weird Sex and Snowshoes and Other Canadian Film Phenomena*, 86.

7   Marc Glassman, 'Rockin' on the Road: The Films of Bruce McDonald,' *Take One* 4.8 (Summer 1995): 18.

8   Gittings, *Canadian National Cinema: Ideology, Difference and Representation*, 154.

9   Ibid., 156.

10   Ibid., 157.

11   Roger Ebert, 'Highway 61,' *Chicago Sun-Times*, 29 June 1992.

12   Hal Hinson, 'Highway 61,' *Washington Post*, 9 June 1992.

13   Peter Stark, 'Punks Mix It Up in Razor-Sharp Comedy,' *San Francisco Chronicle*, 4 Dec. 1998.

14   Wise, ed., *Take One's Essential Guide to Canadian Film*, 55.

15   Later the Turner book was copied/parodied when the making of the film appeared as a diary written by the film's screenwriter, Noel Baker. *Hard Core Road Show* (Toronto: Anansi, 1997) captures the process by which McDonald and crew created Canada's greatest mockumentary.

16   Ken Anderlin, 'Hard Core Logo,' *Take One* 5.13 (Fall 1996): 44.

17   Brian D. Johnson, 'Raw Punk Cooked Pop,' *Maclean's*, 14 Oct. 1996, p. 89.

18   Glassman, 'Rockin' on the Road,' 18.

19   Gayle MacDonald, 'Money Isn't Everything,' *Globe and Mail*, 24 Nov. 2000, p. R1.

20   Peter Godard, 'Bruce McDonald at the Crossroads with *Picture Claire*,' *Take One* 10.35 (Dec. 2001–Jan. 2002): 15.

21   Brian D. Johnson, 'Clarifying Claire,' *Maclean's*, 4 March 2002, p. 54.

22   MacDonald, 'Money Isn't Everything,' R4.

23   Richard Kelly, 'Last Night,' *Sight and Sound* 9.7 (July 1999): 44–5.

24   Jonathan Romney, 'Last Night,' *New Statesman*, 5 July 1999, p. 45.

25   Ibid., 46.

26   Brian D. Johnson, 'French Connection: A Canadian Filmmaker Steps Out at the World's Splashiest Festival,' *Maclean's*, 25 May 1998, p. 60.

27   Ibid.

28 www.canoe.ca/JamMoviesArtists/mckellar, 7 March 2000.
29 Marc Glassman, 'Last Night: In the Year of the Don,' *Take One* 7.21 (Fall 1998): 15.
30 Monk, *Weird Sex and Snowshoes and Other Canadian Film Phenomena*, 307.
31 Adam Richardson, 'A Few Minutes with Lynne Stopkewich,' *The Rice Thresher*, www.riceinfo.ric.educ/projects/thresher/issues/84/970425/ AE/Story 04, 25 April 1997, p. 3
32 Ibid.
33 Brian D. Johnson, 'Death and the Maiden,' *Maclean's*, 14 April 1997, p. 60.
34 Ibid., 61.
35 Roger Ebert, 'Kissed,' *Chicago Sun-Times*, 4 March 1997.
36 Maurie Alioff, 'Sweet Necrophilia,' *Take One* 5.15 (Spring 1997): 15.
37 For a discussion of Parker's career after the success of *Kissed*, see Gayle MacDonald, 'Kissed Again,' *Globe and Mail*, 12 Sept. 2000, p. R1.
38 Andy Sheehan, *Cinemania Online*, www.twincities.sidewalk.com/detail/ 18132, 20 May 1997.
39 Katherine Monk, 'Let's Talk about (Kinky) Sex,' *Globe and Mail*, 5 Sept. 2001, p. R1.
40 Geoff Pevere, 'Kissed,' www.movingpictures.nisa.com/1998/kissed.htm; and Sheehan, *Cinemania Online*, 20 May 1997.
41 'Festival Wraps,' *Take One* 9.30 (Winter 2001): 32.
42 Rick Groen, 'Emotional Vacancy at a Flea-Bag Hotel,' *Globe and Mail*, 5 April 2001, p. R3.
43 Ian Edwards, 'Suburbanators-Distrib Strategy,' *Playback*, 29 July 1996, p. 7.
44 Ibid.
45 Craig MacInnis, 'Kitchen Party: Gary Burns Returns to Suburbia,' *Take One* 6.19 (Spring 1998): 13.
46 Ian Edwards, 'Production in Alberta: Fade to Gray,' *Playback*, 24 Feb. 1997, p. 20.
47 *CBC This Morning* Radio interview with Gary Burns, 20 Nov. 2000, www.infoculture.cbc.ca.
48 Reg Hill, 'Waydowntown a Triumph for Gary Burns,' www.motherstars mag.com/garyburns.
49 Sharon Corder and Jack Blum, 'Waydowntown: The Subversive Charm of Gary Burns,' *Take One* 9.30 (Winter 2001): 10.
50 Ibid., 12.
51 For a discussion of this trend, see Geoffrey Nowell-Smith 'The Resurgence of Cinema,' in Nowell-Smith, ed., *The Oxford History of World Cinema*, 759–66.

15. The Anguished Critic

1 Jonathan Rosenbaum, *Placing Movies: The Practice of Film Criticism* (Berkeley: University of California Press, 1995), 11–12.
2 Stam, *Film Theory: An Introduction*, 257.
3 See Alexander Doty, 'Queer Theory' in Hill and Gibson, eds, *The Oxford Guide to Film Studies*, 148–52.
4 Robert Fulford, *Marshall Delaney at the Movies: The Contemporary World As Seen on Film* (Toronto: Peter Martin Associates, 1974), 29, 81.
5 Delaney, 'Artists in the Shadows: Some Notable Canadian Movies,' in Feldman, ed., *Take Two*, 2.
6 John Hofsess, *Inner Views: Ten Canadian Filmmakers* (Toronto: McGraw-Hill Ryerson, 1975), 33.
7 Ibid., 24.
8 Ibid., 37.
9 Knelman, *This Is Where We Came In*, 35.
10 Martin Knelman, *Home Movies: Tales from the Canadian Film World* (Toronto: Key Porter, 1987), 103–4.
11 Jay Scott, *Midnight Matinées* (Toronto: Oxford University Press, 1985), 81.
12 Karen York, ed., *Great Scott: The Best of Jay Scott's Movie Reviews* (Toronto: McClelland and Stewart, 1994), 294.
13 Ibid., 13.
14 Ibid., 17.
15 Monk, *Weird Sex and Snowshoes and Other Canadian Film Phenomena*, 1.
16 Ibid., 5.
17 Ibid., 129.
18 Angela Stukator, 'Book Review,' *Canadian Journal of Film Studies* 11.2 (Fall 2002): 105.
19 Greg Quill, 'Why Canadian Movies Suck,' *Toronto Star*, 13 April 2001, p. E2.
20 Ibid., E3.
21 Rosenbaum, *Placing Movies*, 12.
22 Observations by Peter Harcourt in an interview with the author in Ottawa, 18 Feb. 2001.
23 Ibid.
24 Reprinted in B. Allan, M. Dorland, and Z.M. Pick, eds, *Responses: In Honour of Peter Harcourt* (Kingston, ON: Responsibility Press, 1992), 248.
25 Ibid., 261.
26 Ibid., 265.
27 R. Bruce Elder, 'The Cinema We Need,' in Fetherling, ed., *Documents in Canadian Film*, 263, 264–5.

28 Ibid.

29 Bart Testa, 'So What Did Elder Say?' in Fetherling, ed., *Documents in Canadian Film*, 281.

30 Piers Handling, 'The Cinema We Need?' in Fetherling, ed., *Documents in Canadian Film*, 291.

31 Geoff Pevere, 'The Rites (and Wrongs) of the Elder; or, The Cinema We Got: The Critics We Need,' in Fetherling, ed., *Documents in Canadian Film*, 325, 332.

32 R. Bruce Elder, 'A Vindication,' in Fetherling, ed., *Documents in Canadian Film*, 315.

33 R. Leach, 'Second Images: Reflections on the Canadian Cinema(s) in the Seventies,' in Feldman, ed., *Take Two*, 102.

34 Ibid.

35 Ibid., 107.

36 Leach, *Claude Jutra: Filmmaker*, 246.

37 Ibid., 249.

38 Michael Dorland, 'Beyond Shame and Glory: Preface to a Critical Dialogue in Canadian/Quebec Cinemas' in Véronneau, Dorland, and Feldman, eds, *Dialogue: Canadian and Quebec Cinema*, 316.

39 Dorland, *So Close to the State/s: The Emergence of a Canadian Feature Film Policy*, 7, 9, 11.

40 The dependent capitalism argument is made by Manjunath Pendakur in *Canadian Dreams and American Control*, and the negotiated dependency argument is made by Ted Madger in *Canada's Hollywood*.

41 Dorland, *So Close to the State/s*, 14.

42 Ibid., 135.

43 See Charles R. Acland, 'From the Absent Audience to Expo-Mentality: Popular Film in Canada,' in Taras and Rasperich, eds, *A Passion for Identity*, 281–95.

44 Michael Dorland, 'Matthew Arnold in Canada: The Lonely Discourse of J. Peter Harcourt,' in Allan et al., eds, *Responses*, 73.

45 Feldman, 'The Silent Subject in English Canadian Film,' in Feldman, ed., *Take Two*, 55.

46 Notes for the Robarts Lecture courtesy of Dr Feldman, p. 3.

47 Ibid., 4.

48 Ibid., 11.

49 Bart Testa, 'When They Pulled the Plug on Canadian National Cinema,' *Literary Review of Canada*, Jan./Feb. 2003, pp. 26–30.

50 Ibid., 26.

51 Ibid.

52 Ibid., 27.

53 Ibid., 29.
54 Gittings, *Canadian National Cinema*, 1.
55 Ibid., 32.
56 Ibid., 75.
57 Brenda Longfellow and Thomas Waugh, 'Introduction,' *Canadian Journal of Film Studies* 10.2 (Fall 2001): 5.
58 Gittings, *Canadian National Cinema*, 195.
59 Martin Levin, in 'A Post-National CanLit,' *Globe and Mail*, 8 June 2002, p. D16, describes an article by Pico Iyer, 'In the Last Refuge: On the Promise of the New Canadian Fiction,' *Harper's*, June, 2002.
60 Kay Armatage et al., 'Gendering the Nation,' in Armatage et al., eds, *Gendering the Nation: Canadian Women's Cinema*, 10.
61 Ibid., 12.
62 Peter Morris, 'The Uncertain Trumpet: Defining a (Canadian) Art Cinema in the Sixties,' *CinéAction* 6 (Spring 1989): 8.
63 Morris, *Embattled Shadows*, 239.
64 Ibid., 240.
65 Ibid.
66 Peter Morris, 'In Our Own Eyes: The Canonizing of Canadian Film,' *Canadian Journal of Film Studies* 3.1 (1994); 34.
67 Will Straw, 'Canadian Cinema,' in Hill and Gibson, eds, *The Oxford Guide to Film Studies*, 526.
68 Interview with Seth Feldman, Toronto, 22 Feb. 2001.
69 Jeffrey Simpson, *Star-Spangled Canadians* (Toronto: HarperCollins, 2000), 6.
70 Dorland, *So Close to the State/s*, 3.
71 Ibid.
72 Ibid., 9
73 Walz, ed., *Canada's Best Features*, xxxiv–xxxv.
74 Marshall, *Quebec National Cinema*, 2.
75 Ibid., 136.
76 Ibid., 15.
77 Ibid., 72.
78 Pallister, *The Cinema of Quebec*, 447.
79 Lefebvre, 'Le Concept de cinéma national,' in Véronneau, Dorland, and Feldman, eds, *Dialogue: Canadian and Quebec Cinema*, 90.
80 Lever, *Histoire générale du cinéma au Québec*, 478.
81 Ibid., 480.
82 Ibid., 482.
83 Ibid., 492.

84 Ibid., 504–5.
85 Lieve Spass, *The Francophone Film: A Struggle for Identity* (Manchester: Manchester University Press, 2000), 250.
86 Ibid., 115.
87 Brian D. Johnson, 'We Like to Watch,' *Maclean's*, 25 Nov. 2002, p. 30.
88 Ibid.

16. The Canadian Film Industry and the Digital Revolution

1 Rebecca Goldfarb, *The Conflict of Two Realities and Two Views: A Comparative Assessment of the Canadian and American Film Industries*, Ref. Doc., no. 5 (Ottawa: D-FAIT, 1998), 3.
2 Ibid., 4, 32.
3 Ibid., 8.
4 Ibid., 14.
5 Ibid., 19.
6 *Report on Business* magazine, a monthly insert in the *Globe and Mail* reported in 2001 that the percentage of Canada's box office revenue that came from Canadian films was a mere 2 per cent or $7.4 million of the $370 million of movie box office sales in Canada in the year 2000! (*Report on Business*, September 2001, p. 96).
7 Denis Seguin, 'The 5% Solution,' *Canadian Business*, 16 Sept. 2002, p. 37.
8 Goldfarb, *The Conflict of Two Realities and Two Views*, 23.
9 Pendakur, *Canadian Dreams and American Control*, 276.
10 *A Guide to Federal Programs for the Film and Video Sector* (Ottawa: Cultural Industries Branch, Canadian Heritage, 1998), 10.
11 Marc Raboy, 'Public Television,' in *The Cultural Industries in Canada: Problems, Policies and Prospects*, ed. Michael Dorland (Toronto: James Lorimer & Co., 1996), 191.
12 Canadian Film and Television Production Association, *The Guide 2000*, 36–41.
13 Ibid.
14 Seguin, 'The 5% Solution,' 36.
15 Ted Madger, 'Film and Video Production,' in Dorland, ed., *The Cultural Industries in Canada*, 175.
16 Ibid., 174.
17 Michel Comte, 'Tax Breaks Lure Cartoon Company to Toronto,' *Business in Vancouver*, 22–8 Jan. 2002, p. 9.
18 The NFB continues its animation work with vigour. In 2002 it announced an 'Animation Hothouse' program for new animators.

19 Karen Mazurkewich, *Cartoon Capers: The History of Canadian Animators* (Toronto: McArthur & Co., 1990), 111.
20 Ibid., 112.
21 Ibid., 113.
22 Bertrand Marotte, 'Cinar Settlement $2 Million,' *Globe and Mail*, 16 March 2002, p. B1.
23 Ibid., B2.
24 See Christopher Shulgan, 'Darth Investor vs. the Cartoon Company,' *Report on Business*, June 2003, pp. 58–70.
25 Pevere and Dymond, *Mondo Canuck: A Canadian Pop Odyssey*, 7; and Simpson, *Star-Spangled Canadians*, 325.
26 Simpson, *Star-Spangled Canadians*, 329.
27 Doug Saunders, 'The Myth of Hollywood North,' *Report on Business*, April 2001, p. 98.
28 Doug Saunders, 'Hollywood's Northern Lights,' *Globe and Mail*, 3 July 2000, p. R1.
29 Saunders, 'The Myth of Hollywood North,' 97.
30 Ibid., 98
31 Jennifer Hunter, 'Northern Exposure,' *Maclean's*, 11 Oct. 1999, p. 70.
32 *Calgary Herald*, 22 Nov. 2002, p. D6.
33 Ibid.
34 Hunter, 'Northern Exposure,' 71.
35 Saunders, 'The Myth of Hollywood North,' 100.
36 Ibid.
37 Gasher, *Hollywood North: The Feature Film Industry in British Columbia*, 142
38 Ibid., 143.
39 www.allianceatlantis.com
40 Ibid.
41 Sarah Hampson, 'Robert Lantos: The Sequel,' *Globe and Mail*, 20 July 2000, p. R1.
42 Ibid., R2.
43 Interview with Michael MacMillan, www.allianceatlantis.com.
44 Press release, www.allianceatlantis.com.
45 David McIntosh, 'Vanishing Point: Proliferations, Purifications and the Convergence of Canadian and Mexican National Cinemas,' *Canadian Journal of Film Studies* 10.2 (Fall 2001): 75.
46 Sarah Scott, 'The Accidental Moguls,' *Report on Business*, December 2000, p. 62.
47 Murray Whyte, 'Oh Yeah, Somebody Told Me That Was Pretty Good,' *National Post*, 29 Jan. 2001, p. D3.

48 McIntosh, 'Vanishing Point,' 75.

49 Michael Posner and James Adams, 'Budget Turns Its Back on TV,' *Globe and Mail*, 20 Feb. 2003, p. R1.

50 Dawn Calleja, 'Manna from Heaven,' *Canadian Business*, 16 Sept. 2002, p. 42.

51 Ibid.

52 Ibid., 44.

53 *Globe and Mail*, 28 Oct. 1999, p. T3.

54 Ibid.

55 Jay Boyar, 'Blair Witch Project Is Making Hollywood Change,' *Calgary Herald*, 21 Oct. 1999, p. E2.

56 Michelle MacAfee, 'Canucks Threatened by U.S. Culture, Poll Finds,' *Calgary Herald*, 1 July 2002, p. A3.

57 Ibid.

58 Pendakur, *Canadian Dreams and American Control*, 29.

59 James Adams, 'Weekend Diary,' *Globe and Mail*, 30 Nov. 2002, p. R3.

60 W.W. Dixon, *Disaster and Memory: Celebrity Culture and the Crisis of Hollywood Cinema* (New York: Columbia University Press, 1999), 6.

61 Seth Feldman, 'What Was Cinema,' *Canadian Journal of Film Studies* 5.1 (Spring 1996): 5.

62 Rick Groen, 'The Neverending Story,' *Globe and Mail*, 31 Dec. 1999, p. R1.

63 Madger, 'Film and Video Production,' in Dorland, ed., *The Cultural Industries in Canada*, 174.

64 A representative sampling of these attitudes is found in Seguin, 'The 5% Solution.'

65 Scott, 'The Accidental Moguls,' 56.

66 Dorland, *So Close to the State/s*, 147.

17. A History of the Future

1 James Adams, 'Genie-Awards: Best-Picture Nominees,' *Globe and Mail*, 2 Feb. 2002, p. R4.

2 Ibid.

3 Liam Lacey, 'No Clean Sweep,' *Globe and Mail*, 8 March 2002, p. R1; and Shannon Kari, 'Taxpayers Help Film Hit Box Office Button,' *Calgary Herald*, 16 March 2002, p. A1.

4 Kari, 'Taxpayers Help Film Hit Box Office Button,' A1.

5 Ibid.

6 Ibid.

7 Gayle MacDonald, 'Canada's Full Monty,' *Globe and Mail*, 23 Feb. 2002, p. R3.

8 Gayle MacDonald, 'Red Green Has It All Wrapped Up,' *Globe and Mail*, 3 April 2002, p. R1.

9 Ibid.

10 See Liam Lacey, 'You Can Stretch Tape Only So Far,' *Globe and Mail*, 19 April 2002, p. R1.

11 Rick Groen, 'The Sublime North,' *Globe and Mail*, 12 April 2002, p. R1.

12 Brian D. Johnson, 'An Arctic Masterpiece,' *Maclean's*, 15 April 2002, p. 53.

13 Margaret Atwood, 'Of Myths and Men,' *Globe and Mail*, 13 April 2002, p. R4.

14 Liam Lacey, 'Against All Odds' *Globe and Mail*, 12 April 2002, p. R4.

15 Ibid. The script is 110 pages, but the abundance of silence in the film makes for a longer than normal film (Liam Lacey, 'Permafrost on the Riviera,' *Globe and Mail*, 18 May 2001, p. A10).

16 Zacharias Kunuk, 'I First Heard the Story of Atanarjuat from My Mother,' *Brick* 70 (Winter 2002): 17.

17 Doug Alexander, 'An Arctic Allegory,' *Beaver* 82.2 (April/May 2002): 49.

18 Raúl Galvez, 'In Conversation: Zacharias Kunuk,' *Montage*, Spring 2002, p. 12.

19 Atwood, 'Of Myths and Men,' R4.

20 Jay Stone, 'Blood Runs Hot in Cold Arctic,' *Calgary Herald*, 12 April 2002, p. E3.

21 Galvez, 'In Conversation: Zacharias Kunuk,' 12.

22 Robert Everett-Green, 'A Filmmaker Worth Remembering,' *Globe and Mail*, 19 June 2002, p. A15.

23 Ibid.

24 Sarah Kilroy, 'Northern Light,' *Globe and Mail*, 28 Dec. 2002, p. R1.

25 Paul Apak Angilirq, *Atanarjuat: The Fast Runner* (Toronto: Coach House Books and Isuma Publishing, 2002). The book has 240 pages.

26 Scott MacKenzie, 'National Identity, Canadian Cinema, and Multiculturalism' *Canadian Aesthetics Journal* 4 (Summer 1999) (http://www.uqtr.uquebec.ca/AE/vol_4/index.htm).

27 Ibid., 2.

28 Ibid., 7.

29 Gittings, *Canadian National Cinema*, 200–201.

30 Wise, ed., *Take One's Essential Guide to Canadian Film*, 89.

31 *Globe and Mail*, 22 Jan. 2003, p. A6.

32 Norman Cohn, 'The Art of Community-Based Filmmaking,' *Brick* 70 (Winter 2002): 23.

33 Ray Conlogue, 'Egoyan Film Sparks Turkish Backlash,' *Globe and Mail*, 18 April 2002, p. R2.

34 Jeremy Rifkin, *The Age of Access: The New Culture of Hypercapitalism* (New York: Jeremy P. Tarcher / Putnam, 2000), 140.

35 Ibid., 170.

36 Ibid., 171.

37 A wire service story from Moscow reported that Russian films make up only 2 per cent of theatre screenings in the age of capitalist globalization, which is a worry for the Russian state (*Calgary Herald*, 18 July 2002, p. E2).

38 A symposium on 'Film in the Age of Electronic Reproduction,' University of Toronto, 14 April 2001, explored this question from a variety of viewpoints, drawing on the participation of major Canadian commentators – Brenda Longfellow, R. Bruce Elder, and Mike Hoolboom.

39 For a discussion of digital versus 35 mm film distribution, see Wheeler Winston Dixon, *The Second Century of Cinema*: *The Past and Future of the Moving Image* (Albany: SUNY Press, 2000), 226–30.

40 Ibid., 246.

41 The term is used by Philip Rosen in his book *Change Mummified: Cinema, Historicity, Theory* (Minneapolis: University of Minnesota Press, 2001) to articulate a theory of cinematic temporality, which seeks to link historical writing with its object (history) in such a way as to show how historical senses of time have played on cinema art.

42 Paul Grosswiler, *Method Is the Message: Rethinking McLuhan through Critical Theory* (Montreal: Black Rose Books, 1998), 77.

43 N. Patrick Peritore, 'Radical Dialectics,' unpublished paper, quoted in Grosswiler, *Method Is the Message*, 56.

44 The theory of Walter Ong, discussed in Grosswiler, *Method Is the Message*, 59.

45 Rifkin, *The Age of Access*, 194–9.

46 Ibid., 206–7.

47 *New Yorker*, 15 July 2002, p. 23.

48 Theodor Adorno and Max Horkheimer, 'The Culture Industry: Enlightenment versus Mass Deception,' in *The Cultural Studies Reader*, ed. Simon During (London and New York: Routledge, 1993), 33.

Bibliography

Acland, Charles R. 'From the Absent Audience to Expo-Mentality: Popular Film in Canada.' In *A Passion for Identity: Canadian Studies for the Twenty-First Century*. 4th ed. Ed. David Taras and Beverly Rasporich. Toronto: Nelson, 2001. 275–91.

Adams, James. 'Genie-Awards: Best-Picture Nominees.' *Globe and Mail*, 2 Feb. 2002, p. R4.

– 'Weekend Diary.' *Globe and Mail*, 30 Nov. 2002, p. R3.

Adorno, Theodor, and Max Horkheimer. 'The Culture Industry: Enlightenment versus Mass Deception.' In *The Cultural Studies Reader*. Ed. Simon During. London and New York: Routledge, 1993. 29–36.

Aitken, Ian. *Film and Reform: John Grierson and the Documentary Film Movement*. London: Routledge, 1990.

Alexander, Doug. 'An Arctic Allegory.' *Beaver* 82.2 (April/May 2002): 49–50.

Alioff, Maurie. 'Childhood Memories.' *Take One* 1.4 (Fall 1992): 17–20.

– 'Haunted by Hitchcock: Robert Lepage's *Le Confessional*.' *Take One* 4.9 (Fall 1995): 9–15.

– 'Sweet Necrophilia.' *Take One* 5.15 (Spring 1997): 12–16.

– 'Denis Villeneuve's *Un 32 août sur terre*: Lost in the Desert.' *Take One* 7.21 (Fall 1998): 29–31.

– 'Andre Turpin: Things That Come from the Deep.' *Take One* 10.35 (Dec. 2001–Feb. 2002): 8–12.

Allan, Blaine. 'Directed by Phillip Borsos.' In *North of Everything: English-Canadian Cinema since 1980*. Ed. William Beard and Jerry White. Edmonton: University of Alberta Press, 2002. 106–21.

Allan, Blaine, Michael Dorland, and Zuzana M. Pick, eds. *Responses: In Honour of Peter Harcourt*. Kingston, ON: Responsibility Press, 1992.

Allor, Martin, Danielle Juteau, and John Shepherd. 'Contingencies of Culture:

The Space of Culture in Canada and Québec.' *Culture and Policy* 6.1 (1994).
    http://www.gu.edu.au/centre/cmp/journal/html.
Amsdem, Cynthia. 'Denis Villeneuve's *Maëlstrom:* Much Ado about a Fish.'
    Take One 9.30 (Winter 2001): 22–4.
Anderlin, Ken. 'Hard Core Logo.' *Take One* 5.13 (Fall 1996): 42–4.
Anderson, Elizabeth. 'Studio D's Imagined Community: From Development
    (1974) to Realignment (1986–1990).' In *Gendering the Nation: Canadian
    Women's Cinema.* Ed. Kay Armatage et al. Toronto: University of Toronto
    Press, 1999. 41–61.
Angilirq, Paul Apak. *Atanarjuat: The Fast Runner.* Toronto. Coach House
    Books, 2002.
Aquin, Hubert. 'The Cultural Fatigue of French Canada.' In *Contemporary
    Quebec Criticism.* Ed. Larry Shouldice. Toronto: University of Toronto Press,
    1979. 54–82.
Arcand, Denys. Interview. www.sundancechannel.com/focus/arcand/5.html.
Armatage, Kay. 'Joyce Wieland, Feminist Documentary and the Body of
    Work.' *Canadian Journal of Political and Social Theory* 13.1–2 (1989): 91–101.
– 'The Feminine Body: Joyce Wieland's *Water Sark.*' In *The Films of Joyce
    Wieland.* Ed. Kathryn Elder. Toronto: Toronto International Film Festival
    Group, 1999. 135–46.
– 'Kay Armatage Interviews Joyce Wieland.' In *The Films of Joyce Wieland.* Ed.
    Kathyrn Elder. Toronto: Toronto International Film Festival Group, 1999.
    153–60.
– *The Girl from God's Country: Nell Shipman and the Silent Cinema.* Toronto:
    University of Toronto Press, 2003.
Armatage, Kay, and Linda Beath. 'Women in Film' and 'Canadian Women's
    Cinema.' In *Documents in Canadian Film.* Ed. Douglas Fetherling.
    Peterborough, ON: Broadview Press, 1988. 167–76.
Armatage, Kay, et al. 'Gendering the Nation.' In *Gendering the Nation: Cana-
    dian Women's Cinema.* Ed. Kay Armatage et al. Toronto: University of
    Toronto Press, 1999. 3–16.
Armatage, Kay, et al., eds. *Gendering the Nation: Canadian Women's Cinema.*
    Toronto: University of Toronto Press, 1999.
Arroyo, José. 'Howls from the Asphalt Jungle.' *Cinema Canada* 141 (May 1987):
    7–11.
Atwood, Margaret. *Strange Things: The Malevolent North in Canadian Literature.*
    Oxford: Oxford University Press, 1995.
– 'Of Myths and Men.' *Globe and Mail,* 13 April 2002, p. R4.
Backhouse, Charles. *Canadian Government Motion Picture Bureau.* Ottawa:
    Canadian Film Institute, 1974.

Bailey, Cameron. 'Standing in the Kitchen All Night: A Secret History of the Toronto New Wave.' *Take One* 9.28 (Summer 2000): 6–11.

Baker, Noel. *Hard Core Road Show*. Toronto: Anansi, 1997.

Banning, Kass. 'Surfacing: Canadian Women's Cinema.' *Cinema Canada* 167 (Oct. 1989): 12–16.

Barac, Victor. 'Dislocation and Postmodern Prairie Film.' In *Dislocations*. Ed. Gilles Hébert. Winnipeg: Winnipeg Film Group, 1995. 25–36.

Beard, William. 'The Visceral Mind: The Major Films of David Cronenberg.' In *The Shape of Rage*. Ed. Piers Handling. Toronto: General, 1983. 1–79.

– *The Artist As Monster: The Cinema of David Cronenberg*. Toronto: University of Toronto Press, 2001.

– 'Thirty-Two Paragraphs about David Cronenberg.' In *North of Everything: English-Canadian Cinema since 1980*. Ed. William Beard and Jerry White. Edmonton: University of Alberta Press, 2002. 144–59.

Beard, William, and Piers Handling. 'The Interview.' In *The Shape of Rage: The Films of David Cronenberg*. Ed. Piers Handling. Toronto: General, 1983. 158–98.

Beard, William, and Jerry White, eds. *North of Everything: English-Canadian Cinema since 1980*. Edmonton: University of Alberta Press, 2002.

Bergan, Ronald. 'Movies Find a Voice.' In *Cinema Year by Year: 1894–2000*. Ed. Robyn Karney. London: Dorling Kindersley, 2000. 213.

Bergman, Brian. 'Maddin Madness.' *Maclean's*, 23 Dec. 2002, pp. 50–1.

Berton, Pierre. *Hollywood's Canada: The Americanization of Our National Image*. Toronto: McClelland and Stewart, 1975.

Beveridge, James. *John Grierson: Film Master*. New York: Macmillan, 1978.

Blaisdell, George. 'Review of Evangeline.' In *Documents in Canadian Film*. Ed. Douglas Fetherling. Peterborough, ON: Broadview Press, 1988. 10–12.

Bonneville, Léo, ed. *Le Cinéma québécois: Par ceux qui le font*. Montreal: Éditions Paulines, 1979.

Bor, Aaron. 'An Interview with Léa Pool.' *Quebec Studies* 9 (Fall 1989/Winter 1990): 63–8.

Boulais, Stéphane-Albert. 'Le Cinéma vécu de l'intérieur: Mon expérience avec Pierre Perrault.' In *Dialogue: Canadian and Quebec Cinema*. Ed. Pierre Véronneau, Michael Dorland, and Seth Feldman. Montreal: Mediatexte, 1987. 161–72.

Bouw, Brenda. 'Baron of Blood Meets Beckett.' *Globe and Mail*, 29 Sept. 2001, p. R8.

Boyar, Jay. 'Blair Witch Project Is Making Hollywood Change.' *Calgary Herald*, 21 Oct. 1999, p. E2.

Bruce, Jean. 'Querying/Queering the Nation.' In *Gendering the Nation: Canadian Women's Cinema*. Ed. Kay Armatage et al. Toronto: University of Toronto Press, 1999. 274–90.

- 'Queer Cinema at the NFB: The "Strange Case" of *Forbidden Love*.' In *Candid Eyes: Essays on Canadian Documentaries*. Ed. Jim Leach and Jeannette Sloniowski. Toronto: University of Toronto Press, 2003. 164–80.

Brunton, Colin. 'Roadkill.' *Cinema Canada* 165 (July/August 1989): 5.

Buchanan, Donald W. 'The Projection of Canada.' In *The National Film Board of Canada: The War Years*. Ed. Peter Morris. Ottawa: Canadian Film Institute, 1965. 13–17.

Burns, Gary. CBC *This Morning* radio interview, 20 Nov. 2000. www. infoculture.cbc.ca.

Cagle, Robert L. 'A Minority on Someone Else's Continent: Identity, Difference, and the Media in the Films of Patricia Rozema.' In *Gendering the Nation: Canadian Women's Cinema*. Ed. Kay Armatage et al. Toronto: University of Toronto Press, 1999. 183–96.

Calleja, Dawn. 'Manna from Heaven.' *Canadian Business*, 16 Sept. 2002, pp. 40–5.

Carrière, Louise. 'Historique des collaborateurs cinématographiques.' In *Les Relations cinématographiques France-Québec*. Ed. Louise Carrière. Montreal: Cinémathèque québécoise, 1994.

- ed. *Les Femmes et cinéma québécois*. Montreal: Boréal Express, 1983.

Clandfield, David. 'From the Picturesque to the Familiar: Films of the French Unit at the NFB (1958–1964).' In *Take Two*. Ed. Seth Feldman. Toronto: Irwin, 1984. 112–24.

- 'Ritual and Recital: The Perrault Project.' In *Take Two*. Ed. Seth Feldman. Toronto: Irwin, 1984. 136–48.

- *Canadian Film*. Toronto: Oxford University Press, 1987.

- 'Linking Community Renewal to National Identity: The Filmmakers' Role in *Pour la suite du monde*.' In *Candid Eyes: Essays on Canadian Documentaries*. Ed. Jim Leach and Jeannette Sloniowski. Toronto: University of Toronto Press, 2003. 71–86.

Cobb, David. 'Day of the Gopher.' *Maclean's*, 1 Nov. 1976, pp. 46–8.

Cohn, Norman. 'The Art of Community-Based Filmmaking.' *Brick* 70 (Winter 2002): 21–3.

Comte, Michel. 'Tax Breaks Lure Cartoon Company to Toronto.' *Business in Vancouver*, 22–8 Jan. 2002), p. 9.

Conlogue, Ray. 'For Michel Brault, the Era Is Over.' *Globe and Mail*, 19 Nov. 1990, p. R3.

- 'NFB: Not Dead Yet.' *Globe and Mail*, 29 Oct. 1999, pp. C1; C6.

- 'Tilting at the U.S. Film Windmill.' *Globe and Mail*, 21 Sept. 2001, p. R3.

- 'In the Head of Andre Turpin.' *Globe and Mail*, 15 Feb. 2002.

- 'Egoyan Film Sparks Turkish Backlash.' *Globe and Mail*, 18 April 2002, p. R2.

- 'Inside Cronenberg's Web.' *Globe and Mail*, 27 Feb. 2003, pp. R1, R7.

– 'Melodrama at Its Exotic Best.' *Globe and Mail*, 4 April 2003, p. R3.
– 'The Bumpy Road to Love.' *Globe and Mail*, 30 Aug. 2003, p. R1.
Cook, Pam, and Mieke Bernink, eds. *The Cinema Book*. 2nd ed. London: British
   Film Institute, 1999.
Cooper, Carol. 'He Filmed the Difficult, Riled the Powerful.' *Globe and Mail*,
   11 Jan. 2003, p. F8.
Corder, Sharon, and Jack Blum. 'Waydowntown: The Subversive Charm of
   Gary Burns.' *Take One* 9.30 (Winter 2001): 8–13.
Cornellier, Bruno. 'Hollywood et le cinéma québécois (I) and (II).' *Cadrage:
   Revue de Cinéma*. www.cadrage.net.
Crawley, F.R. 'A Slick Way to Skin the Public.' *Maclean's*, 13 April 1981, p. 10.
– 'Have Independent Films a Look-In?' *Documents in Canadian Film*. Ed.
   Douglas Fetherling. Peterborough, ON: Broadview Press, 1988. 82–7.
Creed, Barbara. *The Monstrous Feminine: Film, Feminism, Psychoanalysis*. Lon-
   don: Routledge, 1993.
Crofts, Stephen. 'Authorship and Hollywood.' In *The Oxford Guide to Film
   Studies*. Ed. John Hill and Pamela Church Gibson. London: Oxford Univer-
   sity Press, 1998. 310–26.
– 'Concepts of National Cinema.' In *The Oxford Guide to Film Studies*. Ed. John
   Hill and Pamela Church Gibson. London: Oxford University Press, 1998.
   385–94.
Cronenberg, David. *Crash*. London: Faber and Faber, 1996.
Culture Industries Branch, Canadian Heritage. *A Guide to Federal Programs for
   the Film and Video Sector*. Ottawa, September 1998.
Curtis, David. *Experimental Cinema: A Fifty Year Evolution*. London: Studio
   Vista, 1971.
Dawn, Allan. 'Canada Has a Movie Future but Certain Restrictions Must Be
   Removed.' In *Documents in Canadian Film*. Ed. Douglas Fetherling.
   Peterborough, ON: Broadview Press, 1988. 23–32.
Delaney, Marshall. 'It Makes You See the Value of Corruption.' *Saturday Night*,
   January 1974, pp. 38–9.
– 'Wielandism: A Personal Style in Bloom.' In *Canadian Film Reader*. Ed. Seth
   Feldman and Joyce Nelson. Toronto: Peter Martin Associates, 1977. 279–82.
– 'Sex Is Not a Spectator Sport.' *Saturday Night*, 19 Dec. 1978, pp. 59–60.
– 'Artists in the Shadows: Some Notable Canadian Movies.' In *Take Two*. Ed.
   Seth Feldman. Toronto: Irwin, 1984. 2–17.
Desbarats, Carole. 'Conquering What They Tell Us Is "Natural."' In *Atom
   Egoyan*, by Carole Desbarats et al. Paris: Éditions Dis Voir, 1993. 9–32.
Desbarats, Carole, et al. *Atom Egoyan*. Paris: Éditions Dis Voir, 1993.
Dickey, Sara. *Cinema and the Urban Poor in South India*. London: Cambridge
   University Press, 1993.

Dickinson, Peter. 'Critically Queenie: The Lessons of *Fortune and Men's Eyes*.' *Canadian Journal of Film Studies* 11.2 (Fall 2002): 19–42.

Dixon, Wheeler Winston. *Disaster and Memory: Celebrity Culture and the Crisis of Hollywood Cinema*. New York: Columbia University Press, 1999.

– *The Second Century of Cinema: The Past and Future of the Moving Image*. Albany: SUNY Press, 2000.

Donohoe, Joseph, Jr, ed. *Essays on Quebec Cinema*. Lansing: Michigan State University, 1991.

Dorland, Michael. 'Beyond Shame and Glory: Preface to a Critical Dialogue in Canadian/Quebec Cinemas.' In *Dialogue: Canadian and Quebec Cinema*. Ed. Pierre Véronneau, Michael Dorland, and Seth Feldman. Montreal: Mediatexte, 1987. 311–28.

– 'Matthew Arnold in Canada: The Lonely Discourse of J. Peter Harcourt.' In *Responses: In Honour of Peter Harcourt*. Ed. Blaine Allan et al. Kingston, ON: Responsibility Press, 1992. 63–76.

– *So Close to the State/s: The Emergence of a Canadian Feature Film Policy*. Toronto: University of Toronto Press, 1998.

– ed. *The Cultural Industries in Canada: Problems, Policies and Prospects*. Toronto: James Lorimer & Co., 1996.

Doty, Alexander. 'Queer Theory.' In *The Oxford Guide to Film Studies*. Ed. John Hill and Pamela Church Gibson. London: Oxford University Press, 1998. 148–52.

During, Simon, ed. *The Cultural Studies Reader*. London: Routledge, 1993.

Dzeguze, Kaspar. 'Go and See "Goin' Down the Road."' *Maclean's*, September 1970, p. 73.

Ebert, Roger. 'Highway 61.' *Chicago Sun-Times*, 29 June 1992.

– 'Leolo.' *Chicago Sun-Times*, 9 April 1993.

– 'Kissed.' *Chicago Sun-Times*, 4 March 1997.

– 'Truth/Not Truth.' *Calgary Herald*, 6 Dec. 2002, p. D1.

Edwards, Ian. 'Suburbanators-Distrib Strategy.' *Playback*, 29 July 1996, p. 7.

– 'Production in Alberta: Fade to Gray.' *Playback*, 24 Feb. 1997, p. 20.

Egoyan, Atom. *Exotica*. Toronto: Coach House Press, 1995.

– 'Foreword.' In *Inside the Pleasure Dome: Fringe Film in Canada*. 2nd ed. Ed. Mike Hoolboom. Toronto: Coach House Books, 2001. 1.

Elder, R. Bruce. 'Claude Jutra's "Mon Oncle Antoine."' In *Canadian Film Reader*. Ed. Seth Feldman and Joyce Nelson. Toronto. Peter Martin Associates, 1977. 194–9.

– 'Michael Snow's *Wavelength*.' In *Canadian Film Reader*. Ed. Seth Feldman and Joyce Nelson. Toronto. Peter Martin Associates, 1977. 308–22.

– 'Image: Representation and Object – the Photographic Image in Canada's

Avant-Garde Film.' In *Take Two*. Ed. Seth Feldman. Toronto: Irwin, 1984.
246–63.
– 'The Cinema We Need.' In *Documents in Canadian Film*. Ed. Douglas
Fetherling. Peterborough, ON: Broadview Press, 1988. 260–71.
– 'A Vindication.' In *Documents in Canadian Film*. Ed. Douglas Fetherling.
Peterborough, ON: Broadview Press, 1988. 301–15.
– *Image and Identity: Reflections on Canadian Film and Culture*. Waterloo, ON:
Wilfrid Laurier University Press, 1989.
– 'Michael Snow's Presence.' In *Presence and Absence: The Films of Michael
Snow 1956–1991*. Ed. Jim Shedden. Toronto: Art Gallery of Ontario, 1995.
94–139.
Elder, Kathryn. 'Foreword.' In *The Films of Joyce Wieland*. Ed. Kathryn Elder.
Toronto: Toronto International Film Festival Group, 1999. 1–6.
– ed. *The Films of Joyce Wieland*. Toronto: Toronto International Film Festival
Group, 1999.
Elley, Derek. 'Rhythm n' Truths: Norman McLaren.' In *Canadian Film Reader*.
Ed. Seth Feldman and Joyce Nelson. Toronto: Peter Martin Associates, 1977.
94–102.
Ellis, Jack. 'Grierson's First Years at the NFB.' In *Canadian Film Reader*. Ed. Seth
Feldman and Joyce Nelson. Toronto: Peter Martin Associates, 1977. 34–47.
Evanchuk, P.M. 'The Outspoken Hector Ross.' *Motion*, Sept./Oct. 1973, p. 11.
Evans, Gary. *In the National Interest: A Chronicle of the National Film Board of
Canada from 1949 to 1989*. Toronto: University of Toronto Press, 1991.
Everett-Green, Robert. 'A Filmmaker Worth Remembering.' *Globe and Mail*,
19 June 2002, p. A15.
Feldman, Seth. 'The Silent Subject in English Canadian Film.' In *Take Two*. Ed.
Seth Feldman. Toronto: Irwin, 1984. 48–57.
– 'What Was Cinema.' *Canadian Journal of Film Studies* 5.1 (Spring 1996): 1–22.
– 'Paradise and Its Discontents.' In *Allan King: Filmmaker*, Ed. Seth Feldman.
Toronto: Toronto International Film Festival, 2002. 1–46.
– ed. *Take Two*. Toronto: Irwin, 1984.
– ed. *Allan King: Filmmaker*. Toronto: Toronto International Film Festival, 2002.
Feldman, Seth, and Joyce Nelson, eds. *Canadian Film Reader*. Toronto: Peter
Martin Associates, 1977.
Fetherling, Douglas. 'Outrageous.' *Canadian Forum*, December–January
1977–8, p. 65.
– ed. *Documents in Canadian Film*. Peterborough, ON: Broadview Press, 1988.
Forbes, Jill. 'The French Nouvelle Vague.' In *The Oxford Guide of Film Studies*.
Ed. John Hill and Pamela Church Gibson. London: Oxford University Press,
1998. 461–5.

Forrester, James A. *Budge: F.R. Crawley and Crawley Films, 1939–1982.* Lakefield, ON: Information Research Services, 1988.

Fothergill, Robert. 'A Place like Home.' In *Canadian Film Reader.* Ed. Seth Feldman and Joyce Nelson. Toronto: Peter Martin Associates, 1977. 347–63.

– 'Coward, Bully or Clown: The Dream-Life of a Younger Brother.' In *Canadian Film Reader.* Ed. Seth Feldman and Joyce Nelson. Toronto: Peter Martin Associates, 1977. 234–49.

Frampton, Hollis, and Joyce Wieland. 'I Don't Even Know about the Second Stanza.' In *The Films of Joyce Wieland.* Ed. Kathryn Elder. Toronto: Toronto International Film Festival Group, 1999. 161–82.

Fraser, Fil. 'Monkey See, Monkey Do, Monkey Pay.' *Cinema Canada* 71 (Jan./Feb. 1981): 9–10.

Frederick, Jaime. 'Undead Can Dance.' *See* [Edmonton], 21–7 Feb. 2002, p. 13.

Freedman, Adele. 'Goddess, Matriarch, Victim.' *Globe and Mail,* 27 Oct. 2001, p. D12.

Freeman, Alan, 'eXistenZ Draws Crowds in Berlin.' *Globe and Mail,* 17 Feb. 1999, p. D1.

Frye, Northrop. *The Bush Garden.* Toronto: House of Anansi, 1971.

Fulford, Robert. *Marshall Delaney at the Movies: The Contemporary World As Seen on Film.* Toronto: Peter Martin Associates, 1974.

– 'The Apprenticeship of Phillip Borsos.' *Saturday Night,* December 1984, pp. 30–43.

Galvez, Raúl. 'In Conversation: Zacharias Kunuk.' *Montage,* Spring 2002, pp. 10–13.

Garneau, Michèle, and Pierre Véronneau. 'Un cinéma <de genre> révélateur d'une inquiétante américanité québécoise.' In *L'Aventure du cinéma québécois en France.* Ed. Michel Larouche. Montreal: XYZ, 1996. 181–207.

Gasher, Mike. *Hollywood North: The Feature Film Industry in British Columbia.* Vancouver: UBC Press, 2002.

Gatenby, Greg. *The Wild Is Always There: Canada through the Eyes of Foreign Writers.* Toronto: Vintage Books, 1994.

Gaulin, Suzanne. 'Pool's Splash.' *Cinema Canada* 111 (Oct. 1984): 7–9.

Gessell, Paul. 'Snow Reaches the Pinnacle.' *Ottawa Citizen,* 24 March 2000, p. E4.

Gill, Brendan, 'Current Cinema.' *New Yorker,* 24 April 1965, pp. 163–5.

Gilliat, Penelope. 'Duddy-O.' *New Yorker,* 22 July 1974, pp. 65–7.

Gittings, Christopher E. *Canadian National Cinema: Ideology, Difference and Representation.* London: Routledge, 2002.

Glassman, Marc. 'Rockin' on the Road: The Films of Bruce McDonald.' *Take One* 4.8 (Summer 1995): 14–19.

– 'Last Night: In the Year of the Don.' *Take One* 7.21 (Fall 1998): 14–15.

Globerman, Steven, and Aidan Vining. *Foreign Ownership and Canada's Feature Film Distribution Section: An Economic Analysis*. Vancouver: Fraser Institute, 1987.

Godard, Peter. 'Bruce McDonald at the Crossroads with *Picture Claire*.' *Take One* 10.35 (Dec.–Jan. 2001–2): 13–15.

Godwin, George. 'Reclaiming the Subject: A Feminist Reading of "I've Heard the Mermaids Singing."' *Cinema Canada* 152 (May 1988): 23–4.

Goldfarb, Rebecca. *The Conflict of Two Realities and Two Views: A Comparative Assessment of the Canadian and American Film Industries*. Ref. Doc. no. 5. Ottawa: D-FAIT, 1998.

Gomery, Douglas. 'The Hollywood Studio System.' In *Oxford History of World Cinema*. Ed. Geoffrey Nowell-Smith. Oxford: Oxford University Press, 1996. 43–52.

– 'Hollywood As Industry.' In *The Oxford Guide to Film Studies*. Ed. John Hill and Pamela Church Gibson. London: Oxford University Press, 1998. 245–54.

Goslawski, Barbara. 'Reel Experimental.' *Globe and Mail*, 29 Jan. 2001, p. R3.

Green, Mary Jean. 'Léa Pool's *La Femme de l'Hôtel* and Women's Film in Québec.' *Quebec Studies* 9 (Fall/Winter 1989/90): 49–62.

Grescoe, Taras. *Sacré Blues: An Unsentimental Journey through Quebec*. Toronto: Macfarlane Walter & Ross, 2000.

Groen, Rick. 'The Neverending Story.' *Globe and Mail*, 31 Dec. 1999, p. R1.

– 'Emotional Vacancy at a Flea-Bag Hotel.' *Globe and Mail*, 5 April 2001, p. R3.

– 'The Sublime North.' *Globe and Mail*, 12 April 2002, p. R1.

Grosswiler, Paul. *Method Is the Message: Rethinking McLuhan through Critical Theory*. Montreal: Black Rose Books, 1998.

Hamilton, Mark. 'Atom Egoyan and the Art of Denial.' *FFWD* [Calgary], 5–11 Dec. 2002, p. 50.

Hampson, Sarah. 'Robert Lantos: The Sequel.' *Globe and Mail*, 20 July 2000, pp. R1–R2.

Handling, Piers. 'Two or Three Things "Bill Fruet,"' *Cinema Canada* 40 (Sept. 1977): 43–6.

– 'The National Film Board of Canada, 1939–1959.' In *Self-Portraits: Essays on the Canadian and Quebec Cinemas*. Ed. Pierre Véronneau and Piers Handling. Ottawa: Canadian Film Institute, 1980. 42–53.

– 'A Canadian Cronenberg.' In *Take Two*. Ed. Seth Feldman. Toronto: Irwin, 1984. 80–91.

– 'The Cinema We Need?' In *Documents in Canadian Film*. Ed. Douglas Fetherling. Peterborough, ON: Broadview Press, 1988. 284–93.

– ed. *The Shape of Rage: The Films of David Cronenberg*. Toronto: General, 1983.

Harcourt, Peter. *Movies and Mythologies: Towards a National Cinema*. Toronto: CBC Publications, 1977.

– 'Years of Hope.' In *Canadian Film Reader*. Ed. Seth Feldman and Joyce Nelson. Toronto: Peter Martin Associates, 1977. 139–43.

– 'The Beginning of a Beginning.' In *Self-Portraits: Essays on the Canadian and Quebec Cinemas*. Ed. Pierre Véronneau and Piers Handling. Ottawa: Canadian Film Institute, 1980. 64–76.

– 'Allan King: Filmmaker.' In *Take Two*. Ed. Seth Feldman. Toronto: Irwin, 1984. 69–79.

– 'The Old and the New.' In *Take Two*. Ed. Seth Feldman. Toronto: Irwin, 1984. 169–81.

– 'Pierre Perrault and *Le cinéma vécu*.' In *Take Two*. Ed. Seth Feldman. Toronto: Irwin, 1984. 125–35.

– 'Imaginary Images: An Examination of Atom Egoyan's Films.' *Film Quarterly* 48.3 (Spring 1995): 2–14.

– 'Faces Changing Colour Changing Canon.' *CineAction* 45 (Feb. 1998): 2–9.

– *Jean Pierre Lefebvre: Vidéaste*. Monograph. Toronto: International Film Festival Group, 2001.

Hardy, Forsyth. *John Grierson: A Documentary Biography*. London: Faber and Faber, 1979.

– ed. *Grierson on Documentary*. London: Faber and Faber, 1966.

Harkness, John. 'Notes on a Tax-Sheltered Cinema.' *Cinema Canada* 87 (Aug. 1982): 22–6.

Harrison, Marion. '*Mermaids* Singing Off Key?' *CineAction* 16 (May 1989): 25–30.

Hartt, Laurinda. 'Interview with Donald Pleasance.' *Cinema Canada* 8 (June/July 1973): 58–60.

Hayes, Matthew. 'Bye Bye Blues.' *Cinema Canada* 157 (Nov. 1988): 8–9.

– 'Art in the Danger Zone.' *Globe and Mail*, 11 Oct. 2001, p. R1.

– 'The Critics May Groan, but Les Boys Are Back.' *Globe and Mail*, 23 Oct. 2001, p. R5.

Hébert, Gilles. 'Dislocations.' In *Dislocations*. Ed. Gilles Hébert. Winnipeg: Winnipeg Film Group, 1995.

– ed. *Dislocations*. Winnipeg: Winnipeg Film Group. 1995.

Hill, John, and Pamela Church Gibson, eds. *The Oxford Guide to Film Studies*. London: Oxford University Press, 1998.

Hill, Reg. 'Waydowntown a Triumph for Gary Burns.' www.motherstars mag.com/garyburns.

Hinson, Hal. 'Highway 61.' *Washington Post*, 9 June 1992.

Hofsess, John. 'Fortune and Men's Eyes – Report from the Set in a Quebec City Prison.' *Maclean's*, December 1970, pp. 81–2.

– 'Films.' *Maclean's*, November 1972, p. 101.
– *Inner Views: Ten Canadian Filmmakers*. Toronto: McGraw-Hill Ryerson, 1975.
– 'In Praise of Older Women.' *Cinema Canada* 49–50 (Sept./Oct. 1978): 68.
Hofsess, John, and Robert Fothergill, 'The Rich Get Richler: A Dialogue on Duddy Kravitz.' *Canadian Forum*, October 1974, pp. 32–3.
Honey, Kim. 'Welcome to Bollywood North.' *Globe and Mail*, 17 Nov. 2001, p. R9.
Hoolboom, Mike. 'Machines of Cinema: An Interview with Michael Snow.' In *Inside the Pleasure Dome: Fringe Film in Canada*. 2nd ed. Ed. Mike Hoolboom. Toronto: Coach House Books, 2001. 6–23.
– ed. *Inside the Pleasure Dome: Fringe Film in Canada*. 2nd ed. Toronto: Coach House Books, 2001.
Hornaday, Ann. 'Quirky "Maelstrom" Ultimately Flounders.' *Washington Post*, 22 March 2002, p. C05.
Horsman, Mathew, and Andrew Marshall. *After the Nation-State: Citizens, Tribalism and the New World Disorder*. New York: Harper Collins, 1994.
Houle, Michel. 'Some Ideological and Thematic Aspects of the Quebec Cinema.' In *Self-Portraits: Essays on the Canadian and Quebec Cinemas*. Ed. Pierre Véronneau and Piers Handling. Ottawa: Canadian Film Institute, 1988. 159–182.
Humm, Maggie. *Feminism and Film*. Bloomington: Edinburgh and Indiana University Presses, 1997.
Hunter, Jennifer. 'Northern Exposure' *Maclean's*, 11 Oct. 1999, pp. 68–71.
Iyer, Pico. 'In the Last Refuge: On the Promise of the New Canadian Fiction.' *Harper's*, June 2002.
Jacobowitz, Florence, and Richard Lippe. 'Dead Ringers: The Joke's on Us.' *CineAction*, Spring 1989, pp. 64–8.
Jaehne, Karen. 'I've Heard the Mermaids Singing: An Interview with Patricia Rozema.' *Cineaste* 16.3 (1988): 23.
James, Rodney. *Film As National Art: The NFB of Canada and the Film Board Idea*. New York: Arno Press, 1977.
Jean, Marcel. *Le Cinéma québécois*. Montreal: Boreal, 1991.
John Grierson and the NFB. Toronto: ECW Press, 1984.
Johnson, Brian D. 'Rock 'n' Roll Renegades.' *Maclean's*, 26 Feb. 1990, pp. 40–2.
– 'Rebel Masterpiece.' *Maclean's*, 25 May 1992, pp. 51–2.
– 'Raw Punk Cooked Pop.' *Maclean's*, 14 Oct. 1996, pp. 89–90.
– 'Death and the Maiden.' *Maclean's*, 14 April 1997, pp. 60–1.
– 'French Connection: A Canadian Filmmaker Steps Out at the World's Splashiest Festival.' *Maclean's*, 25 May 1998, pp. 60–2.
– 'A Festival Zeroes In on Quebec.' *Maclean's*, 7 Sept. 1998, pp. 52–3.

- 'Virtual Director.' *Maclean's*, 26 April 1999, pp. 62–3.
- 'Atom's Journey.' *Maclean's*, 13 Sept. 1999, pp. 54–8.
- 'Austen Powers.' *Maclean's*, 22 Nov. 1999, pp. 106–8.
- 'Clarifying Claire.' *Maclean's*, 4 March 2002, pp. 54–5.
- 'An Arctic Masterpiece.' *Maclean's*, 15 April 2002, p. 53.
- 'Riviera Rendezvous.' *Maclean's*, 3 June 2002, pp. 46–50.
- 'A Maze of Denial.' *Maclean's*, 18 Nov. 2002, pp. 116–18.
- 'We Like to Watch.' *Maclean's*, 25 Nov. 2002, pp. 28–30.
- 'Down by the Bays.' *Maclean's*, 3 Feb. 2003, pp. 46–7.
- 'An Exquisite Madness.' *Maclean's*, 3 March 2003, pp. 42–3.

Kael, Pauline. 'The Current Cinema.' *New Yorker*, 8 Aug. 1983, pp. 84–9.

Kane, Kathryn. *Visions of War: Hollywood Combat Films of World War II*. Ann Arbor, MI: UMI Research Press, 1982.

Kari, Shannon. 'Taxpayers Help Film Hit Box Office Button.' *Calgary Herald*, 16 March 2002, p. A1.

Karney, Robyn, ed. *Cinema Year by Year: 1894–2000*. London: Dorling Kindersley, 2000.

Kelly, Richard. 'Last Night.' *Sight and Sound* 9.7 (July 1999): 44–5.

King, Allan. 'Pourquoi? Round Two.' *Cinema Canada* 159 (Jan. 1989): 5.

Knelman, Martin. 'A Night at the Pictures in Arcola.' *Saturday Night*, September 1977, pp. 26–32.

- *This Is Where We Came In: The Career and Character of Canadian Film*. Toronto: McClelland and Stewart, 1977.
- *Home Movies: Tales from the Canadian Film World*. Toronto: Key Porter, 1987.
- 'Claude Jutra in Exile.' In *Documents in Canadian Film*. Ed. Douglas Fetherling. Peterborough, ON: Broadview Press, 1988. 215–29.

Koller, George Csaba.'Bill Fruet's *Wedding in White*.' *Cinema Canada* 3 (July–Aug. 1972): 42–7.

Kunuk, Zacharias. 'I First Heard the Story of Atanarjuat from My Mother.' *Brick* 70 (Winter 2002): 17–20.

Kupecek, Linda. 'Loyalties: Anne Wheeler's Film Family.' *Cinema Canada* 123 (Oct. 1985): 6–7.

Lacasse, Germain. *Histoires de scopes: Le Cinéma muet au Québec*. Montreal: Cinémathèque québécoise, 1988.

Lacey, Liam. 'Permafrost on the Riviera.' *Globe and Mail*, 18 May 2001, p. A10.
- 'No Clean Sweep.' *Globe and Mail*, 8 March 2002, p. R1.
- 'Against All Odds.' *Globe and Mail*, 12 April 2002, p. R4.
- 'You Can Stretch Tape Only So Far.' *Globe and Mail*, 19 April 2002, p. R1.
- 'A Socko Québécois Invasion.' *Globe and Mail*, 22 May 2003, p. R1.

Lant, Antonia. 'Britain at the End of Empire.' In *Oxford History of World Cinema*. Ed. Geoffrey Nowell-Smith. London: Oxford University Press, 1996. 361–73.

Larouche, Michel. 'Pierre Perrault et la "parlure" du Québec.' In *L'Aventure du cinéma québécois en France*. Ed. Michel Larouche. Montreal: XYZ, 1996. 145–58.

– ed. *L'Aventure du cinéma québécois en France*. Montreal: XYZ, 1996.

Lauder, Scott. 'A Studio with a View: The NFB's Studio D Is Lifting Women's Filmmaking out of the Basement.' *Canadian Forum*, August-September 1986, pp. 12–15.

Leach, James. 'Second Images: Reflections on the Canadian Cinema(s) in the Seventies.' In *Take Two*. Ed. Seth Feldman. Toronto: Irwin, 1984. 100–10.

– 'The Sins of Gilles Carle.' In *Take Two*. Ed. Seth Feldman. Toronto: Irwin, 1984. 160–8.

– 'The Body Snatchers: Genre and Canadian Cinema.' *Cinema Canada* 141 (May 1987): 18–21.

– *Claude Jutra: Filmmaker*. Kingston and Montreal: McGill-Queen's University Press, 1999.

– 'The Reel Nation: Image and Reality in Contemporary Canadian Cinema.' *Canadian Journal of Film Studies* 11.2 (Fall 2002): 2–188.

Leach, Jim, and Jeannette Sloniowski, eds. *Candid Eyes: Essays on Canadian Documentaries*. Toronto: University of Toronto Press, 2003.

Lefebvre, Jean Pierre. 'Le Concept de cinéma national.' In *Dialogue*: *Canadian and Quebec Cinema*. Ed. Pierre Véronneau, Michael Dorland, and Seth Feldman. Montreal: Mediatexte, 1987. 83–96.

Lerner, Loren R. *Canadian Film and Video: A Bibliography and Guide to the Literature*. 2 vols. Toronto: University of Toronto Press, 1997.

Lever, Yves. *Cinéma et société québécoise*. Montreal: Éditions du Jour, 1972.

– *Histoire générale du cinéma au Québec*. 2nd ed. Montreal: Boréal, 1995.

Levin, Martin. 'A Post-National CanLit.' *Globe and Mail*, 8 June 2002, p. D16.

Levitin, Jacqueline. 'Contrechamp sur les démarches de quelques réalisatrices.' In *Les Femmes et cinéma québécois*. Ed. Louise Carrière. Montreal: Boréal, 1983. 225–45.

Lind, Jane. *Joyce Wieland: Artist on Fire*. Toronto: Lorimer, 2001.

Longfellow, Brenda. 'Gender, Landscape, and Colonial Allegories in *The Far Shore*, *Loyalties*, and *Mouvements du désir*.' In *Gendering the Nation: Canadian Women's Cinema*. Ed. Kay Armatage et al. Toronto: University of Toronto Press, 1999. 165–82.

Longfellow, Brenda, and Thomas Waugh. 'Introduction.' *Canadian Journal of Film Studies* 10.2 (Fall 2001): 2–5.

Lord, Susan. 'States of Emergency in the Films of Anne Wheeler.' In *North of Everything: English-Canadian Cinema since 1980*. Ed. William Beard and Jerry White. Edmonton: University of Alberta Press, 2002. 312–27.

Lowe, Patrick. 'The Winnipeg Film Group Aesthetic.' In *Dislocations*. Ed. Gilles Hébert. Winnipeg: Winnipeg Film Group, 1995. 63–73.

MacAfee, Michelle. 'Canucks Threatened by U.S. Culture, Poll Finds.' *Calgary Herald*, 1 July 2002, p. A3.

MacDonald, Gayle. 'Kissed Again.' *Globe and Mail*, 12 Sept. 2000, p. R1.

– 'Money Isn't Everything.' *Globe and Mail*, 24 Nov. 2000, pp. R1, R4.

– 'Canada's Full Monty.' *Globe and Mail*, 23 Feb. 2002, p. R3.

– 'Red Green Has It All Wrapped Up.' *Globe and Mail*, 3 April 2002, p. R1.

MacInnis, Craig. 'Kitchen Party: Gary Burns Returns to Suburbia.' *Take One* 6.19 (Spring 1998): 12–16.

MacKenzie, Scott. 'National Identity, Canadian Cinema, and Multiculturalism.' *Canadian Aesthetics Journal* 4 (Summer 1999). http://www.uqtr.uquebec.ca/AE/vol_4/index.htm

Maddin, Guy. *Cowards Bend the Knee*. Toronto: The Power Plant, 2003.

Madger, Ted. *Canada's Hollywood: The Canadian State and Feature Film*. Toronto: University of Toronto Press, 1993.

– 'Film and Video Production: Problems, Policies and Prospects.' In *The Cultural Industries in Canada*. Ed. Michael Dorland. Toronto: Lorimer, 1996. 145–77.

Marcel, Jean. 'Jean-Claude Lauzon.' *24 images* 90 (1998).

Marcorelles, Louis. 'Snow Storms Italy.' *Cinema Canada* 6 (Feb./March 1973): 64.

Margetts, Jayne. 'Deepa's Doctrine.' www.thei.aust.com/film97/celiindeepah.html.

Marie, Michel. 'Singularité de l'oeuvre de Perrault.' In *Dialogue: Canadian and Quebec Cinema*. Ed. Pierre Véronneau, Michael Dorland, and Seth Feldman. Montreal: Mediatexte, 1987. 153–60.

Marotte, Bertrand. 'Cinar Settlement $2 Million.' *Globe and Mail*, 16 March 2002, pp. B1–B2.

Marshall, Bill. *Quebec National Cinema*. Kingston and Montreal: McGill-Queen's University Press, 2001.

Mazurkewich, Karen. *Cartoon Capers: The History of Canadian Animators*. Toronto: McArthur & Co., 1990.

McDonald, Bruce. 'Dear Norman, What Is to Be Done?' *Cinema Canada* 122 (Sept. 1985): 10–12.

McGuinness, Richard. 'Gay, Yes but Proud It's Not.' *Village Voice* [New York], 1 July 1972.

McIntosh, David. 'Vanishing Point: Proliferations, Purifications and the Con-
    vergence of Canadian and Mexican National Cinemas.' *Canadian Journal of
    Film Studies* 10.2 (Fall 2001): 59–79.
McKay, Marjorie. *History of the National Film Board of Canada*. Ottawa: National
    Film Board, 1964.
McLaren, Norman. 'Animated Film.' In *The National Film Board of Canada:
    The War Years*. Ed. Peter Morris. Ottawa: Canadian Film Institute, 1965.
    10–12.
McLarty, James. '1,000,000 – Let's Hear It for Duddy.' *Motion* 3.3 (July/Aug.
    1974): 30–3.
McLarty, Lianne M. 'The Experimental Films of Joyce Wieland.' *Ciné Tracts* 17
    (Summer/Fall 1982): 51–9.
Medjuck, Joe. 'The Life and Times of Michael Snow.' In *Canadian Film Reader*.
    Ed. Seth Feldman and Joyce Nelson. Toronto: Peter Martin Associates, 1977.
    290–307.
Melnyk, George. *The Literary History of Alberta*, Volume One: *From Writing-on-
    Stone to World War Two*. Edmonton: University of Alberta Press, 1998. 62–72.
– ed. *Canada and the New American Empire: War and Anti-War*. Calgary: Univer-
    sity of Calgary Press, 2003.
Menard, Louis. 'Paris, Texas.' *New Yorker*, 17 and 24 February 2003, pp. 169–77.
Michener, Wendy. 'Look Who's Looking at the Movies.' In *Documents in
    Canadian Film*. Ed. Douglas Fetherling. Peterborough, ON: Broadview Press,
    1988. 102–11.
Miller, Toby. 'Hollywood and the World.' In *The Oxford Guide to Film Studies*.
    Ed. John Hill and Pamela Church Gibson. London: Oxford University Press,
    1998. 372–82.
Milroy, Sarah. 'Northern Light.' *Globe and Mail*, 28 Dec. 2002.
– 'Peeping Guy.' *Globe and Mail*, 29 March 2003, p. R10.
Monk, Katherine. 'Let's Talk about (Kinky) Sex.' *Globe and Mail*, 5 Sept. 2001,
    p. R1.
– *Weird Sex and Snowshoes and Other Canadian Film Phenomena*. Vancouver:
    Raincoast Books, 2001.
Morris, Peter. *Embattled Shadows: A History of Canadian Cinema 1895–1939*.
    Montreal and Kingston: McGill-Queen's University Press, 1978.
– 'After Grierson: The National Film Board 1945–1953.' In *Take Two*. Ed. Seth
    Feldman. Toronto: Irwin, 1984. 182–94.
– 'Backwards to the Future: John Grierson's Film Policy for Canada.' In
    Flashback: People and Institutions in Canadian Film History. Ed. Eugene Walz.
    Montreal: Mediatexte, 1986. 17–35.
– 'Re-thinking Grierson: The Ideology of John Grierson.' In *Dialogue: Canadian*

and Quebec Cinema. Ed. Pierre Véronneau, Michael Dorland, and Seth
 Feldman. Montreal: Mediatexte, 1987. 21–56.
– 'The Uncertain Trumpet: Defining a (Canadian) Art Cinema in the Sixties.'
 CinéAction 6 (Spring 1989): 6–13.
– *David Cronenberg: A Delicate Balance*. Toronto: ECW Press, 1994.
– 'In Our Own Eyes: The Canonizing of Canadian Film.' *Canadian Journal of
 Film Studies* 3.1 (Spring 1994): 27–44.
– ed. *The National Film Board of Canada: The War Years*. Ottawa: Canadian Film
 Institute, 1965.
National Film Board of Canada. *Annual Reports*. 1977–8, 1992–3, 1999–2000.
Nelson, Joyce. *The Colonized Eye: Rethinking the Grierson Legend*. Toronto:
 Between the Lines, 1988.
Nowell, Iris. *Joyce Wieland: A Life in Art*. Toronto: ECW Press, 2001.
Nowell-Smith, Geoffrey. 'After the War.' In *The Oxford History of World Cinema*.
 Ed. Geoffrey Nowell-Smith. London: Oxford University Press, 1996. 436–42.
– 'Introduction.' In *The Oxford History of World Cinema*. Ed. Geoffrey Nowell-
 Smith. London: Oxford University Press, 1996. 3–5.
– 'The Resurgence of Cinema.' In *The Oxford History of World Cinema*. Ed.
 Geoffrey Nowell-Smith. London: Oxford University Press, 1996. 759–66.
– ed. *The Oxford History of World Cinema*. London: Oxford University Press,
 1996.
Nowry, Laurence. 'The Early Scenario of Ernest Quimet, Grandpère of Film.'
 In *Documents in Canadian Film*. Ed. Douglas Fetherling. Peterborough, ON:
 Broadview Press, 1988. 13–22.
Pageau, Pierre. 'A Survey of the Commercial Cinema, 1963–1977.' In *Self-
 Portraits: Essays on the Canadian and Quebec Cinemas*. Ed. Pierre Véronneau
 and Piers Handling. Ottawa: Canadian Film Institute, 1980. 146–58.
Pageau, Pierre, and Yves Lever. *Cinémas canadien et québécois: Notes historiques*.
 Montreal: College Ahuntsic, 1977.
Pallister, Janis L. *The Cinema of Quebec: Masters in Their Own House*. Madison:
 Associated University Presses, 1995.
Parpart, Lee. 'Political Alignments and the Lure of "More Existential Ques-
 tions" in the Films of Patricia Rozema.' In *North of Everything*: *English-
 Canadian Cinema since 1980*. Ed. William Beard and Jerry White. Edmonton:
 University of Alberta Press, 2002. 294–311.
Pasquariello, Nicholas. 'Jan Kadar.' *Cinema Canada* 68 (Sept. 1980): 20.
Pearson, Roberta. 'Early Cinema.' In *The Oxford History of World Cinema*. Ed.
 Geoffrey Nowell-Smith. London: Oxford University Press, 1996. 13–22.
– 'Transitional Cinema.' In *The Oxford History of World Cinema*. Ed. Geoffrey
 Nowell-Smith. London: Oxford University Press, 1996. 23–42.
Pendakur, Manjunath. *Canadian Dreams and American Control: The Political*

Economy of the Canadian Film Industry. Detroit: Wayne State University Press, 1990.

Perreaux, Les. 'Far from the Maddin Crowd.' *National Post* [Toronto], 11 Sept. 2001, p. B3.

Pevere, Geoff. 'Cronenberg Tackles Dominant Videology.' In *The Shape of Rage: The Films of David Cronenberg*. Ed. Piers Handling. Toronto: General, 1983. 136–48.

– 'Images of Men.' *Canadian Forum*, February 1985, pp. 24–7.

– 'The Rites (and Wrongs) of the Elder; or, The Cinema We Got: The Critics We Need.' In *Documents in Canadian Film*. Ed. Douglas Fetherling. Peterborough, ON: Broadview Press, 1988. 323–36.

– 'Greenland Revisited: The Winnipeg Film Group during the 1980s.' In *Dislocations*. Ed. Gilles Hébert. Winnipeg: Winnipeg Film Group, 1995. 37–52.

– 'No Place like Home: The Films of Atom Egoyan.' In *Exotica*, by Atom Egoyan. Toronto: Coach House Press, 1995. 9–42.

– 'Kissed.' www.movingpictures.nisa.com/1998/kissed.htm.

Pevere, Geoff, and Greig Dymond. *Mondo Canuck: A Canadian Pop Culture Odyssey*. Toronto: Prentice-Hall, 1996.

Picard, Yves. 'Les Succès du cinéma québécois.' In *Dialogue: Canadian and Quebec Cinema*. Eds. Pierre Véronneau, Michael Dorland, and Seth Feldman. Montreal: Mediatexte, 1987. 97–108.

Pick, Zuzana M. 'This Land Is Ours – Storytelling and History in *Kanehsatake: 270 Years of Resistance*.' In *Candid Eyes: Essays on Canadian Documentaries*. Ed. Jim Leach and Jeannette Sloniowski. Toronto: University of Toronto Press, 2003. 181–96.

Pittman, Bruce. 'Shebib Exposes Himself.' *Cinema Canada* 81 (Feb. 1982): 18–21.

Posner, Michael. *Canadian Dreams: The Making and Marketing of Independent Films*. Vancouver: Douglas and McIntyre, 1993.

Posner, Michael, and James Adams. 'Budget Turns Its Back on TV.' *Globe and Mail*, 20 Feb. 2003, p. R1.

Pratley, Gerald. 'Film in Canada.' In *Documents in Canadian Film*. Ed. Douglas Fetherling. Peterborough, ON: Broadview Press, 1988. 89–101.

Quill, Greg. 'Why Canadian Movies Suck.' *Toronto Star*, 13 April 2001, pp. E2–E3.

Raboy, Marc. 'Public Television.' In *The Cultural Industries in Canada: Problems, Policies and Prospects*. Ed. Michael Dorland. Toronto: James Lorimer & Co., 1996. 178–202.

Ramsay, Christine. 'Canadian Narrative Cinema from the Margins: The "Nation" and Masculinity in *Goin' Down the Road*.' *Canadian Journal of Film Studies* 2.2–3 (1993): 27–94.

Ray, Robert B. 'Impressionism, Surrealism, and Film Theory: Path Dependence, or How a Tradition in Film Theory Gets Lost.' In *The Oxford Guide to Film Studies*. Ed. John Hill and Pamela Church Gibson. London: Oxford University Press, 1998. 67–76.

Rees, A.L. 'Cinema and the Avant-Garde.' In *The Oxford History of World Cinema*. Ed. Geoffrey Nowell-Smith. London: Oxford University Press, 1996. 95–104.

Richardson, Adam. 'A Few Minutes with Lynne Stopkewich.' *Rice Thresher*, 25 April 1997. www.riceinfo.ric.educ/projects/thresher/issues/84/970425/AE/Story04.

Rifkin, Jeremy. *The Age of Access: The New Culture of Hypercapitalism*. New York: Jeremy P. Tarcher/Putnam, 2000.

Rodley, Chris. 'Introduction: From Novel to Film.' In *Crash*, by David Cronenberg. London: Faber and Faber, 1996. i–xiv.

– ed. *Cronenberg on Cronenberg*. Toronto: Knopf Canada, 1992.

Romney, Jonathan. 'Last Night' *New Statesman*, 5 July 1999, pp. 45–6.

Rosen, Philip. *Change Mummified: Cinema, Historicity, Theory*. Minneapolis: University of Minnesota Press, 2001.

Rosenbaum, Jonathan. *Placing Movies: The Practice of Film Criticism*. Berkeley: University of California Press, 1995.

Rosenthal, Alan. 'Fiction Documentary: *A Married Couple*.' *Film Quarterly* 23.4 (Summer 1970): 9–32

– 'Interview with Richard Leiterman.' In *Documents in Canadian Film*. Ed. Douglas Fetherling. Peterborough, ON: Broadview Press, 1988. 145–66.

Routt, Bill. 'The Emergence of Australian Film.' *The Oxford History of World Cinema*. Ed. Geoffrey Nowell-Smith. London: Oxford University Press, 1996. 422–6.

Rubin, Mike. 'The Pretty Good Films of Guy Maddin: An Interview.' www.motorbooty.com/maddin.

Russell, Catherine. 'Role Playing and the White Male Imaginary in Atom Egoyan's *Exotica*.' In *Canada's Best Features: Critical Essays on Fifteen Canadian Films*. Ed. Eugene P. Walz. Amsterdam: Rodopi, 2002. 321–46.

Saunders, Doug. 'Hollywood's Northern Lights.' *Globe and Mail*, 3 July 2000, p. R1.

– 'The Myth of Hollywood North.' *Report on Business Magazine*, April 2001, pp. 95–102.

Schneller, Johanna. 'Memo to Hollywood.' *Globe and Mail*, 4 May 2001, p. R1.

Scott, Jay. 'Burn Out in the Great White North.' In *Take Two*. Ed. Seth Feldman. Toronto: Irwin, 1984. 29–35.

– *Midnight Matinées*. Toronto: Oxford University Press, 1985.

Scott, Sarah, 'The Accidental Moguls.' *Report on Business Magazine*, December 2000, pp. 59–64.

Segal, Robert A. *Joseph Campbell: An Introduction*. Rev. ed. New York: Mentor, 1990.

Seguin, Denis. 'The 5% Solution.' *Canadian Business*, 16 Sept. 2002, pp. 35–9.

Shaviro, Steven. 'Fire and Ice: The Films of Guy Maddin.' In *North of Everything: English-Canadian Cinema since 1980*. Ed. William Beard and Jerry White. Edmonton: University of Alberta Press, 2002. 216–21.

Shedden, Jim, ed. *Presence and Absence: The Films of Michael Snow 1956–1991*. Toronto: Art Gallery of Ontario, 1995.

Sheehan, Andy. *Cinemania Online* www.twincities.sidewalk.com/detail/18132. 20 May 1997.

Shek, Ben-Z. 'History As a Unifying Structure in *Le Déclin de l'empire américain*.' *Quebec Studies* 9 (Fall/Winter 1989/90): 9–16.

Sherritt, David. 'Quirky Canadian Film Blends Calm, Chaos, and a Talking Fish.' *Christian Science Monitor*, 1 Feb. 2002.

Shouldice, Larry, ed. *Contemporary Quebec Criticism*. Toronto: University of Toronto Press, 1979.

Shulgan, Christopher. 'Darth Investor vs. the Cartoon Company.' *Report on Business Magazine*, June 2003, pp. 58–70.

Simpson, Jeffrey. *Star-Spangled Canadians*. Toronto: HarperCollins, 2000.

Snow, Michael. 'La Région Centrale.' In *Collected Writings of Michael Snow*. Waterloo, ON: Wilfrid Laurier University Press, 1994. 53–6.

– *The Collected Writings of Michael Snow*. Waterloo, ON: Wilfrid Laurier University Press, 1994.

– 'Interview with Michael Snow.' In *Inside the Pleasure Dome: Fringe Film in Canada*. 2nd ed. Toronto: Coach House Books, 2001.

Spass, Lieve. *The Francophone Film: A Struggle for Identity*. Manchester: Manchester University Press, 2000.

Stam, Robert. *Film Theory: An Introduction*. Oxford: Blackwell, 2000.

Stark, Peter. 'Punks Mix It Up in Razor-Sharp Comedy.' *San Francisco Chronicle*, 4 Dec. 1998.

Stone, Jay. 'Blood Runs Hot in Cold Arctic.' *Calgary Herald*, 12 April 2002, p. E3.

Straw, Will. 'Canadian Cinema.' In *The Oxford Guide to Film Studies*. Ed. John Hill and Pamela Church Gibson. London: Oxford University Press, 1998. 523–6.

Stukator, Angela. 'Book Review.' *Canadian Journal of Film Studies* 11.2 (Fall 2002): 101–5.

Sussex, Elizabeth. *The Rise and Fall of British Documentary: The Story of the Film*

Movement Founded by John Grierson. Berkeley: University of California Press, 1975.

Taras, David, and Beverly Rasporich, eds. *A Passion for Identity: Canadian Studies for the Twenty-First Century.* 4th ed. Toronto: Nelson, 2001.

Taylor, Kate. 'Daring Lepage Crosses Borders and Breeds in Quebec.' *Globe and Mail*, 23 May 2000, p. R1.

Testa, Bart. 'So What Did Elder Say?' In *Documents in Canadian Film.* Ed. Douglas Fetherling. Peterborough, ON: Broadview Press, 1988. 272–83.

– 'An Axiomatic Cinema: Michael Snow's Films.' In *Presence and Absence: The Films of Michael Snow 1956–1991.* Ed. Jim Shedden. Toronto: Art Gallery of Ontario, 1995. 26–83.

– 'Technology's Body: Cronenberg, Genre, and the Canadian Ethos.' www.utoronto.ca/cinema/tests1.htm. 16 Nov. 1998.

Therrien, Denyse. 'Petit à petit, le cinéma des prairies fait son nid.' In *À la recherche d'une identité: Renaissance du cinéma d'auteur canadien-anglais.* Ed. Pierre Véronneau. Montreal: Cinémathèque québécoise, 1991. 143–64.

Toles, George. 'Drowning for Love: Jean-Claude Lauzon's *Léolo.'* In *Canada's Best Features: Critical Essays on Fifteen Canadian Films.* Ed. Eugene P. Walz. Amsterdam: Rodopi, 2002. 275–304.

Topalovich, Maria. *A Pictorial History of the Canadian Film Awards.* Toronto: Stoddart, 1984.

Tousignant, Isa. 'Fated Possibilities: A Conversation with Robert Lepage.' *Take One* 9.30 (Winter 2001): 14–17.

Tremblay-Daviault, Christiane. *Un cinéma orphelin: Structures mentales et sociales du cinéma québécois (1942–1953).* Montreal: Québec/Amérique, 1981.

– 'Avant la Révolution tranquille: Une Terre-Mère en perdition.' In *Les Femmes et cinéma québécois.* Ed. Louise Carrière. Montreal: Boréal Express, 1983. 21–52.

Tschofen, Monique. 'Repetition, Compulsion, and Representation in Atom Egoyan's Films.' In *North of Everything: English-Canadian Film since 1980.* Ed. William Beard and Jerry White. Edmonton: University of Alberta Press, 2002. 166–83.

Usai, Paolo Cherchi. 'Origins and Survival.' In *The Oxford History of World Cinema.* Ed. Geoffrey Nowell-Smith. London: Oxford University Press, 1996. 6–12.

Vallières, Pierre. 'An Account by a Privileged Hostage of *Les Ordres:* Brault Has Missed His Shot.' In *Canadian Film Reader.* Ed. Seth Feldman and Joyce Nelson. Toronto: Peter Martin Associates, 1977. 264–7.

Van Den Hoven, Adrian. '*The Decline of the American Empire* in a North-American Perspective.' In *Essays on Quebec Cinema.* Ed. Joseph Donohoe, Jr. Lansing: Michigan State University Press, 1991. 145–56.

Varga, Darell. 'Desire in Bondage: Guy Maddin's *Careful*.' *Canadian Journal of Film Studies* 8.2 (Fall 1999): 56–70.

Vasey, Ruth. 'The World-Wide Spread of Cinema.' In *The Oxford History of World Cinema*. Ed. Geoffrey Nowell-Smith. London: Oxford University Press, 1996. 53–61.

Vatnsdal, Caelum. *Kino Delirium: The Films of Guy Maddin*. Winnipeg: Arbeiter Ring Publishing, 2000.

Véronneau, Pierre. *Cinéma de l'époque Duplessiste*. Montreal: Cinémathèque québécoise, 1979.

– *Histoire du cinéma au Québec*. Vol. 1. Montreal: Cinémathèque québécoise, 1979.

– 'The First Wave of Quebec Feature Films 1944–1953.' In *Self-Portraits: Essays on the Canadian and Quebec Cinemas*. Ed. Pierre Véronneau and Piers Handling. Ottawa: Canadian Film Institute, 1988. 54–63.

– ed. *À la recherche d'une identité: Renaissance du cinéma d'auteur canadien-anglais*. Montreal. Cinémathèque québécoise, 1991.

Véronneau, Pierre, and Piers Handling, eds. *Self-Portraits: Essays on the Canadian and Quebec Cinemas*. Ottawa: Canadian Film Institute, 1988.

Véronneau, Pierre, Michael Dorland, and Seth Feldman, eds. *Dialogue: Canadian and Quebec Cinema*. Montreal: Mediatexte, 1987.

Wade Rose, Barbara. *Budge: What Happened to Canada's King of Film*. Toronto: ECW Press, 1998.

Walz, Eugene, P., ed. *Flashback: People and Institutions in Canadian Film History*. Montreal: Mediatexte, 1986.

– *Canada's Best Features: Critical Essays on Fifteen Canadian Films*. Amsterdam: Rodopi, 2002.

Warkentin, Germaine. 'Comment on Film.' *Canadian Forum*, October 1964, pp. 157–9.

– 'Norman McLaren.' In *Documents in Canadian Film*. Ed. Douglas Fetherling. Peterborough, ON: Broadview Press, 1988. 68–81.

Warren, Paul. 'Les Québécois et le cinéma: Un mode spécifique d'exhibition.' In *Dialogue: Canadian and Quebec Cinema*. Ed. Pierre Véronneau, Michael Dorland, and Seth Feldman. Montreal: Mediatexte, 1987. 109–22.

Waugh, Thomas. 'Léa Pool's *À Corps Perdu* (Straight for the Heart).' *Cinema Canada* 149 (Feb. 1988): 25–6.

Weinmann, Heinz. *Cinéma de l'imaginaire québécois: De 'La Petite Aurore' à 'Jésus de Montréal*.' Montreal: Hexagone,1990.

White, Jerry. 'Alanis Obomsawin: Documentary Form and the Canadian Nation(s).' *CineAction* 49 (Summer 1999): 26–36.

Whyte, Murray. 'Oh Yeah, Somebody Told Me That Was Pretty Good.' *National Post*, 29 Jan. 2001, p. D3.

Winch, David. 'La Femme de l'hôtel.' *Cinema Canada* 111 (Oct. 1984): 10.

Wise, Wyndham. 'Canadian Cinema from Boom to Bust: The Tax-Shelter Years.' *Take One* 7.22 (Winter 1999): 17–24.

– ed. *Take One's Essential Guide to Canadian Film*. Toronto: University of Toronto Press, 2001.

Wood, Robin. 'Cronenberg: A Dissenting View.' In *The Shape of Rage: The Films of David Cronenberg*. Ed. Piers Handling. Toronto: General, 1983. 115–35.

Wright, Judy, and Debbie Magidson. 'Making Films for Your Own People: An Interview with Denys Arcand.' In *Canadian Film Reader*. Ed. Seth Feldman and Joyce Nelson. Toronto: Peter Martin Associates, 1977. 217–34.

Xie, Shaobo, and Fengzhen Wang, eds. *Dialogues on Cultural Studies*. Calgary: Calgary University Press, 2002.

York, Karen, ed. *Great Scott: The Best of Jay Scott's Movie Reviews*. Toronto: McClelland and Stewart, 1994.

Yuen-Carrucan, Jasmine. 'The Politics of Deepa Mehta's *Water*.' *Bright Lights Film Journal* 28 (April 2000). www.brightlightsfilm.com/28/water.html.

Illustration Credits

Peter Harcourt: Jim Kitses, Jean Renoir, and Peter Harcourt

National Archives of Canada: Ernest Shipman (C-55212); *Carry on Sergeant!* poster (MISA 7606); Abbé Tessier (PA-66712); John Grierson (Ronny Jaques / NFB, PA-179108); Norman McLaren (Jack Long / NFB, PA-169509); Budge Crawley (© Southam / *Montreal Gazette* / Mac Juster, PA-213747); Allan King (Henry Fox, PA-213785); *Entre la mer et l'eau douce* (Pierre Gaudard, PA-166264); Michael Snow (Michael Lambeth, PA-162070); Joyce Wieland (Tess Taconis, PA-137321)

National Film Board of Canada: *Pas de deux*; Pierre Perrault; *Pour la suite du monde*; Alanis Obomsawin

National Film, Television, and Sound Archives Stills Collection: Nell Shipman, no. 4857

Dan Power: Gary Burns

Anne Wheeler: *Cowboys Don't Cry*; *Bye Bye Blues* (Doug Curran)

Winnipeg Film Group: Angela Heck and Michael Gottli; Guy Maddin

Index

Note: Page references in bold refer to photographs.